WASHINGTON STATE

A Literary Chronicle

BOOKS BY W. STORRS LEE

Hawaii: A Literary Chronicle
Maine: A Literary Chronicle
California: A Literary Chronicle

The Islands
The Great California Deserts
The Sierra
Canal Across a Continent
God Bless Our Queer Old Dean
The Strength to Move a Mountain
Yankees of Connecticut
Green Mountains of Vermont
Town Father
Stagecoach North
Father Went to College

A Vanishing America (Contributor)
Bread Loaf Anthology (Editor)
Footpath in the Wilderness (Editor)

WASHINGTON STATE

A LITERARY CHRONICLE

Edited, with Commentaries by

W. STORRS LEE

Illustrations by W. Ralph Merrill

fW

FUNK & WAGNALLS

NEW YORK

Notices of Copyright Holders

To

JUNIE and DORTHEA

Contents

[ix]

xiv] CONTENTS

Contents

Foreword

Connecticut Yankees cherish old place names like Quinebaug, Cos Cob, Naugatuck, and Yantic; Floridians never give a second thought to oddities like Chokoloskee, Kissimmee, or Tallahassee; Midwesterners haven't chuckled for generations over the ridiculous dissonance in Kalamazoo, Kankakee, Chicago, Tecumseh, Tippecanoe, and Pawpaw. No one now considers such carry-overs from the heyday of our aborigines and early settlers particularly barbarous or amusing. But let an outlander from any state cross the border into Washington and he will go into stitches over Chuckanut and Chumstick, Satsop and Snoqualmie, Tumtum, Twisp and Steilacoom, Humptulips and Hyak, Puyallup, Queets, Oyhut and Utsaladdy.

It has always been so. Although American gadabouts long ago became accustomed to the linguistic absurdities spotted on the maps of their home states, they never have quite accepted the cartographic idiosyncrasies of that northwest-corner state. Washington has been providing this gratuitous entertainment since its earliest Territorial days.

"When you enter Washington Territory, your ears begin to be assailed by the most barbarous names imaginable," snickered Charles Nordhoff a century ago. "On your way to Olympia by rail you cross a river called the Skookum-Chuck; your train stops at

places named Newaukum, Tumwater and Toutle; and if you seek
further, you will hear of whole counties labeled Wahkiakum and
Snohomish or Kitsap; and Cowlitz, Hookium and Nenolelops
greet you.

"They complain that Washington Territory gets little immigration. But what wonder? What man, having the whole American
continent to choose from, would willingly date his letters from
the county of Snohomish or bring up his children in the city of
Nenolelops. The village of Tumwater is very pretty indeed, but
surely an emigrant would think twice before he established himself either there or at Toutle. . . . I suspect that the Northern
Pacific Railroad terminus has been fixed at Tacoma because it is
one of the few places on Puget Sound whose name does not
inspire horror."

Nordhoff may have been right; possibly the exotic names did
scare off settlers who jumped to the conclusion that only banshees
and savages would occupy haunts with such cacophonous titles.
But by the same logic, whoever would have been induced to take
up residence in Quonochontaug or Usquepaug, Rhode Island;
Tuscaloosa, Alabama; Chillicothe, Illinois; Tunkhannock, Pennsylvania; or Cuckoo, Virginia?

The state of Washington has been subjected to more than its
share of such fatuous judgments. During the formative years of
the American Republic, there existed so much indifference to the
idea of extending national interests into the Northwest that only
the persistent efforts of a handful of visionaries saved the region
from the clutches of the British Lion. For two generations influential Easterners and Southerners scoffed at the notion of attempting to bring Puget Sound and the Columbia River basin
into the orbit of the United States, reiterating the slippery argument that such expansion would scatter the future population of
the nation all too sparsely.

Once that objection was overcome, it took an inordinately long
time for the Territory to rate anything like adequate protection of
military forces. Washington was treated like a stepchild. In 1867,
even after the Territory was cut down to a state-sized chunk—
divorced from Oregon, Idaho, and Montana—and legislators in

Olympia were pleading for admission to statehood, Congress ignored them.

They tried again in 1876. By that time the Indians were pretty well subdued; towns were settling up both east and west of the Cascade Mountains; stretches of highway here and there were supplementing riverboat and coastal routes; sawmills and salmon canneries were introducing something like an industrial revolution in a wilderness; there were fair prospects of a railroad connection with the East in the foreseeable future; at Seattle was an institution euphemistically called a university; at Walla Walla even a bank; and the population, according to the latest census, was over 20,000.

The Territorial legislators were sure they had a valid case. Nevertheless, they were blackballed a second time by Congressmen who looked upon Olympia as capital of a vast hinterland, an Indian country littered with all those ugly heathen names and too few Christian or classic ones. Gentry of Virginia, savants of Massachusetts, educated plowmen of Ohio were in no hurry to take into their fraternity of states another commonwealth of barbarians. Thirteen more years passed before Washington was considered fit for admission as a state.

Then in the very year that statehood was finally granted, as if to point up the unenlightened nature of the inhabitants, a respected luminary of their own little university at Seattle publicly embarrassed local seekers of learning by putting to them the blunt rhetorical question: "Has Puget Sound a literature?" "No," he answered, before anyone had a chance to take issue with him, "Puget Sound has no literature." The entire population of Washington, he alleged, was much too preoccupied with material affairs and the scramble for wealth to demonstrate interest in any cultural matters or literary production—yet.

If it had been completely true, the charge would have been cruel enough, but it fell short of the truth. Washington had already built up a considerable body of literature. To be sure, relatively little of it had been composed by native-born scriveners: the land was too young to allow them time. Most of the writing had been done by newcomers, short-term residents, and journeyers; but that was no disgrace; even in literate New England the first belles-lettres were the work of immigrants and visiting foreigners. In 1889 Washington possessed a literary wealth that would have been the envy of many an older state.

This volume is a sampling of that wealth and of what has since accrued. Indeed, the accumulation is so great that it is impossible to include more than a modest representation; but it does incorporate pronouncements of all types of contributors: explorers, fur traders, overlanders, settlers, travelers, military observers, missionaries, naturalists, political and industrial pioneers, poets, and professionals—both Washington writers and writers of Washington. Here, pieced together chronologically, is their story of the state. They speak for Washington.

The book is not so much an appraisal of the authors as their appraisal of the state. It is a biography of Washington as revealed by the real recording secretaries of state minutes, by eyewitnesses to major events, by participants in the events, or by historians who, with the advantage of hindsight, later reevaluated and reconstructed them.

Characteristically, their treatment of the subject is modest. Washington is one state whose natural attractions are seldom overwritten, for the simple reason that almost anything reported on them is likely to be understatement. The first sailors to explore Juan de Fuca Strait and Puget Sound taxed the English and Spanish languages to express the magnificence of what they saw, and still failed to do it justice; the glories of the rain forest and mountain range on the Olympic Peninsula have more often inspired silent awe than a flux of words; the majesty of the Cascades, with the white cones of Adams, Baker, and Rainier appearing to occupy space where only clouds should be, leave more viewers fumbling for words than pouring forth poetry; and the grand climax awaiting those unprepared for it is in the dry sagebrush lands to the east where man has gone into partnership with Nature to recreate along the course of the Columbia, its tributaries, and its empty coulees a watered wonderland, a miraculous new realm of recreation, an agricultural empire stretching to horizon after horizon.

In a land so splendidly endowed, understatement and reserve seem to come naturally to the better qualified expositors, and a little of their spirit carries over into historical writing, fiction, journals, verse, even the puffs of publicity agents. All are represented here, though the sheer bulk of the writing on Washington necessitates the exclusion of many authors of standing. Inevitably a few favorites will be missed. Then, suitability of material to the chronology, as well as literary quality, had to be taken into consideration in making the selections; priority was given to primary sources, factual writing was favored over fiction, and in some instances omissions were necessary because of reprint restrictions.

With few exceptions, we have limited the text to the present area of the state in order not to conflict with the efforts of some other editor who may wish to give similar literary treatment to Oregon, Idaho, and Montana, with which Washington was, of course, identified when it was part of the Oregon Territory, or when Washington Territory encompassed most of the two states to the east. However, political and commercial activities affecting the Northwest in general were periodically controlled from places like Nootka Sound, Astoria, Montreal, and the nation's capital, and to present a cohesive story, the self-imposed editorial restrictions occasionally have been broken.

Contrary to appearance, the volume is not an anthology in the usual sense. It has continuity and is intended to be read in sequential order. Anyone who peruses the selections and commentary from beginning to end will get at least a panoramic impression of the emergence of Washington from disputed anyman's land to Spanish and British outpost, a province of the Hudson's Bay Company, American frontier, Territory, state, and finally a model region for industrial, agricultural, and recreational development.

Both the great writers and the less great are given a voice in this collective appraisal of Washington. From the reservoir of buried, forgotten, or long-out-of-print material, we have attempted to restore to circulation at least a few selections. Many writers of earlier generations are virtually unknown to their successors. Through examples of their work, we present to student and general reader alike what we hope will be accepted as an invitation to investigate them further and to reevaluate their contribution to the literature of the state.

In order to keep the length of the collection within bounds, it was not possible to include all selections in their entirety, but for each author we have endeavored to reprint an extract of sufficient length to demonstrate his flavor, style, and message. Expendable amplifications and material not pertinent to an immediate subject have been excised, and the excision indicated by ellipses, which may represent deletion of a few words from a sentence (. . .), deletion of much longer passages (. . . .), or occasional transposition of topical material. Since most of the selections are taken from the body of a longer piece, ellipsis marks at the beginning and end of a selection are omitted.

Represented in the text are samples of English covering almost four centuries, and in that period grammatical usage has been modified so materially that old forms can make for halting reading or even convey unintended meaning. Accordingly, in some of the older documents spelling, punctuation, and obsolete expressions have been modernized; interminable paragraphs have been broken into more digestible nuggets; obscure and outmoded abbreviations have been written out. However, this is a compromise at best; we have made no attempt to dress the selections to grammatical conformity, and where quaintness of spelling or currently unacceptable usage contribute to the character of the composition, they have been retained.

For assistance in solving many problems of source and fact during the preparation of this volume, I am indebted to the librarians of the Bancroft Library at the University of California in Berkeley, and particularly to Mrs. Hazel E. Mills and her assistant Mrs. Nancy Pryor of the Washington-Northwest Room at the Washington State Library in Olympia.

W. S. L.

I

Michael Lok

For more than a century after Christopher Columbus discovered the Americas, European merchants and mariners were inclined to look upon his great landfall less as a beneficial addition to world real estate than as an obstruction to navigation. The continental land mass blocked the way to that treasury of trade, Cathay and the Orient. Surely, reasoned the cosmographers, the Maker of an orderly universe would have provided some sort of water passage across the obstruction to link the Atlantic and the Pacific. It was the search for this "Northwest Passage," or the fabled Strait of Anian, first on the Atlantic side and then on the Pacific, that stirred original interest in the region that was one day to be known as the State of Washington.

Spain, of course, had already let the world know that it held prior rights to all American soil washed by the Pacific. But that claim was warmly disputed by Great Britain, and to challenge it openly—as well as to look for the west-coast mouth of the Passage—in 1579 the illustrious Sir Francis Drake went on a plundering prowl of Spanish shipping in the Pacific. After raising havoc with vessels in South American ports, he sailed his *Golden Hind* far north in search of a shortcut back to England.

Exposed to "most vile, thicke and stinking fogs" north of California, he despaired of carrying out that part of his mission and

[1]

turned back with the rationalization: "Wee conjecture that either there is no passage at all through these Northerne coasts, or if there be, yet it is unnavigable." Nevertheless, on his retreat southward he paused near San Francisco Bay to name all "these Northerne coasts" Nova Albion—New England—and claim them for his Queen.

Drake's sudden appearance in the Pacific thoroughly mystified the Spaniards. They were not at all sure that he had not actually arrived via a secret Northwest Passage. Why would he sail north after his raids if he did not know of some short route home? His actions revived the old rumor of the existence of the Strait of Anian, and provoked new curiosity among the Spaniards to discover the secret for themselves.

Among those who claimed they were sent on that mission of discovery by the Spaniards in Mexico was a Greek mercenary, Apostolos Valerianos, who, long after his alleged expedition, passed his story on to a distinguished merchant of Venice and London, Michael Lok, world traveler and linguist, governor of the Company of Cathay, director of the Muscovy Company, a gentleman respected by kings, queens, and courtiers.

Lok undoubtedly was more gullible than guileful, but he in turn recited the tale to the English historian and curate, Samuel Purchas, who in 1625 saw fit to incorporate it in his monumental anthology of sea yarns. Lok it was—through Purchas—who first revealed to the world the exact location of the Pacific entrance to the Northwest Passage—between Vancouver Island and the Olympic Peninsula.

Tale of a Greek Pilot

When I was at Venice in April, 1596, happily arrived there an old man about threescore yeares of age, called commonly Juan de Fuca, but named properly Apostolos Valerianos, of nation a Greeke, born in the Iland Cefalonia, of profession a mariner, and an ancient pilot of shippes. This man, being come lately out of

Spaine . . . said that he was in the Spanish shippe which, in returning from the Ilands Philippinas and China towards Nova Spania, was robbed and taken at the Cape California by Captaine Candish, Englishman, whereby he lost sixtie thousand duckets of his owne goods.

Also he said that he was pilot of three small shippes which the Viceroy of Mexico sent from Mexico, armed with one hundred men, soldiers under a captain, Spaniards, to discover the Straits of Anian . . . and to fortifie that Strait to resist the passage and proceedings of the English nation, which were feared to passe through those Straits into the South Sea. And that by reason of a mutinie . . . that voyage was overthrowne and the shippes returned back from California coast to Nova Spania without any effect of thing done. . . .

Also he said that shortly after the said voyage was so ill ended, the said Viceroy of Mexico sent him out againe, anno 1592, with a small caravela and a pinnace, armed with mariners onely . . . for discovery of the same Straits of Anian and the passage thereof into the sea, which they call the North Sea, which is our Northwest Sea. And that he followed his course in that voyage . . . all alongst the coast of Nova Spania and California and the Indies, now called North America (all which voyage he signified to me in a great map, and a sea chart of mine owne, which he laid before me), untill he came to the latitude of 47 and 48 degrees.

There finding that the land trended north and northeast, with a broad inlet of sea . . . he entered thereinto, sayling therein more than twentie dayes, and found that land trending still sometimes northwest and northeast and north, and also east and southeastward, and very much broader sea than was at the said entrance, and that he passed by divers ilands in that sayling. And that at the entrance of this said Strait there is on the northwest coast thereof a great hedland or iland with an exceeding high pinacle or spired rocke, like a piller thereupon.

And he said that he went on land in divers places and that he saw some people on land clad in beasts skins, and that the land is very fruitfull, and rich in gold, silver, pearle and other things, like Nova Spania. . . . Finding the sea wide enough everywhere, and to be about thirtie or fortie leagues wide in the mouth of the Straits where he entered, he thought he had now well discharged his office and done the thing which he was sent to doe. . . . Not being armed to resist the force of the savage people . . . he therefore set sayle and returned homewards againe towards Nova Spania, where he arrived at Acapulco, anno 1592, hoping to be rewarded greatly of the Viceroy for his service done in this said voyage. . . .

After his comming to Mexico, he was greatly welcommed by the Viceroy and had great promises of great reward, but having sued there two yeares time and obtained nothing to his content, the Viceroy told him that he should be rewarded in Spaine by the King himselfe very greatly, and willed him therefore to goe into Spaine, which voyage he did performe. . . . He was greatly welcommed there at the Kings Court in wordes after the Spanish manner, but after long time of suite there also, he could not get any reward there either to his content. And therefore at length he stole out of Spaine and came into Italie, to goe home againe and live among his owne kindred and countrimen, he being very old.

Also he said that he thought the cause of his ill reward, had of the Spaniards, to bee for that they did not understand very well that the English nation had now given over all their voyages for discoverie of the Northwest Passage, wherefore they need not feare them any more to come that way into the South Sea, and therefore they needed not his service therein any more.

Also he said that . . . understanding the noble minde of the Queene of England and of her warres maintayned so valiantly against the Spaniards, and hoping that her Majestie would doe him justice for his goods lost by Captain Candish, he would be content to goe into England and serve her Majestie in that voyage for the discoverie perfectly of the Northwest Passage . . . if she would furnish him with onely one ship of fortie tunnes burden and a pinnace, and that he would performe it in thirtie dayes time from one end to the other of the straits. And he willed me to write into England.

. . . I did write thereof accordingly into England unto the right honourable old Lord Treasurer Cecill and to Sir Walter

Raleigh and to Master Richard Hakluyt, that famous cosmographer. . . . And in behalfe of the said Greeke Pilot, I prayed them to disburse one hundred pounds of money to bring him into England with myselfe, for that my owne purse would not stretch so wide at that time.

And I had answere hereof by letters of friends that this action was very well liked and greatly desired in England to bee effected, but the money was not readie, and therefore this action died at that time, though the said Greeke pilot perchance liveth still this day at home in his owne countrie in Cefalonia, towards the which place he went from me within a fortnight after this conference had in Venice.

From *Hakluytus Posthumus or Purchas His Pilgrimes*, Volume XIV, Samuel Purchas (Glasgow: James MacLehose and Sons, 1906).

II

James Cook

Tidings of Juan de Fuca's discovery were bruited about various ports of the world for years before the tale was dignified by publication, and periodically there were flurries of interest after some explorer coasted into the area. But the 48th parallel on the western shores of North America came as near to being one of the outposts of the globe as any place on earth. Only the most venturesome mariners roamed that far from civilization, and inevitably they seemed to encounter in its vicinity fogs, frigid winds, and tempests that forbade any approach to the shelter of the Northwest Passage. The surreptitious Spaniards undoubtedly made repeated attempts to verify its existence, but they remained silent about their navigational failures. For over a century and a half the Greek Pilot's tale might as well have been untold.

In 1741 Vitus Bering sailed south from Kamchatka to the general latitude allegedly penetrated by Juan de Fuca; he hoped to make a legitimate claim for Russia, but foul weather and supply shortages turned him back. In 1774 Spanish explorer Juan Pérez sighted Mount Olympus from the ocean and named it Santa Rosalia. Then, when the weather took a turn for the worse, he sailed across a broad strait without realizing it was a strait and went on to Vancouver Island to reassert its possession by the Spanish Crown.

The next year Bruno Heceta and Juan Francisco de Bodega

landed on the southern shores of the Olympic Peninsula and again claimed all the Northwest for Spain, as if repetition of the ceremony would make that nation's title clearer.

In defiance of that claim, the badgering British were back again in 1778, represented by their foremost living navigator, Captain James Cook (1728–1779). Scientist as well as explorer, Cook had been scouring the South Pacific for unclaimed lands, had just discovered the Sandwich Islands, and was now undertaking the major quest of his cruise—that old occupation of searching for the Northwest Passage. Like mariners before him, he, too, ran into vicious weather as he approached the "long-looked-for coast of New Albion," and appropriately named one of the first points of land he sighted "Cape Foulweather."

Storms drove him back into the high seas for a week; and when a break in the fog at last revealed a headland, he named it "Cape Flattery" because it "flattered us with the hopes of finding a harbour." Although all eyes were peeled for the inlet that Juan de Fuca had described, he missed it, tartly asserting, "We saw nothing like it, nor is there the least possibility that ever any such thing existed."

So he sailed a few leagues north to land at Nootka Sound on Vancouver Island, where his two ships, the *Resolution* and the *Discovery* were soon surrounded by flotillas of Indians, some of whom he concluded came from as far south as the cape he had just named. To be sure, Nootka Sound was never to be incorporated as part of Washington, but what transpired there during his stopover was to have a profound effect on the mainland just to the south. Captain Cook did not find the Northwest Passage, but he did find a local product that was going to be of much more importance, historically and economically, than would have been a charting of all the landmarks of Juan de Fuca Strait and Puget Sound.

Furs for a Song

I lost no time in endeavoring to find a commodious harbor where we might station ourselves during our continuance in the Sound.

. . . A great many canoes filled with natives were about the ships all day, and a trade commenced betwixt us and them, which was carried on with the strictest honesty on both sides.

The articles which they offered for sale were skins of various animals. . . . They also brought garments made of them, and another sort of clothing made of the bark of a tree or some plant like hemp; weapons, such as bows, arrows and spears; fishhooks and instruments of various kinds; wooden visors of many different monstrous figures; a sort of woolen stuff or blanketing; bags filled with red ochre; pieces of carved work; beads; and several other little ornaments of thin brass and iron shaped like horseshoes, which they hang at their noses; and several chisels or pieces of iron fixed to handles.

From their possessing these metals, we could infer that they had either been visited before by some civilized nation or had connections with tribes on their continent who had communication with them. But the most extraordinary of all the articles which they brought to the ships for sale were human skulls and hands, not yet quite stripped of the flesh, which they made our people plainly understand they had eaten. . . . For the various articles which they brought, they took in exchange, knives, chisels, pieces of iron and tin, nails, looking glasses, buttons or any kind of metal. . . .

We counted over a hundred canoes at one time, which might be supposed to contain, at an average, five persons each, for few of them had less than three on board; great numbers had seven, eight or nine; and one was manned with no less than seventeen. . . . If they had any distrust or fear of us at first, they now appeared to have laid it aside, for they came on board the ships and mixed with our people with the greatest freedom.

We soon discovered by this nearer intercourse that they were as light-fingered as any of our friends in the islands we had visited in the course of our voyage. And they were far more dangerous thieves, for possessing sharp iron instruments, they could cut a hook from a tackle or any other piece of iron from a rope the instant that our backs were turned. A large hook weighing between twenty and thirty pounds, several smaller ones, and other articles of iron were lost in this manner.

As to the boats, they stripped them of every bit of iron that was worth carrying away, though we always had men left in them as a guard. They were dexterous enough in effecting their purposes, for one fellow would contrive to amuse the boatkeeper at one end of a boat while another was pulling out the iron work at the other. . . .

A considerable number of the natives visited us daily; and every now and then we saw new faces. On their first coming, they generally went through a singular mode of introducing themselves. They would paddle with all their strength quite round both ships, a chief or other principal person in the canoe standing up with a spear or some other weapon in his hand, and speaking, or rather hollooing all the time. Sometimes the orator of the canoe would have his face covered with a mask, representing either a human visage or that of an animal; and instead of a weapon, would hold a rattle in his hand. . . . After making this circuit round the ships, they would come alongside and begin to trade without further ceremony. Very often, indeed, they would first give us a song in which all in the canoe joined, with a very pleasing harmony.

During these visits they gave us no other trouble than to guard against their thievish tricks. . . . Many of the principal natives who lived near us carried on a trade with more distant tribes in the articles they had procured from us, for we observed that they would frequently disappear for four or five days at a time and then return with fresh cargoes of skins and curiosities, which our people were so passionately fond of that they always came to a good market. . . .

Beads and such other toys, of which I had still some left, were in little estimation. Nothing would go down with our visitors but metal; and brass had by this time supplanted iron, being so eagerly sought after before we left this place that hardly a bit of it was left in the ships, except what belonged to our necessary instruments. Whole suits of clothes were stripped of every button, bureaus of their furniture, and copper kettles, tin canisters, candlesticks and the like all went to wreck, so that our American friends here got a greater medley and variety of things from us than any other nation which we visited in the course of the voyage.

. . . Some strangers in two or three large canoes . . . by signs made our people understand that they had come from the southeast, beyond the bay. They brought several skins, garments and other articles, which they bartered. But what is most singular, two silver tablespoons were purchased from them, which from their peculiar shape, we supposed to be of Spanish manufacture. One of these strangers wore them round his neck by way of ornament. These visitors also appeared to be more plentifully supplied with iron than the inhabitants of the Sound. . . .

Everything being now ready, on the morning of the 26th [of April, 1778] . . . I determined to put to sea at all events. Our friends, the natives, attended us till we were almost out of the Sound, some on board the ships and others in their canoes. One of their chiefs, who had some time before attached himself to me, was amongst the last who left us. Having, before he went, bestowed upon him a small present, I received in return a beaver skin of much greater value. This called upon me to make some addition to my present, which pleased him so much that he insisted upon my acceptance of the beaver-skin cloak which he then wore, and of which I knew he was very fond.

Struck with the instance of generosity, and desirous that he should be no sufferer by his friendship to me, I presented to him a new broadsword with a brass hilt, the possession of which made him completely happy. He, and also many others of his countrymen, importuned us much to pay them another visit, and by way of encouragement promised to lay in a good stock of skins. I make no doubt that whoever comes after me to this place will find the natives prepared accordingly with no inconsiderable supply of an article of trade which they could observe we were eager to possess, and which we found could be purchased to great advantage. . . .

The fur of these animals . . . is certainly softer and finer than

The Traders—skins which do not cost the purchaser sixpence

that of any others we know of, and therefore, the discovery of this part of the continent of North America, where so valuable an article of commerce may be met with, cannot be a matter of indifference.

From *A Voyage to the Pacific Ocean* . . . , Volume II, Captain James Cook (London: H. Hughs, 1785).

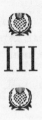

III

John Ledyard

The full value of those beaver pelts and seal skins bartered by Cook's crew for broadswords and brass knobs, kettles, and candlesticks didn't come to light until they were peddled in China at fantastic markups. Every buttonless tar returned to England wealthy by his standards. One of the richest and most impressed was a young marine corporal and inveterate globetrotter, John Ledyard (1751–1789), a Yankee from Connecticut, the first American to have a look at the Northwest.

Ledyard knew Indians, and he also knew something about furs. Before setting out on his wanderings, he had matriculated at Dartmouth, with the notion of qualifying himself as a missionary to the savages. But a few weeks of Eleazar Wheelock's regimen cured him of that objective. He escaped from the dull halls of learning and, without benefit of theological training, moved in for a time with a tribe of New Hampshire Indians. That life, too, failed to meet his expectations, and one night he made off down the Connecticut River in his host's canoe, paddled to Long Island Sound, and signed on a tramp schooner bound for Europe. In England he met Cook, just as the captain was setting sail on his last voyage, and talked his way into a berth on the *Resolution*.

If Cook had survived the brutal assault of the Sandwich Islanders, he might well have regretted his recruitment of Ledyard; for once the expedition returned to England, the Yankee escaped to America during the last months of the Revolution and published his version of the momentous voyage in Hartford long before the official report came from London presses.

Of all the observations made on that voyage of thrills, the one that struck Ledyard most forcibly was the potential market for furs in the Northwest. Fortunes were to be made there, and making such a fortune became an obsession with him. Commuting from Connecticut to Boston, to New York, to Philadelphia, he devoted all his energies to the creation of a Northwest fur company, and met apathy and frustration everywhere he went. He was brushed aside as a crackbrain: the Northwest was incomprehensibly remote; the United States had no claim to it.

Failing in his own country, he sailed off to Europe again to sell his idea to France or any country that would buy it. And in Paris at last he met a gentleman who understood his language—the American Minister, Thomas Jefferson. Jefferson himself summarized that chapter in Ledyard's fantastic career: "While I resided in Paris (in 1787), John Ledyard of Connecticut arrived there . . . panting for some new enterprise. His immediate object was to engage a mercantile company in the fur trade of the western coast of America, in which, however, he failed. I proposed to him to go by land to Kamchatka, cross in some of the Russian vessels to Nootka Sound, fall down into the latitude of the Missouri and penetrate to and through that to the United States."

Jefferson even obtained permission from Catherine the Great for Ledyard to tramp across Siberia. He immediately set out, but just before he reached Kamchatka, the Queen changed her mind and ordered his arrest and expulsion from Russia. It was the end of Ledyard's career as prospector in furs. Brokenhearted, he decided to salve his wounded pride by making a safari across Africa, and died in Egypt at the age of thirty-seven while waiting impatiently for a caravan to set out.

In his book and in his arguments, Ledyard did more than he realized to publicize the wealth of the Northwest. Moreover, he had impressed Thomas Jefferson, who would never forget him and who was going to exert a greater influence than any other statesman on the affairs of that fur-rich country.

Such an Astonishing Profit

The light in which this country will appear most to advantage respects the variety of its animals and the richness of their fur. . . . We purchased while here 1500 beaver, besides other skins, but took none but the best, having no thoughts at the time of using them to any other advantage than converting them to the purpose of clothing. But it afterwards happened that skins, which do not cost the purchaser sixpence sterling, sold in China for $100. Neither did we purchase a quarter part of the beaver and other fur skins we might have done, and most certainly should have done, had we known of meeting the opportunity of disposing of them to such an astonishing profit. . . .

We were visited by a number of natives in their boats, which resemble our bateaux. . . . This was the first fair opportunity that I had of examining the appearance of those unknown aborigines of North America. It was the first time, too, that I had been so near the shores of that continent which gave me birth from the time I at first left it, and though more than two thousand miles distant from the nearest part of New England, I felt myself plainly affected. All the affectionate passions incident to natural attachments and early prejudices played round my heart, and indulged them because they were prejudices. I was harmonized by it. It soothed a homesick heart and rendered me very tolerably happy.

I had no sooner beheld these Americans than I set them down for the same kind of people that inhabit the opposite side of the continent. They are rather above the middle stature, copper-colored, and of an athletic make. They have long black hair, which they generally wear in a club at the top of the head; they fill it, when dressed, with oil, paint and the down of birds. They also paint their faces with red, blue and white. . . . Their clothing generally consists of skins, but they have two others sorts of garments: the one is made of the inner rind of some sort of bark, twisted and united together like the woof of our coarse cloths; the other . . . principally made with the hair of their dogs, which are mostly white and of the domestic kind.

Upon this garment is displayed very naturally the manner of their catching the whale: we saw nothing elsewhere so well done by a savage in our travels. Their garments of all kinds are worn mantlewise, and the borders of them are fringed or terminated with some particular kind of ornament; their richest skins when converted to garments are edged with a great. curiosity. This is nothing less than the very species of wampum so well known on the opposite side of the continent. It is identically the same. . . . It was seldom they covered their heads. When they did, it was a kind of basket covering made after the manner and form of the Chinese and Chinese-Tartars hats. . . .

In their manners they resemble the other aborigines of North America: they are bold and ferocious, sly and reserved, not easily provoked, but revengeful. . . . When a party was sent to procure some grass for our cattle, they would not suffer them to take a blade of it without payment, nor had we a mast or yard without an acknowledgement. . . .

Captain Cook would not credit this fact when he first heard it and went in person to be assured of it, and persisting in a more peremptory tone in his demands, one of the Indians took him by the arm and thrust him from him, pointing the way for him to go about his business. Cook was struck with astonishment and, turning to his people with a smile mixed with admiration, exclaimed, "This is an American indeed!" and instantly offered this brave man what he thought proper to take, after which the Indian took him and his men to his dwelling and offered them such as he had to eat. . . .

Like all uncivilized men they are hospitable, and the first boat that visited us in the cove brought us what no doubt they thought the greatest possible regalia and offered it to us to eat. This was a human arm roasted. I have heard it remarked that human flesh is the most delicious, and therefore tasted a bit, and so did many others, without swallowing the meat or the juices, but either my conscience or my taste rendered it very odious to me.

We intimated to our hosts that what we had tasted was bad, and expressed as well as we could our disapprobation of eating it on account of its being part of a man like ourselves. They seemed to be sensible by the contortions of our faces that our feelings were disgusted and apparently paddled off with equal dissatisfaction and disappointment. . . .

We found a few copper bracelets and three or four rough-wrought knives with coarse wooden hafts among the natives at this place, but could not learn from the appearance of either of these articles or from any information they could give us how they came possessed of them, but it was generally thought they came from a great distance, and not unlikely from Hudson's Bay. Commerce is defusive, and nothing will impede its progress among the uninformed part of mankind but an intervention of too remote a communication by water, and as this cannot be the case with regard to the inhabitants of a continent, it seems entirely conclusive to suppose no part of America is without some sort of commercial intercourse immediate or remote.

From *A Journal of Captain Cook's Last Voyage to the Pacific Ocean* . . . , John Ledyard (Hartford: Nathaniel Patten, 1783).

IV

John Meares

John Ledyard, footing it across the wintry wastes of Siberia on his circuitous route to the American Northwest, would have turned back long before his arrest if he had known that British ships were already on their way to the same destination. His and Cook's reports of that potential fur trade had spread around the world; no longer was the coast of future Washington to be shrouded in mystery.

The news reached desultory skippers in India and China. In Shanghai an enterprising Britisher, James Hanna, electrified by the information, immediately chartered a diminutive sixty-ton brig, crossed the Pacific during the spring of 1785, and in six weeks—at the price of an inordinate slaughter of Indians—picked up a cargo of sea otter that netted him over $20,000.

The English trader Charles Barkley, skipper of the four-hundred-ton *Imperial Eagle,* was honeymooning with his seventeen-year-old bride in Hawaiian waters. He altered his course, headed for the coast, and on a fair day sailed into the strait between Vancouver Island and the Olympic Peninsula as if it were a common commercial channel. When he realized it was still uncharted, he bestowed upon it the name of the now legendary Juan de Fuca. There he filled the ship's hold to the very hatch boards with furs.

Reckless John Meares (c. 1756–1809) learned of the fur bonanza in India, resigned a British lieutenancy, bought a ship, and raced for the North Pacific late in the autumn of 1786. He sailed too late in the season and too far north, and his venture proved a complete fiasco. Half his crew died of scurvy while wintering in Alaska's Prince William Sound, and in the spring he limped back to China with an empty ship. Undismayed, however, in Portuguese Macao he secured two more ships, loaded them with Chinese coolies—on the hunch they might prove useful in constructing a settlement on the coast if he were successful in purchasing suitable land from the Indians—raised the Portuguese flag over his vessels, and pointed east.

Approaching the American coast on July 6, 1788, "a day very unfavorable to the business of making discoveries," he saw a rocky promontory looming ahead through the mist. Hoping it would shelter a harbor, he steered for it but when the water rapidly shoaled, he named it "Cape Disappointment" and sailed on.

As he progressed, his spirits perked up: "The face of the country assumed a very different appearance. Many beautiful spots covered with the finest verdure solicited our attention, and the land rose in a very gradual ascent to the distant mountains, skirted by a white sandy beach down to the sea. As we sailed along, spacious lawn and hanging woods everywhere met the delighted eye—but not a human being appeared to inhabit the fertile country of New Albion."

As he rounded the Olympic Peninsula, however, beings more or less human began to appear, and he was soon to discover that traders before him had already sorely alienated them. He did not get the welcome he expected.

A Thousand Against Thirteen

We had now obtained no inconsiderable knowledge of the coast of America from King George's Sound to Cape Lookout, that is, from the latitude of 45°37' north to the latitude of 49°37' north.

We had not only traced every part of the coast which unfavorable weather had prevented Captain Cook from approaching, but had also ascertained the real existence of the Strait of John de Fuca, which now renewed its claim to our attention. . . . It may not be improper to mention that we took possession of the Straits of John de Fuca in the name of the King of Britain. . . .

It was now the height of summer; the weather was warm and pleasant, and we very sensibly enjoyed the benign influence of the delightful season. Not a single patch of snow was visible on the summits of the lofty mountains which surrounded the sound. We could not, therefore, but derive a most refreshing satisfaction from our temporary repose in this calm and charming situation.

We embraced the present favorable opportunity to dispatch the longboat not only to explore the Straits of de Fuca but to procure if possible some knowledge of the people of Shoalwater Bay. She was therefore properly equipped for the occasion, was manned with thirteen of our people and furnished with provisions for a month. . . . On the 13th [of July, 1788] the boat departed on its voyage of discovery.

The crew employed on this occasion, added to the party we had spared for the service of King George's Sound, had so diminished our ship's company that it became absolutely necessary for us to put ourselves in the best possible state of preparation in case our present neighbors, who are a numerous, bold and powerful people, should be tempted by a knowledge of our weakness to make an attack. All the guns were therefore mounted, the arms got ready for service, and orders issued that none of the natives should on any pretense whatever be suffered to come on board the ship.

Immediately after the departure of the longboat, a considerable number of canoes from the northward came alongside us, few if any of which contained less than thirty men, and many of them more, besides women and children. . . . However, nothing material occurred till the 20th. The weather continued to be extremely fine, and our communication with the natives was on terms of reciprocal good understanding. They daily resorted to us with furs, fish and vegetables, and sometimes an occasional pres-

ent of very fine venison added its luxury to the common plenty of
our table.

But in our present state of inactivity, the situation of the
longboat was continually pressing home upon our minds with the
hopes of success or the fears of calamity. The savage nature of the
people who inhabited the parts which our friends were gone to
explore operated to alarm the one, at the same time that our
confidence in their skill, courage and good conduct animated the
other. While, however, our imaginations were following them in
their voyage with the most affectionate solicitude, they were on
the verge of destruction and threatened with sharing the abhor-
rent fate of their countrymen who were devoured by the canni-
bals of Queenhithe.

On the evening of the 20th we saw the sails of the longboat in
the offing; but the sudden impulse of our unreflecting joy on the
occasion was immediately checked by the apprehensions that
naturally arose in our minds from their early return. The interval
of her arrival at the ship was a period of very painful suspense to
every one on board. At length, to our inexpressible satisfaction,
we observed, on her coming alongside, that not an individual was
missing. Our immediate attention, however, was called to the
assistance of some wounded men who had suffered severely in a
very violent conflict the boat had sustained with the natives of
the Straits, and which was the cause of her sudden return.

The whole attention of the ship was now transferred to our
wounded people; but though several of them were much hurt, we
were consoled with finding that no mortal injury had been received by any. The officer was wounded by a barbed arrow in the
head which would have killed him on the spot if a thick hat had
not deadened the force of the weapon. One of the seamen was
pierced in the breast, and another in the calf of the leg, into
which the arrow had entered so far as to render a very large
incision absolutely necessary in order to discharge it.

A fourth received a wound very near the heart, but the weapon
which gave it very fortunately fell short of the vital parts. The
rest of the people were bruised in a terrible manner by the stones
and clubs of the enemy. Even the boat itself was pierced in a

thousand places by arrows, many of which remained in the awning that covered the back part of it, and which by receiving the arrows and breaking the fall of large stones thrown from slings, in a great measure saved our party from inevitable destruction.

In this engagement the natives behaved with a spirit and resolution that resisted the usual terror of firearms among a savage people, for the contest was close, and for some time our men fought for their lives. One of them had been singled out by an individual savage for his victim and a fierce engagement took place between them. The native was armed with a stone bludgeon and the sailor with a cutlass. They both manifested for some time equal courage and dexterity; but if an intervening oar had not broken a blow armed with all the force of his enemy, our brave countryman must have sunk beneath it.

It, however, failed of its object and gave him an opportunity, by a severe stroke of the cutlass, to deprive the native of an arm, who, notwithstanding such a loss and several other wounds, contrived to swim from the boat, indebted for his life to the noble mercy of his conqueror, who disdained to kill him in the water.

The seaman who was wounded in the leg continued during the action with the arrow in his flesh; and without attempting to rid himself of the torturing weapon, became by his courageous and active exertions a very principal instrument in preserving the boat.

Though we had never had any intercourse or communication with the inhabitants of the Straits, we had indulged ourselves with the hope that our friendly conduct towards their neighbors might by some means have reached the district of their habitation and given them favorable impressions of us. But their conduct marked the most savage and bloody hostility, and the fury of their onset compelled a similar spirit of resistance. . . .

The attack was begun by the savages—who boarded the boat with the design of taking her—in two canoes containing between forty and fifty men, who were most probably some of their choicest warriors. Several other canoes also remained at a small distance to assist in the attempt; and the shore was everywhere lined with people who discharged at our vessel continual showers of stones and arrows.

A chief in one of the canoes who encouraged the advance of the others was most fortunately shot in the head with a single ball, while in the very act of throwing a spear of a most enormous length at the coxswain. This circumstance caused the canoes to draw back and deprived the natives who were already engaged of that support which must have insured them the victory. Indeed, as it was, when we consider that the boat's company consisted only of thirteen men, who were attacked with the most courageous fury by superior numbers, and galled as these were at the same moment by the numerous weapons constantly discharged from the shore, their escape is to be numbered among those favorable events of life which never fail to excite in well ordered minds a mingled sensation of gratitude and astonishment.

The boat had advanced a considerable way up the Straits of de Fuca and had entered a bay or harbor when, as our people were preparing to land for the purpose of examining it, they were attacked by the natives . . . and, of course, effectually obstructed in the pursuit of their original design. From this station, however, they observed that the Straits to the east northeast appeared to be of great extent and to increase rather than diminish.

As they returned down the Straits, they were met by a small canoe paddled by two men . . . from whom they purchased some fish. But words cannot express the surprise and abhorrence of our people when these savages held up two human heads but just cut off and still streaming with blood, by way of offering them for sale. They held these detestable objects by the hair with an air of triumph and exultation. . . . This circumstance threw a damp upon the spirits of the crew, which continued more or less through the whole of the voyage.

Though the boat had not succeeded in the principal object of our expedition, yet it did not return without being able to communicate some knowledge of the Straits of de Fuca. She had sailed near thirty leagues up the Strait, and at that distance from the sea it was about fifteen leagues broad with a clear horizon stretching to the east for fifteen leagues more. Such an extraordinary circumstance filled us with strange conjectures as to the extremity of this Strait, which we concluded at all events could not be any great distance from Hudson's Bay.

From *Voyages Made in the Years 1788 and 1789,* John Meares (London: Logographic Press, 1790).

Manuel Quimper

From Cape Disappointment north to Nootka Sound, before the shores had been explored or mapped, a kind of frantic competition was building up among fur traders. While Meares was still on the coast, the British were joined by two Americans: Captain John Kendrick, who had made a name for himself during the Revolutionary War as an audacious privateer, now commanding the heavily armed, 212-ton *Columbia Rediviva;* and young, energetic, impetuous Robert Gray, skipper of the little sloop *Lady Washington.* The Russians were conspicuously present, too, and occasionally ships under Portuguese, French, or Spanish colors.

The Americans were experimenting with a clever scheme in triangular trade that took a ship first to the Northwest to swap its miscellany of gewgaws, cheap hardware, and gaudy textiles for furs; then to Canton, where the high-priced pelts were exchanged for quantities of low-priced Oriental finery; and finally back to London or Boston for a grand killing in the insatiable market for treasures of Cathay—all carried out by taking advantage of the naïve West Coast Indians and the long-suffering Spaniards, who, according to a Papal edict issued just before Columbus discovered America, controlled all that stretch of Pacific shore.

Naturally Spain resented the trespass, and in 1789 sent out a token naval force to drive off the invaders and fortify Nootka

Sound. The seizure of one of Meares's vessels brought England and Spain to the verge of war; otherwise the military effort was totally ineffective. Rather than flexing military muscles with conviction, the favorite Spanish method of asserting territorial rights was going through a religious ritual here, there, and anywhere along the shores, consecrating the land in the name of the Father, Son, Holy Ghost, and His Majesty the King, Don Carlos IV. Though it carried no political impact, the pageantry was repeated over and over again, as if its very repetition would charm away the enemies of Spain.

In 1790 one of the King's naval functionaries, Manuel Quimper, sailed into the Strait of Juan de Fuca as far as the San Juan Islands. He described in detail the principal landmarks he saw, the ocean currents, impediments to shipping, the nature of the natives, wild life, and the green world, and disregarding the official claim made two years earlier by John Meares for the king of England, solemnly went ashore at four different points to put on the ritual Act of Possession. The pattern set at Neah Bay, which he called Nuñez Gaona, was followed identically at the three other places.

For a More Perpetual Sign of Possession

In the name of the most Holy Trinity, Father, Son and Holy Ghost, three persons and one true God, the first maker and creator of all things and without whom nothing good can be done . . . in His most holy name may it be known to all those to whom the present testimonial, instrument or letter of possession comes, that today, Sunday, August 1, 1790, this sloop, the *Princesa Real* . . . which departed from the Puerto de San Blas, one of those in the South Sea in the jurisdiction of the said viceroyalty, February 3 of the current year, on a voyage of discovery following the coast from Monterey to the north and commanded by Don Manuel Quimper, *alferez de navio* of the royal navy, at anchor in this now newly named "Nuñez Gaona," the said commander and the greater part of the seamen and soldiers having disembarked, took ashore a cross which they adored on their knees and everybody in a loud voice devotedly proclaimed that, in the name of His Majesty the King, Don Carlos IV, our master (whom may the Lord our Master guard for many years with increase of greater estates and kingdoms for the service of the Lord and the prosperity of his vassals and of those very powerful lords, his heirs and successors in the times to come), the commander of this sloop, by virtue of the order and instructions that the said most excellent Señor, viceroy of New Spain, has given him in the same royal name, was taking and took possession of this country where at present he has disembarked, which has been discovered for all time, in the said royal name and that of the royal crown of Castile and Leon as stated, as its own property and which really belongs to it by virtue of the donation and the bull which our most Holy Father, Alexander VI, high Roman pontiff, executed on his own motion as a gift to the very high and Catholic lords Don Fernando V and Doña Isabel his wife, king of Castile and Leon of glorious memory, and to their successors and heirs, of one-half of the world, done in Rome May 4, 1493.

By virtue of this these lands belong to the said royal crown of Castile and Leon and as such he takes and took said possession of these lands and the neighboring seas, river, *ensenadas*, ports, bays, gulfs, archipelagos, and this bay of Nuñez Gaona where at present this vessel is anchored, and places them in subordination to and under the power, possession and domain of the royal crown of Castile and Leon, as stated, as something belonging to it as it does.

In sign of possession, laying hand on his sword which he carried in his belt, he cut with it trees, branches and grass, moved stones, and walked over fields and the beach without contradiction from anyone, asking those present to be witnesses to it and me, Estéban Bañales, the clerk appointed by the commander of this expedition, to make a testimony of it in public form.

Then immediately taking a large cross on their shoulders, the men of the vessel being arranged in martial order with their muskets and other arms, they carried this in procession, chanting a litany with all responding. The procession being concluded, the commander planted the cross and erected a pile of stones at the foot of it as a memorial and sign of possession of all these seas and lands and their districts, continuous and contiguous, and named the bay "Nuñez Gaona."

As soon as the cross was planted, they adored it a second time and all begged and supplicated Our Lord, Jesus Christ, to be pleased, as this would be for His holy service, for the exalting and augmentation of the Holy Catholic Faith, and for the sowing of the Holy Evangel among these barbarous nations, who up to the present have been turned away from the true knowledge and doctrine, to guard them and free them from the devices of the devil and the blindness in which they exist, so that their souls may be saved.

The ceremony being over, the commander, for a more perpetual sign of memorial and possession, had a tree stripped, on which a cross was made and placed on it the following inscription: *Santisimo nombre de Nuestro Señor Jesu Cristo* with these four initials *I.N.R.I.* At the foot of the cross he put *Carolus IV Rex Hispaniarum.* On order that this should be of record, it was signed by the commander, and the witnesses . . . certify to it as a true testimonial.

From *Spanish Explorations in the Strait of Juan de Fuca,* Henry R. Wagner (Santa Ana: Fine Arts Press, 1933).

VI

John Boit

Gloomy weather and the reluctance of skippers to venture too close to an unfamiliar coast were responsible for the long delay in the discovery of the Columbia River. For two centuries mariners passed and repassed its mouth without realizing it was there, though at least one—Bruno Heceta—did sense its existence from the discolored water, the quantities of flotsam, and the strong offshore currents. The actual discovery, however, was left to the intrepid Yankee Robert Gray.

Gray's first trading trip of 1788, with John Kendrick, in the *Columbia* and the *Washington,* as the crew preferred to nickname their ships, was anything but a towering success. Gray scoured the Pacific coast for furs as far north as Alaska, and made some notable barters, including one batch of two hundred prime sea-otter pelts for exactly two hundred twopenny chisels. But aging Captain Kendrick proved first overcautious and later openly perfidious; he stayed put at Nootka the whole season, then exchanged ships with Gray and ordered him to take the *Columbia* back to Boston via the Hawaiian Islands and China. As soon as his partner was out of sight, he loaded the sloop *Washington* with the accumulation of furs stored ashore, carried a profitable cargo to China himself, and there absconded with the returns and the ship.

The Boston backers of that expedition, including a prominent merchant, Joseph Barrell, and the great statehouse architect Charles Bulfinch, never saw their ship or Kendrick again. However, undeterred by the duplicity, Barrell, Bulfinch, and company immediately reoutfitted the *Columbia* and, with Gray in command, sent it back to the Pacific with instructions to get there ahead of all other seasonal competitors, confident that the young captain would redeem the loss of the *Washington*.

"We are willing to go hand in hand in this concern," counseled Barrell, "and sink or swim together; and as we wish no advantage ourselves but what you share with us, so we mean to avoid any partial disadvantage." Gray was to get a generous five per cent of the gross receipts.

It was strictly a commercial venture. Not a word was said in his instructions about discoveries or a search for the Northwest Passage—which every other Pacific voyager was still looking for. Gray fulfilled his charge to the letter; he made an enormously profitable voyage, and as a bonus, returned with news of his discovery of the Columbia River.

In his own log that momentous event was casually mentioned as a minor incident, no more important than his exploration and charting of a dozen other important bays and estuaries. Even John Boit (1774–1829), the quiet Bostonian who sailed with him as fifth mate, treated it almost perfunctorily, though Boit, a blooming artist, poetaster, and fumbling philosopher, as well as a good navigator, sensed at least the historic significance of crossing the perilous bar into the noble river for the first time.

Up This Noble River

May 12, 1792. . . . This day saw an appearance of a spacious harbor abreast the ship. Hauled our wind for it. Observed two sand bars making off, with a passage between them to a fine river. Out pinnace, and sent her in ahead and followed with the ship under short sail. . . . The river extended to the northeast as far

as eye could reach, and water fit to drink as far down as the bars
at the entrance.

We directed our course up this noble river in search of a
village. The beach was lined with natives who ran along shore
following the ship. Soon after over twenty canoes came off and
brought a good lot of furs and salmon, which last they sold two
for a board nail. The furs we likewise bought cheap for copper
and cloth. They appeared to view the ship with the greatest
astonishment and no doubt we were the first civilized people that
they ever saw. We observed some of the same people we had
before seen at Gray's Harbor, and perhaps that was a branch of
this same river.

At length we arrived opposite to a large village situated on the
north side of the river about five leagues from the entrance and
came to in ten fathoms, sand, about one-quarter mile from the
shore. The river at this place was about four miles over. We
purchased four otter skins for a sheet of copper; beaver skins, two
spikes each; and other land furs, one spike each.

We lay in this place till the 20th May, during which time we
put the ship in good order and filled up all the water casks
alongside, it [the water] being very good. These natives talked
the same language as those farther south, but we could not learn
it. Observed that the canoes that came down river brought no
otter skins, and I believe the otter constantly keep in salt water.
They, however, always came well stocked with land furs and
capital salmon. The tide set down the whole time and was rapid.
Whole trees sometimes come down with the stream. The Indians
informed us there were fifty villages on the banks of this river.

    . . . On the 15th took up the anchor and stood up river, but
soon found the water to be shoal, so that the ship took the ground
after proceeding seven or eight miles from our first station.
However, soon got off again. Sent the cutter and found the main
channel was on the south side and that there was a sand bank in
the middle. As we did not expect to procure otter furs at any
distance from the sea, we contented ourselves in our present
situation, which was a very pleasant one. I landed abreast the
ship with Captain Gray to view the country and take possession,

Columbia Rediviva *at the mouth of the river to which the ship gave its name*

leaving charge with the second officer. Found much clear ground, fit for cultivation, and the woods mostly clear from underbrush. None of the natives came near us.

May 18. Shifted the ship's berth to her old station abreast the village Chinook commanded by a chief named Polack. Vast many canoes full of Indians from different parts of the river were constantly alongside. Captain Gray named this river Columbia's; the north entrance Cape Hancock, and the south, Point Adams.

This river in my opinion would be a fine place for to set up a factory. The Indians are very numerous and appeared very civil —not even offering to steal. During our short stay we collected 150 otter, 300 beaver and twice the number of other land furs. The river abounds with excellent salmon and most other river fish, and the woods with plenty of moose and deer, the skins of which were brought us in great plenty; and the banks produce a ground nut which is an excellent substitute for either bread or potatoes.

We found plenty of oak, ash and walnut trees, and clear ground in plenty, which with little labor might be made fit to raise such seeds as are necessary for the sustenance of inhabitants: and, in short, a factory set up here, and another at Hancock's River in the Queen Charlotte Isles, would engross the whole trade of the northwest coast, with the help [of] a few small coasting vessels.

May 20. This day left Columbia's River and stood clear of the bars and bore off to the northward. The men at Columbia's River are straight-limbed, fine-looking fellows, and the women are very pretty.

From "Remarks on the Ship *Columbia's* Voyage from Boston, on a Voyage, Round the Globe," John Boit (Boston: Massachusetts Historical Society *Proceedings*, Volume LIII, June, 1920).

VII

George Vancouver

Captain Gray, in all likelihood, had picked up from the Indians a tip regarding the existence of the Columbia River, and while he was haphazardly poking into bays and inlets, looking for it as well as for bargains in furs, just at sunset on April 28, 1792, a lookout sang down from the rigging that two ships were looming out of the haze. They were British—the huge *Discovery* and its tender, the *Chatham*. The *Discovery* was signaling for a consultation.

Gray hove to and waited for a boat bearing Lieutenant Peter Puget and the physician-naturalist Dr. Alexander Menzies to cross to the *Columbia*. The Yankee captain soon learned that the ships were on a notable expedition under the command of George Vancouver (1758–1798), the man who had accompanied Cook as an ordinary jack tar on his second voyage and as a midshipman on his third, and had since risen so rapidly in the British Admiralty that he was now carrying on where Cook had left off—combing the Pacific for more undiscovered territories, serving as ambassador at large to underprivileged races, and in the Northwest specifically charged with acting as mediator in the crisis John Meares had stirred up and investigating Meares's conclusion that the Strait of Juan de Fuca extended inland so far that it "could not be any great distance from Hudson's Bay": he was to confirm or scotch forever that nagging rumor about the Northwest Passage.

Gray glibly passed on to the emissaries all the information he possessed about the Strait of Juan de Fuca, and even let slip a word on his own quest for the great River of the West—a venture that the Englishmen chose to dismiss at the moment as inconsequential, for they had already observed the turbulent water Gray was talking about and attributed it to spring freshets. They parted amiably, Vancouver to sail north, Gray south.

Vancouver was eminently successful in all phases of his multiple mission, particularly in terminating what had become known as the "Nootka Controversy." For England he made the concession that the British would abandon exclusive claim to the Sound if the Spaniards would do the same. Spain finally accepted the proposal—a checkmate move on the part of great Britain, for that agreement was the beginning of the end to all Spanish territorial claims north of California.

Vancouver surveyed the region more systematically than had anyone before him. He circumnavigated the island that was to bear his name; thoroughly explored the Strait of Georgia and the San Juan Islands; dipped down into Puget Sound; and on learning of Captain Gray's discovery, later sent the *Chatham*, under Lieutenant W. R. Broughton, up the Columbia to Point Vancouver, where Broughton, belittling Gray's accomplishment, "formally took possession of the river and the country in its vicinity in His Britannic Majesty's name."

On his staff Vancouver had a team of distinguished men of science and of the sea, and one by one he memorialized them on the new charts he was drafting, including Menzies, Whidbey, and Puget; in fact, he scattered the names of his officers, friends, and English benefactors all over the map, not overlooking any mountain peak within sight. Of all the lands he saw, the shores and islands of Puget Sound and the straits to the north most delighted him. They were groomed in verdure as if for his reception in the early spring of 1792.

Birthday Present for a King

The evening of the 29th [April, 1792] brought us to anchor . . .
about eight miles within the entrance on the southern shore of
the supposed Straits of De Fuca. The following morning a gentle
breeze sprang up from the northwest, attended with clear and
pleasant weather, which presented to our view this renowned
inlet. . . . We weighed anchor with a favorable wind and
steered to the east along the southern shore . . . composed of
low sandy cliffs falling perpendicularly on beaches of sand or
stones. From the top of these eminences, the land appeared to
take a further gentle ascent and was entirely covered with trees
chiefly of the pine tribe, until the forest reached a range of high
craggy mountains . . . their summits covered with snow. . . .

Every new appearance, as we proceeded, furnished new conjectures; the whole was not visibly connected; it might form a
cluster of islands separated by large arms of the sea or be united
by land not sufficiently high to be yet discernible. About five in
the afternoon a long, low, sandy point of land was observed
projecting from the craggy shores into the sea, behind which was
seen the appearance of a well-sheltered bay. . . . Having turned
up a little way into the bay, we anchored . . . [off] the low,
sandy point of land, which from its great resemblance to Dungeness in the British Channel, I called New Dungeness. . . . The
lofty mountain discovered in the afternoon by the third lieutenant, and in compliment to him called by me Mount Baker, rose
a very conspicuous object. . . .

We had now advanced further up this inlet than Mr. Gray, or,
to our knowledge, any other person from the civilized world
(although it should be proved hereafter to be the same which is
said to have been entered by De Fuca) . . . considering ourselves now on the point of commencing an examination of an
entirely new region. . . .

Our May Day was ushered in by a morning of the most
delightfully pleasant weather. . . . The *Chatham's* cutter, with

the *Discovery's* yawl and cutter, were ordered to be armed and supplied with a day's provision, with which we set off to examine the two apparent openings nearest to us. We found the surface of the sea almost covered with aquatic birds of various kinds, but all so extremely shy that our sportsmen were unable to reach them with their guns. . . . We made the best of our way for land appearing like an island . . . and ascending its eminence, which was nearly a perpendicular cliff, our attention was immediately called to a landscape almost as enchantingly beautiful as the most elegantly finished pleasure grounds in Europe. From the height we were now upon, our conjectures of this land being an island situated before the entrance of an opening in the mainland was confirmed.

The summit of this island presented nearly a horizontal surface . . . which produced a beautiful variety on an extensive lawn covered with luxuriant grass and diversified with an abundance of flowers. To the northwestward was a coppice of pine trees and shrubs of various sorts that seemed as if it had been planted for the sole purpose of protecting from the northwest winds this delightful meadow, over which were promiscuously scattered a few clumps of trees that would have puzzled the most ingenious designer of pleasure grounds to have arranged more agreeably. Whilst we stopped to contemplate these several beauties of nature . . . we gathered gooseberries and roses in a state of considerable forwardness. . . . After taking some little refreshment, we returned towards the ships and arrived on board about midnight, perfectly satisfied with the success of our expedition. . . .

A light, pleasant breeze springing up, we weighed on Wednesday, the 2nd, and steered for the port we had discovered the preceding day. . . . The delightful serenity of the weather greatly aided the beautiful scenery that was now presented; the surface of the sea was perfectly smooth and the country before us exhibited everything that bounteous nature could be expected to draw into one point of view. As we had no reason to imagine that this country had ever been indebted for any of its decorations to the hand of man, I could not possibly believe that any uncultivated country had ever been discovered exhibiting so rich a picture. . . .

Between us and the snowy range, the land . . . rose here in a very gentle ascent and was well covered with a variety of stately forest trees. These, however, did not conceal the whole face of the country in one uninterrupted wilderness, but pleasingly clothed its eminences and checkered the valleys, presenting in many directions extensive spaces that wore the appearance of having been cleared by art. . . .

A picture so pleasing could not fail to call to our remembrance certain delightful and beloved situations in Old England. . . . Our progress brought us before noon abreast the stream that discharges its water from the western shore near five miles within the entrance of the harbor, which I distinguished by the name of Port Discovery, after the ship. . . . We had little trouble in clearing a sufficient space for our encampment. . . . The tents, observatory, chronometers and instruments, guarded by a party of marines, were sent on shore. . . .

A few of the natives in two or three canoes favored us with their company and brought with them some fish and venison for sale. The latter was extremely good and very acceptable. . . . These people, in their persons, canoes, arms, implements, etc., seemed to resemble chiefly the inhabitants of Nootka, though less bedaubed with paint and less filthy in their external appearance. . . . Their bows and implements they freely bartered for knives, trinkets, copper, etc., and what was very extraordinary, they offered for sale two children, each about six or seven years of age, and being shown some copper, were very anxious that the bargain should be closed. This, however, I peremptorily prohibited. . . .

As I was desirous of obtaining some further knowledge of this inlet . . . I directed the *Discovery*'s yawl and launch, with the *Chatham*'s cutter, properly armed and supplied with stores and . . . on the 7th we took our departure for the purpose of becoming more intimately acquainted with the region. . . .

As we advanced, the country seemed gradually to improve in beauty. The cleared spots were more numerous and of larger extent, and the remote lofty mountains covered with snow re-

flected greater lustre on the fertile productions of the less elevated country. . . . [We soon reached] an arm of the sea
stretching to the southeast. . . . Its northern part formed a snug
little port and . . . proved to be a very safe and more capacious
harbor than Port Discovery. . . . To this port I gave the name of
Port Townshend, in honor of the noble marquis of that name.
. . . [The "h" was later discarded]

This new inlet [Puget Sound] appeared to be of no inconsiderable extent . . . and the round, snowy mountain forming its
southern extremity, after my friend Rear Admiral Rainier, I
distinguished by the name of Mount Rainier. . . . This country,
regarded in an agricultural point of view, I should conceive as
capable of high improvement, notwithstanding the soil in general
may be considered to be light and sandy. Its spontaneous productions in the vicinity of the woods are nearly the same, and grow in
equal luxuriance with those under a similar parallel in Europe,
favoring the hope that if nutritious exotics were introduced and
carefully attended to, they would succeed in the highest degree.
The mildness of the climate and the forwardness of every species
of plants afforded strong grounds in support of this opinion. . . .

After the great fatigue our people had lately undergone, [two
days] were well appropriated as holidays. Sunday, the 3rd [of
June] all hands were employed in fishing, with tolerably good
success, or in taking a little recreation on shore; and on Monday,
the 4th, they were served as good a dinner as we were able to
provide them, with double allowance of grog to drink the King's
health, it being the anniversary of His Majesty's birth, on which
auspicious day I had long since designed to take formal possession of all the countries we had lately employed in exploring, in
the name of and for His Britannic Majesty, his heirs and successors.

To execute this purpose . . . I went on shore about one
o'clock, pursuing the usual formalities which are generally observed on such occasions, and under the discharge of a royal
salute from the vessels, took possession accordingly of the coast
from that part of New Albion in the latitude of 39° 20′ north and

longitude 136° 26′ east to the entrance of this inlet of the sea, said to be the supposed straits of Juan de Fuca, as likewise all the coast islands, etc. within the said straits . . . which interior sea I have honored with the name of the Gulf of Georgia, and the continent binding the said gulf, and extending southward to the 45th degree of north latitude, with that of New Georgia, in honor of his present Majesty.

From *A Voyage of Discovery to the North Pacific Ocean and Round the World*, Volume II, George Vancouver (London: John Stockdale, 1801).

VIII

Thomas Jefferson

Geographers now possessed at least some vague conception of the coastal periphery of the Northwest; Vancouver had proved to the satisfaction of most dreamers that there was no easy waterway across the continent. Circuitous river transportation might be possible over much of the distance, as independent trapper-traders and voyageurs of the Hudson's Bay Company, working out of Montreal, had demonstrated, but obviously portages would be necessary from the headwaters of one river to the headwaters of the next.

It was essential that something about the length and number of these portages be learned. Blazing an overland trail to the fur country was the next step in unraveling the geography of North America, and it called for more systematic scouting than what had been done by unscientific trappers and hunters. Visionary John Ledyard, once so eager to blaze that trail, had possessed the right idea.

Even after he became President of the United States, Thomas Jefferson (1743–1826) remembered Ledyard's overtures in Paris. Someone like Ledyard ought to tramp across the continent if for no other purpose than to learn the feasibility of a trade route to the region Vancouver and Gray had reported on so favorably. But as President, Jefferson hesitated to advocate openly or officially such a venture, because it involved what would be interpreted as a hostile invasion of Louisiana—crossing that vast expanse of foreign territory stretching from the Gulf of Mexico to Canada.

However, his convictions were so strong that on January 18, 1803, he finally compromised by assembling a joint meeting of the houses of Congress, and in a closed session delivered a confidential proposal. That address, in which he recommended the appropriation of a parsimonious $2500 to defray the cost of a two-year transcontinental expedition, was the opening wedge for the opening of the Northwest to Americans—the simple, adroit proposal for action, without which the whole basin of the Columbia River, Puget Sound, with its adjacent lands and waters, might soon have fallen permanently into the hands of another nation.

Even to the Western Ocean

The Indian tribes residing within the limits of the United States have for a considerable time been growing more and more uneasy at the constant diminution of the territory they occupy, although effected by their own voluntary sales; and the policy has long been gaining strength with them, of refusing absolutely all further sale, on any conditions. . . .

In order peaceably to counteract this policy of theirs, and to provide an extension of territory which the rapid increase of our numbers will call for, two measures are deemed expedient: first, to encourage them to abandon hunting, to apply to the raising of stock, to agriculture and domestic manufactures, and thereby prove to themselves that less land and labor will maintain them in this better than in their former mode of living. The extensive forests necessary in the hunting life will then become useless, and they will see advantage in exchanging them for the means of improving their farms and of increasing their domestic comforts.

Secondly, to multiply trading houses among them, and place within their reach those things which will contribute more to their domestic comfort than the possession of extensive but uncultivated wilds. Experience and reflection will develop to them the wisdom of exchanging what they can spare and we want for what we can spare and they want. In leading them thus to agriculture, to manufactures and civilization, in bringing together their and our settlements, and in preparing them ultimately to participate in the benefits of our government, I trust and believe we are acting for their greatest good. . . .

The river Missouri, and the Indians inhabiting it are not as well known as is rendered desirable by their connection with the Mississippi and consequently with us. It is, however, understood that the country on that river is inhabited by numerous tribes who furnish great supplies of furs and peltry to the trade of another nation, carried on in a high latitude, through an infinite number of portages and lakes shut up by ice through a long season. The commerce on that line could bear no competition with that of the Missouri, traversing a moderate climate, offering, according to the best accounts, a continued navigation from its source, and possibly with a single portage from the western ocean, and finding to the Atlantic a choice of channels. . . .

An intelligent officer with ten or twelve chosen men fit for the enterprise, and willing to undertake it, taken from our posts where they may be spared without inconvenience, might explore the whole line even to the western ocean; have conferences with the natives on the subject of commercial intercourse; get admission among them for our traders, as others are admitted; agree on convenient deposits for an interchange of articles; and return with the information acquired in the course of two summers.

Their arms and accoutrements, some instruments of observation, and light and cheap presents for the Indians would be all the apparatus they could carry, and with an expectation of a soldier's portion of land on their return, would constitute the whole expense. Their pay would be going on whether here or there.

While other civilized nations have encountered great expense to enlarge the boundaries of knowledge by undertaking voyages of discovery and for other literary purposes in various parts and directions, our nation seems to owe to the same object, as well as to its own interests, to explore this, the only line of easy communication across the continent, and so directly traversing our own part of it. . . . That it should incidentally advance the geographical knowledge of our own continent cannot but be an additional gratification.

The nation claiming the territory, regarding this as a literary pursuit, which it is in the habit of permitting within its own dominions, would not be disposed to view it with jealousy, even if the expiring state of its interests there did not render it a matter of indifference. The appropriation of $2500 "for the purpose of extending the external commerce of the United States," while understood and considered by the executive as giving the legislative sanction, would cover the undertaking from notice and prevent the obstructions which interested individuals might otherwise previously prepare in its way.

From "Confidential Message [to Congress] Recommending a Western Exploring Expedition," Thomas Jefferson. *American State Papers*, Executive Documents, 7th Congress, 2nd Session.

IX

William Clark

Grudgingly Congress put up the $2500 that the President wanted to expend on an expedition to "the western ocean," and Jefferson lost no time in getting it organized. As a substitute for the late John Ledyard, he immediately appointed to head the undertaking his own private secretary and fellow Virginian, Meriwether Lewis, who had earned his army captaincy in assorted frontier skirmishes; and the captain in turn persuaded another frontier campaigner, Lieutenant William Clark (1770–1838) to join him as associate leader.

The detachment of "ten or twelve chosen men" that Jefferson originally proposed gradually multiplied until it comprised four times that number and included an infantry unit of over thirty, two interpreters, and even Clark's indispensable private slave, Yorkland; to these were added along the way native chiefs, Canadian boatmen, porters, volunteer pathfinders, and the heroine of the whole entourage, Sacajawea, the Bird Woman—a loyal squaw taken on as guide and vanguard, who over thousands of miles pushed ahead of the others to prepare Indian villages for the coming of the white men, and saved the expedition many times from certain annihilation.

International politics, too, worked in favor of Lewis and Clark. Shortly before their departure, France's Napoleon, who in a

[43]

secret treaty with Spain had just acquired title to the Louisiana Territory, decided to sell the tract to the United States, so there was no longer any question of trespass between the Mississippi and the Rockies.

Late in 1803 the nucleus of the party gathered near the mouth of the Missouri, and as soon as it was free of ice the following spring, they started up the river. By late fall they reached the site of Bismarck, North Dakota, and wintered there. Then began the hard part of the journey: to the Three Forks of the Missouri, up the Jefferson, across the Continental Divide, over the Bitterroot Mountains, and down the westward-flowing rivers—the Clearwater, the Snake and Columbia—to the coast. Not a day's travel in all that distance was free of suspense, agonizing fatigue, and danger.

They had expected that drifting down the Columbia would be a pleasant climax for their long circuit. Instead it was a climactic ordeal, the most hazardous, nervewracking part of the entire journey. On the upper waters they contended daily with white water, upsets, exhausting portages, tedious Indian visitations, and torment from the swarms of fleas at Indian villages. And as they neared the coast, they found little cause for celebration. November storms swept in, one after another, subjecting them to discomforts, delays, and perils that threatened destruction within sight of their goal.

At the mouth of the Columbia they had hoped they might be picked up by a trading ship returning to the East, but someone had faltered in this detail of the planning. No one had thought even to alert captains to be on the lookout for the party, and ironically, a trader that could have taken them aboard passed unseen almost within hailing distance. Stranded at the mouth of the river, they were obliged to erect a crude shelter—Fort Clatsop—where they fought off starvation through the winter, and the next year they retraced the long trail across the continent. Instead of the "two summers" Jefferson had estimated for the expedition, it took three and a half years. Yet that original appropriation of $2500 was to prove one of the most remunerative investments in United States financial history.

Out of respect for William Clark, who made his journal jottings by campfire light, in pelting rain, frequently in desperate plight—and who was inclined to write phonetically and punctuate sparingly—the excerpts covering the last trying days at the mouth of the Columbia are here freely edited.

By Land

November 7th [1805]. Great joy in camp. We are in view of the ocean, this great Pacific Ocean which we have been so long anxious to see, and the roaring or noise made by the waves breaking on the rocky shores (as I suppose) may be heard distinctly.

November 8th. A cloudy morning with some rain. We did not set out until nine o'clock. . . . We came to at the remains of an old village. . . . Here we found great numbers of fleas, which we treated with the greatest caution and distance. . . .

The swells or waves were so high that we thought it imprudent to proceed. We landed, unloaded and drew up our canoes. Rain all day at intervals. We were all wet and disagreeable, as we have been for several days past. . . . We have not level land sufficient for an encampment and for our baggage to lie clear of the tide. . . . Added to this, the waves are increasing to such a height that we cannot move from the place. . . .

We are not certain as yet if the white people who trade with the Indians . . . are stationary at the mouth or visit this quarter at stated times for the purpose of traffic. . . . The seas rolled and tossed the canoes in such a manner this evening that several of our party were seasick. . . .

November 9th. The tide of last night did not rise sufficiently high to come into our camp, but the canoes, which were exposed to the mercy of the waves . . . all filled; with great attention we saved them until the tide left them dry. . . . At two o'clock the flood tide came in accompanied by immense waves and heavy winds, floated the trees and drift . . . and tossed them about in such a manner as to endanger the canoes very much. Every exertion and the strictest attention by every individual of the party was scarcely sufficient to save our canoes from being crushed by those monstrous trees, many of them nearly two hundred feet long and from four to seven feet through. Our camp entirely under water during the height of the tide. Every man as wet as water could make them all the last night and today all day, as the rain continued.

At four o'clock P.M. the wind shifted about to the southwest and blew with great violence immediately from the ocean for about two hours. Notwithstanding the disagreeable situation of our party, all wet and cold, and one which they have experienced for several days past, they are cheerful and anxious to see further into the ocean. The water of the river being too salt to use, we are obliged to make use of rain water. Some of the party, not accustomed to salt water, have made too free use of it; on them it acts as a purgative. At this dismal point we must spend another night, as the wind and waves are too high to proceed.

November 10th. Rained very hard the greater part of the last night and continues this morning. The wind has layed and the swells are fallen. We loaded our canoes and proceeded on. . . .

The wind rose from the northwest and the swells became so high, we were compelled to return about two miles to a place where we could unload our canoes, which was in a small bay, on driftwood, on which we had also to make our fires to dry ourselves as well as we could, the shore being either a cliff or perpendicular rocks or steep ascents to the height of 400 or 500 feet. . . . The logs on which we lie are all afloat every high tide. The rain continued all day. We are all wet, also our bedding and many other articles. . . . Nothing to eat but pounded fish.

November 11th. A hard rain all the last night. During the last tide the logs on which we lay were all afloat. Sent out Jo Fields to hunt. He soon returned and informed us that the hills were so high and steep and thick with undergrowth and fallen timber that he could not get out any distance. About twelve o'clock five Indians came down in a canoe, the wind very high from the southwest, with most tremendous waves breaking with great violence against the shores, rain falling in torrents. We are all wet as usual, and our situation is truly a disagreeable one. The great quantities of rain . . . have loosened the stones on the hillsides, and the small stones fall down upon us. Our canoes are at one place, at the mercy of the waves, our baggage in another, and ourselves and party scattered on floating logs and such dry spots as can be found on the hillsides and crevices of the rocks.

We purchased of the Indians thirteen red char, which we found to be excellent fish. . . . One of those men had on a sailor's jacket and pantaloons, and made signs that he got those clothes from the white people who lived below the point, etc. Those people left us and crossed the river, which is about five miles wide at this place, through the highest waves I ever saw a small vessel ride. Those Indians are certainly the best canoe navigators I ever saw. Rained all day.

November 12th. A tremendous wind from the southwest about three o'clock this morning with lightning and hard claps of thunder and hail, which continued until six o'clock A.M., when it became light for a short time. Then the heavens became suddenly darkened by a black cloud from the southwest and rained with great violence until twelve o'clock, the waves tremendous breaking with great fury against the rocks and trees on which we are encamped. Our situation is dangerous. We took the advantage of a low tide and moved our camp around a point to a small wet bottom at the mouth of a brook. . . .

It would be distressing to see our situation—all wet and cold, our bedding also wet, and the robes of the party which compose half the bedding are rotten, and we are not in a situation to supply their places, in a wet bottom scarcely large enough to contain us, our baggage half a mile from us, and canoes at the mercy of the waves, although secured as well as possible, sunk with immense parcels of stone to weight them down to prevent their dashing to pieces against the rocks. . . . If we have cold weather before we can kill and dress skins for clothing, the bulk of the party will suffer very much.

November 15th. Rained all the last night at intervals of sometimes of two hours. This morning it became cold and fair. . . . The sun shown until one o'clock P.M., which gave an opportunity for us to dry some of our bedding and examine our baggage, the greater part of which I found wet. Some of our pounded fish spoiled. I had all the arms put in order and ammunition examined. The rainy weather continued without a longer intermission than two hours at a time from the fifth in the morning until the 16th—eleven days rain, and the most disagreeable time I have experienced, confined on a tempest coast, wet, where I can neither get out to hunt, return to a better situation, or proceed on. In this situation have we been for six days past.

Fortunately the wind lay about three o'clock. We loaded in great haste and set out, passed the blustering point, below which is a sand beach . . . on which is a large village of thirty-six houses, deserted by the Indians and in full possession of the fleas. . . . The immense swells from the main ocean, immediately in front of us, raised to such a height that I concluded to form a camp on the highest spot I could find in the marshy bottom and proceed no further by water. . . . The ocean is immediately in front and gives us an extensive view of it from Cape Disappointment to Point Adams. . . . Evening fair and pleasant. Our men all comfortable in the camps they have made of the boards they found in the town above.

November 17th. A fair cool morning. Wind from the east. . . . At half past ten o'clock Captain Lewis returned, having traversed Haley Bay to Cape Disappointment and the seacoast to the north for some distance. Several Chinook Indians followed Captain Lewis and a canoe came up with roots, mats, etc. to sell. . . . This Chinook nation is about 400 souls; [they] inhabit the country on the small rivers which run into the bay below us and on the ponds to the northwest of us, liv[ing] principally on fish and roots. They are well armed with fusees and sometimes kill elk, deer and fowl. Our hunters killed today three deer, four brant and two ducks, and inform me they saw some elk sign. I directed all the men who wished to see more of the main ocean to prepare themselves to set out with me early on tomorrow morning. . . .

November 18th. I set out with ten men and my man York to the ocean by land. . . . At three miles passed a nitch. This rock island is small and at the south of a deep bend in which the natives inform us the ships anchor, and from whence they receive their goods in return for their peltries and elk skins, etc. This appears to be a very good harbor for large ships. Here I found Captain Lewis' name on a tree. I also engraved my name and "BY LAND," the day of the month and year. . . . The men appear much satisfied with their trip, beholding with astonishment the high waves dashing against the rocks and this immense ocean.

From *Original Journals of the Lewis and Clark Expedition,* Volume III, edited by Reuben Gold Thwaites (New York: Dodd, Mead and Company, 1904–5).

X

John R. Jewitt

If the patience of Lewis and Clark and their heterogeneous company had not been exhausted by an interminable winter at Fort Clatsop, and if they had been content to wait a few months longer, they would most certainly have hitched passage back home, for there was now more American traffic than British in the Northwest. Yankee peddlers who once sold their wares from door to door in New England had expanded their beat until it extended from the lower Canadian provinces into the Deep South, and then had taken to sea in search of marts around the globe. In their wanderings they had discovered the Northwest, and for a generation these Yankee sea peddlers, ready to exchange for furs anything from Bibles to boots, outnumbered all other hucksters on the Pacific coast. Their ships were floating general stores.

The brig *Lydia* of Boston was such an emporium. It was the very ship that bypassed Lewis and Clark at the mouth of the Columbia in the fall of 1805; and by chance her Captain Samuel Hill had just completed a mission of mercy in rescuing another stranded adventurer, John R. Jewitt (1783–1821), who for more than two years had been held captive by the Nootka Indians. Jewitt had survived as thrilling an experience as a shipwrecked Robinson Crusoe.

The son of a Lincolnshire blacksmith, and a good smith himself, young John had joined the crew of the American ship *Boston* as armorer at the British port of Hull while she was taking aboard the biggest cargo of Indian trading goods yet sent to the Northwest: "English cloths, Dutch blankets, looking glasses, beads, knives, razors . . . sugar, molasses, about twenty hogsheads of rum, a great quantity of ammunition, cutlasses, pistols and 3000 muskets and fowling pieces."

After a relatively uneventful trip around the Horn, the *Boston* arrived off Vancouver Island on March 12, 1803, and immediately started trading with the Indians. During the barter John was kept busy at his anvil fashioning custom-made hooks, chisels, and daggers for the natives, fascinating them with his dexterity. But the great Nootka chief, Maquina, was insulted while the trading was going on, and stormed ashore, bent on revenge. When the trading resumed on the following day, a pretense of entertainment by the tribesmen was suddenly turned into a gruesome assault, in which the outnumbered crew and officers were indiscriminately massacred. Only the popular blacksmith and sailmaker Thompson were spared.

A riot of pillage, above decks and below, followed, but scarcely half the cargo was appropriated by the Indians before the ship was accidentally set afire and totally destroyed. Then began Jewitt's melancholy months of slaving as blacksmith for his captors. But his craftsmanship and tact won the confidence and affection of Maquina, and also won him privileges of which he took full advantage.

He befriended representatives of other tribes who were trying to lure him into their camps, and through them broadcast missives addressed anonymously to the captain of any ship that might appear on the coast. At last Captain Hill of the *Lydia* was handed one of the appeals and went to the rescue. Although the story belongs more to Vancouver Island than to the state of Washington, it was toward the land of the Chinooks that Jewitt looked for his deliverance, and from whence it came.

The Rescue of John Jewitt

It was now past midsummer, and the hopes we had indulged of our release became daily more faint, for though we had heard of no less than seven vessels on the coast, yet none appeared inclined to venture to Nootka. The destruction of the *Boston*, the largest, strongest and best equipped ship, with much the most valuable cargo of any that had ever been fitted out for the Northwest trade, had inspired the commanders of others with a general dread of coming thither lest they should share the same fate; and though in the letters I wrote, imploring those who should receive them to come to the relief of two unfortunate Christians who were suffering among heathen, I stated the cause of the *Boston*'s capture and that there was not the least danger in coming to Nootka . . . still I felt very little encouragement that any of these letters would come to hand.

Then on the morning of the 19th of July [1805], a day that will be ever held by me in grateful remembrance of the mercies of God, while I was employed with Thompson in forging daggers for the king, my ears were saluted with the joyful sound of three cannon, and the cries of the inhabitants exclaiming, "Weena, weena—Mamethlee," that is, strangers—white men.

Soon after, several of our people came running into the house to inform me that a vessel under full sail was coming into the harbor. Though my heart bounded with joy, I repressed my feelings, and affecting to pay no attention to what was said, told Thompson to be on his guard and not betray any joy, as our release, and perhaps our lives, depended on our conducting ourselves so as to induce the natives to suppose we were not very anxious to leave them.

We continued our work as if nothing had happened, when in a few minutes Maquina came in, and seeing us at work, appeared much surprised and asked me if I did not know that a vessel had come. I answered in a careless manner that it was nothing to me.

"How, John," said he, "you no glad go board?"

I replied that I cared very little about it, as I had become reconciled to their manner of living and had no wish to go away. He then told me that he had called a council of his people respecting us and that we must leave off work and be present at it.

The men having assembled at Maquina's house, he asked them what was their opinion should be done with Thompson and myself now a vessel had arrived, and whether he had not better go on board himself to make a trade and procure such articles as were wanted. . . . Some were for putting us to death and pretending to the strangers that a different nation had cut off the *Boston,* while others, less barbarous, were for sending us fifteen or twenty miles back into the country until the departure of the vessel.

These, however, were the sentiments of the common people, the chiefs opposing our being put to death or injured, and several of them . . . were for immediately releasing us. But this, if he could avoid it, by no means appeared to accord with Maquina's wishes. . . . With regard to his going on board the vessel, which he displayed a strong inclination to do, there was but one opinion —all remonstrating against it, telling him that the captain would kill him or keep him prisoner in consequence of his having destroyed our ship.

When Maquina had heard their opinions, he told them that he was not afraid of being hurt from going on board the vessel, but that he would, however, be guided by John, whom he had always found true. He then turned to me and asked me if I thought there would be any danger in his going on board. I answered that . . . he had almost always experienced good and civil treatment from them, nor had he any reason to fear the contrary now, as they never attempted to harm those who did not injure them, and if he wished to go on board he might do it with security.

After reflecting a few moments, he said with much apparent satisfaction that if I would write a letter to the captain, telling him good of him, that he had treated Thompson and myself kindly since we had been with him, and to use him well, he would go. . . .

I felt much joy at this determination, but knowing that the

least incaution might annihilate all my hopes of escape, I was
careful not to manifest it and to treat his going or staying as a
matter perfectly indifferent to me. I told him that if he wished me
to write such a letter I had no objection, as it was the truth. I then
proceeded to write the recommendatory letter . . . of a somewhat different tenor from the one he had required, for if decep-
tion is in any case warrantable, it was certainly so in a situation
like ours, where the only chance of regaining that freedom of
which we had been so unjustly deprived, depended on it . . . :

Sir,
    The bearer of this letter is the Indian king by the name of Maquina.
He was the instigator of the capture of the ship *Boston,* of Boston in
North America, John Salter captain, and of the murder of twenty-five
men of her crew, the two only survivors being now on shore——
Wherefore I hope you will take care to confine him according to his
merits, putting in your dead-lights and keeping so good a watch
over him that he cannot escape from you. By so doing we shall be
able to obtain our release in the course of a few hours.
                                    John R. Jewitt, *Armourer of*
                                    the Boston *for himself and*
                                    John Thompson, *Sail-maker of*
                                    said ship.

. . . . From my long residence among these people I knew that I
had little to apprehend from their anger on hearing of their king
being confined, while they knew his life depended upon my
release, and that they would sooner have given up five hundred
white men than have had him injured. . . .
    On my giving the letter to Maquina, he asked me to explain it
to him. This I did line by line, as he pointed them out with his
finger, but in a sense very different from the real, giving him to
understand that I had written to the captain that as he had been
kind to me since I had been taken by him, that it was my wish
that the captain should treat him accordingly and give him what
molasses, biscuit and rum he wanted.
    . . . Never did I undergo such a scrutiny or ever experience
greater apprehensions than I felt at that moment. . . . The least
mark of embarrassment on mine or suspicion of treachery on his

part would probably have rendered my life the sacrifice. Fortunately I was able to preserve my composure, and my being painted in the Indian manner . . . prevented any change in my countenance from being noticed. . . . Observing nothing to excite his suspicion, he told me that he believed what I said was true, and that he would go on board, and gave orders to get ready his canoe. . . .

Scarcely had the canoe put off when he ordered his men to stop, and calling to me asked me if I did not want to go on board with him. Suspecting this as a question merely intended to ensnare me, I replied that I did not wish to do it, not having any desire to leave them.

On going on board the brig, Maquina immediately gave his present of skins and my letter to the captain, who on reading it asked him into his cabin, where he gave him some biscuit and a glass of rum, at the same time privately directing his mate to go forward and return with five or six of the men armed. When they appeared, the captain told Maquina that he was his prisoner and should continue so until the two men, whom he knew to be on shore, were released, at the same time ordering him to be put in irons and the windows secured, which was instantly done. . . .

Maquina was greatly surprised and terrified at this reception; he, however, made no attempt to resist, but requested the captain to permit one of his men to come and see him. One of them was accordingly called and Maquina said something to him which the captain . . . supposed to be an order to release us. . . .

In a few minutes, to my inexpressible delight, I once more found myself alongside of a Christian ship, a happiness which I had almost despaired of ever again enjoying. All the crew crowded to the side to see me as the canoe came up and manifested much joy at my safety. I immediately leaped on board, where I was welcomed by the captain, Samuel Hill of the brig *Lydia* of Boston, who congratulated me on my escape, informing me that he had received my letter . . . and immediately proceeded hither to aid me.

I returned him my thanks in the best manner I could for his humanity, though I hardly knew what I said, such was the

agitated state of my feelings at that moment. . . . What with my
strange dress, being painted with red and black from head to foot,
having a bear skin wrapped around me, and my long hair, which
I was not allowed to cut, fastened on the top of my head in a
large bunch with a sprig of green spruce, I must have appeared
more like one deranged than a rational creature, as Captain Hill
afterwards told me that he never saw anything in the form of man
look so wild as I did when I first came on board.

The captain then asked me into the cabin, where I found
Maquina in irons, with a guard over him. He looked very melancholy, but on seeing me his countenance brightened up and he
expressed his pleasure with the welcome of "Wocash John,"
when, taking him by the hand, I asked the captain's permission to
take off his irons. . . . Such was the transport he felt when Captain Hill . . . told him he was at liberty to go that he threw off
his mantle, which consisted of four of the very best skins and
gave it to him as a mark of his gratitude. . . . The captain then
desired me to inform him that he should return to that part of the
coast in November and that he wished him to keep what skins he
should get, which he would buy of him. This Maquina promised,
saying to me at the same time, "John, . . . when you come, make
pow (which means fire a gun) to let me know, and I will come
down." . . . Then grasping both my hands, with much emotion,
while the tears trickled down his cheeks, he bade me farewell and
stepped into the canoe, which immediately paddled him on
shore. . . .

The brig being under weigh immediately on Maquina's quit-
ting us, we proceeded to the northward, constantly keeping the
shore in sight and touching at various places for the purpose of
trading. . . . After a period of nearly four months from our
leaving Nootka, we returned from the northward to Columbia
River for the purpose of procuring masts, etc. for our brig, which
had suffered considerably in her spars during a gale of wind.

We proceeded about ten miles up the river to a small Indian
village where we heard from the inhabitants that Captains Clark
and Lewis from the United States of America had been there
about a fortnight before on their journey overland, and had left

several medals with them, which they showed us. The river at this place is of considerable breadth and both sides of it from its entrance covered with forests of the very finest pine timber, fir and spruce, interspersed with Indian settlements.

From here, after providing ourselves with spars, we sailed for Nootka, where we arrived in the latter part of November. . . . Inquiry was immediately made . . . if John was there, as the king had some skins to sell them if he was. I then went forward and invited them on board, with which they readily complied, telling me that Maquina had a number of skins with him, but that he would not come on board unless I would go on shore for him.

This I agreed to, provided they would remain in the brig in the meantime. To this they consented. . . . I then went on shore in the canoe, notwithstanding the remonstrances of Thompson and the captain who, though he wanted the skins, advised me by no means to put myself in Maquina's power. But I assured him that I had no fear as long as those men were on board.

As I landed, Maquina came up and welcomed me with much joy. On his inquiring for the men, I told him that they were to remain till my return. "Ah, John," said he, "I see you are afraid to trust me. But if they had come with you, I should not have hurt you, though I should have taken good care not to let you go on board of another vessel."

Condensed from *A Narrative of the Adventures and Sufferings of John R. Jewitt* (Middletown: Seth Richards, 1815).

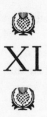

XI

Washington Irving

The success of the Yankee peddlers in the Northwest market and the report of the Lewis and Clark expedition caught the attention of a German immigrant in Manhattan, John Jacob Astor, who had started his career as a shopkeeper, dealing principally in musical instruments, and then switched to the more lucrative trade of furs. An early prescience had convinced young Astor that he would one day be a very rich man, and within twenty years after his 1784 arrival in New York he was well on the way toward holding a monopoly on the American fur market as well as becoming the wealthiest man in the United States.

As head of the American Fur Company, he controlled a wilderness kingdom extending deep into Canada and west beyond the Great Lakes, and by 1810 aspired to an even broader realm. He founded the Pacific Fur Company and entertained ideas of superseding all the Yankee peddlers of the West by establishing a trading capital at the mouth of the Columbia—"the emporium of an immense commerce, and a colony that would form the germ of a wide civilization, that would, in fact, carry the American population across the Rocky Mountains and spread it along the shores of the Pacific."

With the blessings of Thomas Jefferson and the federal government, he proceeded to carry out his plan; he would remain in

New York, but headquarters for the new company would be at Astoria on the other side of the continent. His prospectus was almost too pat: "Posts would be established in the interior, and on all the tributary streams of the Columbia, to trade with the Indians; these posts would draw their supplies from the main establishment and bring to it the peltries they collected. Coasting craft would be built and fitted out, also at the mouth of the Columbia, to trade at favorable seasons all along the northwest coast and return with the proceeds of their voyages to this place of deposit. Thus all the Indian trade, both of the interior and the coast, would converge on this point and thence derive its sustenance. A ship was to be sent annually from New York to this main establishment with reinforcements and supplies, and with merchandise suited to the trade. It would take on board the furs collected during the preceding year, carry them to Canton, invest the proceeds in the rich merchandise of China, and return thus freighted to New York."

Actually there was nothing very original about the scheme. It was borrowed intact from the operations of the Hudson's Bay Company, the North West Fur Company, and the New England coastal traders. He was merely combining and enlarging upon the procedures.

But Astor made one big mistake. In his overweening ambition, he boldly proposed to British officials of the powerful North West Company, which already stretched across Canada to the Pacific, that they form a kind of loose merger. He was turned down summarily, but in making the proposal, he had tipped his hand, informed his competitors of his intentions, and the North West Company at once took steps to invade the Columbia region ahead of him. Astor retaliated by abducting from North West, with promises of partnerships and big returns, experienced men like Alexander McKay. The war of the furs was on.

From the start, the success of Astor's great scheme seemed doomed. The competition with the aggressive British companies proved too stiff, and the War of 1812 came at the wrong time. The one event, however, that crippled the Pacific Fur Company at the beginning was the tragic loss of its first supply ship, the

Tonquin. Her freight had just been unloaded at Astoria and she was sailing up the coast on her initial mission of trade when catastrophe struck. The fur capital, of course, was on the Oregon side of the Columbia and the *Tonquin's* itinerary took her north of Juan de Fuca Strait, but envisioned in Astor's plan was a penetration of every fur-yielding haunt between the Columbia and the Fraser rivers, and the catastrophe accordingly had a far-reaching effect upon the future of the whole region.

Washington Irving (1783–1859), the literary giant of the period and a close friend of Astor's, was employed by the fur merchant to draft the Pacific saga in his *Astoria.*

The Tonquin *Disaster*

The *Tonquin* set sail from the mouth of the [Columbia] River on the fifth of June [1811]. The whole number of persons on board amounted to twenty-three. In one of the outer bays they picked up from a fishing canoe an Indian named Lamazee, who had already made two voyages along the coast and knew something of the language of the various tribes. He agreed to accompany them as interpreter.

Steering to the north, Captain Thorn arrived in a few days at Vancouver's Island and anchored in the harbor of Neweetee, very much against the advice of his Indian interpreter, who warned him against the perfidious character of the natives of this part of the coast. Numbers of canoes soon came off, bringing sea-otter skins to sell. It was too late in the day to commence a traffic, but Mr. McKay [supercargo], accompanied by a few of the men, went on shore to a large village to visit Wicananish, the chief of the surrounding territory, six of the natives remaining on board as hostages. He was received with great professions of friendship, entertained hospitably, and a couch of sea-otter skins was prepared for him in the dwelling of the chieftain, where he was prevailed upon to pass the night.

In the morning, before Mr. McKay had returned to the ship,

great numbers of the natives came off in their canoes to trade,
headed by two sons of Wicananish. As they brought abundance
of sea-otter skins and there was every appearance of a brisk trade,
Captain Thorn did not wait for the return of Mr. McKay, but
spread his wares upon deck, making a tempting display of blankets, cloths, knives, beads and fishhooks, expecting a prompt and
profitable sale.

The Indians, however, were not so eager and simple as he supposed, having learned the art of bargaining and the value of merchandise from the casual traders along the coast. They were
guided, too, by a shrewd old chief named Nookamis, who had
grown gray in traffic with New England skippers and prided himself upon his acuteness. His opinion seemed to regulate the
market. When Captain Thorn made what he considered a liberal
offer for an otter skin, the wily old Indian treated it with scorn,
and asked more than double. His comrades all took their cue from
him, and not an otter skin was to be had at a reasonable rate.

The old fellow, however, overshot his mark and mistook the
character of the man he was treating with. Thorn was a plain,
straightforward sailor who never had two minds nor two prices in
his dealings, was deficient in patience and pliancy, and totally
wanting in the chicanery in traffic. He had a vast deal of stern but
honest pride in his nature and, moreover, held the whole savage
race in sovereign contempt. Abandoning all further attempts,
therefore, to bargain with his shuffling customers, he thrust his
hands into his pockets and paced up and down the deck in sullen
silence.

The cunning old Indian followed him to and fro, holding out a
sea-otter skin to him at every turn, and pestering him to trade.
Finding other means unavailing, he suddenly changed his tone
and began to jeer and banter him upon the mean prices he
offered. This was too much for the patience of the captain, who
was never remarkable for relishing a joke, especially when at his
own expense.

Turning suddenly upon his persecutor, he snatched the
proffered otter skin from his hands, rubbed it in his face, and
dismissed him over the side of the ship with no very complimen-

tary application to accelerate his exit. He then kicked the peltries to the right and left about the deck and broke up the market in the most ignominious manner. Old Nookamis made for the shore in a furious passion, in which he was joined by Shewish, one of the sons of Wicananish, who went off breathing vengeance, and the ship was soon abandoned by the natives.

When Mr. McKay returned on board, the interpreter related what had passed and begged him to prevail upon the captain to make sail, as from his knowledge of the temper and pride of the people of the place he was sure they would resent the indignity offered to one of their chiefs. Mr. McKay . . . went to the captain, who was still pacing the deck in moody humor, represented the danger to which his hasty act had exposed the vessel and urged him to weigh anchor. The captain made light of his counsels and pointed to his cannon and firearms as sufficient safeguard against naked savages. Further remonstrances only provoked taunting replies and sharp altercations. The day passed away without any signs of hostility, and at night the captain retired as usual to his cabin, taking no more than the usual precautions.

On the following morning at daybreak, while the captain and Mr. McKay were yet asleep, a canoe came alongside in which were twenty Indians, commanded by young Shewish. They were unarmed, their aspect and demeanor friendly, and they held up otter skins and made signs indicative of a wish to trade. . . . The officer of the watch, perceiving those in the canoe to be without weapons and having received no orders to the contrary, readily permitted them to mount the deck. Another canoe soon succeeded, the crew of which was likewise admitted. In a little while other canoes came off, and Indians were soon clambering into the vessel on all sides.

The officer of the watch now felt alarmed and called to Captain Thorn and Mr. McKay. By the time they came on deck it was thronged with Indians. The interpreter noticed to Mr. McKay that many of the natives wore short mantles of skins, and intimated a suspicion that they were secretly armed. Mr. McKay urged the captain to clear the ship and get under way. He again made light of the advice; but the augmented swarm of canoes about the ship and the numbers still putting off from shore at length awakened his distrust, and he ordered some of the crew to weigh anchor, while some were sent aloft to make sail.

The Indians now offered to trade with the captain on his own terms, prompted apparently by the approaching departure of the ship. Accordingly a hurried trade was commenced. The main articles sought by the savages in barter were knives; as fast as some were supplied they moved off and others succeeded. By degrees they were thus distributed about the deck, and all with weapons.

The anchor was now nearly up, the sails were loose, and the captain in a loud and peremptory tone ordered the ship to be cleared. In an instant a signal yell was given; it was echoed on every side; knives and war clubs were brandished in every direction and the savages rushed upon their marked victims. The first that fell was Mr. Lewis, the ship's clerk. He was leaning with folded arms over a bale of blankets, engaged in bargaining, when he received a deadly stab in the back and fell down the companionway. Mr. McKay, who was seated on the taffrail, sprang to his feet but was instantly knocked down with a war club and flung backwards into the sea, where he was dispatched by the women in the canoes.

In the meantime Captain Thorn made desperate fight against fearful odds. He was a powerful as well as a resolute man, but he had come upon deck without weapons. Shewish, the young chief, singled him out as his peculiar prey and rushed upon him at the first outbreak. The captain had barely time to draw a clasp knife, with one blow of which he laid the young savage dead at his feet.

Several of the stoutest followers of Shewish now set upon him. He defended himself vigorously, dealing crippling blows to right and left, and strewing the quarter-deck with the slain and wounded. His object was to fight his way to the cabin, where there were firearms, but he was hemmed in with foes, covered with wounds and faint with loss of blood. For an instant he leaned upon the tiller wheel, when a blow from behind with a war club felled him to the deck, where he was dispatched with knives and thrown overboard.

While this was transacting upon the quarter-deck, a chance-medley fight was going on throughout the ship. The crew fought desperately with knives, handspikes and whatever weapon they could seize upon in the moment of surprise. They were soon, however, overpowered by numbers and mercilessly butchered.

As to the seven who had been sent aloft to make sail, they contemplated with horror the carnage that was going on below. Being destitute of weapons, they let themselves down by the running rigging, in hopes of getting between decks. One fell in the attempt and was instantly dispatched; another received a death blow in the back as he was descending; a third, Stephen Weekes, the armorer, was mortally wounded as he was getting down the hatchway. The remaining four made good their retreat into the cabin, where they found Mr. Lewis still alive, though mortally wounded. Barricading the cabin door, they broke holes through the companionway and with the muskets and ammunition which were at hand opened a brisk fire that soon cleared the deck.

. . . The survivors of the crew now sallied forth and discharged some of the deck guns, which did great execution among the canoes and drove all the savages to shore. For the remainder of the day no one ventured to put off to the ship. . . . The night passed away without any further attempt on the part of the natives. When the day dawned, the *Tonquin* still lay at anchor in the bay, her sails all loose and flapping in the wind and no one apparently on board of her.

After a time some of the canoes ventured forth to reconnoiter, taking with them the interpreter. They paddled about her, keeping cautiously at a distance, but growing more and more emboldened at seeing her quiet and lifeless. One man at length made his appearance on the deck, and was recognized by the interpreter as Mr. Lewis. He made friendly signs and invited them on board. It was long before they ventured to comply. Those who mounted the deck met with no opposition; no one was to be seen on board, for Mr. Lewis, after inviting them, had disappeared.

Other canoes now pressed forward to board the prize; the decks were soon crowded, and the sides covered with clambering savages, all intent on plunder. In the midst of their eagerness and exultation the ship blew up with a tremendous explosion. Arms, legs and mutilated bodies were blown into the air, and dreadful havoc was made in the surrounding canoes. The interpreter was in the mainchains at the time of the explosion and was thrown unhurt into the water, where he succeeded in getting into one of the canoes. According to his statement, the bay presented an awful spectacle after the catastrophe.

The ship had disappeared, but the bay was covered with fragments of the wreck, with shattered canoes, and Indians swimming for their lives or struggling in the agonies of death, while those who had escaped the danger remained aghast and stupefied, or made with frantic panic for the shore. Upwards of a hundred savages were destroyed by the explosion; many more were shockingly mutilated and for days afterwards the limbs and bodies of the slain were thrown upon the beach.

The inhabitants of Neweetee were overwhelmed with consternation at this astounding calamity which had burst upon them in the very moment of triumph. The warriors sat mute and mournful, while the women filled the air with loud lamentations. Their weeping and wailing, however, was suddenly changed into yells of fury at the sight of four unfortunate white men brought captive into the village. They had been driven on shore in one of the ship's boats and taken at some distance along the coast.

The interpreter was permitted to converse with them. They proved to be the four brave fellows who had made such desperate defense from the cabin. The interpreter gathered from them some of the particulars already related. They told him further that after they had beaten off the enemy and cleared the ship, Lewis advised that they should slip the cable and endeavor to get to sea. They declined to take his advice, alleging that the wind set too strongly into the bay and would drive them on shore. They resolved as soon as it was dark to put off quietly in the ship's boat, which they would be able to do unperceived, and to coast along back to Astoria. They put their resolution into effect, but Lewis refused to accompany them, being disabled by his wound, hopeless of escape, and determined on a terrible revenge.

. . . He now declared his intention to remain on board of the ship until daylight, to decoy as many of the savages on board as possible, then to set fire to the powder magazine and terminate his life by a signal act of vengeance. . . . His companions bade him a melancholy adieu and set off on their precarious expedition. They strove with might and main to get out of the bay, but found it impossible to weather a point of land, and were at length compelled to take shelter in a small cove. . . . Exhausted by fatigue and watching, they fell into a sound sleep, and in that state were surprised by the savages.

Better had it been for those unfortunate men had they remained with Lewis and shared his heroic death: as it was they perished in a more painful and protracted manner, being sacrificed by the natives to the manes of their friends with all the lingering tortures of savage cruelty. Some time after their death, the interpreter, who had remained a kind of prisoner at large, effected his escape and brought the tragical tidings to Astoria. . . .

Mr. Astor was well aware of the perils to which ships were exposed on this coast from quarrels with the natives and from perfidious attempts of the latter to surprise and capture them in unguarded moments. He had repeatedly enjoined it upon Captain Thorn, in conversation, and at parting, in his letter of instructions, to be courteous and kind in his dealings with the savages, but by no means to confide in their apparent friendship, *nor to admit more than a few on board of his ship at a time.* . . .

The loss of the *Tonquin* was a grievous blow to the infant establishment of Astoria, and one that threatened to bring after it a train of disasters. The intelligence of it did not reach Mr. Astor until many months afterwards. He felt it in all its force and was aware that it must cripple, if not entirely defeat, the great scheme of his ambition.

From *Astoria*, Washington Irving (New York: G. P. Putnam's Sons, 1868).

XII

Wilson Price Hunt

In his youth at Asbury, New Jersey, Wilson Price Hunt (1783–1879) heard the call of the wild, as well as the call of merchandising, and combined his talents as woodsman and tradesman so admirably that in 1810 he was offered—and accepted—a partnership in the Pacific Fur Company. According to Astor's plans for setting up an establishment at the mouth of the Columbia, two parties were to be dispatched to the site: one by sea on the *Tonquin,* the other by land. Partner Hunt was delegated to conduct the overland expedition.

At Michilimacinac, Michigan, one of the northern fur-trade centers, he recruited some sixty trail-hardened Canadian voyageurs, assembled them in St. Louis, and from there was to proceed up the Missouri and across the Rocky Mountains to the Columbia by the best route he could locate, spotting along the way sites for future Pacific Fur Company trading posts.

But Hunt did not arrive at Astoria until the middle of February, 1812, weeks after the *Tonquin,* and considered himself lucky to get there then. His trip had taken him through the tortures of a purgatory. Time and again he and his seasoned cohorts had suffered every misfortune known to the trapping trade. Not infrequently they had lost their way and become separated; they had been hunted down by Indians, ambushed by them, robbed

[67]

by them; for weeks on end they had been exposed to starvation; in the rapids of the Snake River the expedition had been wrecked and indispensable supplies lost; men had been drowned; all had taken a turn at fighting off a mysterious disease that dogged them; they had barely escaped being frozen to death; and finally, not knowing where to turn for help, had cached their trading goods, subdivided into small groups on the chance that some of them at least might find game enough for survival, and proceeded on different routes.

Late in January, 1812, the stragglers reassembled on the banks of the upper Columbia to begin their canoe-and-saddle trip down the river. Hunt described that last part of the journey in the rhetoric of a very tired man—language in which one can almost hear the sighs of exhaustion between the monotonously short sentences. After that experience, he was content to hoof it back to relatively civilized St. Louis and settle into the safety and security of a postmastership. Thousands of overlanders later were to make his acquaintance as the dispenser of the last communication from the East they would receive for a long time.

So Long Our Goal

On the 21st [of January, 1812] we at last reached the banks of the Columbia, for so long the goal of our desires. We had traveled 1751 miles; we had endured all the hardships imaginable. With difficulty I expressed our joy at sight of this river. It was three-fourths of a mile wide. Its shores were bare of trees, and were formed of pebbles and, in some places, of steep rocks.

They were inhabited by the Akaitchis, miserable Indians who have neither moccasins nor hose; their clothing consists of only a scanty mantle of the skin of bison, deer, rabbit or fox, or else of duck. They sometimes add to this a pair of sleeves of wolfskin. Their lodges are well made of mats, are in the shape of the roof of a house, and are very light and warm. Holes dug in the ground and furnished with mats are the abode of the women.

They usually are naked; some few have a scrap of robe which covers their shoulders, but all have around the waist a leathern belt which passes between the thighs and proves that they aspire to be decent. Also these Indians are better provided with food than are the Snakes, for it seems that dried salmon abounds with them. They gave us a large quantity of salmon-trout. . . . This fish is excellent. Their canoes are of pine trunks split in two; consequently they are not raised at bow and stern. Having no sort of tool, they have recourse to fire for hollowing these trees.

I crossed the river because I was told that the trail ran along the right or north bank. I left on the 23rd after purchasing fresh fish and nine dogs. The trail along the river was very good. We settled ourselves near a camp of Indians who had some fifty canoes. I bought nine dogs, which were very fat, and we made a delicious meal. Their flesh seemed to us well flavored, healthful and strengthening, whereas horsemeat, however well cooked, did not nourish, no matter how much one ate of it. The weather was fine and very mild, like the fine days of October.

From the 24th to the 28th we followed the river. . . . We frequently encountered huts of Indians. They sold us some dogs. They placed such a high price on the meat of elk and deer that I could not buy it. Moreover they caused us great inconvenience because they stole the ropes of the horses, which escaped and made us lose much time in recapturing them. Sometimes they took away these animals and hid them. These Indians ate acorns. . . .

On the 28th the country became very mountainous. The Indians seemed more prosperous. They talked to me of whites who had built a large house at the mouth of the river, had surrounded it with palisades, etc. They had not been there, but they informed me that the whites were in great trouble, expected a large number of their friends, constantly looked toward Big River and when we arrived, would dry their tears and would sing and dance.

The mountains and rocks along the river became more frequent on the 29th. The Indians whom we saw had many horses. We began to maintain a guard during the night. On the 30th we camped opposite the mouth of Chochoni River [Deschutes].

. . . The Indians had assembled in great number to dance in honor of our arrival. But this large crowd made me apprehensive and I accordingly pretended to be indisposed and begged them to leave me alone. They complied with my wishes after a little while.

On the 31st we passed the falls of the Columbia. . . . The bed of the river is blocked by rocks, across which the water violently plunges by several channels. . . . I arrived early at the village of Ouichram [Wishram] at the entrance of a long defile, in which the river has cut into the rock a canal from 200 to 240 feet wide and several miles long. This is the site of the great fishery of the Columbia. It resembles one of the small fishing ports on the eastern coast of the United States. On both sides of the river are to be seen large flakes, well made of interlaced sticks for drying fish. The ground is covered with the bones and heads of fish. In the springtime, when the waters of the river are high, the salmon come in schools so large that the Indians catch them with dip-nets attached to the end of poles. They station themselves for this purpose on the tips of the most projecting rocks.

The Indians of this place are the most intelligent I have yet seen. One of them knew several words of English. . . . He re-counted to me the catastrophe of Mr. McKay and of the ship *Tonquin*. . . .

February 1st. Last evening a great many Indians assembled near my camp. Not finding an opportunity to steal horses or goods, they devised an unusual stratagem to get something. They informed us that some forty Indians were coming from down-stream to attack us and take our horses. We paid little attention to their talk. Later some of the village chiefs arrived armed with knives, spears, etc., reiterating the story and adding that they wished to stay with us. I received them with extreme coldness and gave them a pipe to smoke. Then I collected all my people and placed sentinels at different points. . . . The rogues imag-ined that by frightening me I would have given them two or three horses to assure myself of the rest. . . .

I could procure only one canoe, and for this I traded a horse. The Indians have a great many [canoes]. They are very well

Indians fishing with dip-nets

made of pine wood, raised at bow and stern, and some of them are able to carry three thousand pounds. Despite my injunctions that careful watch be kept, the Indians had filched an axe. Emboldened by this success, several followed us on the 2nd and stole two guns; and at eleven o'clock in the evening, though our horses were in our camp, made off with one of them. On the 3rd I embarked in the canoe with all our goods and sent our horses ahead.

I met my party at a village on the right bank at the mouth of the Oatarack [Klickitat], and there purchased three canoes, each of which cost me a horse. While I was trading, the Indians pilfered a hatchet and our last axe. They also made off with Dorion's horse. . . . On the 4th the violence of the wind forced me, much against my wish to remain among this gang of thieves. . . .

The next day at a village where I arrived I traded the three remaining horses for canoes. It seemed that the trail ends at this village. The hills changed to mountains, which for the most part are snow-covered. One sees here some pines; they fringe both sides of the river. . . . The extremely heavy rain and the storm detained me several days opposite an Indian village. A Clatsop came to see us and talked to me of the establishment at the mouth of the river, as also of Mr. McKay's disaster. He was the third one to give me this distressing news. This Indian, who knew several English words, asked me for news of Messrs. Lewis and Clark and some of their companions. He already had heard of the death of Mr. Lewis.

On the 10th, the wind having abated, we embarked early. On reaching the commencement of the great rapids, I examined the portage on the left bank. The trail was good for a mile. We landed all the canoes at ten o'clock and were below the rapids before one o'clock. They are very great; the water, in dashing against the rocks, produces some very high waves. No boat could pass, at least in the present state of the river. . . .

On the 11th some rapids two miles in length forced us again to land our canoes. Finally eight miles from the great rapid we encountered the last one. Below it the river regains its usual width, which is three-fourths of a mile, and the hills diminish in height and recede from its banks. . . . On the 13th I passed the mouth of the Quicksand River [the Sandy]. . . . Twenty miles further down and on the same side the Columbia receives another river [Willamette], which is approximately 1800 feet wide. A large island lies in front of its mouth. There are several small ones a bit further down. The Columbia is here a mile and a quarter wide. On both sides of the vast brush-covered spaces we saw sometimes small prairies and frequently ponds. Seals were numerous. Much more distinctly than before, we saw the mountain which . . . must be the Mount Hood of Vancouver. For two days the wind had blown violently from the east. It hailed, rained and snowed.

On the 14th the mountains again drew close. We camped on the right bank at the mouth of a small river. Indians talked to us of our fellow-countrymen's establishment, adding that we should have no more than one night to sleep before reaching there. . . . On our voyage we frequently encountered huts of Indians who sold us dogs, dried salmon, beaver skins. . . . On the 16th we started early. It had rained all night. The fog was so thick that we could see only the lowlands and some small islands; all was covered by it. It disappeared in the afternoon at high tide. I found that we were navigating along a large bay, and shortly afterward I saw the fort of Astoria on the southerly bank.

I had the pleasure there of again meeting Messrs. Mackenzie and McClellan, who had arrived more than a month before, after having suffered incredible hardships. . . . It was a very real pleasure for travelers harassed by fatigue to rest in quiet and be surrounded by friends after so long a journey in the midst of savages, of whom it is always prudent to be wary. We had covered 2073 miles since leaving the Aricaras' village.

From "Journey of Mr. Hunt and His Companions from St. Louis to the Mouth of the Columbia," Wilson Price Hunt, as incorporated in *The Discovery of the Oregon Trail, Robert Stuart's Narratives*, edited by P. A. Rollins (New York: Charles Scribner's Sons, 1935).

XIII

David Thompson

The first important visitor at Astoria, once it was in business, was the trail-blazing trapper—years later to be recognized as a foremost North American geographer—David Thompson (1770–1857). But in 1811 he was not paying a courtesy call at John Jacob's establishment. Ostensibly he was mapping landmarks of the Columbia for posterity; actually he was sleuthing for the North West Company, by whom he had been employed for fifteen years.

Thompson had started out as an apprentice in the Hudson's Bay Company, emigrated to Canada from England at the age of fourteen, served out his apprenticeship as a fur trader on Hudson's Bay and then diverted his allegiance to North West. Though lacking formal education in any branch of science, he had schooled himself and so impressed his new employees with his talent for making geodetic and astronomical observations, as well as with his delicacy in dealing with Indians, that he was given carte blanche to roam, trap, trade, and map wherever he chose, as long as he showed up back East once a year with pelts and a progress report.

With a company of Canadians he started West on an exploratory jaunt to the Pacific that took twenty-seven years. En route he set up a string of trading "houses," most lucrative of which were Kootenae House, far north in the Canadian Rockies, and Killyspell House on Pend Oreille Lake. The maps he executed in his spare time were so accurate that many of them remained in use for the next century and a half. For years he lived within a few weeks' striking distance of the Pacific Ocean, but postponed that last leg of his cartographic tour as if he were reserving it for the grand climax of his old age.

However, as soon as word was out that the Americans planned to promote a trading center on the coast, he put everything else aside and hurried down the Columbia. Anticipating that Astor's company would soon be posting claims all through the region, he jumped them for North West by pausing at the juncture of the Snake and Columbia rivers to erect a conspicuous pole, on which he tacked a half-sheet of foolscap with the public declaration: "Know hereby that this country is claimed by Great Britain as part of its Territories and that the N.W. Company . . . do hereby intend to erect a factory at this place for the commerce of the country around."

Preparing the way for that commerce, he stopped at the major villages along the river to smoke with the Indians, propagandize the benefactions North West would bring them, and undercut the Astorians. He sighted Mount Hood and other eminences, made comprehensive notes on the countryside, portaged the Dalles, and then descended into more attractive country—inhabited by less attractive natives.

He had been accustomed to dealing with Indians of the interior uncorrupted by white civilization, and was thoroughly depressed by the wretched specimens he found on nearing the coast. Those last miles followed the same course Lewis and Clark and Hunt had traveled, a course that countless others were to pursue, but the reaction to it always differed: what impressed newcomers was conditioned by the background they brought with them, the purpose of their coming, and their preconceived notion of the geography. Thompson appeared almost to regret that he had ever bothered to penetrate to the Pacific.

From Sea to Sea

The country in appearance has improved, the grass somewhat green, and a few trees in places. . . . Having proceeded sixteen miles [below the Dalles], we saw the first ash trees, with willow and aspen, a most agreeable change from bare banks and monotonous plains. Continuing nine miles, we saw two mountains to the westward, each isolated and heavily capped with snow. . . . Both sides of the river have woods of aspen, cedar, ash and willow, but none of fine growth—they are full of branches.

Having descended forty miles, the greatest part fine, steady current, we came to a village of houses built of logs, the people of which are called Wawthlarlar [Wahclellahs]. . . . At the desire of the chief of the Wawthlarlar, we camped near his village at five P.M. and bought two good salmon. These people are a distinct race from those above the Dalles; they are not so tall, but strongly built, brawny, fat people, the face round, the eye black or hazel, the hair brown, that of the women and children light brown, the cheek bones not too high, the nose full and rather flat, the mouth rather large, the lips thick, the teeth good and the neck short. Except for a few of both sexes who were clothed, they were all naked. The female sex had scarcely a trace of the decency and modesty of the upper country women. Some of them offered their favors, but they were so devoid of temptation that not one pretended to understand them. What a change in a few miles!

The chief came and invited me to his house, which was near to us; it was well and strongly built of logs, the inside clean and well arranged, separate bed places fastened to the walls and raised about three feet above the floor, which was of earth, and clean. A number of small poles were fixed, in the upper part on which were hanging as many salmon, drying and smoking, as could be placed. . . . I stayed about an hour in the house; he kept talking to me, pointing out the arrangements of his house, and making use of as many English words as he had learned from the ships when trading with them—some of them not the best.

The fireplace was on the left-hand side of the door, for which some earth had been taken away to keep the wood steady on the fire. There was no aperture for the smoke, in order to give the salmon the full benefit of it. The fireplace was surrounded with rush mats; the whole appeared comfortable to naked people, but to me was intolerably close and warm. I was glad to breathe fresh air and get to my men. The last five or six villages we have passed, as well as these people, appear to live wholly on salmon, without berries, roots or any other vegetable, yet all appeared healthy, and no cutaneous disorders were perceived. . . .

We stayed till 9:30 A.M. but could not procure a guide for the rapids and falls [the Cascades]. We proceeded three miles, of which we carried one mile at a steep rapid. We continued our course and . . . passed several houses on each side of the river; they all appeared constructed as I have already described. At one of them we put ashore and traded a few half-dried salmon; and a native in his canoe came to us and gave us a salmon. We camped a short distance above Point Vancouver. . . .

We continued our journey, amused with the seals playing in the river. On the 15th, near noon, we arrived at Tongue Point, which at right angles stretches its steep rocky shores across the river for a full half mile, and brought us to a full view of the Pacific Ocean, which to me was a great pleasure. But my men seemed disappointed; they had been accustomed to the boundless horizon of the Great Lakes of Canada and their high rolling waves; from the ocean they expected a more boundless view, a something beyond the power of their senses which they could not describe; and my informing them that directly opposite to us, at a distance of five thousand miles, was the Empire of Japan added nothing to their ideas, but a map would.

The waves being too high for us to double the point, we went close to the river bank where there is a narrow isthmus of one hundred yards, and carried across it. From thence near two miles to the fur-trading post of Mr. J. J. Astor of the city of New York—which was four low log huts—the far-famed Fort Astoria of the United States. The place was in charge of Messieurs McDougall and Stuart, who had been clerks of the North West Company, and by whom we were politely received. They had been here but a few months, and arriving after a long voyage round Cape Horn, in the rainy season, without sufficient shelter from tents, had suffered from ague and low fever, from which most of them had recovered.

This place was about seven miles from the sea and too much exposed to the undulations of the waves. The quality of their goods for trade was very low, but good enough for the beggarly natives about them, . . . a race of worthless, idle, impudent knaves without anything to barter, yet begging everything they saw. They were all accustomed to trade with the ships, mostly of the United States, and had learned a great part of the worst words of their language.

The next day in my canoe with my men I went to Cape Disappointment, which terminates the course of this river, and remained until the tide came in. At ebb tide we noticed the current of the river riding in waves over the surface to the sea for about four miles; on all the shores of this ocean the agitation of the sea is constantly breaking against the rocky shore with high surges, and my men now allowed the great volume of water forming these high surges to be far superior to those of any lake.

Thus I have fully completed the survey of this part of North America from sea to sea, and . . . have determined the positions of the mountains, lakes and rivers and other remarkable places of the northern part of this continent, the maps of all of which have been drawn and laid down in geographical position, being now the work of twenty-seven years.

From *David Thompson's Narrative, 1784–1812*. Publications of the Champlain Society. Richard Glover, Editor (Toronto: Champlain Society, 1962).

XIV

Alexander Ross

Astoria, of course, was across the river from the future state of Washington, but its short-lived jurisdiction spread over more fur country north of the Columbia than south. Of equal importance to the vessels that picked up pelts at Indian coastal settlements were the posts deep in the interior, usually at a confluence of rivers. These posts were manned by strong, silent men who rarely articulated their experiences. Alexander Ross (1783–1856), a Scottish schoolteacher who had migrated to Canada and then joined the Astor enterprises, was the exception. Not only was he articulate, but he possessed culture, wit and sagacity, and his writings on the Western fur trade yielded more authentic information on the subject than came from any other one source.

He was among the company that sailed around the Horn on the ill-fated *Tonquin,* and shortly after his arrival was assigned to a new trading post near the mouth of the Okanogan River, six hundred miles up the Columbia. From Astoria he set out with a party of twenty-one, including experienced Canadians, two Sandwich Islanders, and David Stuart, one of the Astor partners, in two overloaded Chinook canoes.

The three or four "gentlemen" attached to the entourage looked upon the venture as a lark and boarded their canoe, "one with a cloak on his arm, another with his umbrella, a third with pamphlets and newspapers for amusement, preparing, we thought, for a pleasure trip." The pleasure lasted less than three miles, when the craft was swamped and grounded, passengers and goods drenched. It was only a foretaste of what was to follow. The umbrella, cloak, and light reading were cast over the side and the "gentlemen" faced up to the sober nature of their employment.

They expected to return within a few weeks; they were gone nearly eight months. Ross's experiences were later incorporated in one of the finest volumes ever written on the fur era, narrated unpretentiously, with more life, authenticity, and amusement than Irving's classic *Astoria*. Though Ross was under the thumb of John Jacob Astor, he pulled no punches in detailing exactly what he thought of the great man dictating company policy from a plush office in New York. During his lonely vigil on the Okanogan he began to see through Astor's operation and the incompetence of the whole organization.

In no particular was the bad management more obvious than in the selection of trading goods the bigwig had provided. "None knew better than Astor himself what was necessary and suitable for that market," he exploded; "but we had got nothing of this kind. Instead of guns, we got metal pots and gridirons; instead of beads and trinkets, we got white cotton; and instead of blankets, molasses. In short, all the useless trash and unsaleable trumpery which had been accumulating in his shops and stores for half a century past were swept together to fill his Columbia ships. That these cargoes were insured need not be told; sink or swim, his profits were sure."

At his outpost Ross could brood over the fact that he and his associates were dupes, but the brooding never succeeded in clouding his humor and horsesense.

A Specimen of Our Trade

The mouth of the Okanogan is situated six hundred miles up the Columbia, and enters it through a low level plain a mile wide. This plain is surrounded on all sides by high hills, so that in no direction does the view extend far. . . . On the south bank of the

river, half a mile from its mouth, was the site pitched upon for the
new establishment. The general aspect of the surrounding country is barren and dreary. On the west the hills are clothed with
thick woods—a dense forest; on the south and east the scene is
bare; but on the north the banks of the river were lined with the
willow and poplar, and the valley through which it meanders
presents a pleasing landscape. . . .

As soon as we could dismiss the distant tribes, who had come to
welcome our arrival, we commenced erecting a small dwelling
house, sixteen by twenty feet, chiefly constructed of driftwood,
being more handy and easier got than standing timber; but while
the building was in a half-finished state, . . . Mr. Stuart and the
remaining men set off on a journey towards the north, or headwaters of the Okanogan, intending to return in the course of a
month, while I was to remain alone at the establishment till Mr.
Stuart's return, my only civilized companion being a little Spanish pet dog from Monterey, called Weasel.

Only picture to yourself, gentle reader, how I must have felt
alone in this unhallowed wilderness, without friend or white man
within hundreds of miles of me, and surrounded by savages who
had never seen a white man before. Every day seemed a week,
every night a month. I pined, I languished, my head turned
gray, and in a brief space ten years were added to my age. Yet
man is born to endure, and my only consolation was in my Bible.

The first thing I did after my friends left me was to patch up
the house a little and put the few goods I had, so tempting to
Indians, into a kind of cellar, which I made in the middle of the
house. This done, I set to in earnest to learn the Indian language,
and wrote vocabulary after vocabulary; and although the task
was a hard one, I soon found from my progress that perseverance
would overcome many difficulties.

The novelty of white men, and particularly of a white man
alone, drew crowds of inquisitive Indians about the place. I
mixed with them, traded with them, and at last began to talk with
them, and from a constant intercourse soon came to understand
them; but still the evenings were long and the winter dreary.
Every night before going to bed I primed my gun and pistol anew

and barricaded the door of my lonely dwelling; and the Indians, friendly inclined, always withdrew from the house at dusk. Yet they often had alarms among themselves and often gave me to understand that enemies or ill-disposed Indians were constantly lurking about; and whenever they began to whoop or yell in the night, which they frequently did, I, of course, partook of the alarm.

One night I was suddenly awakened out of my sleep by the unusual noise and continual barking of Weasel, running backwards and forwards through the house. Half asleep, half awake, I felt greatly agitated and alarmed. My faithful gun and pistol were at hand, for they lay always at my side in bed; but then all was dark: I could see nothing, could hear nothing but the barking of Weasel, which was continually growing louder and louder.

I then thought there must be somebody in the house, for I was ready to put the worst construction on appearances. In this perplexing dilemma I got my hand, with as little noise as possible, to the muzzle of my gun, and gradually drawing out the ramrod, tried, with my right arm stretched out, to stir up the embers so that I might see; but here again a new danger presented itself: I was exposing myself as a mark to a ball or an arrow, without the chance of defending myself, for the light would show me to the enemy before I could see my object. But there was no alternative and something must be done.

Between hope and despair I managed to stir up the ashes, so that I could see little Weasel running to and fro to the cellar door. I concluded that the enemy must be skulking in the cellar. I then, but not without difficulty, got a candle lighted. Holding the candle in my left hand, I laid hold of my pistol. With the lynx eye and wary step of a cat ready to pounce on its prey, I advanced rather obliquely, with my right arm stretched out at full length holding the cocked pistol, till I got to the cellar door, the little dog all the while making a furious noise; when, lo! what was there but a skunk sitting on a roll of tobacco!

The shot blew it almost to atoms, and so delicately perfumed everything in the house that I was scarcely able to live in it for days afterwards. But that was not all. The trivial incident was productive of very bad consequences. Several hundreds of Indians being encamped about the place at the time, no sooner did they see the light, or hear the shot than they all rushed into the house, thinking something serious had happened. So far, however, there was no great harm; but when they beheld two rolls of tobacco and two small bales of goods, it appeared such wealth to their eyes that they could scarcely recover from the surprise.

These tempting articles I had endeavored all along to keep as much as possible out of their sight and dealt them out with a sparing hand, and as long as the Indians did not see them in bulk all went well. But after the overwhelming exhibition of so much property, there was no satisfying them. They became importunate and troublesome for some time and caused me much anxiety.

The time fixed for Mr. Stuart's return had now arrived, and I most anxiously looked for him every hour. Often I had reason to curse the intrusion of the skunk into my house. After some time, however, things settled down again to their usual level, and good order and good feelings were again renewed between us.

October had now passed by and November also, but no Mr. Stuart came, and various reports were circulated by the Indians as to his fate; and I myself now began to despair of his return. The delay of Mr. Stuart's party had a visible effect on the conduct of the Indians: they became more bold, neglected their hunting and loitered about the place, as if in expectation of some sudden change. Strange Indians were every day swelling the camp; they held councils, too; altogether they were a changed people.

Seeing this unfavorable change fast spreading among the Indians in consequence of Mr. Stuart's delay, I set about counteracting it. I assembled all the chiefs and other great men, and after smoking the pipe of friendship, told them not to be uneasy at Mr. Stuart's absence, that I could easily account for it; that finding the country rich in furs as he went along, and the Indians peaceable and well disposed, he had most probably gone off to the white men's land for more goods, and would be back early with a rich supply and many people, so that all their wants would be satisfied; that those who hunted best would get most; that they had better exert themselves in hunting and procuring furs; that their success would entitle them to the favor of Mr. Stuart and the great white chief; and that I would not fail to represent their conduct in the fairest light.

This harangue had the desired effect. The Indians set to hunting in earnest, and kept bringing in furs regularly, and in other respects behaved exceedingly well during the whole of the winter. Thus I wished to make them believe what I did not believe myself, because in my critical situation safety required it. . . .

December now was passed, and the new year of 1812 ushered in, but still there was no account of the absent party. January passed, and likewise February, but no Mr. Stuart; nor was it until the 22nd of March that little Weasel announced early in the morning the approach of strangers, and I was rejoiced to meet again at my lonely dwelling my long-expected friends all safe and well.

During Mr. Stuart's absence of 188 days I had procured 1,550 beavers, besides other peltries, worth in the Canton market 2,250 d. sterling, and which on an average stood the concern in but 5½d. apiece, valuing the merchandise at sterling cost, or in round numbers 35l. sterling—a specimen of our trade among the Indians!

Here follows Mr. Stuart's account of his journey: "After leaving this place," said he, "we bent our course up the Okanogan, due north for upwards of 250 miles till we reached its source; then crossing a height of land fell upon Thompson's River. . . . The snow fell while we were in the mountains and precluded our immediate return, and after waiting for fine weather the snows got so deep that we considered it hopeless to attempt getting back and therefore passed our time with the She Whaps and other tribes in that quarter. The Indians were numerous and well disposed, and the country throughout abounds in beavers and all other kinds of fur; and I have made arrangements to establish a trading post there. . . . The distance may be about 350 miles."

From *Adventures of the First Settlers on the Oregon or Columbia River*, Alexander Ross (London: Smith, Elder and Company, 1849).

XV

Gabriel Franchère

A fellow passenger of Ross's on the voyage of the *Tonquin* to Astoria was a French Canadian, Gabriel Franchère (1786–1863), who on hearing about Astor's projected establishment in the West had paddled down from Montreal to New York—via the St. Lawrence, Lake Champlain, and the Hudson River—and signed up with the Pacific Fur Company as an apprentice clerk for a term of five years.

The overseers at Astoria, however, quickly sized Franchère up as too good a man to tie down as a mere clerk, and soon had him out on the beaver trails as crack ambassador among the Indians, trapper, trader, boatman, and general handy man. But the jinx that seemed to be pursuing the Pacific Fur Company interrupted his service and cut short his five-year commitment. The company's predicament this time originated with the War of 1812.

When word of British-American hostilities belatedly reached the Scottish managers at Astoria, along with rumors that English warships were on their way to storm the vulnerable little American fort, they were confronted with an irksome quandary: Should they abandon the post? Put up a futile resistance? Destroy it before it was destroyed or captured? The situation was complicated by the fact that a majority of the key employees were Canadian, with divided allegiance. "All of us who were British subjects or Canadians," Franchère confessed, "wished ourselves in Canada, but in the dead of winter had no way of getting there."

As it was impossible to get in touch with Astor on the other side of the continent for his counsel, the partners at Astoria had to reach a decison by themselves. And only a Scotchman would have thought of the obvious expedient: Since the North West Company was already trying to strangle the American competitors, the sensible move was to sell out to North West and salvage what could be salvaged before all was lost.

They did—much to the later disgruntlement of John Jacob Astor. A majority of the employees merely transferred their contracts to the new owners, but Franchère declined to accept that easy way out; he insisted on return transportation to Montreal. During all his adventures in the Northwest, he had been keeping a journal, with which he thought he might entertain a few of his friends upon his return to civilization. But once he was back in Montreal, the friends considered the journal much too absorbing to keep to themselves. They soon found a publisher to edit, print, and acclaim it; and the youngster who had gone West as an apprentice clerk returned as a popular author and authority on the Indian tribes of the Columbia.

Good Fathers, Good Fishermen

The natives inhabiting on the Columbia from the mouth of that river to the falls, that is to say on a space extending about 250 miles from east to west, are, generally speaking, of low stature, few of them passing five feet six inches, and many not even five feet. They pluck out the beard in the manner of the other Indians of North America, but a few of the old men only suffer a tuft to grow upon their chins.

On arriving among them we were exceedingly surprised to see that they had almost all flattened heads. This configuration is not a natural deformity, but an effect of art, caused by compression of the skull in infancy. It shocks strangers extremely, especially at first sight; nevertheless, among these barbarians it is an indispensable ornament, and when we signified to them how much this mode of flattening the forehead appeared to us to violate nature and good taste, they answered that it was only slaves who had not their heads flattened.

The slaves, in fact, have the usual rounded head, and they are not permitted to flatten the foreheads of their children. . . . The natives of the Columbia procure these slaves from the neighboring tribes and from the interior, in exchange for beads and furs. They treat them with humanity while their services are useful, but as soon as they become incapable of labor, neglect them and suffer them to perish of want. When dead, they throw their bodies without ceremony under the stump of an old decayed tree or drag them to the woods to be devoured by the wolves and vultures.

The Indians of the Columbia are of a light copper color, active in body and, above all, excellent swimmers. They are addicted to theft, or rather they make no scruple of laying hands on whatever suits them in the property of strangers, whenever they can find an opportunity. The goods and effects of European manufacture are so precious in the eyes of these barbarians that they rarely resist the temptation of stealing them.

These savages are not addicted to intemperance, unlike in that respect the other American Indians, . . . regarding intoxicating drinks as poisons and drunkenness as disgraceful. . . .

The men go entirely naked, not concealing any part of their bodies. Only in winter they throw over the shoulders a panther's skin or else a sort of mantle made of the skins of wood-rats sewed together. In rainy weather I have seen them wear a mantle of rush mats, like a Roman toga or the vestment which a priest wears in celebrating mass; thus equipped, and furnished with a conicle hat made from fibrous roots and impermeable, they may call themselves rain-proof.

The women, in addition to the mantle of skins, wear a petticoat made of the cedar bark, which they attach round the girdle and which reaches to the middle of the thigh. It is a little longer behind than before, and is fabricated in the following manner: They strip off the fine bark of the cedar, soak it as one soaks hemp, and when it is drawn out into fibers, work it into a fringe; then with a strong cord they bind the fringes together. With so poor a vestment they contrive to satisfy the requirements of modesty. . . .

Cleanliness is not a virtue among these females, who in that respect resemble the other Indian women of the continent. They anoint the body and dress the hair with fish oil, which does not diffuse an agreeable perfume. Their hair—which both sexes wear long—is jet black; it is badly combed, but parted in the middle . . . and kept shining by the fish oil.

Sometimes, in imitation of the men, they paint the whole body with a red earth mixed with fish oil. Their ornaments consist of bracelets of brass, which they wear indifferently on the wrists and ankles; of strings of beads of different colors (they give a preference to blue), and displayed in great profusion around the neck and on the arms and legs; and of white shells called *haiqua,* which are their ordinary circulating medium. These shells are found beyond the straits of Juan de Fuca and are from one to four inches long; . . . the longest are most valued. The price of all commodities is reckoned in these shells; a fathom string of the largest of them is worth about ten beaver skins.

Although a little less slaves than the greater part of the Indian women elsewhere, the women on the Columbia are, nevertheless, charged with the most painful labors: they fetch water and wood, and carry the goods in their frequent changes of residence; they clean the fish and cut it up for drying; they prepare the food and cook the fruits in their season. Among their principal occupations is that of making rush mats, baskets for gathering roots, and hats very ingeniously wrought. As they want little clothing, they do not sew much, and the men have the needle in hand oftener than they.

The men are not lazy, especially during the fishing season. Not being hunters and eating consequently little flesh meat (although they are fond of it), fish makes their principal diet. They profit, therefore, by the season when it is to be had, by taking as much as they can, knowing that the intervals will be periods of famine and abstinence, unless they provide sufficiently beforehand.

Their canoes are all made of cedar, and of a single trunk. We saw some which were five feet wide at midships and thirty feet in length; these are the largest, and will carry from twenty-five to thirty men. The smallest will carry but two or three. The bows terminate in a very elongated point, running out four or five feet from the water line. It constitutes a separate piece, very ingeniously attached, and serves to break the surf in landing or the wave on a rough sea. In landing they put the canoe around, so as to strike the beach stern on. Their oars or paddles are made of ash and are about five feet long, with a broad blade in the shape of an inverted crescent, and a cross at the top, like the handle of a crutch. . . . All their canoes are painted red and fancifully decorated.

Their houses, constructed of cedar, are remarkable for their form and size; some of them are one hundred feet in length by thirty or forty in width. . . . An oblong square of the intended size of the building is dug out to the depth of two or three feet; a double row of cedar posts is driven into the earth about ten feet apart; between these the planks are laid, overlapping each other to the requisite height. The roof is formed by a ridgepole laid on taller posts, notched to receive it, and is constructed with rafters and planks laid clapboardwise and secured by cords for want of nails.

When the house is designed for several families, there is a door for each and a separate fireplace; the smoke escapes through an aperture formed by removing one of the boards of the roof. The door is low, of an oval shape, and is provided with a ladder cut out of a log to descend into the lodge. The entrance is generally effected stern-foremost.

The kitchen utensils consist of plates of ash wood, bowls of fibrous roots and a wooden kettle. With these they succeed in cooking their fish and meat in less time than we take with the help of pots and stewpans. See how they do it! Having heated a number of stones red-hot, they plunge them one by one in the vessel which is to contain the food to be prepared; as soon as the water boils, they put in the fish or meat, with some more heated stones on top, and cover up the whole with small rush mats to retain the steam. In an incredibly short space of time the article is taken out and placed on a wooden platter, perfectly done and very palatable. The broth is taken out also with a ladle of wood or horn.. . . .

We did not find among them a single hatchet. Their only tools consisted of an inch or half-inch chisel, usually made of an old file, and of a mallet, which was nothing but an oblong stone. With these wretched implements, and wedges made of hemlock knots steeped in oil and hardened by fire, they would undertake to cut down the largest cedars of the forest, to dig them out and fashion them into canoes, to split them and get out the boards wherewith to build their houses. Such achievements with such means are a marvel of ingenuity and patience.

The politics of the natives of the Columbia are a simple affair: each village has its chief, but that chief does not seem to exercise a great authority over his fellow-citizens. Nevertheless, at his death they pay him great honors: they use a kind of mourning which consists in painting the face with black, in lieu of gay colors; they chant his funeral song or oration for a whole month. The chiefs are considered in proportion to their riches; such a chief [as] has a great many wives, slaves and strings of beads is accounted a great chief.

As all the villages form so many independent sovereignties, differences sometimes arise. . . . Before commencing hostilities, however, they give notice of the day when they will proceed to attack the hostile village, . . . embark in their canoes, which on these occasions are paddled by the women, repair to the hostile village, enter into parley, and do all they can to terminate the affair amicably. Sometimes a third party becomes mediator between the first two and, of course, observes an exact neutrality.

If those who seek justice do not obtain it to their satisfaction, they retire to some distance and the combat begins, and is continued for some time with fury on both sides; but as soon as one or two men are killed, the party which has lost these, owns itself beaten and the battle ceases. If it is the people of the village

attacked who are worsted, the others do not retire without receiving presents. When the conflict is postponed till the next
day—for they never fight but in open daylight . . . —they keep
up frightful cries all night long, and when they are sufficiently
near to understand each other, defy one another by menaces,
railleries and sarcasms like the heroes of Homer and Virgil. The
women and children are always removed from the village before
the action.

Their combats are almost all maritime, for they fight ordinarily
in their pirogues, which they take care to careen so as to present
the broadside to the enemy, and half lying down avoid the
greater part of the arrows let fly at them. But the chief reason of
the bloodlessness of their combats is the inefficiency of their
offensive weapons, and the excellence of their defensive armor.

Their offensive arms are merely a bow and arrow, and a kind of
double-edged sabre about two and a half feet long, and six inches
wide in the blade; they rarely come to sufficiently close quarters
to make use of the last. For defensive armor they wear a cassock
or tunic of elskin double, descending to the ankles, with holes
for the arms. It is impenetrable by their arrows, which cannot
pierce two thicknesses of leather; and as their heads are also
covered with a sort of helmet, the neck is almost the only part in
which they can be wounded.

They have another kind of corslet, made like the corsets of our
ladies, of splinters of hard wood interlaced with nettle twine. The
warrior who wears this cuirass does not use the tunic of elskin;
he is consequently less protected but a great deal more free, the
said tunic being very heavy and very stiff. . . . In their military
expeditions, they have their bodies and faces daubed with different paints, often of the most extravagant designs. . . .

Marriages are conducted with a good deal of ceremony. When
a young man seeks a girl in marriage, his parents make the
proposals to those of the intended bride, and when it has been
agreed upon what presents the future bridegroom is to offer to
the parents of the bride, all parties assemble at the house of the
latter, whither the neighbors are invited to witness the contract.
The presents, which consist of slaves, strings of beads, copper

bracelets, *haiqua* shells, etc., are distributed by the young man, who on his part receives as many and sometimes more, according to the means or the munificence of the parents of his betrothed. The latter is then led forward by the old matrons and presented to the young man. . . . The men are not very scrupulous in their choice and take small pains to inform themselves what conduct a young girl has observed before her nuptials, and it must be owned that few marriages would take place if the youth would only espouse maidens without reproach on the score of chastity. . . . Polygamy is permitted, indeed is customary. . . .

There are charlatans everywhere, but they are more numerous among savages than anywhere else, because among these ignorant and superstitious people the trade is at once more profitable and less dangerous. As soon as a native is indisposed, no matter what the malady, they send for the medicine man, who treats the patient in the absurd manner usually adopted by these imposters, and with such violence of manipulation that often a sick man, whom a timely bleeding or purgative would have saved, is carried off by a sudden death.

They deposit their dead in canoes, on rocks sufficiently elevated not to be overflowed by the spring freshets. By the side of the dead are laid his bow, his arrows and some of his fishing implements; if it is a woman, her beads and bracelets. The wives, the relatives and the slaves of the defunct cut their hair in sign of grief and for several days at the rising and setting of the sun go to some distance from the village to chant a funeral song. . . . The natives believe that the men who have been good citizens, good fathers, good husbands and good fishermen, who have not committed murder, etc., will be perfectly happy after their death, and will go to a country where they will find fish, fruit, etc., in abundance; and that on the contrary, those who have lived wickedly will inhabit a country of fasting and want, where they will eat nothing but bitter roots and have nothing to drink but salt water. . . .

In spite of the vices that may be laid to the charge of the natives of the Columbia, I regard them as nearer to a state of civilization than any of the tribes who dwell east of the Rocky

Mountains. They do not appear to be so attached to their customs that they could not easily adopt those of civilized nations; they would dress themselves willingly·in the European mode if they had the means. . . . They possess in an eminent degree the qualities opposed to indolence, improvidence and stupidity; the chiefs above all are distinguished for their good sense and intelligence. Generally speaking, they have a ready intellect and a tenacious memory.

From *Narrative of a Voyage to the Northwest Coast of America,* Gabriel Franchère. Translated and edited by J. V. Huntington. (New York: Redfield, 1854).

XVI

Alexander Henry

On December 13, 1813, the Union Jack was briskly raised over the rude stockade and ramshackle log huts built by the Pacific Fur Company pioneers; a bottle of Madeira was broken against the new flagstaff; everyone cheered; HMS *Raccoon*, which had arrived too late to blow Astoria off the map, respectfully fired a salute; and American Astoria became British Fort George, under ownership of the North West Company.

The new tenants had generously purchased John Jacob Astor's cast-off store stock at "ten per cent above cost" and agreed to pay $40,000 for some ten tons of beaver and other skins in storage—hardly a bargain according to Astor, who whimpered in New York months later when he learned of the sale that the pelts were worth $100,000 in the market.

The British had won the first round in the battle for the Columbia fur country, through which they had already spread their own trading posts. But the North West Company also fell heir to an unenviable dilemma: the Hudson's Bay Company was invading the same territory with formidable competition; most of their supplies and their furs had to be freighted overland to Montreal; unlike the Yankees, they could not ship furs directly to China, for the English East India Company held an exclusive monopoly on that commerce; and, worst of all, they inherited all the grievances of the Indians, who had to be depended upon for bringing in the furs and who were increasingly resentful of the white man's intrusion.

A typical expression of that resentment echoed through the lower Columbia valley little more than a year after North West took over Astoria. On January 3, 1814, the winter "express" to Spokane, Kooteney, and the remote interior posts was dispatched upriver from Fort George, with thirty men in their canoe flotilla. Stowed aboard were some eighty different items—208 axes of different sizes, 50 bright new rifles and a quarter of a ton of ammunition, 335 brass and copper kettles, 1,000 darning needles, 2,000 cheap rings, 3,000 thimbles, sacks of Chinese beads, 500 pounds of tobacco, quantities of blankets, yard goods, shirts, and wholesale foodstuffs ranging from rice, salt, and dried salmon to molasses and vinegar. In charge were two experienced company woodsmen, Alexander Stuart and James Keith. No one at the Fort expected to see them again for months.

On January 9 the remnants of the express reappeared off Fort George, slowly returning in two canoes. They struggled ashore to report that they had advanced only as far as the Cascades, had been ambushed by Indians, one man had been killed, and Stuart "looked almost dead." The entire cargo had been captured by the Indians.

It was a staggering loss even for the great North West Company. Immediately all the white men in the area who could be spared—Hudson's Bay employees as well as North West—were assembled to make a "peaceful assault" on the Cascade villages in an attempt to recover the goods. There were conferences with local friendly Indians, too. A few of them agreed to go along, and a chief named Casino, with his sister-in-law, "Coalpo's wife," were hired to accompany them as mediators. The fur dealers could ill afford to incur the wrath of the natives at a strategic point like the portage of the Cascades, so every effort was to be made to secure the pilfered goods without recourse to firearms.

A party of sixty-nine laboriously paddled up the Columbia, against severe winter winds and rain, in an armada of seven canoes under the command of a North West partner, Alexander

Henry (d. 1814), who was also chronicler for the expedition,
later recognized as one of the authorities on frontier life of the
North country.

Troublesome Visitors

At eleven we set off [from an overnight encampment north of
Point Vancouver] with a strong head wind, and pushed on until 2
P.M., when we landed on the north side to put our arms in order
and prepare for our arrival at the villages. These are at no great
distance from us—the first one but six miles. The highlands we
here enter are entirely covered with snow; from the shore to their
rocky summits all is white.

We had another conference with Casino, who knows more
about the subject [the pillage of the canoes] than we imagined.
He informed us that the principal instigator of that affair was a
chief called Canook, of the Cathlathlaly village on the north. This
fellow, it seems, on seeing our party of two canoes only, passing
up river, formed a plan to pillage them. He assembled the warriors of the two villages below and made a long speech, telling
them that we never traded anything of consequence with them,
but took our property further up to their enemies, the Nez Percés,
and that here was a favorable opportunity to better themselves.

They agreed, and all went armed up to the Cathlayackty
village, where the harangue was repeated. That village also
joined the party and crossed over to the Cathlayackty village on
the south, where a similar speech was made, and that village also
joined. Then they all came down to meet our people at the
portage on the south, with Canook as their war chief. Another
village, of the Thlamooyackoack tribe, situated a few miles above
the portage on the north was invited down to join, which they
soon did. Early in the affair a chief of the latter village and one
belonging to the Cathlayackty village were both killed; these two
were all that fell.

This afternoon we finished our stock of dried salmon and meat, being thus left without one mouthful for sixty-five of us and four Indians—on the eve of encountering enemies.

January 14. A gale all night. At 6 A.M. we embarked. Our progress was slow; twice my canoe was driven back to our fires, and then we crossed the river to the south side before we could bring her up. We put out the line and towed her along the beach; the other canoes followed our example, by which means we got on slowly. At ten we came nearly abreast of the Soto village, where we saw the natives running into a low point of wood at the upper end of their village. They seemed to be in great hurry and confusion, and we soon perceived they all wore large white war garments.

Directly opposite the village we crossed over to a stony beach about 150 yards from the woods, in which some natives were posted behind trees in a posture of defense, armed with bows and arrows, clubs and axes—bows bent and arrows across them, ready to let fly. All was still as death. We did not land, but desired Casino to assure them of our pacific disposition. After some time a chief came to the edge of the woods and made a long speech with many gestures, as if violently agitated.

Finding that none of them could be induced to leave the woods, we put Casino and Coalpo's wife ashore to go up to the village to demand the guns and the kettles. The natives then retired from the woods to the village, where a long parley was held. An old woman was the first person who ventured down to the canoes; but a man soon followed her example. We proposed to trade with them for dogs, to which they readily agreed. . . . We soon secured sixteen dogs and then crossed over to the south, where we made a fire, as by this time we were benumbed with cold. While here we saw two horsemen set off at full speed for the village above, as we presumed to carry the news of our arrival.

Having warmed ourselves, we returned to the village, where they delivered to us nine loaded guns. This was all the property we could recover here. They assured us all the rest was in the hands of the natives above. We then assembled them on the beach and presented the pipe, hoping to allay all suspicion by this pacific measure, that we might find the upper villages off their guard and be thus enabled to seize this famous Canook and keep him prisoner until all the property should be returned. For the present we demanded only guns and kettles, without mentioning other goods—the guns being our principal object.

At 1 P.M. we continued our voyage . . . and soon came in sight of the second village, which is that of the Cathlathlaly tribe, and could see the natives hurrying to the woods with their baggages, while others in their war garments posted themselves behind trees and among rocks. We loaded our guns and put everything in order to pass up the rapids along Strawberry Island.

On coming abreast of the village we could see the natives stationed on the hill behind trees and rocks, and thence as far up river as we could see along the portage, all armed for defense. . . . Such a menace was more than we expected, considering our pacific measures at the first village; and we feared that, on our pushing over to the village, they would shoot at us in desperation, and thus oblige us to fire upon them—a thing we ardently wished to avoid.

However, we could not but go over, which we did after Casino had made a short speech to them. None moved from his lurking place while we were crossing to the north shore. Casino went up to the village and soon the natives seemed to leave the woods and assemble at Canook's house, where a long parley was held, with the result that Casino came back to us with four loaded guns, and thirty armed men accompanied him. None of us left our canoes, but we desired them to be seated on the beach.

They did so, but their looks were suspicious, for they had their bows bent and arrows ready to let fly in a twinkling. A pipe was filled for them, and we pretended friendship. Canook smoked and then came to the water's edge, but with the eye of a hawk, watching our every movement. After the long parley we crossed the river to Strawberry Island and camped on an open level spot. . . . Here we prepared for defense in case of attack. Casino, whom we had left at the village to collect property, soon brought two more guns. . . . Our orders for guard duty were four watches of three hours each. . . .

January 15. At eight we loaded our canoes and went over to the village, where we traded nine dogs and one horse for food; the dogs were knocked on the head with an ax, and the horse was shot through the head. Here we lay three hours, exposed to a heavy rain, before we set off with our stock of provisions. . . . We then crossed and went to the portage on the south. . . . This portage is six hundred paces long at present low water, over an ugly point of huge rocks to the place where the scuffle took place. We got everything over excepting one of our birch canoes. . . .

Casino asked permission to go up to the village to his relatives to demand the property, which we granted. At the east end of the portage we found the remains of our basket of kettles, hoops, staves, etc., and a quantity of wet powder was strewn on the sand. On the spot where the Indian fell, whom Mr. McKay shot, some blood was still to be seen. I also traced over the portage many spots of blood which I presume fell from Mr. Stuart's wounds on his retreat.

At 2 P.M. we went up to the Cathlayackty village by land, the men *en canot;* there we found on the beach Casino with seven natives, who delivered to us one gun, a few kettles and two cotton shirts. . . . Nothing more being expected by fair means, we crossed the river to the other Cathlayackty village, consisting of eight houses. . . . We landed Casino who parleyed with them while we went in search of a camp on an island about half a mile above the village, telling him to bring the kettles and guns to us there.

Having landed on this island and set camp for the night, we fired all our guns and the brass swivel, which we then reloaded. Seeing four loaded canoes cross to the village on the south, we began to suspect Casino's fidelity, fearing that he was acting a double part in sending some of his friends to the village, which he supposed we would not molest on this account; but it would have been imprudent to show any suspicions of him. He soon came to us with sixteen natives, who brought five guns, some kettles, balls, and a few trifling articles, besides some dried salmon. Guard was mounted as usual. . . .

January 16. I sent a canoe with eight men to the village to trade dogs; they returned with nine. Having breakfasted at noon, we embarked and went down to the Cathlayackty village on the north. . . . We demanded horses to trade, which they sent for; and Canook arrived on horseback with seven others. . . . Our intention was to seize Canook, but he kept in the crowd and could not be prevailed upon to approach, though he and all the others were invited to come and smoke.

Having bought, butchered and shipped three horses, we pushed over to the Cathlayackty village on the south. The chief, whose house we entered, was a portly old man who looked more respectable than any other I had seen on the Columbia. . . . We talked with the chief for some time, but to no purpose; no property was produced and he appeared uneasy in our presence. We then went down to the portage, where we camped for the night on the spot where the scuffle had happened. Shortly afterward Casino brought us a few more kettles, which he said were all he could get. He asked to be allowed to sleep at the village under a pretense of getting more property. Strict watch was kept as usual. . . .

This evening we received information from Coalpo's wife respecting Casino's duplicity. He even tried to bribe her at the last village this afternoon by offering her two fathoms of red shrouds and other things, but she rejected the offer and upbraided him for his double dealing. Had we known as much on landing at this portage yesterday as we do now, we probably would have recovered every article there was in both villages; but we had placed confidence in Casino. . . . This afternoon our men regaled themselves on the offals of the horses. Puddings were made of the blood and fat. The guts were boiled or roasted, and the marrow-bones cracked—in short nothing was lost, and had I not seen the horsehides I could have imagined we were just in from a buffalo hunt.

January 17. At 7 A.M. we began to carry over the portage. A few natives came to us, but they were shy and cautious, as they had no arms. . . . At noon Casino came over in a canoe, accompanied by a chief, a boy and a woman. . . . [The chief] came to our tent and we gave him tobacco to smoke with Casino. We determined to take him, having given up hope of getting hold of Canook. Three men . . . were ordered to seize him. They did so; his bow and quiver were taken and his legs and arms bound. He appeared surprised, but not terrified, and said not a word.

Casino, who was sitting near him, started up instantly, but we desired him to explain to the prisoner our intention of keeping him until our property was returned; that not only the guns and kettles were wanted, but every article they had taken from us; that we had heretofore been trifling, but were now in earnest, must have our goods and were ready to fight if necessary. The boy and woman were told the same and then allowed to go over to the village to communicate our intentions to the natives. . . . We fired our swivel to show them we had such a thing and . . . paraded all our people on the field facing the village, fired a round of musketry, and marched and countermarched. . . . We then called out to the Indians that we were ready for peace or war, as they thought fit. . . .

Two wives of the prisoner soon brought us three guns and thirteen kettles, and then all was quiet. Later on . . . the women again came over with nine guns and a few articles of bale goods. During a long conference between them and the prisoner, both parties appeared much affected, sobbing and crying. He desired them to collect the property quickly, and we told them we would remain two nights to give them time, when, if the goods were not returned, we would take him to the sea with us. . . . We fired the swivel and sent up two sky rockets, which must have alarmed the natives, who had never seen or heard of anything of the kind. . . .

January 19. There being no hope of recovering anything more, we prepared to depart. Before embarking we held a sham council on the beach, during which the women came again to ask us to remain one day longer, which we agreed to do. . . .

January 21. The women came over with a few trifles and told us they could get nothing more; they had even sold a slave to Canook for beads. However, we sent Casino with Mr. Franchère and a party of armed men to harangue the village once more, while we breakfasted on lean horseflesh and fat seal, after which not a mouthful of anything remained for seventy persons, and there was no hope of a supply from the natives. Mr. Franchère returned with their answer, which was that we must be a bad lot to want all our property back after killing two chiefs, and they would give no more. . . .

This closed the business. We, therefore, dropped down to the Soto village with the prisoner, accompanied by a canoe of his own, in which were his two wives and some other relations. . . . We pushed off, not less pleased to be on our way home than the natives must have been to get rid of such troublesome visitors.

From *New Light on the Early History of the Greater Northwest: The Manuscript Journals of Alexander Henry and David Thompson, 1799–1814*, Volume II. Edited by Elliott Coues (New York: Francis P. Harper, 1897).

XVII

Peter Corney

Between 1814 and 1819, five crucial years in the Pacific fur trade, a free-lance shipper, Peter Corney (d. 1836) put in frequent appearances at North West's Fort George headquarters, often running charter service to China for the company. Although he was born a Britisher, and presumably retained his native citizenship, his family lived in Honolulu and he commonly regarded the Sandwich Islands as base for his commercial activity. He took full advantage of a certain vagueness about the location of his home port and unhesitatingly freighted cargoes of furs to the Orient in defiance of the East India Company's monopoly.

Nor did he limit his shipping to furs. He roamed up and down the American coast or among the islands of the Pacific, taking aboard anything from California hides and beef to Hawaiian sandalwood. He was a smart trader, and also an incisive journalist—keeping a careful record of his experience and observation wherever he went. There were sparkling accounts of Hawaii and the Sandwich Islanders, the Russians and their persistent attempts at American colonization, pirates of the Pacific, California cattlemen, coastal Indian tribes, the animosity between British and Americans in the Northwest—all of which went into his *Voyages in the Northern Pacific*, originally published in 1821 in the *London Literary Gazette*. His first visit to Fort George, trade

capital for the territory on both sides of the Columbia, was in
July, 1814.

Trader in Port

On the 6th of July [1814] we saw Cape Disappointment, the
north point of Columbia River, . . . stood close in with the bar,
fired a gun and tacked ship . . . about a mile from the breakers.
Next day we stood in. The tide setting in strong and drifting us
fast toward the bar, I went to the masthead to look for a channel,
and perceived an Indian canoe paddling toward us. She soon after
came alongside; . . . we then lowered the boat and I took one of
the Indians with me to sound before the ship. . . .

On rounding Cape Disappointment, an Indian village opened
to our view, consisting of about fifty miserable-looking huts. The
Indians were all busily employed launching their canoes and
pushing off toward the ship, which was a novel spectacle to us all,
as we had never seen people of this description before. At three
o'clock P.M. we anchored under Cape Disappointment in Baker's
Bay, about a mile from the village, and were soon visited by
about thirty canoes, with men, women and children, most of
whom had flat heads. We put sentries on immediately and ran our
boarding defense out, to the great astonishment of the natives.

The natives of the Columbia brought us plenty of fine salmon,
sturgeon and fruit, such as strawberries, blackberries and rasp-
berries, for which we gave them in exchange, knives, buttons,
etc. . . . They are a very warlike people and extremely dangerous, taking every advantage of you if you are off your guard.
So hostile and treacherous were they that we never allowed the
men of this tribe [Chickeloes] to come on board. . . .

The next morning we weighed and ran up the river, passed two
Indian villages belonging to the Chinook tribe, and came to
above Village Point. . . . A large canoe came across from Fort
George, in which was the governor, John George McTavish,

Esq. . . . After the necessary precautions, we crossed the river
. . . and anchored under Fort George. . . .

The North West Company's Establishment lies about seven
miles from Point Adams, on the south side of the river, above a
small bay, where ships are in great safety out of the strength of
the tide. There is a very good wharf with a crane for landing or
shipping goods. The settlement is a square of about two hundred
yards, surrounded by pickets about fifteen feet high, and protected by two bastions, one on the southwest and the other on the
northeast corner. Each of these bastions mounts eight guns, four
and six pounders; and there are loopholes for musketry. The
grand entrance is through a large double gate on the north side,
above which there is a platform for the sentry to walk; on this are
several swivels mounted.

As you enter the fort, or square, there is a two-story house, with
two long eighteen-pounders in front of it on the south side; on the
east is a range of low buildings where the clerks have their apartments, and in the same row stands the grand hall where the
gentlemen assemble to dinner, etc. The houses for the men are on
the same side and behind the two-story or governor's house. In
the southwest corner is the magazine well secured; along the west
side stands a range of stores, tailor's shop and Indian trading
shop; in the southeast corner the blacksmith's and cooper's shops,
and on the northeast corner a granary for the corn. In the northwest corner stands a very high flagstaff, erected by the crew of
the *Columbia.* The whole of the settlers here do not exceed 150
men, most of whom keep Indian women, who live inside of the
fort with them. Nearly all the settlers are Canadians. The clerks
and partners are Scotch. . . .

The Company's canoes arrive here from the interior in the
spring and fall; they bring the furs that are collected at the different posts on the west side of the Stoney Mountains [the Rockies],
and take back stores for the posts. The canoes are manned with
Euroque Indians and Canadians under the direction of a partner
and several young clerks. When they arrive in the fall, the boatmen encamp outside the fort; they are each served out with a half
pint of rum and their year's clothing, and orders are issued that

those men who do not get drunk must go to the wood and cut timber. The liquor shop is then opened and kept by one of the clerks. A scene of drunkenness and all manner of vice follows. A frolic of this kind will cost them a year's pay and upwards; they generally agree for two years, at the end of which time they find themselves in debt, are therefore obliged to agree for two years longer, and in this manner are kept in the service till they are gray-headed.

The Company have a train of posts from the Columbia River to the Rocky or Stoney Mountains, and from thence to Montreal. All the furs that are collected on the west side of these mountains are brought to the Columbia, and sent from thence to China; and all that are collected on the east side are sent to Montreal and from thence to England. . . .

This trade having been prosecuted with such success by the British, the Americans seem in like manner resolved to profit by the vast tract of similar territory to which they have access. . . . By establishing a port which would gradually grow up into a village or a town at the mouth of the Columbia River on the Pacific Ocean, they could thence transport their cargoes to the great Indian markets, in exchange for the valuable produce of the East. Such is the project contemplated and if it succeed, it would have this important consequence, that it would lay the foundation of an American colony on the shores of the Pacific Ocean.

The peopling of the American continent is at present going on at a rapid rate; but by this means the seeds of population would be scattered with a more prodigal hand, and having once taken root, the shores of the Pacific would be quickly overspread with civilized inhabitants, drawing their support from the country in which they were settled, and in this respect independent of the parent state.

From *Voyages in the Northern Pacific*, Peter Corney (Honolulu: Thrum, 1896).

XVIII

Hall Jackson Kelley

The surrender of Astoria did not mean in any sense that the Americans were yielding to the British their claim to "Oregon"—as the whole territory north of California was beginning to be called. Rather, the loss graphically reminded Easterners that they had just as much right to the territory as Great Britain; and the public outcry for reassertion of those rights was so resounding that within four years after the Treaty of Ghent ended the War of 1812, representatives of the two nations were again at the conference table arguing out a compromise under which "vessels, subjects and citizens" of both were to share freely all the country "westward of the Stony Mountains." This "Convention of 1818" was all that was needed to activate a new burst of public spirit for American occupation of the West.

The most vociferous single advocate of northwesterly expansion and settlement was Hall Jackson Kelley (1790–1874), and his was the voice of a fanatic. He had attended Middlebury College in Vermont, then a missionary-minded institution that was inculcating in its students an urge to carry both the Christian gospel and the Jeffersonian gospel to far places and benighted peoples. Kelley's college mates were choosing fields for ministration like India, Brazil, Sierra Leone, Liberia, Syria, Egypt, Palestine, Ceylon, the Sandwich Islands. Kelley chose a field then considered no less distant, dangerous, and benighted—Oregon.

In countless speeches, in letters to newspapers, in circulars and tracts, in memorials to Congress, in books, and in private persuasion he rooted for the settlement of Oregon. He gave up schoolteaching and textbook writing in Boston to devote full time to his mania, and to found the "American Society for Encouraging the Settlement of Oregon." His revelations of the wonders of the territory were humorless, grandiose, incessant. He was dubbed "The Prophet of Oregon" and talked the part.

Occasionally dissenters struck back at him and his self-righteousness, or tried to cut him down to size. Countered the editor of the *Boston Herald:*

> We can see no advantage in Oregon which the emigrant may not secure in the state of Maine. The sea washes the shores of both. The soil is good in both. There are fisheries pertaining to both. If the climate of Oregon is milder, it is not proved that it is better. There is waste land in both. There is plenty of timber in both. Maine has these advantages: her inhabitants are under the protection of laws. . . . They have free communication with every part of the world. . . . All that can be done in Oregon within a hundred years is already done in Maine. Above all, she has no Indians to root out with fire and sword, fraudulent treaties or oppressive enactments.

But Kelley was astonishingly resistant to abrasion.

Not until 1833 did he actually set out for Oregon himself, and that brief tour was hardly a triumph. Before then he gathered all his information second-hand from sources like Lewis and Clark, from Washington Irving, from Congressional debates and the tales of Boston skippers, and concocted his tracts and oratory out of them. Yet he so thoroughly convinced himself that he was the one true champion of Oregon emigration that once people began to trend toward his utopia, he immodestly declared to the world that it was indebted to him for the whole migration; and in large measure it was.

For Men of Virtue Only

The settlement of the Oregon country has been so long contemplated . . . the time has fully come, in the order of Providence, when that uncultivated tract is to be changed into a fruitful field; that haunt of savages and wild beasts to be made the happy abode of refined and dignified man.

. . . No portion of the globe presents a more fruitful soil, or a milder climate, or equal facilities for carrying into effect the great purposes of a free and enlightened nation. A country so full of those natural means which best contribute to the comforts and conveniences of life is worthy the occupancy of a people disposed to support a free representative government, and to establish civil, scientific and religious institutions, energized by the mild and vital principles of our Republic.

Life in that country may be made easy with comparatively little effort. . . . Its local position, its physical appearance and productions, its qualities of soil and climate suggest not only the practicability of founding a colony in it, but the consequent beneficial results to our Republic and the many valuable blessings it might be made to yield to the settlers and to their posterity. . . .

The occupancy of it by three thousand of the active sons of American freedom would secure it from the possession of another nation and from augmenting the power and physical resources of an enemy. It might save that and this country from the disastrous consequences of a foreign and corrupt population, and benefit mankind by a race of people whose past lives, affording the most honorable testimony of their characters, would be a pledge for their future conduct and a full indemnity for all expenses incurred in their behalf. It is not a doubtful hypothesis that unless our legitimate rights on the waters and in the territory of Oregon are protected by planting a colony in it, or by means no less effectual, they will in a few years more become entirely lost to our merchants or to the benefits of our country. . . .

Men of steady habits, virtuous intentions, endeavoring to cultivate practical knowledge and honest industry, will be deemed worthy of the enterprise; and such persons may in Oregon secure to themselves a pleasant home and competency of good things, subserve individual happiness and sustain the great objects of founding the settlement. . . .

Enlistments should be made of properly educated persons to fill the civil, military and literary rolls: of clergymen and physicians; of persons possessing a scientific knowledge of the different branches of mathematics and natural philosophy to constitute corps of engineering, surveying, astronomy, geology and botany; of farmers; of the following mechanics, viz., master shipbuilders, millwrights, wheelwrights, carpenters, blacksmiths, tinmen, tanners, curriers, shoemakers, tailors, hatters, etc.; of capitalists, taking with them vessels suitable for the lumber trade and whale and salmon fisheries; of capitalists who will carry out the iron parts of gristmills, sawmills, of nail-making machinery, etc., who will establish a paper mill, a printing press, a manufactory of window glass and a foundry of ironware. . . .

A free and exclusive trade with the Indians and with the colony in Oregon would very considerably increase the resources and promote the commercial and manufacturing interests of our country. The fur trade has been and still is found vastly lucrative to those who pursue it. The contemplated colony would find it productive of great pecuniary advantage and a fruitful source of their prosperity. The traffic carried on with the Indians will become more reciprocal and equal in the diffusion of its comforts, as industry and the peaceful arts are sustained by them, for a trade with any people is commensurate with their real wants; these with the Indians must naturally increase as they assimilate their customs and habits to those of their refined and civilized neighbors. . . .

The fisheries might be more extensively and profitably pursued. They have long constituted a valuable branch of our commerce, and a perennial and vital source of our comforts and prosperity. Fish in vast shoals and of the most useful kinds abound in the Western ocean. Whales, both the black and spermaceti, throng those waters and sport in the very seas and bays of Oregon. . . . A colony, therefore, affording to the fisheries the advantage of greater facilities, would render them more valuable. . . .

A port of entry and a naval station at the mouth of the Columbia or in De Fuca Straits would be of immense importance to the protection of the whale and other fisheries and of the fur trade, and to a general control over the Pacific Ocean, where millions of our property are constantly afloat. The great abundance of excellent timber for shipbuilding and the small comparative expense at which ships of war might be built on the banks of the Columbia would justify the making of navy yards, and building in them the principal part of our public and private vessels. Incalculable would be the advantage of some safe place in that part of the globe, where to build, repair vessels and get supplies—where in time of war to enter with prizes and make preparation for common defence. . . .

By cultivating a friendly intercourse and coalition with the Indians, they might not only be prevented from cooperating with an enemy but, if desirable, be induced to oppose his attacks. The American people at present are too far remote to effect this purpose. . . . Indians love their ease and seldom leave it, unless compelled, to supply animal wants or excited by revenge or by triumph of victory. Nevertheless, they may be made to acquire habits of industry and practice labor, and even to seek moral and intellectual improvement.

Let kindness and affection invite them to moderate but regular exercise, under excitements of curiosity and self-gratification. Let them be directed and assisted in cultivating at first small parcels of fertile ground, and let them receive the entire products. Let them furthermore share variously in the benefits of society—their children be educated in the common schools of the Colony, and they will be made happy and useful in the present generation, and commence on another under the blessings of improved natures and progressive civilization. . . .

The settlement of the Oregon country would conduce to a freer intercourse and a more extensive and lucrative trade with the East Indies. Commerce would break away from its present narrow and prescribed limits and spread into new and broader channels, embracing within its scope China, Korea, the Philippine and Spice islands, Japan and its provinces. . . . Such an extension and enjoyment of the East India trade would provoke the spirit of American enterprise to open communications from the Mississippi valley and from the Gulf of Mexico to the Pacific

Ocean and . . . conduct the full tide of a golden traffic into the reservoir of our national finance. . . .

All nations who have planted colonies have been enriched by them. . . . The present period is propitious to the experiment. The free governments of the world are fast progressing to the consummation of moral excellence, and are embracing within the scope of their policies the benevolent and meliorating principles of humanity and reform.

The most enlightened nation on earth will not be insensible to the best means of national prosperity. Convinced of the utility and happy consequences of establishing the Oregon colony, the American Republic will found, protect and cherish it . . . and extend the peculiar blessings of civil polity and of Christian religion to distant and destitute nations.

From *A Geographical Sketch of that Part of North America Called Oregon,* Hall J. Kelley (Boston: J. Howe, 1831) and *A General Circular to the Persons of Good Character Who Wish to Emigrate to the Oregon Territory* (Charlestown: W. W. Wheildon, 1831).

XIX

Bernard A. DeVoto

Of all the unpleasant obstacles that Kelley overlooked in his extravagant visions for planting an American colony on the Northwest shores, the thorniest was the nationality of the white tenants who already controlled the region—the British. Despite pledges of amity, official agreements to share and share alike, despite international treaties, the North West and Hudson's Bay companies ruled there. They had to be contended with, and even between those two would-be landlords there was a sea of contention.

The veteran Hudson's Bay Company had been in business on the Atlantic side of the American continent for over a century before upstart North West corporatively took to the beaver trails in 1787. From the first, "The Company" regarded the youthful competitor as an impostor, hardly worth its contempt. After all, since 1670 the old fur dealers had possessed exclusive trading rights in Hudson's Bay and virtual sovereign rights over the infinitely immense area drained by all the rivers flowing into the Bay. And those rights were backed by the full authority of the king of England, Parliament, and the Admiralty.

But over the years the Company had succumbed to the ills of old age: overconfidence in its own power and prestige, lassitude, loss of vitality. By contrast North West had youth, vigor, aggression, and an obsessive spirit of competition. With those endowments the young rival in little more than a decade had swept across the continent from Montreal to the northern Pacific, established a thriving and steadily growing line of trading posts, openly or surreptitiously invading the sacred precincts of Hudson's Bay wherever such invasion was advantageous.

All this was more than the old company could tolerate. Suddenly the descendants of those "gentlemen adventurers trading into Hudson's Bay" were taunted, shamed, or inspired to new life. There were shake-ups in management, reorganization, adoption of more aggressive policies, a rebirth of competitive spirit—conflict and bloody battle wherever and whenever representatives of the two companies crossed paths. As a grand climax to the contest, the rivals met at the Red River Settlement—near the site of Winnipeg—for the Battle of the Seven Oaks in June, 1816. So many died in that encounter that the British Government finally intervened and virtually ordered an end to hostilities and an amalgamation of Hudson's Bay and North West.

It took five years for the effects of that battle to reach Fort George on the Columbia River, but in 1821 North West closed its books there and reopened them under the new corporation title of Hudson's Bay Company; out of respect for seniority the younger firm surrendered even its name. The merger brought peace among the trappers, still further reorganization, and a stronger British monopoly than ever to Oregon. As a major trading center, Fort George was shortly abandoned, and headquarters moved across the river, a hundred miles further up, to Vancouver.

Bernard A. DeVoto (1897–1955), historian, critic, writer of fine fiction, poet, and professor, who on occasion could introduce a Churchillian roll into his prose, reconstructed the episode in *Across the Wide Missouri.*

A Touch of the Durbar

Fort Vancouver was built in 1825, following the merger of the North West Company and the Hudson's Bay Company, and a great man had been put in charge of it. Doctor John McLoughlin was a physician who had found the life of a North West partisan more fascinating than medicine; physically a giant, an imperious man and an imperial mind, a despot and a statesman, a master of leadership and administration. And in Oregon he had shown what monopoly could do with the fur trade. The Hudson's Bay Company had the wisest of all systems—or what would have been the wisest if history had co-operated. It farmed the fur country, practicing conservation, taking only a calculated percentage from a given field and then letting it lie fallow till the animal population had been restored.

It maintained a steady market and a fixed price for furs, and so stabilized its economy. It established a hierarchy of organization and command but preserved the career open to talent. It enforced a military government on its employees. It extended the same rigid control to the Indians, managing them with the wily wisdom amassed in more than a century and a half, and governing them with a code of wilderness law the infraction of which invariably meant punishment. So much so that the name of the Company was justice to the Indian, and Hudson's Bay men in twos and threes, or alone, could travel any of the Company's wilderness in safety.

The Company's history in the Pacific Northwest is not a chronicle of solitary murder and impromptu war, the bloody history of the American fur trade, but the orderly record of the British imperial caste dealing wisely, sternly, and profitably with any set of natives—that is, in places where the Company was a monopoly. It conserved the fur crop in its private fields, but exhausted it as rapidly as anyone else where there was competition. It neither gave, traded, nor sold liquor to Indians so long as no other traders invaded its preserves; when they did, it had more and cheaper liquor than anyone else. Its chivalrousness seems courtly beside the rough trail hospitality of the Americans—and it fought competition more bloodily than they ever did.

The American Fur Company's dealings with the Missouri or the mountain opposition were gentle and bush-league compared to the Hudson's Bay Company's century and a half of annihilating French, Canadian and rival British enterprises. Its final competi-

The Voyageurs who farmed the fur country

tion with the North West Company, which made the best fight and usually won it, meant many years of theft, hijacking, ambush and solitary murder more deliberate than anything the American companies ever saw, and rose to a small civil war with pitched battles—whereupon His Majesty's government had at last stepped in and forced peace and amalgamation.

The Company, hiring the North West partisans who had out-skilled its own, thereupon applied its peaceful system to Oregon. Back in the mountains it fought the Americans with the weapons the Americans used, but west of the mountains it was the just, paternal despotism of a monopoly managed by experts and em-pire-builders. It could have run the Columbia country as a profitable fur farm forever. . . .

McLoughlin's ten years as resident king had made the Depart-ment of the Columbia as neat as a blueprint. He moved the head-quarters from Astoria . . . to Fort Vancouver, not only to locate it on presumably permanent British soil but to get it into farming country and away from the coastal Indians. These tribes, whose culture differed greatly from that of the Plains tribes, had had thirty years of the coasting trade. Our history knows no bloodier or more depraved toughs than the sailors and sea captains—American, British and Russian—who traded into the inlets and river mouths from the sea. The Indians were just as bloody and depraved; and the China trade, of which this business was a part, rested on a confused warfare.

When the continent-girdling North West Company came down from the north to pirate Astor's business, its partisans had no choice but to continue the practices which the sailors had insti-tuted. . . . By the time it merged with the Hudson's Bay Com-pany it had, at a considerable cost in the lives of its employees, reduced the Indian population fifty per cent by means of murder, alcohol and disease. It had broken the culture and morale of the coastal tribes and developed to an extreme their talents for theft, beggary, treachery and murder.

McLoughlin changed all that. Locating upriver among less debauched Indians, he made Hudson's-Bay-Company subjects of them. For the most part they were well-behaved and scrupulous in keeping business contracts, and the life of a Company man was secure in Oregon. To be sure, he had had the help of an agent always powerful in the white man's burden. Long before Lewis and Clark got to the Columbia, venereal and other diseases brought by the ships had begun to cut down the Indian population. The slow, sure process was accelerated by the establishment of civilization at Vancouver. The mysterious epidemics that followed settlement everywhere in a new country here proved extraordinarily lethal to Indians. . . . A single generation accomplished in Oregon results that would have required three generations in the East. This also was convenient for the emigration that was to come.

However, here was the King of Oregon, "The White Eagle," and here was his kingdom. He had developed a system. . . . The home farm at Fort Vancouver covered nearly two thousand acres. . . . He had sawmills, blacksmith shops, cooperage shops, shipyards, salt works, fisheries. . . . He had a series of trading posts—as far east as the Flathead country in the United States, along the northern rivers, and while New Caledonia remained part of his territories, almost as far north as Alaska. . . .

At Fort Vancouver . . . [was] a mixture of aristocratic and barbaric splendor that would be perfectly familiar to a Scotch nobleman. The partners who came down the white river from the tremendous northern forests, where for months partisans and voyageurs alike experienced the full severity and squalor of wilderness life, stepped ashore into an ordered, ceremonious life as punctilious as a court. They dressed according to the requirements of their station—and their wives were the most expensively clad of all Indian women, with the Company ship bringing China silks and French laces and London busks. . . .

They dined in exact precedence and full ceremony. On the most delicate chinaware, elk roasts and grizzly steaks were borne in state by halfbreed or Kanaka servants dressed in a kind of livery. Here were an Englishman's port and the toasts proper to gentlemen. . . . At such an outpost of the British Empire in the nineteenth century there were always scientists, scholars and noblemen making their extemporized colonization and maintaining a nostalgic perfume of the court in a society of natives . . . the miscellany of Canucks, halfbreeds, Indians, Kanakas, the traffic upriver from the sea, the traffic downriver from Canada, the traffic overland from the States and Mexico.

And [there was] the superb spectacle when the canoe fleets landed or the pack trains departed—British spectacle, more ordered and more quiet than the American kind, with brighter colors and more seemly songs, with a touch of the durbar and many touches of His Majesty's Guards setting out for foreign service. A microscopic but complex nucleus of civilization on the rim of the world, with the great North over one horizon, and the great West—here made the East—over another, California to the south, China across the water. Forever England on the edge of forests whose trees rose a hundred feet or more to the first branch, on the bank of the River of the West rolling its tide westward to the ocean of Drake and Cook.

From *Across the Wide Missouri*, Bernard DeVoto (Boston: Houghton Mifflin Company, 1947).

XX

Jonathan S. Green

In the vicinity of his new headquarters at Fort Vancouver, generous John McLoughlin had seen to it that the Indians were accorded at least some semblance of humanitarian treatment, but in a moment of truth, he would have been the first to admit that his paternalistic policy was instituted primarily for the long-range protection and welfare of his business. It was in the interests of the Company to be merciful to Indians. Among all the representatives of Christian lands that had been visiting the coast for decades, not one had yet conceived of a scheme devoted to betterment of the Indians for their own sake, without reference to the material betterment of would-be benefactors.

But there was something different in the wind. Ever since the creation of the American Board of Commissioners for Foreign Missions at Boston in 1810, the Northwest had been on its list of prospective "fields ripe for gospel harvest." Action undoubtedly would have been taken earlier, but there were never enough funds, and calls for Protestant missionaries in a dozen countries of Asia, in Africa, in the Near East and among the frontier settlements of the American Midwest and South, always appeared more urgent. In 1820 a missionary band had been sent to the Sandwich Islands; and it had been extremely successful, so successful, in fact, that converted Hawaiians were already considering the promotion of foreign missions of their own.

The Congregational station nearest to Oregon was in Honolulu, and it was from there that the first overtures came for establishing a center for the enlightenment and salvation of savage souls of the Northwest. "A mission to the Northwest Coast will soon be expedient," announced the American Board in July, 1827. "It had better be attempted probably by the missionaries from the Sandwich Islands . . . and regarded as a branch of the Sandwich Island mission."

As usual, the principal deterrent to the project was a matter of cost. The expense would be much less if a team were dispatched from Hawaii than "if sent originally from this country." "How desirable," expatiated a Board secretary in Boston, "that the natives of the wilderness should hear the Gospel before they are prejudiced against it by the fraud, injustice and dissolute lives of men who give up the blessings of Christianity that they may not be troubled with its restraints."

The missionary to Hawaii chosen to investigate this new field was the Reverend Jonathan S. Green (1796–1878), a practical Yankee with a disarming sense of humor, a green thumb, and a rare ability to bring out talent in the underprivileged. Neither dreamy idealist nor stuffy pulpiteer, on the island of Maui he was about to establish a pioneer seminary for young ladies and put his parishioners to work raising and milling wheat. The Boston Board could have searched the length and breadth of the country and not found a man with wider perspective and sounder wisdom to look over the projected field. Yet when he came to turn in a report late in 1829, he was thoroughly pessimistic; things had gone from bad to worse among the Indians of Oregon. The Board had delayed too long. Dissolute men had already prejudiced the natives against the gospel.

Most of Green's scouting was done among northern coastal tribes. He had planned to conduct a special survey of the lower Columbia, but inclement weather and high seas prevented his entering the river, so for that area he had to rely on cross-examination of responsible captains who knew the region. Information received from them convinced him that this would be the most practical place for establishing a mission.

Trifling with Damnation

On the subject of religion, the ideas of the Indians are exceedingly vague. I have taken much pains to ascertain what notions they cherish of a Supreme Being and of a future state of existence, and I think it may emphatically be said of them, "They are atheists, head and heart." Of a Creator, powerful, wise and good, they seem to have no idea. In answer to the inquiry which I have frequently made, "Who formed the sea, the land and the creatures which inhabit them?" they have generally replied, "We know not." . . .

Of a future state of existence, their ideas are equally confused. They imagine that those who die of sickness go into the interior to some undefined place; those who are drowned continue to exist, but remain in the sea; those who die in battle go to the house of the sun. This they regard as highly honorable, and most of their warriors choose to die in this manner, and some of their chiefs have obtained a military suit in which they wish to be dressed when they fall. All who are killed in war are burned. The reason for this practice I could not ascertain. If the warrior thus slain be a chief, a slave is killed to accompany him.

They seem to have no idea of a future retribution for deeds done in the body. In conversing with them on this subject, I have supposed and stated a case as strong as possible—that of a drunken, thieving, quarrelsome Indian, who should first embrue his hands in the blood of his family and then destroy himself; and that of a sober, honest, peaceable man who should devote himself to the good of his family and tribe. And I have asked them what distinction there would be in their condition, and they have uniformly replied, "We know of none." . . .

The Indians on the Northwest Coast . . . are atheists in heart. That they live "without God" and are devoid of all consciousness of accountability is certain. They appear to have no sense whatever of obligation. Gratitude is a flame which no favor can kindle in their icy bosoms. Indeed, with scarcely an exception, to do them a kindness is to increase their insolence, so that the man who *today* should heap on them the richest benefits, they would stab to the heart *tomorrow*, should he refuse to accede to their unreasonable demands.

In their barter (exchanging furs for goods) they are to the highest degree insolent. They are exceedingly skillful in the disgusting phraseology of magnifying the value of their own property and depreciating that of their neighbor. They will also give him the lie with the greatest possible impudence. Not only are they destitute of everything that is lovely and of good report, but they are inconceivably wicked. The smallest confidence can not be placed in their statements, when they have a motive to dissemble.

All their movements on board ship must be narrowly watched, for they will *steal* whatever they can lay their hands upon, even if it is of no conceivable value to them; and when detected they seem devoid of shame. They are exceedingly fond of spirituous liquors and when intoxicated they are wrought up to the highest pitch of frenzy. Murders are frequent among them, and the different tribes are almost constantly involved in quarrels which result in bloody wars. Revenge is sweet to them. The most inconsiderable provocation awakens their vengeance; nor will they cease to hunt their foe till they drink his blood.

With regard to foreign influence, I am fully of the opinion that in every respect it has been baneful. I know not of a single benefit which it has conferred upon these unhappy men, while the miseries which through this channel have flowed in upon them, are incalculably great. Some years since, a trader left a few English potatoes . . . and instructed the natives in the cultivation of them. This is doubtless a benefit to the Indians, but not less so to the traders themselves. For years, at very little expense, they have been able to furnish their vessels with most excellent potatoes. Last year, I am told, Captain B. left swine. . . . These, if they increase, will be another benefit. I mention these things as I would do justice to the gentlemen concerning whose movements and influence I have been obliged to speak.

With their bows and arrows the Indians once roamed their

forests and hunted their game, the skins of which afforded them comfortable clothing, while they subsisted upon their flesh. They were perhaps often engaged in petty warfare with each other, though they say they were not; but as they had no firearms, nor *poisoned water*, their wars were less bloody and destructive. The introduction of these has opened upon them the flood gates of desolation.

Besides, most men from Christian countries have seemed to forget that, in these ends of the earth, the Omniscient God has watched their movements and marked in the book of his remembrance all their aberrations from the path of duty. Hence they have exhibited anything but a Christian spirit. They have plunged into the slough of sensual indulgence and have thus strengthened the practice of infanticide, if they did not introduce it.

Lest they should fail to reap their golden gains, they have suffered the Indians to be insolent, till every idea of justice is eradicated from their minds. They have taught them—if example may be said to teach what a people so intelligent easily learn—to dissemble and defraud, to profane the name of God, and trifle with damnation. They have put into their mouths the elements of mischief and into their hands the implements of death. And now it is said they are savage and blood-thirsty. And what wonder? They may, indeed, have the ferocity of the roamers of their own native wilds, may naturally resemble ravening wolves; but foreign intercourse has added to their ferocity *disease* and *madness*. And who now shall tame them? . . .

Nootka Sound . . . was formerly much visited by traders, but as furs have been scarce, vessels have not been there for several years. The natives had become hostile long before their trade ceased. The Straits of Juan de Fuca . . . are now becoming a place of resort for the purpose of trade. They are easily entered, and the country about them is said to be an excellent one. The natives are unacquainted with the use of firearms and ardent spirits.

About the Columbia River and its branches the Indians are exceedingly numerous. From a Mr. McKay, who has resided in that country seventeen years, I have the names of thirty-four tribes, many of which he represents as powerful. They are said to be a superior race of men, and though savage, are less bloody than the tribes further north. One of the Chinook tribe who resides near the mouth of the Columbia, I saw on board Captain Dominis' brig. I was pleased with his appearance. He gave me several words of his own language, but I had no medium through which I could converse with him.

These Indians have suffered from their intercourse with foreigners. Captain Simpson, an officer of the Hudson Bay Company, assured me that they had learned every vice, but not a single virtue of their white neighbors. . . . Captain Thompson of the brig *Convoy,* who left the Columbia River about a month since . . . regards the Indians there as *friendly.* Respecting the loss of an English brig there last March, Captain Thompson says there is no evidence that a solitary individual reached the shore or that the Indians had the slightest agency in their death—on the contrary, that the probability is that all the crew perished in the river.

Captain Thompson saw the brig soon after she struck the bar and he immediately sent a boat to her assistance. The crew of the boat went as near the brig as safety would permit; they saw no one on board, nor could assistance be afforded. The English, from evidence circumstantial and slight, came to the conclusion that a part of their friends were murdered by the Indians, and according to their uniform custom, they determined to seek redress. They applied to Captain Dominis (This he told me) for men to chastise the Indians. He humanely refused to aid them.

After several weeks, they obtained a large party of men, marched to the Indian village occupied by the tribe whom they charged with the murder of their countrymen and demanded the goods which had been taken from the wreck of the brig. The Indians brought out a few articles and delivered them up. The English were dissatisfied and demanded a large quantity of goods which they averred the Indians had taken, and they declared that unless their demands were speedily complied with, death was their portion!

What could be done? The poor savages were in the power of the English. In vain did they plead their innocency. Many of them were massacred, their village burned and the head of a chief taken as a memento of their love of justice. This was brought to Honolulu . . . and exhibited. Captain Thompson . . . after the murder of these Indians, spent a considerable time, several weeks . . . on shore among the Indians with perfect safety. . . .

Indeed, to seek a place on the coast where the Indians have not suffered in consequence of their intercourse with foreigners, will be, I am persuaded, a fruitless attempt. The Russian Fur, the North West and the Hudson Bay companies, and traders from the United States, have occupied every post of importance from Norfolk Sound to the Columbia River. The love of gain brought these men hither and to secure this object all their movements have concentrated.

It is useless to inquire what might have been done here forty years ago. What can be done, or what should be attempted now? And there can be no doubt, I think, that a counteracting influence might and should be exerted. The natives of the Northwest Coast are an intelligent race of men—they certainly have perceived the spirit by which men who have visited them have been influenced. This spirit they have caught, and this spirit they now breathe. But let them have an illustration of that charity which "seeketh not her own"; let them become acquainted with those who breathe the temper of the gospel, and they would learn and acknowledge its heavenly origin and by the blessings of God become subjects of its purifying and saving efficacy.

But, for the commencement of operations which shall ultimately bless the whole coast, a regard to Christian economy would urge to the selection of the most favorable situation. In making this decision it would be exceedingly pleasant, were the limits of the United States on this coast permanently defined. For though your benevolent wishes and efforts embrace all lands, yet, as we have territory on this coast, it seems desirable that missionary efforts should commence here. This would be especially desirable should the mission be connected with a small colony.

Somewhere in the vicinity of the Columbia River such a colony, I doubt not, would find a salubrious climate, a fertile soil and ultimately a country of great importance. . . . An establishment here, in addition to the good which might be effected in behalf of the native inhabitants, would have a happy influence on the interests of the Sandwich Island mission. Timber, fish and other necessities could be obtained for the islands, while it would afford a better than New England climate for those whose strength had withered beneath the influence of a tropical sun.

From *Journal of a Tour on the Northwest Coast of America in the Year 1829*, Jonathan S. Green (New York: Chas. Fred. Heartman, 1915).

XXI

Nathaniel J. Wyeth

"Salubrious climate . . . fertile soil . . . ultimately a country of great importance"—this was just what an industrious young ice dealer in Cambridge, Massachusetts, Nathaniel J. Wyeth (1802–1856), was looking for. It appealed to him even more than the prospect of preaching to the Indians, though he could be broad-minded about helping to enlighten them. A colony on the Columbia River! Certainly life there would be more romantic than cutting ice on Fish Pond and shipping the crop to the iceless West Indies; ice was good business, and highly remunerative, but furs, salmon, tobacco, potatoes in Oregon might provide a better business.

The energetic iceman was undoubtedly influenced by the report of Jonathan Green, but he was much more influenced by the extravagant propaganda of Hall Jackson Kelley. He joined Kelley's American Society for Encouraging the Settlement of Oregon, became one of its most outspoken enthusiasts, and finally in 1831 agreed to abandon the ice concern and accompany Kelley and the cross-country expedition he was organizing for Oregon settlers.

But Kelley was a better talker than organizer. His first company broke up in disagreement and bitter argument—a complete failure. However, once Wyeth had made up his mind on a course of action, nothing was likely to dissuade him. Kelley returned to his preoccupation with writing ponderous prose about the virtues of Oregon; Wyeth ignored him, quickly formed a little company of his own, stowed aboard a ship bound for Oregon the heaviest of the supplies they would need there, and headed West on foot.

Thirty-five of them set out overland early in the spring of 1832. Only eleven checked in at Fort Vancouver a long six months later, on October 29, and if it had not been for the everlasting drive, dexterity, and brazen determination of their leader, the eleven never would have made it. On the trail they had proven themselves the tenderest of tenderfeet. Bad luck followed misfortune; discord followed disaster. Even Wyeth's own brother and a cousin deserted him en route. The trip was a nightmarish series of calamities, and those calamities were capped by a final one: the ship on which they had forwarded their supplies foundered on the way.

On learning of that loss at Fort Vancouver, Wyeth concluded he had no choice but to turn around, tramp across the continent and, profiting from his errors, form a new company. Only a man of iron will could have exposed himself to such punishment. He did it. And the second venture—a corporation organized to pack salmon, raise tobacco, and trade for furs—too, was a failure. After that, Wyeth was happy to return to his Cambridge pond and carry on as an iceman.

At Vancouver he had been welcomed by John McLoughlin and entertained cordially, yet made to feel that he was trespassing on British soil. He was keenly aware that the monopoly of the Hudson's Bay Company was complete, all-embracing, and inviolable. It could be broken only by an agency as powerful as the United States Government; and he was convinced it was high time the Government did step in and assert its rights. Despite his liberality, McLoughlin had managed to thwart every American attempt to establish a permanent enterprise on the Columbia River. And so Wyeth reported, thoroughly disenchanted with Oregon.

The Unknown American

The coast trade was early in the hands of the Americans, who with expert navigators and swift vessels explored its numerous inlets and harbors in search of the sea otter, beaver and other valuable furs, which were traded by the Indians. This part of the trade is now, like that inland, passing into the hands of the Hudson's Bay Company. . . . The vigilance of this company allows of no accumulation of furs in the hands of the Indians; their emissaries are constantly on the move, with the best assortment of Indian goods, to pick up the skins one by one as fast as the Indians obtain them, and thus no motive is left for an American vessel to stop on the coast. . . .

The [American] fur trade, although trifling as to amount in a national view, is far otherwise in regard to its bearing on the Indians and their political relations with the country from which the trade emanates: whatever nation has the exclusive trade of an Indian tribe may wield the whole power of that tribe for such purposes, consistent with Indian character, as it may choose, provided it identifies itself as a nation with that trade.

This the United States have never done, and perhaps the aversion to monopolies among us will prevent their ever doing so. . . . At present the United States as a nation are unknown west of the mountains; Americans are designated only by some peculiarity of themselves or their leaders, and the different parties are considered as different tribes. This state of things subjects the traders to much danger, for the Indians, seeing perhaps a dozen men whom they consider as the whole of that concern, have no fear except that of the immediate contest to restrain them from plundering and scalping. . . .

By the indiscriminate trading of all persons with the Indians, individual safety, profit, national policy and good of the Indians are alike sacrificed. Where one murder is committed on English parties or individuals, I am certain there are more than ten upon our people. With the British traders everything is different; one company has the exclusive control of the trade in all places, except where the Americans have enjoyed an equal right west of the mountains.

They can trade as many beaver from a district as they think it will bear without diminishing the breeding stock, and thus continue their trade instead of destroying it. They can prevent the beaver being taken except at the best season. They can refuse supplies of ammunition beyond necessary and immediate consumption and thereby prevent any accumulation dangerous to themselves.

Besides—and stranger than all—is the fact that the white man's inventions in the hands of one tribe at once become articles of absolute necessity to all others, and there being but one party from whom to obtain them, they must be at peace with that party. Thus the trader who is without competition in an Indian country, however weak his force, not only may compel the Indians to respect him and his property, but if he chooses, prevent one tribe from warring with another, the practical illustration of which is that in all the countries where the Hudson's Bay Company have exclusive control, they are at peace with the Indians, and the Indians among themselves. Wars with the Indians on the British frontiers have long since ceased. . . .

A further evil that attends our loose laws and their looser execution is that the Indian country is becoming a receptacle for fugitives from justice. The preponderance of bad character is already so great amongst traders and their people that crime carries with it little or no shame. I have heard it related among white American trappers as a good joke that a trapper who had said he would shoot any Indian whom he could catch stealing his traps, was seen one morning to kill one, and on being asked if the Indian had stolen his traps, he answered no, but he looked as if he was going to. An Indian was thus wantonly murdered and white men were found to laugh at the joke. . . .

Experience has satisfied me that the entire weight of the Hudson's Bay Company will be made to bear on any trader who shall attempt to prosecute his business within its reach. . . . No sooner does an American concern start in these regions than one of these trading parties is put in motion, headed by a clerk of the company, whose zeal is stimulated by the prospect of an election to a partnership in it, fitted out with the best assorted goods from their ample stores, and men who have long been in the service of the company, and whose wages of many years are in its hands as security for their fidelity.

Under these circumstances we come in contact. If there are furs in the hands of the Indians, their superior assortment of goods will obtain them. . . . In this way the American companies are broken up. . . . The people employed by Hudson's Bay are about one-fourth from the Sandwich Islands, about one-fourth Orkney men and the residue Canadians; their discipline is strict and hard, and subordination from the highest officers to the lowest engagé is as perfect as that of the army. . . .

In their personal intercourse with Americans who come into the country, they are uniformly hospitable and kind. But the circumstances under which we meet them are mortifying in the extreme, making us too often but the recipients of the bounty of others instead of occupants to administer it, as should be the case. . . .

In conclusion I will observe that the measures of this Company have been conceived with wisdom, steadily pursued, and have been well seconded by their government, and the success has been complete. And, without being able to charge on them any very gross violations of the existing treaties, a few years will make the country west of the mountains as completely English as they can desire. Already the Americans are unknown as a nation, and as individuals their power is despised by the natives of the land. A population is growing out of the occupancy of the country whose prejudices are not with us, and before many years they will decide to whom the country shall belong, unless in the meantime the American Government make their power felt and seen to a greater degree than has yet been the case.

From "Mr. Wyeth's Memoir," Nathaniel J. Wyeth. *Territory of Oregon,* Report of the Committee on Foreign Affairs, H. R., 25th Congress, Third Session, Appendix 1, 1839.

XXII

John K. Townsend

On his second expedition to Oregon, Wyeth had more congenial company than on his first. In the retinue were Daniel and Jason Lee, uncle and nephew, who were to establish the first American settlement in the future state of Oregon; Harvard botanist Thomas Nuttall, on the prowl for plant specimens to add to his collections; and Philadelphia physician-naturalist John K. Townsend (1809–1851), who had been drafted by the American Philosophical Society to make a study of Western ornithology.

Except for time out for a brief excursion to the Sandwich Islands, Townsend remained in Oregon for two years, assembled a valuable collection of birds, and identified many more that still bear his name. But he was not able to cast off entirely his role as physician and was persuaded to pinch hit for several months as resident doctor at the makeshift hospital which the Hudson's Bay Company had opened at Fort Vancouver.

He took almost as much interest in observing Indian diseases and native treatments as in his contracted duties as ornithologist, declaring that the medicine men, with their chanting, wailing, stick-beating, and ear-splitting shouts, were utter imposters, completely "inefficacious," and that all their attempted cures were involved in superstition. "They believe in black spirits and white, blue spirits and gray," he asserted.

He deplored the Indian custom of mutilating their own bodies as a demonstration of their courage, pointing out that the slashes and self-inflicted flesh distortions often became infected and failed to heal, and cited a cocky chief who proudly displayed gunshot wounds in his chest and back from deliberately shooting himself through the lungs. When asked if he had no fear of death from the wound, the chief had replied that "his heart was strong and that a bullet would never kill him."

He was appalled at the absence of sympathy for the sick and dying and was haunted for days by the recollection of a sightless urchin being ridiculed, tortured, and barely kept alive by scraps of filthy food thrown to him as to a dog. From the kneadings and brutal manipulations of a medicine man, he rescued another fever-stricken, desperately ill child and cured her within two days with a little quinine. It was Townsend who sounded the warning that the Indians of the lower Columbia were disappearing so fast that unless something were done for their physical salvation soon, there would be no need for concern over their spiritual salvation.

Gathered to Their Fathers

The Indians of the Columbia were once a numerous and powerful people; the shore of the river for scores of miles was lined with their villages; the council fire was frequently lighted, the pipe passed around, and the destinies of the nation deliberated upon. War was declared against neighboring tribes; the deadly tomahawk was lifted and not buried until it was red with the blood of the savage; the bounding deer was hunted, killed, and his antlers ornamented the wigwam of the red man; the scalps of his enemies hung drying in the smoke of his lodge, and the Indian was happy.

Now, alas! where is he? Gone. Gathered to his fathers and to his happy hunting grounds; his place knows him no more. The spot where once stood the thickly peopled village, the smoke curling and wreathing above the closely packed lodges, the lively children playing in the front, and their indolent parents lounging on their mats, is now only indicated by a heap of undistinguished ruins.

The depopulation here has been truly fearful. A gentleman told me that only four years ago as he wandered near what had formerly been a thickly peopled village, he counted no less than sixteen dead men and women, lying unburied and festering in the sun in front of their habitations. Within the houses all were sick; not one had escaped the contagion; upwards of a hundred individuals, men, women and children, were writhing in agony on the floors of the houses, with no one to render them any assistance. Some were in the dying struggle; and clenching with the convulsive grasp of death, their disease-worn companions shrieked and howled in the last sharp agony.

Probably there does not now exist one, where five years ago there were a hundred Indians, and in sailing up the river from the Cape to the Cascades the only evidence of the existence of the Indian is an occasional miserable wigwam with a few wretched, half-starved occupants. In some other places they are rather more numerous, but the thoughtful observer cannot avoid perceiving that in a very few years the race must in the nature of things become extinct; and the time is probably not far distant when the little trinkets and toys of this people will be picked up by the curious and valued as mementos of a nation passed away forever from the face of the earth. The aspect of things is very melancholy. It seems as if the fiat of the Creator had gone forth, that these poor denizens of the forest and the stream should go hence, and be seen of men no more.

In former years when the Indians were numerous, long after the establishment of Fort Vancouver, it was not safe for the white men attached to it to venture beyond the protection of its guns without being fully armed. Such was the jealousy of the natives towards them that various deep-laid schemes were practiced to obtain possession of the post and massacre all whom it had harbored; now, however, they are submissive as children. Some have even entered into the service of the whites, and when once the natural and persevering indolence of the man is worn off, he will work well and make himself useful.

About two hundred miles southward, the Indians are said to be in a much more flourishing condition, and their hostility to the white people to be most deadly. They believe that we brought with us the fatal fever which has ravaged this portion of the country, and the consequence is that they kill without mercy every white man who thrusts himself amongst them. . . .

I have just had a visit from an old and intelligent Indian chief who lives near. It is now almost midnight, but for the last hour I have heard the old man wandering about like an unquiet spirit in the neighborhood of my little mansion, and singing snatches of the wild but sweetly musical songs of his tribe. It is a bitter night, and supposing the old man might be cold, I invited him to a seat by my comfortable fire.

He says, "Eighty snows have chilled the earth since Maniquon was born." Maniquon has been a great warrior; he has himself taken twenty scalps between the rising and setting of the sun. Like most old people, he is garrulous, and, like all Indians, fond of boasting of his warlike deeds. I can sit for hours and hear old Maniquon relate the particulars of his numerous campaigns, his ambushes and his "scrimmages," as old Hawk-eye would say.

When he once gets into the spirit of it, he springs upon his feet; his old, sunken eyes sparkle like diamonds set in bronze, and he whirls his shrunken and naked arm around his head as though he still held the deadly tomahawk. But in the midst of his excitement, seeming suddenly to recollect his fallen state, he sinks to his chair: "Maniquon is not a warrior now—he will not raise his ax again—his young men have deserted his lodge—his sons will go down to their graves, and the squaws will not sing of their great deeds."

I have several times heard him speak the substance of these words in his own language, and in one instance he concluded thus: "And who made my people what they are?"

This question was put in a low voice, almost a whisper, and was accompanied by a look so savage and malignant that I almost quailed before the imbecile old creature. I, however, answered quickly without giving him time to reply to his own question: "The Great Spirit, Maniquon," pointing with my finger impressively upwards.

"Yes, yes—it *was* the Great Spirit; it was not the *white man!*"

I could have been almost angry with the old Indian for the look of deadly hostility with which he uttered these last words, but that I sympathized with his wounded pride, and pitied his sorrows too much to harbor any other feeling than commiseration for his manifold wrongs.

From *Narrative of a Journey Across the Rocky Mountains and the Colorado River to the Sandwich Islands,* John K. Townsend (Philadelphia: Henry Perkins, 1839).

XXIII

William Walker

Before action was taken on Jonathan Green's report by the necessarily slow-moving American Board of Commissioners for Foreign Missions, there took place down in St. Louis an uncanny incident that was to bring a much quicker response from the Methodist Church than the Congregationalists seemed ready to give.

The incident was reported by a sympathetic Wyandotte Indian Chief, William Walker (c.1800–1874), one of the tribesmen who had migrated to Missouri and Kansas from Ohio to escape the invasion of white men there. Walker, like many of his fellow Wyandottes, had received a reasonably good education in Ohio and was a responsible, respected leader, later to be appointed the first provisional governor of Kansas.

Chief Walker picked up his information on "The Four Wise Men from the West" from William Clark of the Lewis and Clark expedition, who had been elevated to the post of Superintendent of Indian Affairs at St. Louis; the Chief passed the account on to Methodist businessman G. P. Disosway in New York, and Disosway in turn submitted it, with his commentary, to the editors of the official Methodist Organ, *The Christian Advocate and Journal.*

Four Wise Men from the West

Immediately after we landed in St. Louis on our crossing to the West, I proceeded to General [William] Clark's, Superintendent of Indian Affairs, to present our letters of introduction from the Secretary of War and to receive the same from him to the different Indian agents in the upper country. While in his office and transacting business with him, he informed me that three chiefs from the Flat Head nation were in his house, and were sick, and that one (the fourth) had died a few days ago. They were from the west of the Rocky Mountains.

Curiosity prompted me to step into the adjoining room to see them. I was struck by their appearance. They differ from any tribe of Indians I have ever seen: small in size, delicately formed, small limbs, and the most exact symmetry throughout, except the head. I had always supposed from their being called Flat Heads that the head was actually flat on the top, but this was not the case. . . . The head is flattened . . . from the point of the nose to the apex of the head; there is a perfect straight line; the protuberance of the forehead is flattened and leveled, . . . as produced by a pressure upon the cranium while in infancy.

The distance they had traveled on foot was nearly three thousand miles, to see General Clark, their "Great Father," as they called him, he being the first American officer they ever became acquainted with, and having much confidence in him. They had come to consult him, as they said, upon very important matters. General Clark related to me the object of their mission. . . .

It appeared that some white men had penetrated into their country and one of them happened to be a spectator to one of their religious ceremonies. . . . He informed them that their mode of worshiping the Supreme Being was radically wrong, and instead of being acceptable and pleasing, it was displeasing to Him; he also informed them that the white people away toward the rising of the sun had been put in possession of the true mode of worshiping the Great Spirit; they had a book containing directions on how to conduct themselves in order to enjoy His favor and hold converse with Him; and with this guide, no one need go astray, but everyone that would follow the directions laid down there, could enjoy in this life His favor, and after death would be received into the country where the Great Spirit resides, and live forever with Him.

Upon receipt of this information, they called a national council to take this subject into consideration. Some said, if this is true, it is certainly high time we were put in possession of this mode, and if our mode of worshiping be wrong and displeasing to the Great Spirit, it is time we had laid it aside. We must know something about this. It is a matter that cannot be put off. The sooner we know it the better.

They accordingly deputed four of their chiefs to proceed to St. Louis to see the Great Father, General Clark, to inquire of him, having no doubt that he would tell them the whole truth about it. They arrived in St. Louis and presented themselves to General Clark. The latter was somewhat puzzled, being sensible of the responsibility that rested upon him; he, however, proceeded by informing them that what they had been told by the white man in their own country was true.

Then he went into a succinct history of man from his creation down to the advent of the Savior; explained to them the moral precepts contained in the Bible, expounding to them the Decalogue; informed them of the advent of the Savior, his life, precepts, his death, resurrection, ascension, and the relation he now stands to man as mediator—that He will judge the world, etc.

Poor fellows, they were not all permitted to return home to their people with the intelligence. Two died in St. Louis, and the remaining two, though somewhat indisposed, set out for their native land. Whether they reached home or not is not known. If they died on the way home, peace be to their manes! They died, inquirers after the truth. I was informed that the Flat Heads as a nation have the fewest vices of any tribe of Indians on the continent of America.

Postscript of G. P. Disosway

How deeply affecting is the circumstance of the four natives traveling on foot three thousand miles through thick forests and extensive prairies, sincere searchers after truth! The story has scarcely a parallel in history. . . . There are immense plains, mountains and forests in those regions whence they came, the abodes of numerous savage tribes. But no apostle of Christ has yet had the courage to penetrate into their moral darkness.

Adventurous and daring fur traders only have visited these regions, unknown to the rest of the world. . . . May we not indulge the hope that the day is not far distant when the missionaries will penetrate into these wilds where the Sabbath bell has never yet tolled since the world began! . . . Not a thought of converting or civilizing them ever enters the mind of the sordid, demoralizing hunters and fur traders. These simple children of nature even shrink from the loose morality and inhumanities often introduced among them by the white man. Let the Church awake from her slumbers and go forth in her strength to the salvation of these wandering sons of our native forest!

From "The Flat-Head Indians," letter by William Walker to G. P. Disosway, as published in *The Christian Advocate and Journal, and Zion's Herald*, March 1, 1833.

XXIV

Samuel Parker

Ironically, the white trapper who had advised the "Four Wise Men" that they were using the wrong approach in addressing the Almighty, was in all probability a Roman Catholic, but the sign language used in the presence of Superintendent Clark failed to convey the distinction between Protestant and Papist, so that any denomination could interpret the message as seemed appropriate; other details of the incident may have been equally garbled. Nevertheless, the effect of that "Macedonian cry" was dramatic and immediate in Eastern Protestant circles.

"Hear! Hear! Who will respond to the call from beyond the Rocky Mountains?" clarioned New England's foremost Methodist spokesman, Dr. Wilbur Fisk, President of Wesleyan University at Middletown, Connecticut. "The communication of G. P. Disosway . . . has excited in many of this section intense interest. And to be short about it, we are for having a mission established there at once. . . . Let two suitable men, unencumbered with families and possessing the spirit of martyrs, throw themselves into the nation, live with them—learn their language—preach Christ to them. . . . Who will go? Who? . . . Were I young and healthy and unencumbered, how joyfully would I go. But this honor is reserved for another. Bright will be his crown; glorious his reward."

The first couple to answer the call were Jason and Daniel Lee. They had gone out with Nathaniel Wyeth, but instead of ministering to the Flatheads of the Bitterroot Valley, whence came the call, they had chosen to go further west to the Willamette Valley.

In Boston the Presbyterians and Congregationalists of the American Board heard the cry too, and dispatched a curiously ill-chosen volunteer, an erudite Biblical scholar and eloquent evangelist with total ignorance of and aptitude for frontier life, the fifty-six-year-old Dr. Samuel Parker (1779–1866). With two companions he was to travel to St. Louis and there join the annual trade caravan bound for the Northwest.

But at St. Louis Parker missed connections with the caravan, and sensing that he was running out of money, hastened back to Boston to report the predicament and start raising funds for another try. He set out for upstate New York to campaign in familiar home ground, and while barnstorming there during the following fall providentially encountered first a young country doctor, Marcus Whitman, burdened with a conscientious urge to help the Flatheads, and then a spirited choir leader, Narcissa Prentiss, entertaining the same passion. He arranged a get-together for the two and, without benefit of courtship, Narcissa and Marcus decided they should wed—provided Parker could fit them into his plans.

Parker postponed the marriage, but with replenished funds he again headed for St. Louis, taking Marcus along as mule skinner, campfire cook, and handyman. This time Parker got as far as Wyoming, where he learned from trappers that the Lees had bypassed the Flatheads and the need for missionaries among inland tribes was great indeed. So after due consideration, Marcus was sent back to New England for reinforcements, and Parker went on to Oregon to scout the territory for the best mission sites.

The aging scholar spent a comfortable winter at Fort Vancouver; over a period of several months he toured much of the lower Columbia basin, selected Fort Walla Walla as a desirable place for a first mission, and then, without waiting for Whitman's return, inexplicably took ship for home via the Sandwich Islands.

In his *Journal,* published shortly after his return to the East, he echoed what Dr. Townsend had already reported, and seemed to argue that the need for men like Marcus Whitman was much greater than that for men like Samuel Parker.

The Vanishing Savage

I have found the Indian population in the lower country—below the falls of the Columbia—far less than I had expected, or what it was when Lewis and Clark made their tour. Since the year 1829 probably seven-eighths—if not, as Dr. McLoughlin believes, nine-tenths—have been swept away by disease, principally by fever and ague [smallpox].

The malignancy of this disease may have been increased by predisposing causes, such as intemperance and the influence of intercourse with sailors. But a more direct cause of the great mortality was their mode of treatment. In the burning stage of the fever they plunged themselves into the river and continued in the water until the heat was allayed, and rarely survived the cold stage which followed.

So many and so sudden were the deaths which occurred that the shores were strewed with the unburied dead. Whole, and large, villages were depopulated, and some entire tribes have disappeared; but where there were any remaining persons they united with other tribes. This great mortality extended not only from the vicinity of the Cascades to the shores of the Pacific but far north and south. . . . After one or two seasons it abated, partly from the want of subjects and partly from medical assistance obtained from the hospital at Fort Vancouver. . . .

Whether the Indians are to pass away before the increasing power and numbers of the white men, or whether enlightened and improved by their philanthropy so they may arise in the scale of intellectual and moral existence is a problem which time alone can solve. . . . I hesitate not to say that I can see no reason existing in the nature of things, or in their present condition, which necessarily dooms the race to annihilation on the one hand, or on the other necessarily makes them objects of apprehension as the future hordes who shall in coming time, like the northern barbarians of Roman days, be reserved as the scourge of an overgrown and decaying republic.

If to do good be an object worthy of humanity or religion, I see not why a consistent and persevering attempt to raise a race of freemen from their depression, and to place them in the rank of intelligent men, be not an undertaking fraught with as much promise and encouragement as it was in earlier days to elevate our ancestors. . . . I tremble for the consequences when I reflect on the wrongs inflicted upon this race of men. Able pens have portrayed in vivid colors their injuries and abuses, and humanity has wept. Were but one-hundredth part spread out to view, we should recoil at the sight.

The life of an Indian, in the estimation of our border and refugee men who visit their country, is worth nothing. Theirs is a land where white men regard no law; but superior cunning and superior force bear rule. . . . I quote as expressing very fully my own sentiments: "Among these tribes our imported diseases produce frightful ravages, our ardent spirits deprave and consume their population, our unjust laws exclude them from enjoying that first element of well-ordered societies—judicial protection. . . . It is impossible for us as men, patriots, philanthropists or Christians to behold without anxiety the ruin of the people whom we are accessory in supplanting, unless our future modes of colonization be directed with greater humanity and wisdom than in times past."

From *Journal of an Exploring Tour Beyond the Rocky Mountains,* Samuel Parker (Ithaca: Andrus, Woodruff and Gauntlett, 1844).

XXV

William A. Slacum

The confusion of reports and complaints emanating from Oregon fur dealers, Yankee traders, trappers, would-be settlers and planters, naturalists, ship captains—and missionaries—at last convinced even the President of the United States that it was time the truth was sifted out of the mass of accumulated misinformation, bias, and fabrication. Supposedly the British and Americans were sharing freedom of enterprise amicably in the area. Surely the Hudson's Bay Company couldn't be violating so patently the terms of the extended and reëxtended "Convention of 1818." What President Jackson wanted was the analysis of a competent, experienced, unprejudiced investigator, and to get it, a secret agent of the State Department, William A. Slacum, was nominated.

"To obtain some specific and authentic information in regard to the inhabitants of the country in the neighborhood of the Oregon or Columbia River" was the substance of his assignment. In drafting the orders, the Secretary of State discreetly avoided mentioning any particular foreign power by name; he did instruct Slacum to make a survey of the Indian tribes; but all the emphasis was on a full report of the Hudson's Bay Company activities.

"Upon your arrival on the northwest coast of America," wrote the Secretary, "you will embrace the earliest opportunity to proceed to and up the river Oregon and ascertain the sentiments entertained by all in respect to the United States . . . and generally endeavor to obtain all such information, political, physical, statistical and geographical, as may prove useful or interesting to the Government." Otherwise he was given a free hand to operate as he saw fit.

To cloak his mission in appropriate mystery, Slacum made the roundabout approach. He journeyed first to Mexico, and from there took off for the Sandwich Islands. In Honolulu he picked up an alarming Hawaiian version of British high-handedness and hostility on the coast and concluded that any dependence on English transportation would handicap, if not jeopardize, his whole mission; so he took the expensive precaution of chartering the American brig *Loriot* for his cruise to the Columbia. "I considered it necessary to have a vessel under my entire control," he explained, "in order to be independent of the Hudson's Bay Company, who have absolute authority over the inhabitants on either side of the Columbia River, and from whom alone the commonest wants or supplies could be procured; at the same time, to have a shelter under the flag of my country."

Off Cape Disappointment, just before Christmas, 1836, he was accosted by a Chinook chief with the question: "Is this King George or Boston ship?" and upon confessing that the *Loriot* was a "Boston" or American vessel, Slacum immediately became suspect and was placed under surveillance. All the trouble he had taken to disguise his purpose was for naught; he might as well have arrived by canoe. And at Fort Vancouver McLoughlin fingered him as a spy upon their first meeting. Nevertheless, in the following weeks he succeeded in obtaining a clear, though occasionally exaggerated—and always biased—picture of the Company's realm and machinations.

The Company

The Hudson's Bay Company have extended their enterprises over an extent of country almost incalculable. . . . A large ship arrives annually from London and discharges cargo at Vancouver:

chiefly coarse woolens, cloths, baizes and blankets; hardware, cutlery, calicoes, cottons and cotton handkerchiefs; tea, sugar, coffee and cocoa; tobacco, soap, beads, guns, powder, lead, rum, playing cards, boots, shoes, ready-made clothing, etc., etc., besides every description of sea stores, canvas, cordage, paints, oils, chains and chain cable, anchors, etc. to refit the company's ships that remain on the coast.

These are the ship *Nereide,* the brig *Llama,* the schooner *Cadborough* and sloop *Broughton;* the steamboat *Beaver* of 150 tons, two engines of thirty horsepower each, built in London last year. These vessels are all well armed and manned; the crews are engaged in England to serve five years at two pounds per month for seamen. The London ship with the annual supply usually arrives in the Columbia in early spring, discharges, and takes a cargo of lumber to the Sandwich Islands; returns in August to receive the furs that are brought to the depot (Fort Vancouver) once a year from the interior via the Columbia River, from the Snake country and from the American rendezvous west of the Rocky Mountains, and from as far south as San Francisco in California.

Whilst one of the company's vessels brings in the collections of furs and peltries made at the different depots along the coast at the north, the steamboat is now being employed in navigating those magnificent straits from Juan de Fuca to Sticken. Immense quantities of furs, sea otter, beaver, martin and sable can be collected along the shores of these bays and inlets. The chief traders at Nisqually, Fort Langley, Fort McLoughlin and Fort Simpson purchase all the furs and peltries from the Indians in their vicinity and as far as New Caledonia, in the interior, and supply them with guns, powder, lead, tobacco, beads, etc., all of which supplies are taken from the principal depot at Port Vancouver.

An express, as it is called, goes out in March annually from Vancouver and ascends the Columbia 900 miles in bateaux. One of the chief factors, or chief traders, takes charge of the property and conveys to York Factory on Hudson's Bay the annual returns of the business conducted by the Hudson's Bay Company west of

the Rocky Mountains in the Columbia district. This party like-
wise conveys to the different forts along the route goods suitable
to the Indian trade. Other parties take up supplies, as they may
be required, to Walla Walla, 250 miles above Vancouver; to
Colville, 600 miles above; to the fort at the junction of Lewis's
River, 700 miles above; to the south to Fort McKoys on the river
Umpqua; and last year chief trader McLeod took up to the
American rendezvous a large supply of British manufactures.

This assemblage of American trappers and hunters takes place
annually on the western side of the Rocky Mountains, generally
in the month of July, and amounts to 450 to 500 men, who bring
the result of their year's labor to sell to the American fur traders.
These persons purchase their supplies for the trappers at St.
Louis, though after being subject to the duties on these articles
(chiefly of British manufacture) they transport their goods about
1,400 miles by land to sell to citizens of the United States within
our acknowledged lines of territory.

Last year they met a powerful opponent in the agent of this
foreign monopoly, chief trader McLeod, who could well afford to
undersell the American fur trader *on his own ground*—first by
having the advantage of water communication on the Columbia
and Lewis's rivers for a distance of seven or eight hundred miles,
and, secondly, by introducing the goods free of duty, which is
equal to at least 25 to 30 per cent.

But a greater evil than this exists in the influence the Hudson's
Bay Company exercises over the Indians by supplying them with
arms and ammunition, which may prove at some future period
highly dangerous to our frontier settlements. Besides this, the
policy of this company is calculated to perpetuate the institution
of slavery, which now exists and is encouraged among all the
Indian tribes west of the Rocky Mountains. . . .

The price of a slave varies from eight to fifteen blankets.
Women are valued higher than men. If a slave dies within six
months of the time of purchase, the seller returns one-half the
purchase money. As long as the Hudson's Bay Company permit
their servants to hold slaves, the institution of slavery will be
perpetuated, as the price is too tempting for an Indian to resist.

Many instances have occurred where a man has sold his own child. . . .

The slaves are generally employed to cut wood, hunt and fish for the families of the men employed by the Hudson's Bay Company, and are ready for any extra work. Each man of the trapping parties has from two to three slaves who assist to hunt and take care of the horses and camp; they thereby save the company the expense of employing at least double the number of men that would otherwise be required on these excursions. . . .

From what I have seen, I feel perfectly satisfied that no individual enterprise can compete with this immense foreign monopoly established in our own waters. For instance, an American vessel, coming from New York or Boston to trade on the Northwest coast or the Columbia, would bring a cargo chiefly of British manufacture on which the duties had been paid, . . . whereas the Hudson's Bay Company's vessels come direct from London, discharge at Vancouver, pay no duty, nor are they subject to the expense and delay of discharging and reloading in a foreign port.

Since the year 1828 a party of forty or fifty trappers (Canadians) with their women, slaves, etc., generally amounting to 150 to 200 persons and 300 horses, go out from Vancouver towards the south as far as 40° north latitude. These parties search every stream and take every beaver skin they find, regardless of the destruction of the young animals. Excesses, too, are unquestionably committed by these hunting parties on the Indians, with the result that every small American party, save one, that has passed through the same country has met defeat and death. The parties being much smaller than those of the Hudson's Bay Company, the Indians attack them with success, and the Americans hesitate not to charge the subordinate agents of the Hudson's Bay Company with instigating the Indians to attack all other parties.

In 1829 the American brig *Owyhee*, Captain Domines of New York, entered the Columbia and commenced trading with the Indians for beaver skins and peltries. In the course of nine months Captain Domines procured a cargo valued at $96,000. It happened that this year the fever that has since desolated the Columbia from the falls to Oak Point appeared, and Dr. Mc-

Loughlin, the chief factor of the Hudson's Bay Company, with all the gravity imaginable, informed me the Indians to this day believe that Domines, of *the Boston ship*, brought the fever to the river. How easy was it for the Hudson's Bay Company's agents to make the Indians believe this absurdity! . . .

The Indians are taught to believe that no vessels but the Company's ships are allowed to trade in the river, and most of them are afraid to sell their skins but at Vancouver or Fort George. . . . The next American vessel that entered the river after the *Owyhee* was the brig *May Dacre* of Boston. She arrived in 1835 to procure a cargo of salmon. . . . The owner and agent agreed not to purchase furs, provided Dr. McLoughlin would throw no impediment in his way of procuring salmon. This enterprise failed; only 800 to 900 pounds of salmon were obtained.

Stock of the Hudson's Bay Company is held in shares (100). Chief traders and chief factors who reside in America are called partners . . . but they are not stockholders in perpetuity, as they cannot sell out to other stockholders, but have only a life estate in the general stock. A council annually assembles at York Factory, where reports from the different districts east and west of the Rocky Mountains are read and recorded, and their proceedings forwarded to London to the Hudson's Bay House. Chief factors and chief traders hold a seat at this council board, and Governor Simpson presides.

It is here that every new enterprise is canvassed, expense and probable profits carefully inquired into, as each member feels a personal interest in every measure adopted. If it is ascertained that in certain districts the quantity of beaver diminishes, the trappers are immediately ordered to desist for a few years, that the animals may increase, as the wealth of the country consists in its furs. And so strict are the laws among many of the northern Indian tribes that to kill a beaver out of season is a crime punished with death.

The enforcement of this law is strongly encouraged by the Hudson's Bay Company. Not so careful, however, are the company of the territory not their own . . . [where] the Indians are encouraged to trap the streams at all seasons. . . .

The price of a beaver skin in the Columbia district is ten shillings, or $2, payable in goods at 50 per cent on the invoice cost. Each skin averages one and a half pounds, and is worth in New York or London $5 per pound—value $7.50. The beaver skin is the circulating medium of the country. . . .

The navigation of the Columbia is absolutely necessary to the Hudson's Bay Company; without this they have no passage into the heart of their finest possessions in the interior. I know not what political influence they command, but this monopoly is very wealthy, and when the question of our western lines of territory is settled, they will make the most strenuous efforts to retain free navigation of the Columbia—more important to them than the free navigation of the St. Lawrence is to the people of the United States.

I beg leave to call your attention to the topography of Puget Sound and urge in the most earnest manner that this point should never be abandoned. . . . In a military point of view, it is of the highest importance to the United States. If it were in the hands of any foreign power, especially Great Britain, with the influence she could command through the Hudson's Bay Company over the Indians at the north on those magnificent straits of Juan de Fuca, a force of 20,000 men could be brought by water in large canoes to the sound in a few days; from thence to the Columbia, the distance is but two days' march via the Cowlitz. . . .

I am now more convinced than ever of the importance of the Columbia River, even as a place where for eight months in the year our whalers from the coast of Japan might resort for supplies. . . . A custom house established at the mouth of the Columbia would effectually protect the American trader from the monopoly which the Hudson's Bay Company enjoy at this time, and a single military post would be sufficient to give effect to the laws of the United States, and protect our citizens in their lawful avocations.

From "Mr. Slacum's Report," William A. Slacum. *Report of Committee on Foreign Affairs*, H.R., "Territory of Oregon," 25th Congress, 3rd Session. Appendix 1, 1839.

XXVI

Narcissa Whitman

The salvation of the Indians was far too urgent a matter to await the construction of customs houses and military posts that federal agents like William Slacum were proposing for the protection of American citizens. In disregard for any harassment he might receive from disapproving Company men or savages not yet ready to be cured or converted, Marcus Whitman stalked into Fort Vancouver early in September, 1836, ready to take up his duties as medical missionary at Waiilatpu.

With phenomenally good luck and an incredible expenditure in energy, he had raced across the country and back again in just over a year. Moreover, he had performed the feat of piloting the first two white women across the plains, over the Rockies, and down the Columbia. True to her provisional pledge, Narcissa Prentiss (1802–1847) had submitted to matrimony, joined her husband on the march, and was already a bride of seven months, conspicuously pregnant.

But in his recruitment of other "reinforcements," Whitman had been less fortunate. Three were all he could rally—the dour Reverend Henry H. Spalding, with his ailing and unprepossessing wife, and a chronically disgruntled lay assistant, William Gray, who had carried a chip on his shoulder all the way across the country and still cherished it. It was anything but a congenial team. And adding to the lack of harmony was an odd storybook circumstance—probably never confided to Marcus—that Spalding had once been an ardent suitor of Narcissa and had never recovered from the sting of her rejection. The gruelling transcontinental journey, by wagon, bateau, canoe, and frequently afoot, necessarily in close company, had aggravated old wounds and created new ones. From start to finish the couples had grated on each other, though they had finally reached agreement on one issue: to take up their labors in entirely separate stations.

In the Snake River country Whitman had picked up the first intimation that Parker had quit after selecting Waiilatpu, near Walla Walla, as site for a mission; but not until the doctor reached Vancouver did he learn that his superior had actually left, and that he was now in charge. Quickly the decision was reached that the Whitmans should establish themselves at Waiilatpu, and the Spaldings at Lapwai on the Clearwater—a sufficient distance to the northwest to discourage frequent commuting. However, the wives would have to remain at the Fort until the men had constructed some semblance of a mission shelter.

Whitman and Spalding paddled back up the Columbia from Vancouver, and while Eliza sulked and felt sorry for herself, Narcissa cheerfully took on the tutorship of McLoughlin's daughter, organized a singing school for half-breed children, and luxuriated in the lavish hospitality provided by the Hudson's Bay Company. To her, a sheltered farm girl from upstate New York, Vancouver was "The New York of the Pacific," while the table service and British-accented drawing-room conversation symbolized the crest of high society.

But that interlude was of short duration. Once the mission house at Waiilatpu was nearing completion, she gave up her classes and durbar life to be ushered upriver to the harsh realities of missionary life. Occasionally during the ensuing months of dawn-to-dusk labor, she found a moment to write fragmentary reports of her experience in letters to her family back East. The doctor, of course, was obliged to spend much of his time on the trail answering distant sick calls, and her principal company con-

sisted of Indians of uncertain loyalty, and her Hawaiian house-
boy, John.

We Love Them Most Sincerely

The greatest trial to a woman's feelings is to have her cooking and
eating room always filled with four or five or more Indians—
men—especially at meal time. . . . They are so filthy they make
a great deal of cleaning wherever they go, and this wears a
woman very fast. We must clean after them, for we have come to
elevate them and not to suffer ourselves to sink down to their
standard. . . . So many Indians have come recently that it was
impossible for all to get into our house. . . .

When they began to return from their winter quarters we told
them it would be good for them to build a large house—which
they often do by putting several lodges together—where it would
be convenient for all to attend worship and not meet in the open
air. They said they should not do it, but would worship in our
new house, and asked us if there were not houses in heaven to
worship in.

We told them our house was to live in and we could not have
them worship there, for they would make it so dirty and fill it so
full of fleas that we could not live in it. We said to them further
that they did not help us build it and that people in other places
built their houses of worship and did not let one man do it all
alone, and urged them to join together by and by and build one
for themselves of adobe. But it was of no avail to them; they
murmured still and said we must pay them for their land we lived
on. Something of this kind is occuring almost all the time when
certain individuals are here—such as complaining because we do
not feed them more, or that we will not let them run all over the
house.

They are an exceedingly proud, haughty and insolent people
and keep us constantly upon the stretch after patience and fore-
bearance. We feed them far more than any of our associates do
their people, yet they will not be satisfied. Notwithstanding all

this, there are many redeeming qualities in them. . . . They are making farms all about us, which to us is a favorable omen. . . .

There has been much sickness among them and several deaths —some of them were our firmest friends. Their sickness causes us a great deal of perplexity, care and anxiety. They are anxious to take medicine, but they do not feel satisfied with this alone: they must have their jugglers playing over them or they will surely die. We have had two or three instances where some have died without being played over. They are such miserable nurses that they die by their own neglect. We have been kept much of the time occupied in visiting and preparing food and medicine for them. . . .

They have attended quite generally upon instructions; some to hear for the benefit of their souls, and others for the gratification of their pride and vanity. . . . They love to hear something new and marvelous—scripture names and history, or any subject that does not touch the heart. These they will repeat day after day and night after night, as if their salvation depended upon it; indeed, they make it their religion and are displeased the moment we attempt to shake the foundations of their hopes. They are supremely selfish and would compel us to do everything for them if they could, without compensation. . . .

They are so impressed with the idea that all who work are slaves and inferior persons that the moment they hear of their children doing the least thing they are panic-stricken and make trouble. We have had a school for them . . . and much of the time our kitchen has been crowded, and all seem very much attached. We will soon commence teaching them to read their own language. . . . We appear to have every encouragement missionaries could possibly expect for the short time we have been here.

We see great improvement in them. . . . All seem to manifest a deep interest in the instruction given them, though some feel almost to blame us for telling them about eternal realities. One said it was good when they knew nothing but to hunt, eat, drink

Whitman Mission—the Cradle of Civilization

and sleep; now it is bad. . . . The aged ones appear to be as much interested as the children. We have been teaching them the Ten Commandments, with which they are very much pleased.
. . .

A most important transaction during one meeting was the formation of a temperance society for the benefit of the Indians. All the chiefs and principal men of the tribe who were here readily agreed to the pledge and gave in their names to become members of the society. I have recently been informed that two of them have been tempted to drink, but have refused and turned their backs upon it, saying they would never drink again. They are truly an interesting people. We love them most sincerely, and long to see them turning unto the Lord. . . .

A Catholic priest has recently been at Walla Walla and held meetings with the Indians and used their influence to draw the people away from us. Some they have forbidden to visit us again, and filled their minds with distraction about truths we teach, and their doctrine—say we have been talking to them about their bad hearts long enough and too long—say we ought to have baptized them long ago, etc. etc. The conflict has begun. What trials await us we know not. . . .

I got dreadfully frightened last night [in her husband's absence]. About midnight I was awakened by someone trying to open my bedroom door. At first I did not know what to understand by it. I raised my head and listened a while and then lay down again. Soon the latch was raised and the door opened a little. I sprang from the bed in a moment and closed the door again, but the ruffian pushed and pushed and tried to unlatch it, but could not succeed. Finally he gained upon me until he opened the door again, and as I supposed, disengaged his blanket. At the same time I was calling John, and as soon as he came in, the Indian ran for his life.

Had the ruffian persisted, I do not know what I should have done. I did not think of the war club, but I thought of the poker. Thanks be to our Heavenly Father, He mercifully "delivered me

from the hand of a savage man." . . . Doubtless it is not safe for
me to remain alone any longer. . . . The Lord only knows what
he has for us to pass through in this world. Frequently I feel as if
our stay would not be long here.

Excerpts topically quoted from "Letters written by Mrs. Whitman from Oregon
to Her Relatives in New York." Oregon Pioneer Association *Transactions* for 1891
(Portland: Anderson, 1893).

XXVII

Thomas Jefferson Farnham

Less than three years after Marcus and Narcissa Whitman opened their mission at Waiilatpu, it was visited by Thomas Jefferson Farnham (1804–1848), who was just beginning to be recognized as one of the most vigorous writers on the West. As a well-educated, traveled reporter, he was qualified to look at it objectively and give a candid evaluation of the Whitmans' accomplishment.

Farnham had come all the way from Maine, where he had been trained as a lawyer. For a few years he had practiced in Illinois; then, still unable to overcome his wanderlust, he had assembled a group of eighteen dubbed the "Oregon Dragoons" and headed further west carrying the banner "Oregon or the Grave." The lawyer held the dubious distinction of serving as their captain—dubious because he and they were woefully disorganized, ill-equipped, and conditioned for a holiday jaunt rather than a battle with the elements and Western geography.

By the time the party reached Independence, Missouri, on the last day of May, 1839, the lighthearted mood had vanished, as had most of their supplies, and mutiny was in the ranks. Then they made the mistake of following the Santa Fe rather than the safer Oregon Trail. As they progressed, the Dragoons gradually diminished to five. But Farnham's enthusiasm never flagged. In

Colorado he engaged a competent guide and pushed on with a handful of followers.

But even the original leader separated from the rest of the company as they approached the Columbia region, and went off on his own. He did not pause long even in Oregon, but kept on his westward course as far as Hawaii before turning back to California and the States. The books on his travels were soon in such demand that they went into a dozen editions, several of them published after his early death.

Not only did Farnham laud Waiilatpu, but after descending the Columbia, after visiting Willamette Valley and Fort Vancouver, he declared the country to be "one of the most favored portions of the globe," and helped settlers compose a petition to Congress, pleading that the United States take Oregon under its protective wing.

This Cradle of Civilization

About three o'clock [on September 22, 1839] we came into the camp of a middle-aged Cayuse Indian, Crickie, who was on his homeward march from the buffalo hunt in the mountain valleys east and northeast of Fort Hall. He was a spare man of five feet eight inches, dressed in a green camlet frock coat, a black vest, striped cotton shirt, leather pants, moccasins and a white felt hat. There were two children, boys, neatly clad in deerskin. His camp equipage was very comfortable—four or five camp kettles with tin covers, a number of pails with covers, a leathern tent and an assortment of fine buffalo robes.

He had had a very successful hunt. Of the seventeen horses in his caravan, six were loaded with the best flesh of the buffalo cow, cured in the best manner; two others bore his tent, utensils, clothing, robes, etc.; four others were ridden by himself and family; the five remaining were used to relieve those that from time to time might tire. These were splendid animals, as large as the best horses of the States, well knit, deep and wide at the shoulders; a broad loin and very small lower limbs and feet; of extreme activity and capacity for endurance.

Learning that this Indian was proceeding to Dr. Whitman's mission establishment, where a considerable number of his tribe had pitched their tents for the approaching winter, I determined to leave the cavalcade and accompany him there. . . . Crickie (in English "poor crane") was a very kind man. Immediately . . . he turned my worn-out animals loose and loaded my packs upon his own, gave me a splendid saddle horse to ride and intimated by significant gestures that we would go a short distance that afternoon in order to arrive at the mission early the next day.

I gave my assent and we were soon on the way. Our course was northeasterly over sharp swells, among which ran many clear and beautiful brooks; soil gravel, loam, sand and clay, and well covered with dry bunch grass, incapable of producing the grains without irrigation. The swells and streams run northwesterly from the Blue Mountains. Our course was diagonally across them.

Having made about ten miles at sunset, we encamped for the night. I noticed during the drive a degree of forbearance towards each other in this family of savages which I had never before observed in that race. When we halted for the night the two boys were behind. They had been frolicking with their horses and as the darkness came on lost the trail. It was a half-hour before they made their appearance, and during this time the worthy parents exhibited the most affectionate solicitude for them.

One of them was but three years old and was lashed to the horse he rode; the other only seven years of age. Young pilots in the wilderness at night! But the elder, true to the sagacity of his race, had taken his course and struck the brook on which we had encamped, within three hundred yards of us. The pride of the parents at this feat, and their ardent attachment to their children, were perceptible in the pleasure with which they received them at their evening fire and heard the relation of their childish venture.

The weather was so pleasant that no tent was pitched. The willows were beat, and buffalo robes spread over them. Underneath were laid other robes, on which my Indian host seated himself with his wife and children on one side, and myself on the other. The fire burned brightly in front. Water was brought, and the evening ablutions having been performed, the wife presented a dish of meat to her husband and one to myself. There was a pause. The woman seated herself between her children. The Indian then bowed his head and prayed to God! A wandering savage in Oregon calling upon Jehovah in the name of Jesus Christ! After the prayer, he gave meat to his children and passed the dish to his wife.

While eating, the frequent repetition of the words Jehovah and Jesus Christ in the most reverential manner led me to suppose they were conversing on religious topics; and thus they passed an hour. Meanwhile, the exceeding weariness of a long day's travel admonished me to seek rest.

I had slumbered I know not how long when a strain of music awoke me. I was about rising to ascertain whether the sweet notes of Tallis's Chant came to these solitudes from earth or sky, when a full recollection of my situation, and of the religious habits of my host, easily solved the rising inquiry and induced me to observe instead of disturbing. The Indian family was engaged in its evening devotions. They were singing a hymn in the Nez Percés language. Having finished it, they all knelt and bowed their faces upon the buffalo robes and Crickie prayed long and fervently. Afterwards they sang another hymn and retired.

This was the first breathing of religious feelings that I had seen since leaving the States. A pleasant evidence that the Oregon wilderness was beginning to bear the rose of Sharon on its thousand hills, and that on the barren soil of the Cayuse heart was beginning to bud and blossom and ripen the golden fruits of faith in Jehovah and hope in an afterstate.

23rd. We were on our way before the sun rose. The dawn on an Oregon sky, the rich blue embankment of mountains over which the great day star raised his glowing rim, the blandness of the air, the lively ambling of the caravan towards the neighboring abode of my countrymen, imparted to my mind and body a most agreeable exhilaration. Crickie, and his wife and children also, appeared to enjoy the atmosphere and scenery of their native valley; and we went on together merrily over the swelling plains and murmuring streams till about eight o'clock when Crickie spurred his horse in advance of the cavalcade and motioned me to follow him.

We rode very rapidly for about three hours. . . . The dust had risen in dark clouds during our ride, and rendering it necessary to bathe before presenting ourselves at the mission. We therefore halted on the bank of a little brook. . . . A small mirror, pocket comb, soap and towel were immediately produced, and the dust was taken from his person and wardrobe with a nicety that would have satisfied a town exquisite.

A ride of five miles afterward brought us in sight of the groves around the mission. The plains far and near were dry and brown. Every form of vegetation was dead save the forest trees. . . . We crossed the river, passed the Indian encampment hard by and were at the gate of the mission fields in presence of Dr. Whitman. He was speaking Cayuse at the top of his voice to some lazy Indians who were driving their cattle from his garden, and giving orders to others to yoke their oxen, get the axes and go into the forest for the lower sleepers of the new mission house. . . .

All seemed desirous to ask me how long a balloon line had been running between the States and the Pacific, by which single individuals crossed the continent. The oxen, however, were yoked, and axes glistened in the sun, and there was no time to spend if they would return from their labor before nightfall. So that the whence and wherefore of my sudden appearance among them were left for an after explanation. The doctor introduced me to his excellent lady and departed to his labor.

The afternoon was spent in listless rest from the toils of my journey. At sunset, however, I strolled out and took a bird's-eye view of the plantation and plain of the Walla Walla. The old mission house stands on the northeast bank of the river . . . at the northeast corner of an enclosure containing about 250 acres, 200 of which are under cultivation. . . . The products are wheat, Indian corn, onions, turnips, ruta baga, water-, musk- and nutmeg melons, squashes, asparagus, tomatoes, cucumbers, peas, etc., in the garden—all of good quality, and abundant crops.

The Walla Walla is a pretty stream. . . . On the opposite bank is a line of timber and underwood, interlaced with flowering brambles. Other small groves occur above and below along the banks. The plain about the waters of this river is about thirty miles square. . . . But I suppose there to be scarcely two thousand acres of this vast extent of surface which can ever be made available for the purposes of cultivation. . . .

The doctor returned near night with his timber. . . . Tea came on, and passed away in earnest conversation about native land and friends left there—of the pleasure they derived from their present occupation—and the trials that befell them while commencing the mission and afterwards. Among the latter was mentioned the drowning of their child in the Walla Walla the year before, a little girl two years old. She fell into the river at the place where they took water for family use. . . . They and others rushed to the stream and sought for their child with frantic eagerness. But the strong heavy current had carried it down and lodged it in a clump of bushes under the bank on which they stood. They passed the spot where it lay, but found it too late. Thus these devoted people were bereft, in the most afflicting manner, of their only child—left alone in the wilderness.

The morning of the 24th opened in the loveliest hues of the sky. Still none of the beauties of the harvest field—none of the fragrance of the ripened fruits of autumn were there. The wild horses were frolicking on the plains; but the plains smoked with dust and dearth. The green woods and the streams sent up their harmonies with the breeze, but it was like a dirge over the remains of the departed glories of the year.

And yet when the smoking vegetables, the hissing steak, bread white as snow and the newly churned golden butter graced the breakfast table, and the happy countenances of countrymen and countrywomen shone around, I could with difficulty believe myself in a country so far distant from, and so unlike, my native land in all its features. But during breakfast this pleasant illusion was dispelled by one of the causes which induced it. Our steak was of

horse flesh! On such meat this poor family subsist most of the
time. They do not complain. It enables them to exist to do the
Indian good and thus satisfies them. But can it satisfy those who
give money for the support of missionaries! . . .

The breakfast being over, the doctor invited me to a stroll over
his premises. The garden was first examined; its location on the
curving bank of the Walla Walla; the apple trees growing thrift-
ily on its western border; the beautiful tomato and other vegetables burdening the grounds. . . . Next to the "caral." A fine
yoke of oxen, two cows, an American bull, and the beginning of a
stock of hogs were thereabout. And last to the gristmill on the
other side of the river. It consisted of a spherical wrought-iron
burr four or five inches in diameter, surrounded by a counter-
burred surface . . . firmly fastened to timbers in such a position
that when the water wheel was put in motion the operation of the
mill was similar to that of a coffee mill. It was a crazy thing, but
for it the doctor was grateful.

It would, with the help of himself and an Indian, grind enough
in a day to feed his family a week, and that was better than to
beat it with a pestle and mortar. It appeared to me quite remarkable that the doctor could have made so many improvements since the year 1834, . . . fence, plough, build, plant an
orchard and do all the other laborious acts of opening a plantation on the face of that distant wilderness; learn an Indian
language and do the duties, meanwhile, of a physician to the
associate stations on the Clearwater and Spokane.

In the afternoon Dr. Whitman and his lady assembled the
Indians for instruction in reading. Forty or fifty children between
the ages of seven and eighteen, and several other people gathered
on the shady side of the new mission house at the ringing of a
hand-bell, and seated themselves in an orderly manner on wooden
benches. The doctor then wrote monosyllables, words and instructive sentences in the Nez Percés language on a large black-
board suspended on the wall and proceeded to teach the nature
and power of the letters in representing the simple sounds of the
language. . . .

The sentences written during these operations were at last

read, syllable by syllable and word after word, and explained until the sentiments contained in them were comprehended; and it was delightful to notice the undisguised avidity with which these people would devour a new idea. It seemed to produce a thrill of delight that kindled up the countenance and animated the whole frame. A hymn in the Nez Percés language, learned by rote from the teachers, was then sung, and the exercises closed with prayer by Dr. Whitman in the same tongue.

25th. I was awakened at early dawn by the merry sounds of clapping boards, the hammer, the axe and the plane—the sweet melodies of the parent of virtue at this cradle of civilization. When I rose everything was in motion. Dr. Whitman's little herd was lowing in the river; the wild horses were neighing at the morning breeze; the birds were caroling in the groves. I said everything was alive. Nay, not so. The Cayuse village was in the deepest slumber. . . . Their conical skin lodges dotted the valley above the mission and imparted to the morning landscape a peculiar wildness. As the sun rose, the inmates began to emerge from them.

It was a chilly hour, and their buffalo robes were drawn over their shoulders, with the hair next the body. The snow-white flesh side was fringed with the dark fur that crept in sight around the edges, and their own long black glistening tresses fell over it far down the back. The children were out in all the buoyancy of young life, shouting to the prancing steed or betting gravel stones that the arrows upon their little bows would be the first to clip the sturdy thistle head upon which they were waging mimic war. The women were busy at their fires, weaving mats from the flag, or sewing moccasins, leggings or hunting shirts. Crickie was giving meat to his friends, who the past winter had fed him and taken care of him while lying sick.

This is the imperial tribe of Oregon. They formerly claimed a prescriptive right to exercise jurisdiction over the country down the Columbia to its mouth, and up the North and South Forks to their sources. . . . They own large numbers of horses. A Cayuse is thought to be poor who has but fifteen or twenty of them. They generally have many more. One fat, hearty fellow owns something more than two thousand—all wild except as many as he needs for use or sale. . . .

I attended the Indian school today. Mrs. Whitman is an indefatigable instructress. The children read in monosyllables from a primer lately published at the Clearwater station. After reading, they repeated a number of hymns in the Nez Percés. . . . These were afterwards sung. They learn music readily.

At nightfall I visited the Indian lodges in company with Dr. Whitman. In one of them we saw a young woman who imagined that the spirit of a Medicine man, or conjuror, had entered into her system and was wasting her life. She was resorting to the native remedy for such evils—singing wild incantations and weeping loudly. This tribe, like all others west of the mountains, believe in witchcraft under various forms, practice slight-of-hand, fire-eating, etc. They insert rough sticks into their throats and draw them up and down till the blood flows freely, to make them long-winded on march. . . .

The 29th was the Sabbath, and I had an opportunity of noticing its observance by the Cayuse. I rose before the sun. The stars were waxing dim on the morning sky, the most cheering dawn I ever witnessed. Every possible circumstance of sublimity conspired to make it so. . . . The light poured over the Blue Mountains like a cataract of gold; . . . it gilded the plain with a flood of brightness, mellow, beautiful brightness—the charms of morning light on the brown, boundless solitudes of Oregon. . . .

At ten o'clock the Cayuse assembled for worship in the open air. The exercises were according to the Presbyterian form: the invocation, the hymn, the prayer, the hymn, the sermon, a prayer, a hymn and the blessing—all in the Nez Percés tongue. The principal peculiarity about the services was the mode of delivering the discourse. When Dr. Whitman arose and announced the text, the Indian, who had been instructed on the previous night, rose and repeated it, and as the address proceeded, repeated it also by sentence or paragraph, till it was finished. This is the custom of the Cayuse in all their public speaking. The benefit resulting from it in this case apparently was giving the doctrines which the doctor desired to inculcate a clearer expression in the proper idiom of the language.

During the recess the children were assembled in Sabbath School. In the afternoon the service was similar to that of the morning. Everything was conducted with much solemnity. After worship the Indians gathered in their lodges and conversed together concerning what they had heard. If doubt rose as to any point, it was solved by the instructed Indian. Thus passed the Sabbath among the Cayuse.

On the 29th I hired Crickie to take me to the Dalles, and Mrs. Whitman having filled my sacks with bread, corn meal and other edibles, I lashed my packs once more for the lower Columbia.

From *Travels in the Great Western Prairies,* Thomas J. Farnham (London: Richard Bentley, 1843).

XXVIII

Charles Wilkes

Almost as soon as it was in operation, the Whitman Mission became an oasis in the wilderness for white travelers as well as for
Indian opportunists. It was a haven for overlanders, a showplace
for settlers and missionary societies, a life-saving station as important as any of the fur company outposts, and a great political
asset to the United States Government. Everyone who visited the
Northwest had to include Waiilatpu in his itinerary. A delegation
from the United States Exploring Expedition called there in 1841
and was as surprised at what they found as T. J. Farnham. The
endorsement of the Exploring Expedition, however, carried considerably more weight in the nation's capital than any civilian
judgment.

Actually the Northwest visit of that Expedition, under the
command of Commodore Charles Wilkes (1798–1877), was a
mere incident in a round-the-world good-will tour. Prior to his
arrival at the mouth of the Columbia in April, his squadron of six
ships, staffed with a galaxy of American scientists and artists, had
rounded South America; toured the Antarctic, where they had discovered Wilkes Land; roamed through the South Seas, where two
ships of the squadron had been left to conduct more exhaustive
studies; visited Fiji and the Hawaiian chain. From it all Wilkes

had obtained a fair perspective with which he could view the wonders of the Northwest.

The Commodore was not a timid officer, but on first sighting the mouth of the mighty Columbia, he declined to permit any of the ships with him to enter it. "Mere description can give little idea of the terrors of the bar of the Columbia," he cautioned. "The wildness of the scene and the incessant roar of the waters, . . . one of the most fearful sights than can possibly meet the eye of the sailor, . . . the difficulty of its channel, . . . the necessity of approaching close to unseen dangers, the transition from clear to turbid water—all cause doubt and distrust."

Wilkes sailed on to the more placid Straits of Juan de Fuca and Puget Sound, and echoed the very words of Vancouver in his glorification of them: "Nothing can exceed the beauty of these waters and their safety; not a shoal exists . . . that can in any way interrupt their navigation by a seventy-four-gun ship. I venture nothing in saying there is no country in the world that possesses waters equal to these."

On horseback he later explored the Cowlitz River and continued in the same vein: "The park scenery increased in beauty, and it was almost impossible to realize that we were in a savage and wild country, and that nature, not art, had perfected the landscape. Beautiful lakes, with greensward growing to the water edge, with deer feeding fearlessly on their margin, and every tint of flower . . . strewn in profusion around; in galloping along we could hardly but expect to see some beautiful mansion as a fit accompaniment to such scenery."

When he reached the Columbia again, his awe returned: "The flood is a very grand sight . . . as it passes swiftly by, bearing along the gigantic forest trees, whose immense trunks appear as mere chips." And he soon learned that his terror was not overstated, for when the U.S.S. *Peacock* belatedly arrived from the South Seas, her captain defiantly headed the warship across the bar. The attempt was the most exciting and disastrous occurrence of the whole tour. At the time it convinced the maritime world that the Columbia was, indeed, a river to be reckoned with.

The Wreck of the Peacock

The *Peacock* made Cape Disappointment on the afternoon of the 17th of July [1841], and throughout the night experienced light airs and calms, accompanied by a dense fog. On the morning of the 18th, between seven and eight o'clock, the fog cleared off, with the wind from the southward and eastward. Cape Disappointment was then about nine miles distant. At nine they sounded in forty fathoms water; at ten, fifteen. It being Sunday, Captain Hudson as usual performed divine service, which being finished at 11:50, they again tacked to stand in. . . .

At meridian the wind came out from the southward and westward, with the weather a little cloudy; soon after which time the ship was off the entrance, and all hands were called to work her into port. Lieutenant Emmons was now sent aloft on the foretopsailyard, while Captain Hudson attended personally to the piloting of the ship . . . running a north-east-quarter-east course, heading for Cape Disappointment, until the proper bearing of Chinook Point east-north-east was reached, when they discovered the sea breaking ahead of them.

He now believed himself too far to the southward, wore ship and ran off a short distance until clear of the breakers, after which they again stood in, where the passage appeared clear and smooth, both from below and aloft. In less than five minutes the ship touched. . . .

The helm was immediately put alee, and every practical effort was made to bring her by the wind and haul off. These efforts were not successful, and the ship, which hung by the keel, began to thump heavily. Every sea forced her further upon the shoal, and as she had now become completely unmanageable, the sails were furled. The stream cable and anchor were got ready, and the first cutter was hoisted out. Lieutenant Emmons was sent to sound around the ship in various directions in one of the waist boats.

At this time the wind, having veered to the northward and westward, was freshening; the air was hazy and a fog was forming; the ebb tide had begun to run strong and, meeting not only the ocean waves but an opposing wind, in a short time formed breakers which completely enveloped the ship. These breakers soon stove in the first cutter and rendered her useless. Such was the fury of the sea that it was with great difficulty Lieutenant Emmons reached the ship and the boat was secured.

With every sea the ship lifted and struck heavily, and much solicitude was therefore felt lest it should be impractical to get the launch afloat; but no boat could have lived alongside of the vessel for more than a few moments.

The lighter spars were now sent down and the pumps were rigged; every exertion was made to save the masts and lower yards, by which the launch might be hoisted out as soon as the sea would permit it.

Captain Hudson, finding that the ship was leaking badly, ordered the watches in gangs to the pumps, which were thenceforward kept in action until the vessel was abandoned. Every possible exertion was made to bring the ship's head to the sea, but without much effect, for the rudder was soon disabled in consequence of the iron tiller being broken off. The rudder was thus left to thresh about with such violence as to threaten to tear away the stern frame.

At last by heaving the shot overboard and starting the water, the ship was so much lightened that by means of the larboard anchor, which had been cast free of the ship, she was hove round with her head to the sea. At low water, which occurred about dark, there was only nine feet depth of water alongside. At 8:45 the chain cable parted, the ship was again thrown broadside to the sea and began again to strike heavily.

At 11:30 it was high water; at 1 P.M. the sea was rapidly increasing; and at 2 A.M. the breakers were making a continued breach over the vessel, by which the bulwarks were stove in and the spar deck flooded. The water was knee-deep on the gun deck and the shot lockers were buried in it. The night passed heavily, with little hope of the ship's holding together till morning. At last the day dawned, and with the coming light, and at the extreme fall of the tide, the sea providentially abated.

At six o'clock in the morning a large canoe boarded the vessel, manned by a crew of Chinook Indians . . . for the purpose of rendering assistance. The launch and boats were also hoisted out, a few provisions put in them, and a part of the men and officers embarked, with as little delay as possible, and just as they stood, for fear of overloading the boats and thus causing the loss of all. In these, Lieutenant Perry, with Purser Spieden, the sick, the naturalists, and the charts, books and ship's papers, were sent off to be landed in Baker's Bay. The boats landed all not necessary to row them in safety, and succeeded in making a second trip, in which all who had remained on board were taken to the shore, except Captain Hudson, Lieutenant Walker, the boatswain, the carpenter, and about thirty men.

Towards noon the breakers again increased; and the sea was making a breach in all directions over the ship, which was filling fast, the water having risen above the level of the berth deck. The masts were cut away and the vessel lay a complete wreck, with nothing standing but the stump of the mizzenmast.

Lieutenant Emmons, who had charge of the boats, was, during this time, using every possible exertion to make a third trip, but without success; and the crews of the boats were the anxious witnesses of the condition of the ship, without being able to relieve those on board from their perilous situation. They persevered, however, in their fruitless and laborious endeavors, until one of the boats . . . was thrown end over end, and with her crew engulfed. Lieutenant De Haven was fortunately close at hand and succeeded in saving those on board, all of whom were injured, and one of them severely by the breaking of his hip bone.

The intense excitement, both of those in the vessel and in the boats at this moment may be readily imagined. The accident was seen from the ship: Captain Hudson was satisfied that any immediate attempt to relieve him and his companions must be fruitless, and that the only chance that remained was to preserve the boats for a future occasion.

He therefore ordered the ensign to be hoisted on the stump of the mizzenmast as a signal for the boats to return to the land, which was obeyed by them, although with the feeling that they were abandoning their commander and those with him to their fate. Those on board, on the other hand, were released from their anxiety for the boats, on which alone they could depend for being relieved, if the wreck should remain together for a few hours. Of this, however, the prospect was far from promising amid the struggle between the waters of the great river and those of the mighty ocean, when every surge seemed to forebode the utter dissolution of the fabric of the ship.

The light articles were now removed to the spar deck, to give them a chance of reaching the shore by the action of the waves and winds, should the ship go to pieces.

In the midst of this trying scene, the ordinary routine of ship's duty was carried on, even to the piping to dinner. . . . By three o'clock Lieutenant Emmons with the boats was again approaching the ship, but the sea was still too rough to venture near her, and it was not until five o'clock that he succeeded in getting alongside, when the remaining men were distributed among the boats and embarked in good order, Captain Hudson being the last to leave the ship.

After a pull of two miles, they landed in Baker's Bay, where Captain Hudson was received by the other officers and men with three hearty cheers, the spontaneous expression of their admiration and gratitude for the courage and conduct he had exhibited in his efforts for the preservation of the ship, and in finally preserving the lives of all.

The exertions of the officers and men were not yet at an end, for some faint hopes were entertained that a portion of the property might still be saved from the wreck, as a relief in their state of utter destitution; and, in consequence, the boats were dispatched the next morning at daybreak to the bar. But nothing was there to be seen of the *Peacock* except the cap of her bowsprit. . . .

When all hopes of getting anything from the wreck were at an end, Captain Hudson sent the crew to Astoria in the boats, with orders to form an encampment there, where they found an ample

supply of provisions in the stores that had been sent from the
Sandwich Islands, and were supplied with clothing by the kind-
ness of Dr. McLoughlin and the officers of the Hudson Bay
Company.

From *Narrative of the United States Exploring Expedition,* Volume IV, Charles
Wilkes (Philadelphia: Lea and Blanchard, 1845).

XXIX

Sir George Simpson

Two ships of the United States Exploring Expedition did manage to cross the bar of the Columbia without mishap. They anchored off Fort Vancouver, and, by chance, Lieutenant Wilkes happened to reach there just in time to help celebrate the arrival of the grand panjandrum of the Hudson's Bay Company, Sir George Simpson (1792–1860).

Simpson was on an inspection tour of his far-flung dominion, a globe-girdling trip by land almost as ambitious as the Exploring Expedition's itinerary by sea. As he explained his incentive, with characteristic lack of modesty: "Ledyard and Cochrane, to the best of my knowledge and belief, were the only travelers that ever attempted before myself to accomplish an overland journey around the world; they both returned . . . without having seen the American continent. If either of them had engaged his peculiar advantages, the task would not have been left for me to achieve."

In the shake-up of management after the merger of the North West Company with Hudson's Bay, the mantle of governor had fallen upon the broad, arrogant shoulders of George Simpson, a pompous, conceited, brilliant fireball of energy. Never shrinking from self-imposed responsibility, he traveled and retraveled the wilderness routes between Company posts, keeping in intimate touch with their affairs, and was now off on a more comprehensive tour.

But his mode of travel was hardly that of penniless, threadbare, footsore Ledyard, with whom he deigned to compare himself. Simpson's feet rarely touched the soil. Dressed immaculately in a dark suit, pressed, strap-bottomed trousers and white shirt with spotless ruffles to the ears, elegant black beaver top hat, frock coat trimmed with velvet, and over that a magnificent greatcoat lined with scarlet, he was always carried pickaback by one of his lackeys to his canoe, deposited preciously on a cushioned seat, and by another lackey handed a lighted pipe.

Though his journeys frequently took him a thousand miles from nowhere, no emperor ever traveled in greater style or comfort, continually fussed over and catered to by a retinue of servants, sheltered from annoyance and inconvenience. With his insatiable demands and indefatigable energy, he drove his voyageurs to despair. On tour, camp was struck precisely at two A.M.; at eight there was a pause for breakfast; at noon another brief stop for a cold cut and a glass of wine; then on until dusk, when a camp fit for a pharaoh was erected and an elaborate dinner served.

If fewer than a hundred miles were covered in an eighteen-hour day, the brigade was expected to make up the mileage in the following twenty-four hours. On long portages the pace was the same; grooms were obliged to hurry ahead to have horses tethered, saddled, and ready for mounting. And whenever the entourage approached an important post, the coming of His Honor was heralded with bugles, bagpipes, and gun salutes, while the voyageurs joined in a well-rehearsed chorus to give the impression that they always traveled in such a happy, spirited mood.

This was the kind of regal advent that Wilkes witnessed. Sir George's own accounts of his journeyings, however, barely mention the pomp, ceremony, and luxurious services provided by his attendants.

Huckster in a Hurry

About sunset we called at the Company's saw and grist mills, distant six miles from the Fort, while the Company's schooner *Cadboro*, that was lying there, honored us with a salute, which served also as a signal of our arrival to the good folks of Vancouver. Being anxious to approach headquarters in proper style, our men here exchanged the oar for the paddle, which, besides being more orthodox in itself, was better adapted to the quick notes of the voyageur's song. In less than an hour afterwards, we landed on the beach, having thus crossed the continent of North America at its widest part, by a route of about five thousand miles, in the space of twelve weeks of actual traveling. . . .

At Vancouver we found two vessels of the United States Exploring Squadron, under the command of Commodore Wilkes . . . and we here spent a week all the more agreeably on this account. . . . Fort Vancouver, the Company's grand depot on the west side of the Rocky Mountains, is situated about ninety miles from the sea, the Columbia in front of it being about one mile in width. Within an oblong enclosure of upwards of six hundred feet by two hundred, which is surrounded by pickets, there are contained several houses, stores, magazines, granaries, workshops, etc., while the dwellings of the servants, the stables, the hospital, etc., form a little village on the outside of the walls.

The people of the establishment, besides officers and native laborers, vary in number according to the season of the year from one hundred and thirty to upwards of two hundred. They consist of Canadians, Sandwich Islanders, Europeans and half-breeds; and they contain among them agriculturists, voyageurs, blacksmiths, tinsmiths, carpenters, masons, tailors, shoemakers, etc., etc., etc. Their weekly rations are usually twenty-one pounds of salted salmon and one bushel of potatoes for each man; and in addition to fish there are also venison and wild fowl, with occasionally a little beef and pork.

Most of the men are married to aboriginal or half-breed

Fort Vancouver, the Company's grand depot

women, and the swarms of children in the little village present a strongly suggestive contrast with the scantiness of the rising generation in almost every native village on the Lower Columbia. Amid so large a population the surgeon of the establishment finds ample employment; to the hospital the most serious cases are removed, seldom exceeding eight or ten in number, and generally consisting of fevers, fractures and neglected syphilis.

There is an elementary school for the children of both sexes. Though at present there is no clergyman at Vancouver, yet divine service is regularly performed every Sunday, in English to the Protestants and in French to the Catholics. The same chapel, a building, by the by, unworthy of the establishment, served both purposes at the time of our visit. . . .

The farm of Fort Vancouver contains upwards of twelve hundred acres under cultivation, which have this year produced four thousand bushels of wheat, three thousand five hundred of barley, oats and peas, and a very large quantity of potatoes and other vegetables. The wheat, which has yielded ten returns, is of very fine quality, weighing from sixty-five to sixty-eight pounds and a half a bushel. There are, moreover, fifteen hundred sheep and between four and five hundred head of cattle. . . .

On the 1st of September my party, now strengthened by the accession of Mr. Douglas, took leave on the beach of Commodore Wilkes and his officers, with mutual wishes for safety and success; and by eleven in the forenoon we were under way in a large and heavy bateau with a crew of ten men . . . to call at the Company's dairy [up the Willamette River] . . . At the dairy we found about a hundred milch cows, which were said to yield on an average not more than sixty pounds of butter each in a year; and there were also two or three hundred cattle that were left, merely with a view to their breeding, to roam about at will. The whole were under the charge of three or four families that resided on the spot. . . .

About sunset we again entered the Columbia, endeavoring to reach Deer's Island for supper. Failing in this attempt, we snapped up a hasty meal on the left bank of the river; and then after wrapping ourselves in a blanket each, we lay down to sleep in the boat while she should be drifting down the stream all night.

In the morning we were toiling up the Cowlitz, a northerly feeder of the Columbia, its lofty banks being crowned with beautiful forests whose leafy bowers, unencumbered by brushwood, realized the poet's "boundless contiguity of shade." As a proof of the occasional height of the waters of this narrow and rapid river, driftwood and other aqueous deposits were hanging high and dry on the overshadowing branches at an altitude of thirty or forty feet above the present level of the stream. When the Cowlitz thus fills its bed, it ceases to be navigable, at least for upward crafts, by reason of the violence of the current. . . . Even at present, the current was so powerful that our rate of progress never exceeded two miles an hour.

When I descended the Cowlitz in 1828 there was a large population along its banks, but since then the intermittent fever, which commenced its ravages in the following year, had left but few to mourn for those that fell. During the whole of our day's course, till we came upon a small camp in the evening, the shores were silent and solitary, the deserted villages forming melancholy monuments of the generation that had passed away. Along the river large quantities of an imperfect coal are found on the surface.

Our bateau carried as curious a muster of races and languages as perhaps had ever been congregated within the same compass in any part of the world. Our crew of ten men contained Iroquois, who spoke their own tongue; a Cree half-breed of French origin, who appeared to have borrowed his dialect from both his parents; a North Briton, who understood only the Gaelic of his native hills; Canadians, who, of course, knew French; and Sandwich Islanders, who jabbered a medley of Chinook, English and their own vernacular jargon. Add to all this that the passengers were natives of England, Scotland, Russia, Canada and the Hudson's Bay Company's territories, and you have the prettiest congress of nations, the nicest confusion of tongues, that has ever taken place since the days of the Tower of Babel.

At the native camp near which we halted for the night we enriched our many clans with one variety more by hiring a canoe and its complement of Chinooks to accompany us. Next morning Mr. Douglas, in company with our Chinook allies, started a little before us in order to get horses, etc., ready for us at the landing place; and by noon when we reached the spot in question we found that, in his lighter craft, he had gained four hours on us, having thus had time to bring our steeds from the Cowlitz Farm about ten miles distant. Right glad we were to leave the clumsy bateau after an imprisonment of eight and forty hours.

Between the Cowlitz River and Puget Sound—a distance of about sixty miles—the country, which is watered by many streams and lakes, consists of an alternation of plains and belts of wood. It is well adapted both for tillage and for pasturage, possessing a genial climate, good soil, excellent timber, water power, natural clearings and a seaport, and that too within reach of more than one advantageous market. When this tract was explored a few years ago, the Company established two farms upon it, which were subsequently transferred to the Puget Sound Agricultural Association, formed under the Company's auspices, with the view of producing wheat, wool, hides and tallow for exportation.

On the Cowlitz Farm there were already about a thousand acres of land under the plow, besides a large dairy, an extensive park for horses, etc.; and the crops this season had amounted to eight or nine thousand bushels of wheat, four thousand of oats, with due proportions of barley, potatoes, etc. The other farm was on the shores of Puget Sound, and as its soil was found to be better fitted for pasturage than tillage, it had been appropriated almost exclusively to the flocks and herds, so that now, with only two hundred acres of cultivated land, it possessed six thousand sheep, twelve hundred cattle, besides horses, pigs, etc.

In addition to these two farms, there was a Catholic mission with about a hundred and sixty acres under the plow. There were also a few Canadian settlers, retired servants of the Hudson's Bay Company; and it was to this same neighborhood that emigrants from Red River were wending their way. The climate is propitious, while the seasons are remarkably regular. . . . The temperature is so mild that the cattle and sheep not only remain out of doors but even find fresh grass for themselves from day to day.

Of the aborigines there are but three small tribes in the neighborhood, the Cowlitz, the Checaylis and the 'Squally, now all quiet, inoffensive and industrious people; and as a proof of their character, they do very well as agricultural servants, thereby forming an important element in estimating the advantages of the district for settlement and cultivation.

Having halted five miles beyond the Cowlitz Farm, we raised camp next morning at four. The belts of wood which separated the plains from each other were composed of stately cedars and pines, many of them rising without a branch or a bend to a height of a hundred and fifty feet . . . and by actual measurement one fallen trunk, by no means the largest that could have been selected, was found to be two hundred and fifty feet long and to be twenty-five around at eight feet from the root.

. . . These plains also have their mysterious stone. This rudely carved block, the only thing of the kind in the neighborhood, was carried to its present position from a considerable distance by a mighty man of old times who could lift a horse by stooping under its belly and carry about the brute, all alive and kicking for a whole day. It is perhaps a blessing that the human race in these parts has degenerated, for otherwise horses would have been as likely to bridle and spur men as men to bridle and spur horses. The stone, which weighs about a ton, still remains where the Skookoom, to use the native term, dropped it, a monument of the degeneracy of all succeeding sojourners in the country, whether red or white.

We breakfasted at the Checaylis, a navigable stream falling into Gray's Harbor about forty miles to the north of Cape Disappointment. . . . Beyond the Checaylis the plains became more extensive, with fewer belts of wood, though there was still more than a sufficiency of timber for every purpose. Towards the 'Squally, or as the whites term it by way of elegance, the Nisqually River, we passed over a space of ten or twelve miles in length covered with thousands of mounds or hummocks, all of a perfectly round shape, but of different sizes. They are from twelve to twenty feet in diameter and from five to fifteen in height. . . . Whatever has been their origin, they must be very ancient, inasmuch as many of them bear large trees.

After crossing the 'Squally River, we arrived at Fort Nisqually on the evening of our fourth day from Fort Vancouver. Being unwilling to commence our voyage on a Sunday, we remained here for six and thirty hours inspecting the farm and dairy and visiting Dr. Richmond, an American missionary stationed in the neighborhood. The surrounding scenery is very beautiful. . . . Near the fort, there was a small camp of 'Squallies under the command of Luckalett, a good friend of the traders. The establishment is frequented also by . . . other tribes, amounting in all, the 'Squallies included, to nearly four thousand souls.

At noon on Monday, the 6th of September, we embarked on board of the *Beaver* steamer, Captain McNeill. . . . Starting under a salute of seven guns, we pushed along against a strong breeze till we anchored about five in the afternoon to enable the engineer to repair some damage which the machinery had sustained; but the job being completed by nine, we then steamed on all night.

About seven in the morning we passed along the inner end of Fuca's Straits, the first of the numberless inlets of this coast that was ever discovered by civilized man. The neighboring country . . . is well adapted for colonization, for in addition to a tolerable soil and a moderate climate, it possesses excellent harbors and abundance of timber. It will doubtless become in time the most valuable section of the whole coast above California.

Sunday, the 17th of October [on the return trip], we had a beautiful run with smooth water and fine weather. We passed close along Whidbey's Island, being about forty miles long. It is well fitted for settlement and cultivation. The soil is good; the timber is excellent; and there are several open plains which have been prepared by natives for the plow. We anchored for the evening about five miles to the south of this island; and by making a very early move we breakfasted ashore at Nisqually about five in the morning. Thus had I twice traversed the most extraordinary course of inland navigation in the world. . . .

This labyrinth of waters is peculiarly adapted for the powers of steam. . . . But independently of physical advantages, steam may be said to exert an almost superstitious influence over the savages; besides acting without intermission on their fears, it has in a great measure subdued their very love of robbery and violence. In a word, it has inspired the red man with a new opinion—new not in degree but in kind—of the superiority of his white brother. . . . A Cree of the name of Bras Croche took a short trip on the *Beaver*. When asked what he thought of her, "Don't ask me," was his reply; "I cannot speak; my friends will say that I tell lies when I let them know what I have seen; Indians are fools and know nothing; I can see that the iron machinery makes the ship to go, but I cannot see what makes the iron machinery itself to go." . . .

Let me still farther illustrate the character of the tribes of the Northwest Coast by a summary sketch of the condition of their slaves. These thralls are just as much the property of their masters as so many dogs, with this difference against them, that a man of cruelty and ferocity enjoys a more exquisite pleasure in tasking or starving, or torturing or killing a fellow creature than in treating any one of the lower animals in a similar way. Even in the most inclement weather a mat or a piece of deer skin is the slave's only clothing, whether by day or by night, whether under cover or in the open air.

To eat without permission, in the very midst of an abundance which his toil has procured, is as much as his miserable life is worth; and the only permission which is ever vouchsafed to him is to pick up the offal thrown out by his unfeeling and imperious lord. . . . But all this is nothing when compared with the purely wanton atrocities to which these most helpless and pitiable children of the human race are subjected. They are beaten, lacerated and maimed—the mutilating of fingers or toes, the splitting of noses and the scooping out of eyes being ordinary occurrences. They are butchered—without the excuse or the excitement of a gladiatorial combat—to make holidays; and as if to carry persecution beyond the point at which the wicked are said to cease from troubling, their corpses are often cast into the sea to be washed in and out by the tide. . . .

To return to my narrative, we almost immediately departed from Nisqually in the steamer for the Chutes River, about five miles farther up Puget Sound, having dispatched a band of horses to meet us there. . . . Next day we reached the Cowlitz Farm, where on the following morning the Reverend Mr. Demers of the Roman Catholic Church breakfasted with us. He had just returned from visiting the country situated between Nisqually and Fraser's River. . . . Everywhere the natives received him with the greatest respect. They had, however, been very much puzzled with regard to the sex of their visitor. From his dress they took him for a woman, but from his beard for a man; but feeling that such inconsistencies could not both be true, they pursued a middle course by referring to him as a distinct species.

About noon we embarked in a bateau on the Cowlitz, and encamped about eight in the evening at its mouth, where we met Mr. Steel, the principal shepherd of the Puget Sound Company, driving a flock of rams to Nisqually. By two in the morning we were again on the water, and with the first dawn descried the Hudson's Bay Company's barque *Columbia*, which was returning, like ourselves, from the Northwest Coast, beating her way up the stream. Having overtaken her near the lower branch of the Willamette, we boarded her in time for breakfast. . . . After doing ample justice to the ship's good things, we again shot ahead as far as the Cattlepootle River; and having there gladly exchanged the bateau for horses, we enjoyed an exhilarating ride across a succession of luxuriant prairies. . . . Ten or twelve miles of this beautiful country brought us by four in the afternoon to Fort Vancouver. . . .

Hardly had the *Columbia* reached Vancouver when the *Cowlitz*, which had made a voyage to the Sandwich Islands and California, was reported to be off the bar, and soon afterwards her papers came up by boat from Fort George. . . .

Towards the close of November the two barques dropped down the river, first the *Columbia* bound for England, and then the *Cowlitz*, destined to convey me to California, the Sandwich Islands and Sitka.

From *Overland Journey Round the World During the Years 1841 and 1842*, Sir George Simpson (Philadelphia: Lea and Blanchard, 1847).

XXX

Pierre Jean De Smet

That Macedonian cry from the Flatheads that had excited so
many conscientious churchmen a decade before had still not been
answered by the Protestants. All the missionaries who had set out
from the East with the intention of responding to it had somehow
been diverted to other Indian nations. The Whitmans and Spaldings were nearest to the Flathead legions, and although a few of
them occasionally spilled over into the Walla Walla region, the
contact had little effect.

But, alas, the plea had been acknowledged, without fanfare or
public recognition, by the church to which it was originally addressed. The self-effacing Jesuits had stolen the march on the
Methodists and Congregationalists, and they had sent to the
Flatheads one of their most distinguished padres, a leader of
quality, of profound scholarship, of great humanity, Father Pierre
Jean De Smet (1801–1873). Born in Belgium and educated in
Europe, he had come to America in 1821, served as Indian missionary in western Iowa for three years, and then had been transferred to the Bitterroot Valley, where he founded St. Mary's Mission in 1841.

The Catholics had a major advantage over the Protestant
missionaries. Their ceremony and symbols, their black robes and
colorful ornaments, set them apart and offered to Indians an eye

appeal that no amount of gospel hymn singing, long-winded pray-
ing, and hell-fire preachment could possibly match in ear appeal.
The Protestants could present an exemplary demonstration of
family life that the priests, of course, could not; but that hardly
made up for the splendor of ecclesiastical show. In sincerity, in
persuasiveness, in their threats of discomfort in an afterlife as the
penalty for not accepting the Word, the two were about even.
Both were very disturbing to the Indians.

Father De Smet was no less severe in belittlement of Protestant
accomplishments than the Protestants were of his, but unquestionably he exerted a broader influence in the Northwest. He was
loved, protected, all but worshipped by the Flatheads, and his
reputation spread rapidly among Indian tribes far beyond St.
Mary's; eventually he held the confidence of every tribe from
Minnesota to the Oregon coast. And he was as well known in the
civilized world. For years the only address he used, and needed,
was "St. Mary's, Rocky Mountains."

Between 1840 and 1847 he traveled an estimated fifty thousand
miles creating new missions and seeking their support. Later he
was to become renowned as the most apt Indian mediator in
America, in constant demand as diplomat and government emis-
sary. His journeyings took him to every part of the United States
and to eastern Europe; he made nineteen crossings of the Atlantic, one voyage around Cape Horn, and two trips from East to
West by way of Panama. In the spring of 1841 his trip from St.
Mary's to Fort Vancouver was on a smaller scale, but the punish-
ing schedule of clerical activity he inflicted upon himself during
his sojourn helped to explain why the black-robes were drawing
into the Catholic fold far greater numbers of Indian converts than
were their less aggressive competitors whom he scornfully referred to as "ministers."

The Right Kind of Black-Robe

Not having been able this year to obtain either provisions or
sufficient clothes to supply the wants of our mission, I started
April 13, 1842 for Fort Vancouver, the great mart of the honor-

able Hudson Bay Company, and distant about a thousand miles from our establishment [via Coeur d'Alene and the Spokane River].

The Spokane River is wide, swift and deep in the spring, and contains, like all rivers of Oregon, many rapid falls and cascades. The navigation of the waters of this immense territory is generally dangerous and few risk themselves on them without being accompanied by experienced pilots. In descending Clark's River we passed by some truly perilous and remarkable places, where the pilots have full opportunity to exhibit their dexterity and prudence.

The rapids are numerous and the roar of the waters incessant, the current sweeping on at the rate of ten or twelve miles an hour; the rugged banks and projecting rocks creating waves resembling those of the troubled sea. The skilful pilot mounts the waves, which seem ready to engulf us; the canoe speeds over the agitated waters, and with the aid of the paddle, skilfully plied, bears us unharmed through numberless dangers.

The most remarkable spot on this river is called the Cabinets; it consists of four apartments, which you have hardly time to examine, as you are scarcely half a minute passing by them. Represent to yourself chasms between two rocky mountains of a stupendous height, the river pent in between them in a bed of thirty or forty feet, precipitating itself down its rocky channel with irresistible fury, roaring against its jagged sides and whitening with foam all around it. In a short space it winds in four different directions, resembling very much forked lightning. It requires very great skill, activity and presence of mind to extricate yourself from this difficult pass.

The Spokane lands are sandy, gravelly and badly calculated for agriculture. The section over which I traveled consisted of immense plains of light, dry and sandy soil and thin forests of gum pines. We saw nothing in this noiseless solitude but a buck, running quickly from us and disappearing almost immediately. From time to time the melancholy and piercing cry of the wood snipe increased the gloomy thoughts which this sad spot occasioned.

Here . . . two ministers have settled themselves with their wives, who had consented to share their husbands' *soi-disant* apostolical labors. During the four years they have spent here, they have baptized several of their own children. They cultivate a small farm, large enough, however, for their own maintenance and the support of their animals and fowls. It appears they are fearful that should they cultivate more they might have too frequent visits from the savages. They even try to prevent their encampment in their immediate neighborhood, and therefore they see and converse but seldom with the heathens whom they have come so far to seek. A band of Spokanes received me with every demonstration of friendship and were enchanted to hear that the right kind of Black-robes intended soon to form an establishment in the vicinity. I baptized one of their little children who was dying.

It was in these parts that in 1836 a modern Iconoclast named Parker broke down a cross erected over the grave of a child by some Catholic Iroquois, telling us emphatically in the narrative of his journey that he did not wish to leave in that country an emblem of idolatry. Poor man!—not to know better in this enlightened age! Were he to return to these mountains he would hear the praises of the holy name of Jesus resounding among them; he would hear the Catholics chanting the love and mercies of God from the rivers, lakes, mountains, prairies, forests and coasts of the Columbia. . . . Were he who destroyed that solitary, humble cross now to return, he would find the image of Jesus Christ crucified borne on the breast of more than 4,000 Indians; and the smallest child would say to him: "Mr. Parker, we do not adore the cross; do not break it because it reminds us of Jesus Christ who died on the cross to save us—we adore God alone."

In the beginning of May I arrived at Fort Colville on the Columbia River. This year the snow melted away very early; the mountain torrents had overflowed and the small rivers that usually moved quietly along in the month of April had suddenly left their beds and assumed the appearance of large rivers and lakes, completely flooding all the lowlands. This rendered my journey to Vancouver by land impossible, and induced me to wait, *nolens volens,* at the fort for the construction of the barges, which were not ready until the 30th of the same month, when I was again able to pursue my journey on the river.

On the same day that I arrived among the Skoyelpi or Chaudière tribe, who resided near the fort, I undertook to translate our prayers into their language. This kept me only one day, as their language is nearly the same as that of the Flatheads and Kalispels, having the same origin. They were all very attentive in attending my instructions, and the old as well as the young tried assiduously to learn their prayers. I baptized all the younger children who had not received the sacrament before . . . with the most gratifying success. The great chief and his wife had long sighed for baptism, which holy sacrament I administered to them, naming them Martin and Mary. This chief is one of the most intelligent and pious I have become acquainted with.

The work of God does not, however, proceed without contradictions. . . . I have had some hard trials in all my visits. I expected them when on the 13th of May I started to see the Okanogan tribe, who were desirous to meet a priest. The interpreter Charles and the chief of the Skoyelpi wished to accompany me.

In crossing the Columbia River my mule returned to the shore and ran at full speed into the forest; Charles pursued her and two hours afterward I was told that he had been found dead in the prairie. I hastened immediately and perceived from a distance a great gathering of people. I soon reached the spot where he was lying, and to my great joy perceived that he gave signs of life. He was, however, senseless, and in a most pitiful state. A copious bleeding and some days of rest restored him and we resumed our journey. This time the mule had a large rope tied around her neck and we crossed the river without any accidents; we took a narrow path that led us by mountains, valleys, forests and prairies, following the course of the river Skarameep.

Toward evening we were on the borders of a deep impetuous torrent, having no other bridge than a tree, which was rather slight and in constant motion from the rushing of the waters. . . . We were fortunate enough to cross the trembling bridge without accident. We soon pitched our camp on the other side, and in spite of the warring waves, which in falls and cascades thundered all night by our side, we enjoyed a refreshing sleep.

The greater part of the next day the path conducted us through a thick and hilly forest of fir trees; the country then became more undulating and open. From time to time we perceived an Indian burial ground, remarkable only for the posts erected on the graves and hung with kettles, wooden plates, guns, bows and arrows, left there by the nearest relatives of the deceased—humble tokens of their grief and friendship.

We encamped on the shore of a small lake . . . where was a Skoyelpi village. I gave these savages several instructions and baptized their infants. In memory of my visit they gave the name of Leêeyou Pierre (Father Peter) to an immense rocky mountain which dominates the whole region. At my departure the whole village accompanied me. . . . Toward evening we came up with the men of the first Okanogan encampment, who received us with the greatest cordiality and joy. The chief who came out to meet us was quite conspicuous, being arrayed in his court dress—a shirt made of horse skin, the hair of which was outside, the mane partly on his chest and back, giving him a truly fantastic and savage appearance.

The camp also joined us, and the fact of my arrival having been soon noised abroad in every direction, we saw issuing from the defiles and narrow passes of the mountains, bands of Indians who had gone forth to gather their harvest of roots. Many sick were presented to me for baptism, of which rite they already knew the importance.

Before reaching the rendezvous assigned us on the borders of the Okanogan Lake, I was surrounded by more than 200 horsemen and more than 200 others were already in waiting. We recited together night prayers and all listened with edifying attention to the instruction I gave them. The interpreter and Martin continued the religious conversation until the night was far advanced. . . .

All the next day was spent in prayer, instructions and hymns. I baptized 106 children and some old people, and in conclusion named the plain where these consoling scenes occurred "The

Plain of Prayer." It would be impossible for me to give you an idea of the piety, the happiness of these men, who are thirsting for the life-giving waters of the divine word. . . . After some regulations and advice, I left this interesting people, and pursuing my journey for three days over mountains and through dense forests, arrived safely at Fort Colville.

Amongst the innumerable rivers that traverse the American continent and afford means of communication between its most distant portions, the Columbia River is one of the most remarkable. . . . I embarked on this river on the 30th of May in one of the barges of the Hudson Bay Company; Mr. [Peter Skeen] Ogden, one of the principal proprietors, offered me a place in his. I shall never forget the kindness and friendly manner with which this gentleman treated me throughout the journey, nor the many agreeable hours I spent in his company. I found his conversation instructive, his anecdotes and *bon mots* entertaining and timely; it was with great regret that I parted with him.

. . . From its source in the mountains to the cascades the river is but a succession of dangers. I will endeavor to give you some idea of one of its largest rapids, called by the Canadian voyageurs the Great Dalles. . . . Here the river is divided into several channels separated from one another by masses of rocks, which rise abruptly above its surface. Some of these channels are navigable at certain seasons of the year, although with very great risk even to the most experienced pilot. But when, after the melting of the snow, the river rises above its usual level, the waters in most of these channels make but one body, and the whole mass of these united streams descends with irresistible fury. At this season the most courageous dare not encounter such dangers. . . .

If arrested for a moment, its accumulated waters proudly swell and mount as though instinct with life, and the next moment dash triumphantly on, enveloping the half smothered waves that preceded them as if impatient of their sluggish course, and wild to speed them on their way. . . . Never shall I forget the sad and fatal accident which occurred on the second day of our voyage at a spot called "The Little Dalles."

I had gone ashore and was walking along the bank, scarcely

thinking of what might happen, for my breviary, papers, bed, in a word my little all had been left in the barge. I had proceeded about a quarter of a mile when, seeing the bargemen push off from the bank and glide down the stream with an easy careless air, I began to repent having preferred a path along the river's side, so strewn with fragments of rocks that I was compelled at every instant to turn aside or clamber over them. I still held on my course when all at once the barge was so abruptly stopped that the rowers can hardly keep their seats.

Regaining, however, their equilibrium, they ply the oars with redoubled vigor, but without any effect upon the barge. They are already within the power of the angry vortex; the waters are crested with foam; a deep sound is heard, which I distinguish as the voice of the pilot encouraging his men to hold to their oars— to row bravely. The danger increases every minute, and in a moment more all hope of safety has vanished. The barge, the sport of the vortex, spins like a top upon the whirling waters—the oars are useless—the bow rises—the stern descends, and the next instant all have disappeared.

A deathlike chill shot through my frame—a dimness came over my sight as the cry "We are lost!" rang in my ears and told but too plainly that my companions were buried beneath the waves. Overwhelmed with grief and utterly unable to afford them the slightest assistance, I stood a motionless spectator of this tragic scene. All were gone, and upon the river's breast there was not the faintest trace of their melancholy fate.

Soon after, the whirlpool threw up in various directions the oars, poles, the capsized barge and every lighter article it had contained. Here and there I beheld the unhappy bargemen vainly struggling in the midst of the vortex. Five of them sank never to rise again. My interpreter had twice touched bottom and after a short prayer was thrown upon the bank. An Iroquois saved himself by means of my bed; and a third was so fortunate as to seize the handle of an empty trunk, which helped sustain himself above water until he reached land.

The rest of our journey was more fortunate. We stopped at Forts Okanogan and Walla Walla, where I baptized several children. . . . We arrived at Fort Vancouver on the morning of the 8th of June. I enjoyed the happiness and great consolation of meeting in these distant parts two respectable Canadian priests— the Reverend Mr. Blanchet, grand vicar of all the countries west of the mountains claimed by the British crown, and the Reverend Mr. Demers. They are laboring in these regions for the same object that we are trying to accomplish in the Rocky Mountains. . . .

They assured me that immense good might be done in the extensive regions that border on the Pacific if a greater number of missionaries, with means at their command, were stationed in these regions, and they urged me very strongly to obtain from my superiors some of our Fathers. . . . The Governor of the honorable Company of Hudson Bay, Dr. McLoughlin, who resides at Fort Vancouver, after having given me every possible proof of interest as a good Catholic, advised me to do everything in my power to gratify the wishes of the Canadian missionaries.

His principal reason is that if Catholicity was rapidly planted in these tracts where civilization begins to dawn, it would be more quickly introduced thence into the interior. Already a host of ministers have overrun a part of the country, and have settled wherever they may derive some advantages for the privations their philanthropy imposes on them. Such is the state of these regions of the new world as yet so little known. . . .

Pray then that the Lord of such a rich harvest may send us numerous fellow laborers, for in so extensive a field we are but five, and beset with so many dangers that at the dawn of day we have often reason to doubt whether we will live to see the sun go down. . . . Of one hundred men who inhabit this country, there are not ten who do not die by some or other fatal accident.

From *Life, Letters and Travels of Father Pierre Jean De Smet*, S.J. Edited by H. M. Chittenden and A. T. Richardson (New York: Francis P. Harper, 1905).

XXXI

Jesse Applegate Applegate

Missionaries like Father Pierre and Dr. Whitman, adventurers, voyageurs, and victims of "Oregon fever" had already beaten trails of a sort to the Northwest; but vast expanses west of the Rockies were still unexplored and unmapped, and no one knew whether the easiest and safest route had yet been located. Anticipating that settlers in increasing numbers might soon be demanding such a route, in 1843 the Federal Government sent out John Charles Frémont to explore the whole terrain between the Rocky Mountains and the Pacific, to scout and map the best trails and tie in his findings with the coastal surveys Charles Wilkes had just completed.

Frémont chose to devote most of his energies to regions south of Oregon, but he did make a perfunctory side trip down the Columbia as far as Fort Vancouver—to replenish his supplies and be able to report that he had "connected our reconnaissance with the surveys of Captain Wilkes." And like other transients, he, too, called on Narcissa Whitman at Waiilatpu to pick up the usual lunch basket of goodies that paddlers munched on the journey down the river.

But that official "reconnaissance" had been delayed too long. To Frémont's astonishment, he found the Oregon trail already clogged with traffic—heavy enough in places even to impede the progress of his imposing train—and along the Columbia he found the best campsites already occupied by overlanders who had preceded him. "Oregon fever" had suddenly reached epidemic proportions. In long columns, over a thousand men, women, and children were heading for the Columbia country, driving herds of cattle that numbered—depending on who did the counting—up to five thousand head, maneuvering over impossible trails strings of oxcarts that stretched out for miles, burdened with everything from churns and rocking chairs to plows and pipe tobacco.

The Applegate family was a fair representation of those gypsy travelers that Frémont overtook on the road. They had frontiersmanship in their blood. One generation had advanced from New Jersey to Kentucky; the next from Kentucky to Missouri; and now a third was on its way to Oregon under the veteran guidance of Marcus Whitman.

The doctor had run into disagreement with the American Board in Boston over the desirability of continuing the mission at Waiilatpu and once more had traipsed across North America to settle it. The fact that he had won the argument was attested by the presence of the Applegates and the throng that joined them—all indoctrinated in the trail philosophy of the peripatetic Whitman: "Travel, travel, TRAVEL! Nothing else will take you to the end of your journey; nothing is wise that does not help you along; nothing is good for you that causes you a moment's delay."

It was that counsel that brought the forerunners of the unwieldy multitude to Waiilatpu and Fort Walla Walla by the early fall of 1843, still with enough zest, at least among the young fry, to pick a squabble with the Indians who assembled to gawk at the latest influx of intruders. Jesse Applegate Applegate (1836–1919) celebrated his seventh birthday on the Oregon Trail. Years later, as a senior citizen, after service as a soldier in the Rogue River War, teaching and school superintending in Polk County, law practice in Dallas and in Salem, Oregon, he harkened back nostalgically to those vagabond days and recorded the recollections of his youthful experience in the "cow column," the march across the plains and mountains, and the two-week pause at Fort

Walla Walla, where members of the company gradually broke away to proceed to their separate destinations.

Battle of the Potato House

The train which arrived here [at Fort Walla Walla] was a detachment of the company which came out to Oregon this season and numbered ten families and probably twenty wagons. The entire emigration of 1843 has been computed at about a thousand souls. This detachment included the three Applegate families— families of three brothers, Charles, Lindsay and Jesse. . . . Besides the oxen of the teams, there was a small herd of stock cattle. Jesse Applegate [the elder] had probably thirty head and others had a few cows and calves. There were also a few horses. This train of wagons corraled for the last time about one hundred yards . . . up the river from the fort and very near where the Walla Walla River flows into the Columbia.

The train of wagons with their once white, now torn, grease- and dust-stained covers, parked on the bank of the Columbia River, was a novel spectacle. Such had never been seen there before. The faithful oxen, now sore-necked, sore-footed and jaded, which had marched week after week and month after month drawing those wagons with their loads from the Missouri River to the Columbia, had done their task and were unhitched for the last time, and I hope all recovered from their fatigue and lived to enjoy a long rest on the banks, "where rolls the Oregon and hears no sound save its own dashing."

Mr. McKinley was in charge of the post of Walla Walla and was very kind and accommodating to the emigrants. There were many Indians here: bucks, squaws and papooses, and these were often visitors at our camp. Some of the bucks talked English fairly well, and all were clever at sign language. There had been at this place mission establishments, both Catholic and Protestant, and this trading post [of the Hudson Bay Company] had been for several years in this part of the country, and so the Indians were to some extent accustomed to modify their manners and dress. They were not naked like Indians we had been among before. . . .

The Indians' tribal names were Cayuse, Nez Percés and Walla Walla, and we had many visitors from all these tribes. I think there was no hostile feeling among these people against us, but some of the emigrants were prejudiced against Indians of whatever kind and were annoyed by the familiarity assumed by them in their intercourse with the whites. This probably came near leading to very serious consequences. We boys, I think, were more or less tinctured with this prejudice and, besides, did not realize the fact that to arouse a spirit of vengeance among this horde of barbarians who could muster a thousand painted warriors in a single night, meant certain destruction to every man, woman and child of our little party.

The first unpleasantness was between us white boys and the Indian boys. One day we were trading nails and scraps of iron of all kinds to the Indian boys for a root they called yampa—a small root half an inch thick or less, and two or three times as long as thick—which when dried was almost as white as chalk and easily ground between the teeth. Of the parsnip family, it is sweet and rich and very pleasant to the taste.

This barter was going on on the drifts some three feet above the common level; it looked like an abrupt-sided sand drift. The barter was going on very sociably. We were munching our yampa with great humor and filling our pockets with the surplus roots. But some of the boys did not have pockets (some mothers will not make pockets in their boys' trousers because if boys have pockets they fill them so full of rocks, strings, dead beetles, dried fish worms, chewing wax, nails, tops, toy pistols, crullers, doughnuts, fishing tackle, bullets, buttons, jewsharps, etc., that the strain on the suspenders often becomes too great) and were holding the surplus roots in one hand held up against the stomach.

When the hand was full of yampas, they would spill and fall to the ground, and this much I know to be true. I saw some fall and picked them up and put them into my pockets, for I did not want such valuable property to "waste its sweetness in the desert air." I saw other boys, both white and Indian, picking up something, and then I saw an Indian picking himself up.

It appeared from the official report of this battle afterwards that the Indian who was picking himself up had stooped down to to pick up a yampa when one of the boys attacked him in the rear with his foot, and the young warrior toppled over on his head. A race war broke out now instantly and the battle became general. Cries of vengeance arose from the whites and yells of defiance from the reds. It was now a hand to hand fight, for we were all mixed up together when the battle began.

How we became separated I never knew, but presently we were some distance from the enemy and throwing pebbles about the size of black walnuts and Irish potatoes at them. They returned the fire with arrows and pebbles. The arrows at first alarmed us a little, and to admit the truth, I believe that if the Indians had charged us just then we would have been routed, but we very soon discovered that we could see the arrows approaching and dodge them, as the range was not very close.

As we pressed forward towards the enemy, throwing finger stones with great fury and dangerous precision, they fell back to the shelter of the potato house. As we had no field artillery heavy enough to batter down a sand hill, we charged over and around the ends of the potato house, taking the enemy in front and on both flanks. The assault was made at a speed of about four double quicks, and was so impetuous as to be irresistible.

The enemy now became demoralized and fled into the fort through an open gate. But we were not far behind and entering the courtyard of the fort, gathered up more dangerous weapons and proceeded to slay and spare not. We found a pile of pack saddles, and one of the boys armed himself with a cinch, with which he attacked an Indian, striking him on the head with the iron ring on one end of the cinch, and another Indian boy was cut on the head with some kind of projectile put in motion by the sinewy arm of one of our boys.

But this ridiculous affair was not allowed to proceed further, for McKinley, the commandant of the fort, in some way very suddenly pacified us and sent us to our corral. Our boys began the fight . . . but it was claimed that the Indians were picking up the yampas that fell to the ground and selling them to us again. However this may have been, relations between us and the Indian boys became so strained by this affair that we got no more roots.

The boys also had a skirmish with a young buck who was mounted on a pony. This was on a sand flat some distance from the camp, and I remember only that the Indian came galloping his pony towards us with his spear poised in his hand and pointed towards us; that we gave him and his pony a volley of finger stones; that he threw his spear in our direction and it stuck fast in the sand. I also remember that he got away from there as fast as his pony could carry him and left his spear behind.

After the battles of the "tater-house" and of the sand flat had been fought and won by the kids, we noticed that the Indians visiting our camp were sulky and not talkative. One evening after the camp fires had been burning some time and it was fairly dark, Indians began to drop in singly or by twos, with that noiseless tread peculiar to that people. So snakelike was their approach that a big Indian with a blanket drawn around him would be seen standing or squatting by the fire before his approach had been noticed by us.

After a while there were half a dozen or more of them about the campfires and each one had his blanket over his shoulders and it completely enveloped his body. I don't know that this alarmed the whites or caused them to suspect danger, but the big bucks were sometimes standing and squatting in the way of people about the fires and were indifferent to the fact.

One of our young men who did not like Indians gave a buck a push to get him out of his way, and when the Indian resisted, seized a brand from the fire and struck him a severe blow with it on the shoulders. I heard the blow and saw the sparks fly. The blow was probably aimed at the Indian's head, but he ducked and saved his cranium. This somewhat rough affair, coming up so unexpectedly, created some excitement in camp for a moment, but it was soon over, for some of our party caught the young man who was now fairly on the warpath with his "brand snatched from the burning" and pacified him.

The chances are that had not this been done promptly there would have been a sanguinary battle fought then and there, for there were many more Indians skulking near our corral, prepared for mischief and only waiting for a signal from the Indians in camp, who were spies and had weapons under their blankets. By the time the trouble arose in camp I think the spies had discovered that our men were on the alert and prepared for anything the redskins wanted, and having become satisfied of this, they did not wish to precipitate a fight, so were willing to drop the matter as it was.

This scrimmage at the campfire between the white man and Indian did not much alarm me, for soon after quiet was restored I became drowsy, went to bed and went to sleep, listening to a monotonous song and grunt accompanied by a tapping noise on the spoke of a wagon wheel. Years afterward I heard the same song and noise made by Indians gambling.

Probably the next day the commander of the fort, McKinley, visited our camp and remained quite a while. I understood afterwards that he invited, or rather advised, us to sleep in the fort, as the Indians were not well disposed toward us. I remember sleeping in the fort after this, and think it probable that the women and children retired to the fort of nights while the men remained in and guarded the corral.

From *Recollections of My Boyhood,* Jesse A. Applegate (Roseburg, Oregon: Press of Review Publishing Company, 1914).

XXXII

Marcus Whitman

During his hurried third visit to the East to defend the interests of his mission, Dr. Marcus Whitman (1802–1847) had taken the time to go to Washington for a personal confrontation with Secretary of War James M. Porter on the desperate need for some sort of law and order on the trails leading from Missouri to Oregon, and the Secretary had unexpectedly responded by requesting him to rough out a bill which he might get into the Congressional hopper for dealing with the dangers of that two-thousand-mile stretch of wilderness highway.

Whitman begged for a little time to think out the best solution. Until he reached Independence, Missouri, it had never occurred to him that such crowds of emigrants were eager to settle in the Northwest. That cavalcade inspired him to expand his vision. Suddenly he saw the need for many more posts along the route than he had indicated in his talks with the Secretary of War. Back at Waiilatpu it developed into a plan so revolutionary that he thought it best to propose it in an informal letter rather than a bill.

It called for the establishment of a whole string of what he called "agricultural posts or farming stations" at intervals of every one or two hundred miles all the way from Independence to Vancouver. The posts would be manned by government "superintendents," and would be, at the outset, virtually fortified hamlets, each including cultivated farmland "not exceeding 640 acres," where travelers could purchase supplies of fresh vegetables, grain, and other necessities. There would be suitable quarters for invalid migrants, storehouses, a blacksmith's shop, gunsmith's shop, and carpenter's shop, at which equipment could be repaired.

Unquestionably it was the brightest, most practical idea anyone had yet thought of for easing the suffering of emigrants, and in two years might have advanced the cause of westward expansion half a century. But it was all too visionary for a textbook Secretary of War used to thinking in terms of regiments, quartermasters, armament, and ammunition; and probably the most far-fetched idea of all was the notion of elevating the Indians to policemen. Herein lay the irreconcilable difference between the points of view of the missionary and the warrior.

To Keep the Peace

The government will doubtless for the first time be apprised, by means of this communication, of the immense migration of families to Oregon which has taken place this year. I have been instrumental in piloting across . . . the only eligible wagon road no less than . . . one thousand persons of both sexes, with their wagons, amounting in all to more than one hundred and twenty, six hundred and ninety-four oxen and seven hundred and seventy-three loose cattle.

The emigrants are from different states, but principally from Missouri, Arkansas, Illinois and New York. The majority of them are farmers, lured by the prospect of bounty in lands, by the reported fertility of the soil and by the desire to be first among those who are planting our institutions on the Pacific Coast. Among them are artisans of every trade, comprising with farmers the very best material for a new colony.

As pioneers these people have undergone incredible hardships, and having now safely passed the Blue Mountain Range with their wagons and effects, have established a durable road from Missouri to Oregon which will serve to mark permanently the route for larger numbers each succeeding year, while they have practically demonstrated that wagons drawn by horses or oxen can cross the Rocky Mountains to the Columbia River, contrary to all the sinister assertions of all those who pretended it to be impossible.

In their slow progress these persons have encountered . . . the continual fear of Indian aggression, the actual loss through them of horses, cattle and other property, and the great labor of transporting an adequate amount of provisions for so long a journey. . . . The present party is supposed to have expended no less than $2000 at Laramie's and Bridger's forts, and as much more at Fort Hall and Fort Boise, two of the Hudson's Bay Company's stations. These are at present the only stopping places in a journey of 2,200 miles, and the only places where additional supplies can be obtained, even at the enormous rate of change called "mountain prices," i.e., $50 the hundred for flour and $50 the hundred for coffee, the same for sugar, powder, etc.

Many cases of sickness and some deaths took place among those who accomplished the journey this season, owing in great measure to the uninterrupted use of meat—salt and fresh—with flour, which constitute the chief articles of food they are able to convey on their wagons. . . . Those who rely on hunting as an auxiliary support are at present unable to have their arms repaired when out of order; horses and oxen become tender-footed and require to be shod on this long journey, sometimes repeatedly, and the wagons repaired in a variety of ways.

I mention these as valuable incidents to the proposed measure [for establishing a line of supply posts along the route] as it will also be found to tend in many other incidental ways to benefit the migratory population of the United States choosing to take this direction, and on these accounts, as well as for the immediate use of the posts themselves, they ought to be provided with the necessary shops and mechanics, which would at the same time exhibit the several branches of civilized art to the Indians.

The outlay in the first instance would be but trifling. Forts like those of the Hudson's Bay Company, surrounded by walls enclosing all the buildings and constructed almost entirely of adobe, or sun-dried bricks, with stone foundations only, can be easily and cheaply erected.

There are very eligible places for as many of these as the government will find necessary, at suitable distances not further than one or two hundred miles apart, at the main crossing of the principal streams that now form impediments to the journey, and consequently well supplied with water . . . and generally well wooded.

If I might be allowed to suggest the best sites for the posts, my personal knowledge and observation enable me to recommend, first, the main crossing of the Kansas River, where a ferry would be very convenient to the traveler and profitable to the station having it in charge; next, and about eighty miles distant, the crossing of the Blue River, where in times of unusual freshet a ferry would be in like manner useful; . . . distant from one hundred to one hundred and fifty miles, the Little Blue or Republican Fork of the Kansas; . . . the point of intersection of the Platte River; . . . the crossing of the South Fork of the Platte River; and about one hundred and eighty or two hundred miles distant, Horseshoe Creek, which is about forty miles west of Laramie's Fork in the Black Hills.

Here is a fine creek for mills and irrigation, good land for cultivation, fine pasturage, timber and stone for building. Other locations may be had along the Platte and Sweetwater, on the Green River . . . and at suitable places down the Columbia. These localities are all of the best description, so situated as to hold a ready intercourse with the Indians in their passage to and from the ordinary buffalo hunting grounds, and in themselves so well situated in all other respects as to be desirable to private enterprise, if the usual advantage of trade existed. Any of the farms above indicated would be deemed extremely valuable in the states.

The government cannot long overlook the importance of superintending the savages that endanger this line of travel, and that are not yet in treaty with it. Some of these are already well known to be led by desperate white men and mongrels, who form bandits in the most difficult passes and are at all times ready to cut off some lagging emigrant in the rear of the party, or some adventurous one who may proceed a few miles in advance, or at night to make a descent upon the sleeping camp and carry away or kill horses and cattle.

This is the case even now in the commencement of our western immigration, and when it comes to be more generally known that large quantities of valuable property and considerable sums of money are yearly carried over this desolate region, it is to be feared that an organized banditti will be instituted. The posts in contemplation would effectually counteract this.

For that purpose they need not, nor ought to be, military establishments. The trading posts in this country have never been of such a character, and yet with very few men in them, have for years kept the surrounding Indians in the most pacific disposition. . . . By investing the officers in charge with competent author-ity, all evil-disposed men, refugees from justice or discharged vagabonds from the trading posts might be easily removed from among the Indians and sent to the appropriate states for trial. The Hudson's Bay Company's system of rewards among the savages would soon enable the posts to root out these desperadoes. A direct and friendly intercourse with all the tribes, even to the Pacific, might be thus maintained. . . .

Instead of sending to the state courts a manifestly guilty Indian to be arraigned before a distant tribunal and acquitted for the want of testimony by the technicalities of lawyers and of laws unknown to them, and sent back into the wilderness loaded with presents as an inducement to further crime, the posts should be enabled to execute summary justice. . . . There are many powers which ought to reside in some person on this extended route for the convenience and even necessity of the public. . . .

At present no person is authorized to administer an oath or legally attest a fact from the western line of Missouri to the Pacific. The immigrant cannot dispose of his property at home, although an opportunity ever so advantageous to him should occur after he passes the western border of Missouri. No one here can make a legal demand and protest of a promissory note or bill of exchange. No one can secure the valuable testimony of a mountaineer or of an immigrating witness after he has entered this lawless country. . . .

The very existence of such a system suggests the utility of post offices and mail arrangements, which it is the wish of all who now live in Oregon to have granted them, and I need only add that contracts for this purpose will be readily taken at reasonable rates for transporting the mail across from Missouri to the mouth of the Columbia in forty days, with fresh horses at each of the contemplated posts.

The ruling policy proposed regards the Indians as the police of the country, who are to be relied upon to keep the peace, not only for themselves, but to repel lawless white men and prevent banditti, under the solitary guidance of the superintendent of the several posts, aided by well directed system to induce the punishment of crime. It will only be after the failure of these means to procure the delivery or punishment of violent, lawless and savage acts of aggression that a band or tribe should be regarded as conspirators against the peace or punished accordingly by force of arms.

From a letter written by Dr. Marcus Whitman to the Secretary of War James M. Porter, 1843, reprinted in the Oregon Pioneer Association *Transactions* for 1891 (Portland: Anderson, 1893).

XXXIII

George H. McDuffie

To a great many prominent and vociferous Americans, this idea of creating highways to the West and encouraging citizens to use them was pure mischief, disruptive to the nation, a threat to the peace and prosperity of the East, an encroachment on alien soil: these wanderers ought to stay put and develop the country where they were born, where they belonged. The population was being spread too thin. If the English coveted the Northwest, let them have it; certainly there was nothing in that wilderness worth the risk of another struggle with Great Britain. If American malcontents insisted on transplanting themselves to a God-forsaken region over which the United States held no clear title, they should do it at their own peril, not expect a Government 3000 miles distant to protect them.

The Louisville *Journal*, barking for needed support of Kentucky enterprise, voiced the sentiment of thousands of conservatives in its excoriation of Oregon: "Of all the countries on the face of the earth, it is one of the least favored by Heaven. It is the mere riddlings of creation. It is almost as barren as the desert of Africa. . . . Russia has her Siberia and England has her Botany Bay; and if the United States should ever need a country to which to banish her rogues and scoundrels, the utility of such a region as Oregon would be demonstrated. Until then, we are perfectly willing to leave this magnificent country to the Indians."

No less a figure than Daniel Webster was credited with the denunciation: "What do we want of the vast, worthless area, this region of savages and wild beasts, of deserts of shifting sands, of cactus and prairie dogs? To what use could we ever hope to put these great deserts, or these endless mountain ranges, impenetrable and covered to their base with eternal snow? . . . What can we hope to do with the Western Coast, a coast of three thousand miles, rock-bound, uninviting and not a harbor on it? What use have we for such a country? I will never vote one cent from the public treasury to place the Pacific coast one mile nearer Boston than it is now."

Even poet William Cullen Bryant helped to cloud matters by coupling the wilds of "the Oregon" (Columbia) with the wilds of "Barca" (Africa) in his grandiloquent meditation on death, "Thanatopsis":

> All that tread
> The globe are but a handful of the tribes
> That slumber in its bosom.—Take the wings
> Of morning, pierce the Barcan wilderness,
> Or lose thyself in the continuous woods
> Where rolls the Oregon, and hears no sound
> Save its own dashings—yet the dead are there:
> And millions in those solitudes, since first
> The flight of years began, have laid them down
> In their last sleep—the dead reign there alone.

From the press, from pulpit, from halls of law everywhere echoed the pros and cons of spending money on Oregon, sponsoring establishments there, risking trouble with Great Britain. The fiery dispute went on for five years, reaching a culmination in 1843 and 1844. It had been prompted originally by an appeal to Congress signed by thirty-six Oregon settlers, who asserted that their settlement had "prospered beyond the most sanguine expectations of its first projectors," but alleged that the prosperity could not now continue if they were obliged to remain dependent upon a British Hudson's Bay Company.

"We flatter ourselves," continued the petitioners, "that we are the germ of a great State, and are anxious to give an early tone to the moral and intellectual character of its citizens." But, they conceded, it was not within their power to control the character of immigrants; only Congress could do that, by offering at once some civil code, some show of strength, at least some protection to life and property. "There are, in our opinion," they reiterated, "strong inducements for the Government of the United States to take formal and speedy possession. We urge this step, as promising to the general interests of the nation; but the advantages it may confer upon us, and the evils it may avert from our posterity, are incalculable."

The petition, like other such requests, was referred to the House Committee on Foreign Affairs, and at last the House resolved that the Committee should come up with some tangible recommendations "on the expediency of establishing a post on the River Columbia for the defense and occupation of the territory," an estimate of the cost of such action, and a summary description of the whole area and its problems.

The Committee labored, assembled documents, maps, and statements, produced a forbidding estimate of a quarter of a million dollars as the first-year cost of setting up a military post, and a recommendation that the status quo be maintained, for if action were taken it might conflict with "the letter as well as the spirit" of the existing treaties between the United States and Great Britain. The report, of course, set off a new explosion of forensic fireworks in both houses of Congress. The Honorable George H. McDuffie (1790–1851), ex-chairman of the Ways and Means Committee, former Governor of South Carolina and now Senator from that state, took the stand for Oregon opposition.

Stay East, Young Man, Stay East

What do we want with this territory? What are we to do with it? What is to be the consequence of our taking possession of it? . . . Why, it is neither more nor less than an act of colonization, for the first time proposed since the foundation of this Government. If this were a question of gradual and continuous and progressive settlement—if the territory to which our citizens are invited were really to become a part of this Union, it would present a very different question. But does any man seriously suppose that any state which can be formed at the mouth of the Columbia River, or any of the inhabitable parts of that territory, would ever become one of the states of this Union? . . .

Even in the most sanguine days of my youth I never conceived the possibility of embracing within the same Government people living five thousand miles apart. The worthy senator from New Hampshire [Levi Woodbury] seems to have discovered a principle much more potent than the representative principle. He refers you to *steam* as far more potent. I should doubt very much whether the elements, or powers, or organization of the principles of government will ever be changed by steam. Steam!

How are we to apply steam in this case? Has the senator examined the character of the country? What is the character of the country? Why . . . about seven hundred miles this side of the Rocky Mountains is uninhabitable, where rain scarcely ever falls—a barren sandy soil. On the other side . . . are three successive ridges of mountains extending toward the Pacific, and running nearly parallel, which mountains are totally impassable, except in certain parts where there are gaps or depressions, to be reached only by going some hundred of miles out of the direct course. . . .

How are you going to apply steam? Have you made anything like an estimate of the cost of a railroad running from here to the mouth of the Columbia? Why, the wealth of the Indies would be insufficient. You would have to tunnel through mountains five hundred or six hundred miles in extent. . . . With a bankrupt treasury and a depressed and suffering people, to talk about constructing a railroad to the western shore of this continent manifests a wild spirit of adventure which I never expected to hear broached in the Senate of the United States. . . .

Who are to go there, along the line of military posts, and take possession of the only part of the territory fit to occupy—that part lying along the seacoast, a strip less than one hundred miles in width, for the rest of the territory consists of mountains almost inaccessible, and low lands which are covered with stone and volcanic remains, where rain never falls except during the spring; and even on the coast no rain falls from April to October, and for the remainder of the year there is nothing but rain. Of what use will this be for agricultural purposes? I would not for that purpose give a pinch of snuff for the whole territory. I wish to God we did not own it. . . .

Do you think your honest farmers in Pennsylvania, New York, or even Ohio or Missouri will abandon their farms to go upon any such enterprise as this? God forbid! If any man who is to go into that country was my child—if he was an honest and industrious man, I would say to him, for God's sake, do not go there. You will not better your condition. You will exchange the comforts of home and the happiness of civilized life for the pains and perils of a precarious existence. But if I had a son whose conduct was such as made him a fit subject for Botany Bay, I would say, in the name of God, go. This is my estimate of the importance of the settlement. . . .

The country is inhabited by fierce and warlike savages. It is a country abounding with recesses to which they can retreat and in which they will be inaccessible; and if we ever get to war with them (and we know by experience that the most certain way to get to war is to go among them) we shall find another Florida; and every person knows how much the expenses of that unfortunate war had exceeded the anticipations of those who foreboded the worst. . . . I venture to say that for the next twenty years there is not a congressional district in this Union, costing the Government nothing, but on the contrary contributing to its support, which will not be more valuable to the United States than the whole of this territory. It never can be of any value for agricultural purposes.

. . . The fur trade is in rapid course of deterioration. The animals which yield furs are disappearing; and the time is not remote when even the British fur company will abandon the country, if you leave them alone. . . . But if the British had no

claim to this territory, and there were nothing which impelled us
to go with our military establishments and agricultural settlements, I would not consent—if there was an embankment of even
five feet to be removed, I would not consent to expend five dollars
to remove that embankment to enable our population to go there.
I do not wish to tempt the people to form settlements there.

I wish this to be a great empire, grown up by the natural
course of civilization, and the natural extension of population. I
thank God for his mercy in placing the Rocky Mountains there. I
believe, if it had not been for these mountains, we would have
been already on the Pacific. You cannot civilize men if they have
an indefinite extent of territory over which to spread their numbers; for so long as they spread their numbers, instead of becoming civilized, they become semi-savage. All agree that civilization
can best be effected when the country is hedged in by narrow
boundaries. . . .

It is not proper to hold out inducements to our citizens to
engage in these adventurous pursuits. There are no advantages to
be derived from them. The advantages of the fur trade have been
highly extolled, but I have seen no results but the enormous
wealth of John Jacob Astor and one or two others to justify the
commendation. Are the honest mechanic and agriculturist, engaged in honest pursuits of industry, to be taxed that inducements may be held out to the adventurous to engage in this trade
which has enriched so few?

. . . I cannot think any man who has a strong feeling of
patriotism—who has a heart bound to his country as it ought to
be, and endearing associations inseparably connected with home
—would abandon his friends and family and all endeared to him,
to emigrate to that country. No, sir. Captivating as it may be to
one portion of the Union, this is a spirit we ought not to encourage: we ought rather to induce the honest and industrious classes
to remain among us, and contribute to the support of their
Government.

From "The Oregon Territory," address in the Senate, January 25, 1843, by
Senator George McDuffie. *Congressional Globe*, Third Session, 27th Congress,
Volume XII (Washington: Globe Office, 1843).

XXXIV

Joel Palmer

Oregonians couldn't wait for action from an unsympathetic, uncomprehending Congress. They had to move ahead. The steady influx of new emigrants decreed it. they set up their own provisional government in 1843, took a firm stand about making boundary concessions to Great Britain by helping to promulgate the slogan "Fifty-four Forty or Fight," and elevated it into a major issue in the Presidential campaign of 1844; in 1845 the Oregon Trail was extended all the way to Tumwater, and three thousand settlers plodded over it.

Then in 1846 the political tide turned in favor of the Yankee occupation. The United States pulled in its horns, gave up the "Fifty-four-Forty" fight and accepted the forty-ninth-parallel boundary compromise; and the unpopular Hudson's Bay Company agreed to evacuate its headquarters at Fort Vancouver and move north to Victoria.

Regardless of oratorical and editorial pleas for stabilization of citizenry in the East, Opportunity was located in the West for an ever-increasing restless multitude, and more than anything else, they wanted to know how to get there, what to take, the best kind of vehicle and draft animal, the most desirable route, the worst hazards to be avoided. As if in answer to a prayer, the exact, practical information they were calling for came at last from the

pen of General Joel Palmer (1810–1881), who conducted the
vanguard of that bewildering throng of three thousand souls
across the country in 1845—losing less than two hundred to the
attraction of California.

Take No Useless Trumpery

For burthen wagons, light four-horse or heavy two-horse wagons
are the size commonly used. They should be made of the best
material, well seasoned, and should in all cases have falling
tongues. The tire should not be less than one and three-fourths
inches wide, but may be advantageously used three inches; two
inches, however, is the most common width. In fastening on the
tire, bolts should be used instead of nails; it should be at least five-
eighths or three-quarters inches thick. Hub boxes for the hubs
should be about four inches. The skeins should be well steeled.

The Mormon-fashioned wagon bed is the best. They are usually made straight, with sideboards about sixteen inches wide and
a projection outward of four inches on each side, and then
another sideboard of ten or twelve inches; in this last set the bows
for covers, which should always be double. Boxes for carrying
effects should be so constructed as to correspond in height with
the offset of the wagon bed, as this gives a smooth surface to
sleep upon.

Ox teams are more extensively used than any others. Oxen
stand the trip much better and are not so liable to be stolen by
the Indians, and are much less trouble. Cattle are generally
allowed to go at large when not hitched to the wagons, whilst
horses and mules must always be staked up at night. Oxen can
procure food in many places where horses cannot, and in much
less time. Cattle that have been raised in Illinois or Missouri
stand the trip better than those raised in Indiana or Ohio, as they
have been accustomed to eating the prairie grass upon which
they must wholly rely while on the road. Great care should be

taken in selecting cattle; they should be from four to six years old, tight and heavy-made.

For those who fit out but one wagon, it is not safe to start with less than four yoke of oxen, as they are liable to get lame, have sore necks or to stray away. One team thus fitted up may start from Missouri with twenty-five hundred pounds, and as each day's rations make the load that much lighter, before they reach any rough road their loading is much reduced. Persons should recollect that everything in the outfit should be as light as the required strength will permit; no useless trumpery should be taken.

The loading should consist of provisions and apparel, a necessary supply of cooking fixtures, a few tools, etc. No great speculation can be made in buying cattle and driving them through to sell, but as the prices of oxen and cows are much higher in Oregon than in the States, nothing is lost in having a good supply of them, which will enable the emigrant to wagon through many articles that are difficult to be obtained in Oregon.

Each family should have a few cows, as the milk can be used the entire route, and they are often convenient to put to the wagon to relieve oxen. They should be so selected that portions of them would come in fresh on the road. Sheep can also be advantageously driven. American horses and mares always command high prices and with careful usage can be taken through, but if used to wagons or carriages, their loading should be light.

Each family should be provided with a sheet-iron stove, with boiler; a platform can easily be constructed for carrying it at the hind end of the wagon; and as it is frequently quite windy and there is often a scarcity of wood, the stove is very convenient. Each family should also be provided with a tent, and to it should be attached good strong cords to fasten it down.

The cooking fixtures generally used are of sheet iron; a dutch oven and skillet of cast metal are very essential. Plates, cups, etc., should be of tinware, as queensware is much heavier and liable to break, and consumes much time in packing up. A reflector is sometimes very useful. Families should each have two churns, one for carrying sweet and one for sour milk. They should also have one eight- or ten-gallon keg for carrying water, one ax, one shovel, two or three augers, one hand saw, and if a farmer, he should be provided with one cross-cut saw and a few plow moulds, as it is difficult getting such articles. When I left the, country, plows cost from twenty-five to forty dollars each.

A good supply of ropes for tying up horses and catching cattle should also be taken. Every person should be well supplied with boots and shoes, and in fact every kind of clothing. It is also well to be supplied with at least one feather bed, and a good assortment of bedding. There are no tame geese in the country, but an abundance of wild ones; yet it is difficult procuring a sufficient quantity of feathers for a bed.

Each male person should have at least one rifle gun, and a shot gun is also very useful for wild fowl and small game, of which there is an abundance. The best-sized calibre for the mountains is from 32 to 56 to the pound, but one of from 60 to 80 or even less is best when in the lower settlements. The buffalo seldom range beyond the South Pass and never west of Green River. The larger game are elk, deer, antelope, mountain sheep or bighorn and bear. The small game are hare, rabbit, grouse, sage hen, pheasant, quail, etc. A good supply of ammunition is essential.

In laying in a supply of provision for the journey, persons will doubtless be governed in some degree by their means, but there are a few essentials that all will require. For each adult there should be two hundred pounds of flour, thirty pounds of pilot bread, seventy-five pounds of bacon, ten pounds of rice, five pounds of coffee, two pounds of tea, twenty-five pounds of sugar, half a bushel of dried beans, one bushel of dried fruit, two pounds of saleratus, ten pounds of salt, half a bushel of corn meal; and it is well to have a half-bushel of corn, parched and ground; a small keg of vinegar should also be taken.

To the above may be added as many good things as the means of the person will enable him to carry, for whatever is good at home is none the less so on the road. The above will be ample for the journey, but should an additional quantity be taken, it can readily be disposed of in the mountains and at good prices, not for cash, but for robes, dressed skins, buckskin pants, moccasins, etc. It is also well for families to be provided with medicines. It is seldom, however, that emigrants are sick; but sometimes eating too freely of fresh buffalo meat causes diarrhoea, and unless it is checked soon prostrates the individual and leaves him a fit subject for disease.

The time usually occupied in making the trip from Missouri is about five months, but with the aid of a person who has traveled the route with an emigrating company, the trip can be performed in about four months.

Much injury is done to teams in racing them, endeavoring to pass each other. Emigrants should make an every-day business of traveling; resting upon the same ground two nights is not good policy, as the teams are likely to ramble too far. Getting into large companies should be avoided, as they are necessarily compelled to move more tardily. From ten to twenty-five wagons is a sufficient number to travel with safety. The advance and rear companies should not be less than twenty; but between, it may be safe to go with six.

The Indians are very annoying on account of their thieving propensities, but if well watched they would seldom put them into practice. Persons should always avoid rambling far from camp unarmed, or in too small parties; Indians will sometimes seek such opportunities to rob a man of what little effects he has about him, and if he attempts to get away from them with his property, they will sometimes shoot him. . . .

Emigrants should endeavor to arrive at St. Joseph early in April, so as to be in readiness to take up the line of march by the middle of April. Companies, however, have often started as late as the tenth of May, but in such cases they seldom arrive in Oregon until after the rainy season commences in the Cascade range. . . .

Farmers would do well to take along a good supply of horse gear. Mechanics should take such tools as are easily carried, as there are but few in the country and those are held at exorbitant prices. Every family should lay in a good supply of school books for their children. In case of emergency, flour can be bought at Fort Hall and Fort Boise, two trading posts of the Hudson's Bay

Company, at $20 per hundred . . . but the company will take nothing in payment but cash or cattle.

At Dr. Whitman's station, flour can be bought at $5 per hundred, corn meal at $4, beef at six and seven cents per pound, potatoes at fifty cents per bushel. It is proper to observe that the flour at Spalding's and Whitman's stations will be unbolted. Emigrants, however, should be cautious and lay in a sufficient supply to last them through.

From *Journal of Travels Over the Rocky Mountains,* Joel Palmer (Cincinnati: J. A. and U. P. James, 1852).

XXXV

Hubert Howe Bancroft

Until American emigrants took up residence on Puget Sound and the Lower Columbia in sufficient numbers to rely on their own community industry for sustenance, a majority of them had been dependent for their very survival upon one man—John McLoughlin. Hundreds were deeply indebted to him. The beneficence of this single Scotchman, in defiance of the corporation policy of the Hudson's Bay Company, made possible the early settlement of the Northwest by emigrants from the East.

The prolific Pacific coast historian Hubert Howe Bancroft (1832–1918), book salesman, publisher, rare book collector, and operator of the San Francisco "history factory" that periodically employed as many as six hundred researchers to produce the thirty-nine tomes of his *Works*, composed the most eloquent of tributes ever paid McLoughlin.

More American than British

"Is it right for us to kill the Americans?" asked a Cascade chief of McLoughlin one day.

"What!" roared the Doctor.

"They or we must die," the chief calmly continued. "Not only do they spoil our forests and drive away our game, thus depriving us of food and clothing, but with their accursed morals and religion they sow broadcast the seeds of disease and death. Shall we kill them or let them kill us?"

"Only a dog would talk so," replied McLoughlin, ineffable scorn conspicuous in voice and features. "You are not a gentleman; you are not a chief; you are only a little man; never speak to me again; I will not look at you."

The savage slunk abashed away, and never again was seen at Fort Vancouver. . . .

The good that a man does lives after him, saith the seer. . . . I have encountered few characters which stand out in such grand and majestic proportions as John McLoughlin. Few persons have done him justice. His life should be written by the recording angel and pillared at the crossing of the two chief highways of the universe. His fiery gentleness, his mild energy, his innate goodness and nobleness of heart, his magnanimity, his benevolence, his unfathomable integrity, and his clearness and firmness of intellect have all been told.

Search these shores from Darien to Alaska, and you will find none such; take your books and study them from the coming of Europeans to your last municipal or state election, and you will discover no such person portrayed. His life, though quiet and untrumpeted, was full of glory; yet like many another good man, his end was not a happy one, for in his old age he was caught in a web of legal technicalities which proved his winding-sheet.

It was the sad ending of a long career of usefulness and benevolence. His record is one of which any man, however high or holy, might be proud. It is absolutely stainless, wholly noble. . . . Englishmen as well as Americans may blush for their treatment of him, for their heaping of sorrow upon his venerable head, for their lacerating of his pure and sensitive heart. . . . McLoughlin's associates, whom he had served for more than a quarter of a century with intelligent zeal and strict fidelity, raising his department from a comparatively low estate to wealth, power and importance second to none, disliked him, reproached him, if indeed they did not spurn him because out of the purest dictates only of a humane heart, he befriended famishing strangers, the United States settlers, whose presence they hated.

Nor was this always a pleasing task, even for the kind-hearted Scotchman. These lean, cadaverous, dirt-tanned ox-drivers, with bushy heads and dull unintelligent eyes sunken in sorrow, followed by famine-visaged women and children, cold and ill, barefooted, and with only rags for raiment, arriving in the wet autumn absolutely without a dollar in any kind of property, having lost their all upon the way, and many of their former companions even their lives, what were they going to do in this cold, cheerless wilderness, without house or tent or hut, without blankets, or clothes or meat or bread? Simply starve.

And this was exactly what the Hudson's Bay Company, as a consciousless corporation would have them do. It was to the interest of the company to have these emigrants die as fast as they arrived. As a corporation, they would assuredly have left them to die; but as men, and eye-witnesses of those sufferings, there never was a Scotchman or an Englishman that traded furs in America or held stock in any British fur company who would have turned his back upon them. McLoughlin could not do it, not for all England could he, and yet his company theoretically blamed him for not doing what not one of them individually could have been brought to do under any circumstance. . . .

To the better behaved of United States frontiersmen it had been the custom of McLoughlin to give employment. Among other industries that of shingle-making was introduced. Shingles were wanted for the old buildings as well as for those now constantly being built; they were likewise wanted for the Hawaiian Islands. The Yankees were expert shingle-makers; and in 1844 several of them . . . under the encouragement of McLoughlin proceeded to Puget Sound and there engaged in the manufacture of shingles. At their head was Michael Simmons, who erected the first sawmill on Puget Sound; since that time boards enough have been shipped hence to house a nation. . . .

Emigrants were flocking in from the United States in such

numbers as greatly to overshadow the English. . . . McLoughlin had reached the height of his power, from which position fate
ever ordains decline. Not that he was a man ambitious of authority; patronage fell to him naturally, and by force of circumstances. He was a born sovereign; and his rule, mingled as it was
with a broad humanity, was not such as in all cases met the
approval of his more mercenary London associates. Indeed, there
were now those who wished his retirement, who would prefer one
less liberal, less philanthropic, of narrower views favoring a more
selfish policy. This man, they said, was becoming more American
than English, more farmer than fur trader. . . .

Finally, in order to curtail his power and eventually drive him
from his position, a board of management for Pacific coast affairs
was organized by the London directors. . . . McLoughlin finally
retired in the spring of 1846, to Oregon City, where he died in
1857. . . .

He is not a statesman, for his hands are clean, his tongue is
single, and self comes not always before duty. He is not a money
magnate, for looking into his breast and then beyond the stars he
sees some things more brightly fair, more worthy of attention of
immortal man than golden calves. He is not a divinity man, nor a
conventional morality man; he teaches and preaches only as does
a shining mark upon a hilltop, beckoning pilgrims onward and
upward; furthermore, he walks within no circle of tradition, and
opens not his mouth with musty sayings to ears attuned to
unreason and conventional hypocrisy. . . .

I think of him as if present; and so he is, though he were dead
this quarter century and more. I never saw him, and yet I see
him; I never heard him, and yet he speaks to me now; I never
grasped his hand, but I feel his presence, and am the better for it.

Condensed and edited, with transposition of topical material, from *History of
the Northwest Coast*, Volume II, Hubert Howe Bancroft (New York: The Bancroft
Company, undated).

XXXVI

Peter Skene Ogden

"Frequently I feel as if our stay would not be long here," Narcissa Whitman had confided plaintively in one of her letters to relatives in the East, as Indian misunderstandings mounted and mission charity seemed to be rewarded with increasing hostility. Her premonition was not far wrong. Everywhere the tribes were showing resentment over the white intrusion, regardless of worthy intentions, and the tragedy that took place at Waiilatpu late in 1847 was only a foretaste of what was to come during the next decade.

Peter Skene Ogden (1794–1854), one of McLoughlin's lieutenants at Vancouver and his successor as chief factor for Hudson's Bay before the company moved north, narrated the grim tale of the tragedy, humbly disguising himself as "A Fur Trader." He was that and more. His life spanned the whole range of the big fur trade, both in time and territory. As a Quebec youth of sixteen, he first went into the employ of the North West Company. He came to the Columbia River country in 1818 and shifted to Hudson's Bay employment after its merger.

From Fort Spokane he led the fur brigades on expeditions that opened to the public much of Idaho, Nevada, Utah, and northern California. His most detailed explorations were on the northern and western shores of Great Salt Lake, and both the Ogden River and the city of Ogden were to perpetuate his name. The modest, courageous, and durable "fur trader" risked his own life to rescue the survivors of the assualt on Waiilatpu, and he it was who paid off the ransom demanded by the truculent savages.

The Whitman Massacre

On the evening of the 6th of December [1847] we were seated around our cheerful fireside, "holding sweet converse" on the different topics of news we had lately received from Canada and England by our overland express, when a loud knocking at the door attracted the attention of all present, and a Mr. H—— from the Dalles mission made his appearance, accompanied by a servant of the Company from Walla Walla. . . . They announced to us the melancholy tidings of the murder of Dr. and Mrs. Whitman and twelve Americans, with the entire destruction of Waiilatpu Mission. . . .

For some time previous to the massacre, a number of the Cayoux Indians who resided in the vicinity of the mission had died of the measles and dysentery, which prevailed in every part of the country. The worthy doctor had been most constant in his attendance on the sufferers, administering not only medicines, but such other comforts as, indeed, he could ill afford from his slender stock. Unhappily, his efforts for their relief were vain; the mortality increased rather than diminished; and the horrid idea became impressed on the superstitious minds of the Indians that Dr. Whitman and others had conspired to exterminate them by means of poison!

This idea, however it may have originated, received corroboration, as has since been ascertained, from the instigations of one Joseph Louis, a Spanish Creole, who for upwards of a year had been employed about the mission. . . . The number of deaths continuing to increase daily confirmed the diabolical suspicion once entertained, and soon these wretched men resolved on

revenging their supposed wrongs and securing their future safety
by murdering all the inmates of the mission.

. . . The hour of ten in the morning was selected for the
butchery, and before many minutes had elapsed no less than
twelve victims had been sacrificed to their wild and revengeful
superstition. The first was a tailor, killed on the bench where he
was seated at his daily labor. . . . The next was the worthy
doctor himself, who had entirely devoted the last ten years of his
life to the instruction of those very savages. . . . He was seated
at a desk writing when he heard the yell of the murderers, and
going to the door, received his first wound.

He did not for an instant lose his composure, but calmly returning into the house, drew a chair toward the fire and sat down, his
hands clasped together in prayer, resigned to whatever fate might
await him. During this brief interval the bloody work was going
on outside, and the good, kind-hearted Mrs. Whitman, who was
upstairs and had rushed to the window on hearing the report of
firearms, had instantly received from one wretched miscreant a
ball in her breast.

Bleeding profusely, she hastily descended to her husband's
room, and embracing him, began to wipe with her handkerchief
the blood that was trickling from his wounds. He fondly returned
the caresses of her who for the last fifteen years had been the
devoted partner of his joys and sorrows in the missionary field,
and who in this last dark hour proved herself the same affectionate wife, regardless of her own sufferings. . . . Thus embraced,
and perfectly resigned to their fate, the blood-thirsty wretches,
armed with guns and axes, rushed into the room, and they were
instantly torn asunder never more to meet in this world.

The chief with his axe so mutilated the face and head of the
worthy doctor that he soon ceased to suffer. The fate of Mrs.
Whitman was still more cruel; she was thrown down and dragged
by the hair of her head into the mud, where with blows and kicks
the inhuman monsters terminated her existence. . . .

The next victim was Dr. Whitman's assistant, who, as several
eye-witnesses have alleged, not only implored the Indians to
spare him, but acknowledged it was too true that the doctor had

administered poison to kill them. . . . After making this admission, the savages promised to spare his life and left him. A few minutes after, however, an Indian who was at some distance when the promise was made, and was not aware of it, came up with him, and in another moment his earthly career was ended.

While these scenes were enacting, two Americans who had concealed themselves managed to effect their escape—one with his family, consisting of a wife and four children. This little party took the road to the Company's establishment, but the poor woman, having just risen from a bed of sickness, soon became too faint and exhausted to follow; she therefore entreated her husband to save her children and leave her to her fate. As there was a ray of hope that all might be preserved, he carefully concealed her with three of the children in the bushes, and taking one in his arms, succeeded in reaching the fort, a distance of twenty-five miles, in safety.

No time was lost by the gentlemen in charge there in sending relief and assistance to the poor woman, but strange to relate, after a search of two days, the husband despaired of finding her and concluded that she was lost . . . murdered by the Indians. He was on the eve of abandoning his search, but a friendly Indian who had accompanied him from the fort was far from losing all hope. . . . He renewed the search and succeeded in finding the now almost lifeless woman, lying concealed with her children in the very spot where they had been left, with scarcely any covering and without food or fire to keep them warm, in which deplorable state they had now remained four days and nights. The whole party reached the fort in safety. . . .

The other American escaped by following, in his wounded state, a mark [trail] which he struck upon by mere chance, and which led him, by a course of two hundred miles, to the Clearwater Mission, where he had never been before, and which he reached after six days and nights traveling, though without food. . . .

After Mr. Rodgers had fallen, and the two surviving Americans had thus baffled pursuit, or escaped unnoticed, there remained but the now desolate women and children, who had been eye-witnesses of the massacre of their husbands and fathers. The number of these unfortunates exceeded fifty. . . . Their lives, indeed, were spared them, but three of the young women were reserved for a more cruel fate, over which I must draw a veil.

The other women and children were detained in captivity and doomed by their cruel masters to toil day and night until all of them, including the three women mentioned above, were fortunately released . . . with the exception of three children who had died. During this period—a long interval to them of nearly a month—they were suffering every indignity and being threatened with death. . . .

The object of these wretches in detaining them was to procure a ransom, and having their victims so completely in their power, they too well succeeded. Late one evening the poor captives reached the Company's establishment, strongly guarded by not less than forty Indians, each of whom had some claim to make which dire necessity compelled us to satisfy. . . .

Another incident worthy of record . . . was the almost miraculous escape of the Rev. Mr. Spalding, for which, indeed, he was indebted to the timely aid and advice of the Rev. Mr. Brouillet of the Roman Catholic Mission. The former gentleman was on his return from the Umatilla River . . . when within a short distance of the mission at Waiilatpu . . . he was happy enough to meet the Rev. Mr. Brouillet, who had just left the scene of bloodshed.

He had gone there, it appears, to administer baptism to two children . . . [only] to find the bodies of twelve of his fellow-creatures so shockingly mutilated, and lying like dogs in the mud and dirt with scarcely any covering. With the assistance of his interpreter, he dug one grave for all, and having procured shrouds, he had the satisfaction . . . of rendering them the last kind office that one mortal owes to another. Had the remains been exposed one night longer, they would have become a prey to wolves and dogs. . . .

The Rev. Mr. Brouillet was returning from the performance of this duty, being accompanied by his interpreter and an Indian who had evil designs on Mr. Spalding, when they met the latter about six miles from the mission. . . . It required some presence of mind on the part of Mr. Brouillet to warn Mr. Spalding of his danger without creating any suspicion in the mind of the Indian. . . . He ordered the interpreter to stop and light his pipe, and by the same ruse detained the Indian in the rear to strike fire. The two divines proceeding on in company, Mr. Spalding was soon made acquainted with the particulars of the late occurrence and strongly advised to escape, his Catholic friend assisting him from his own small stock of provisions.

The advice was acted upon in the same haste that it was given. . . . In an instant he left the trail and proceeded toward the mountains. Mr. Brouillet meanwhile made all dispatch to reach his own mission, and when almost within sight of it, the Indian interpreter overtook him. The former, finding Mr. Spalding no longer in company, cast a savage and threatening look on Mr. Brouillet and immediately retraced his steps in pursuit of his victim. Fortunately a dense fog and . . . the darkness of night frustrated his evil designs, and thus the life of Mr. Spalding was preserved . . . though wandering for six days and nights among the mountains, losing his horse and provisions, and at last reaching home barefoot. . . .

"Revenge is sweet!" May it fall on the savages tenfold, for richly do they deserve it!

From *Traits of American Indian Life and Character,* A Fur Trader (London: Smith, Elder and Company, 1853).

XXXVII

Samuel C. Damon

The First Regiment, U.S. Artillery, did not arrive in time to fulfill Peter Ogden's prayer that the Whitman Massacre be avenged, but the carnage at Waiilatpu at least helped to justify in the public mind the wisdom in the 1848 organization of Oregon as a Territory, as well as the need for its proper defense. Late in May, 1849, the regiment pitched tents at Fort Vancouver, just as the British were slowly moving out.

Astonishing changes had occurred in the West during the brief interim of eighteen months between the Massacre and the coming of the defenders. The War with Mexico had been terminated and California was now a part of the United States. But the most disrupting event was the discovery of gold on the American River in January, 1848; that, indeed, had upset the equilibrium of the whole nation.

Prior to the American occupation of California and to John Marshall's lucky find, for every emigrant bound for Mexican California, there were approximately ten bound for Oregon. Suddenly the statistics were reversed, and all roads from the East led to the Sierra gold fields. The need for improvement of the Oregon Trail was no longer so urgent; Oregonians were already deserting their clearings for a gamble at the California diggings; and if Congress had not previously committed itself to token defense of the Columbia region, the First Regiment would probably have been dispatched to the Golden Gate. Almost overnight the course of ocean traffic changed, too. New England shippers who had been seeking markets in the Northwest altered their bills of lading for San Francisco and Sacramento.

U.S.S. *Massachusetts*, transporting the 161 members of the First Regiment, followed the old itinerary of American whaleships and came by way of Honolulu, Pacific capital of the whaling industry. In the Hawaiian Islands the arrival of the transport had stirred considerable excitement, for it drifted into the port of Honolulu "without the help of sails or other visible means of locomotion"— only the second operating steamship to call there.

The event had been duly chronicled by the Reverend Samuel C. Damon (1815–1885), seamen's chaplain in Honolulu, world traveler, well-known lecturer both in America and England, and a talented penman, who upon taking up his residency in the Islands had also turned editor and started publishing a newspaper, *The Friend and Temperance Advocate*, for the benefit of his local and seafaring congregations.

In fact, the vivacious pastor was so impressed at the sight of the mighty 750-ton vessel that he immediately boarded her, befriended the captain, and shortly had an invitation to join her on a cruise to the Columbia River. It was too good a junket to turn down. Damon preached a farewell sermon at his Bethel Seamen's Chapel, suspended publication of his newspaper, and temporarily transferred his chaplaincy to the *Massachusetts*. Three weeks later he was steaming into the mouth of the Columbia.

His leave, however, was only for a few months. Before fall he was back in his pulpit—and back at his editorial desk, where he drafted for *The Friend* his impressions of the new Oregon Territory.

As Parson Damon Saw It

Sabbath, May 13th, the vessel came to anchor off Fort Vancouver, and although it was not convenient to have public service on

shipboard amidst the necessary confusion attending the ship's
duties, yet it was pleasant when we arrived off the pier and the
pilot asked, "Where are all the gentlemen of the fort?" to listen to
the reply, "They are at church."

How, methought, can gentlemen be better employed during
the hours of the holy Sabbath than in worshipping God! Would
that all who profess themselves gentlemen were thus to be found
on God's holy day. I much regretted, however, to hear the firing
of salutes from ship to shore. Such things but illy comport with
the sacredness of the Sabbath, or roughly harmonize with the
command, "Remember the Sabbath to keep it holy." . . .

Our sailing up the Columbia was exceedingly pleasant. This
river abounds with much beautiful scenery, agreeably diversified
by valleys, hills and mountains. At present the whole country
along the river's banks abounds with a heavy growth of forest
trees, some of which are of immense dimensions. . . . From the
mouth of the river as far up as Fort Vancouver, a distance of
ninety miles, probably the number of settlements or small clearings in the forest would not exceed twenty, including three or
four sawmills. Even the view of a log cabin was exceedingly
pleasant to the eye. On Sabbath morning, May 13th, we passed
"New Plymouth," where there was a very good log house. . . .
The master of the establishment came to the door and welcomed us with a tune from his flute, the soft and melodious
sounds coming over the gentle waters, wafted by the morning
breeze. . . .

Having ascended the Columbia to the highest point which I
expected to advance and expecting to spend some weeks in
traveling among the settlements . . . I endeavored to inform
myself with reference to the general outlines of the Territory of
Oregon . . . equal in extent to all of New England and the
middle states, with the addition of Virginia, North and South
Carolina and a good part of Georgia . . . an area of 400,000
square miles, watered by the Columbia and its numerous tributaries.

It is distinctly divided into three grand divisions: Lower,
Middle and Upper Oregon. 1. Lower Oregon embraces the terri-

tory lying between the ocean and the President or Cascade Mountains, the Willamette being the principal river of this division. 2. Middle Oregon lies between the Cascade and the Blue Mountains, the Shutes and Umatilla being the principal rivers of this division. 3. And Upper Oregon lies between the Blue and Rocky Mountains, the Lewis and its tributaries being the rivers of this division. . . . Clatsop County is near the mouth of the Columbia River; Lewis about the Nisqually settlement on the Straits of Juan de Fuca; and Vancouver about the Fort of Vancouver.

May 14th I visited the Fort, stores, storehouses and offices of the Hudson Bay Company. The extensive mechanical operations which have, in the estimation of former visitors, imparted so much animation to the central depot of the "Company," are now almost entirely suspended. Scores of the company's servants are now seeking their fortunes in the mines of California. It is clearly apparent that affairs at the Fort are in a transition state. The old and rigid discipline is relaxing; a new order of things is gradually coming about; and one is inclined to think that the glory of Vancouver's Fort is departing. The introduction of United States laws into the territory necessarily will have a powerful influence upon the government of the company's servants. . . . Mr. Douglass, hitherto at the head of the company's establishment, is to remove with his family to Vancouver's Island, there to officiate as Governor. Mr. Ogden is to become his successor at the Fort. . . .

Every visitor to Oregon will very soon after his arrival learn that there is in use a new language, which has been created by the necessities of the situation in which emigrants, Hudson Bay Company officers and others found themselves in relation to the aborigines of the country. Indians have learned a few English and French words, foreigners have learned a few Indian words, so that ere long a mode of communication was introduced, which answered all the common purposes of trading and intercourse between the Indians and the white population.

I was particularly struck with the frequent use which is made of this jargon. . . . There was one word which was in constant use, but its derivation I could not learn. This word is *cultus*. If a man was inefficient, he was *cultus;* and if any instrument was useless, it was *cultus.* The frequency with which the word was introduced into conversation led me to imagine that almost everything and everybody, animate and inanimate in Oregon, must be *cultus.* Webster's spelling book has already been republished in Oregon, and when the time arrives for an edition of his dictionary, it may be expected that *cultus* and numerous other words of the jargon will take their station by the side of words and terms derived from the French, Latin, Greek and Anglo-Saxon: . . . chain—*chinkamin;* handkerchief—*hankachim;* crow—*kawkaw;* molasses—*lomaslas;* mountain—*lemonte;* name—*neim;* old—*oldman;* paper—*papa;* mad, angry—*salluks;* warm—*wam;* wood—*stick;* cat—*puss;* Americans—*Bostons;* Englishmen—*King George men.* . . .

On my return to the *Massachusetts* [after a tour of other settlements] I found quite a new state of things. Both officers and soldiers with all their tents and warlike equipage were removed on shore. Their tents were erected in rear of the Fort. Although it is now the middle of June, the weather was quite cool, and I deeply sympathized with officers and men encamped upon the "tented plain." The soldier as well as sailor has surely many hardships to encounter, and it truly is no trifling hardship during times of peace to be sent to a remote part of the country and there stationed for years . . . spending a quiet and monotonous life, receiving their daily rations and contriving all kinds of sports to kill the time. I was glad to know that the officers and soldiers had taken the precaution to supply themselves with a good quantity of entertaining books. . . . I doubt not that officers and privates will find ample time for reading. . . .

On the following morning the *Massachusetts* left the Fort. Really a more pleasant, mild and propitious day could not have been asked for wherein to glide down the Columbia. Its banks were clothed in the richest foliage. I am sure spring never decked the country with a robe of deeper and richer green. As steam and tide rapidly bore us down the stream, I gazed probably for the last time upon the mountains, hills and forests of Lower Oregon.

. . . I had witnessed the enterprising and intelligent citizens of the country busy in their various employments, but laying the foundations of civil, religious, political and literary institutions which were to bless posterity.

Condensed from "A Journey from the Sandwich Islands to Lower Oregon and Upper California," Samuel C. Damon, *Seamen's Friend and Temperance Advocate,* November 15, 1849, and following issues.

XXXVIII

Ulysses S. Grant

The original Oregon Territory remained intact for only five years. A small third of it, between the Columbia River and the northern bounds of California, assumed the title in 1853, and the remainder, extending far inland across the Rockies to the headwaters of the Missouri, was given the name of Washington Territory. Though Olympia was accorded the honor of standing as its capital, Fort Vancouver was still its principal political and commercial center; there, too, were the barracks for its defenders.

One of the officers who took a turn of service at the barracks during the transition was a recent graduate of West Point and veteran of the War with Mexico, First Lieutenant Ulysses S. Grant (1822–1885). His orders cast him as regimental quartermaster, and so inconspicuous a figure was he that not even the most impressionable private under him would have put him down as potential material for the position of commander in chief of the army, much less President of the United States. As the product of an Ohio farm, in 1853 Grant was more interested in raising potatoes on the banks of the Columbia than in becoming a military or political hero.

With Sword and Plowshare

My regiment spent a few weeks at Benicia barracks [California] and then was ordered to Fort Vancouver on the Columbia River, in Oregon Territory. During the winter of 1852–53 the territory was divided, all north of the Columbia River being taken from Oregon to make Washington Territory.

Prices for all kinds of supplies were so high on the Pacific coast from 1849 until at least 1853 that it would have been impossible for officers of the army to exist upon their pay, if it had not been that authority was given them to purchase from the commissary such supplies as he kept, at New Orleans wholesale prices. A cook could not be hired for the pay of a captain. The cook could do better. At Benicia in 1852 flour was twenty-five cents per pound; potatoes were sixteen cents; beets, turnips and cabbage, six cents; onions, thirty-seven and a half cents; meat and other articles in proportion.

In 1853 at Vancouver vegetables were a little lower. I, with three other officers, concluded that we would raise a crop for ourselves and by selling the surplus realize something handsome. I bought a pair of horses that had crossed the plains that summer and were very poor. They recuperated rapidly, however, and proved a good team to break the ground with. I performed all the labor of breaking up the ground, while the other officers planted the potatoes. Our crop was enormous.

Luckily for us the Columbia River rose to a great height from the melting of the snow in the mountains in June, and overflowed and killed most of our crop. This saved digging it up, for everybody on the Pacific coast seemed to have come to the conclusion at the same time that agriculture would be profitable. In 1853 more than three-quarters of the potatoes raised were permitted to rot in the ground, or had to be thrown away. The only potatoes we sold were to our own mess.

While I was stationed on the Pacific coast we were free from Indian wars. There were quite a number of remnants of tribes in the vicinity of Portland in Oregon and of Fort Vancouver in Washington Territory. They had generally acquired some of the vices of civilization, but none of the virtues, except in individual cases. The Hudson's Bay Company had held the Northwest with their trading posts for many years before the United States was represented on the Pacific coast. They still retained posts along the Columbia River and one at Fort Vancouver when I was there.

Their treatment of the Indians had brought out the better qualities of the savages. Farming had been undertaken by the company to supply the Indians with bread and vegetables; they raised some cattle and horses; and they had now taught the Indians to do the labor of the farm and herd. They always compensated them for their labor and always gave them goods of uniform quality and at uniform price.

Before the advent of the American, the medium of exchange between the Indian and the white man was pelts. Afterward it was silver coin. If an Indian received in the sale of a horse a fifty-dollar gold piece, not an infrequent occurrence, the first thing he did was to exchange it for American half dollars. These he could count. He would then commence his purchases, paying for each article separately as he got it. He would not trust anyone to add up the bill and pay it all at once. At that day fifty-dollar gold pieces, not the issue of the government, were common on the Pacific coast. They were called slugs.

The Indians along the lower Columbia as far as the Cascades and on the lower Willamette died off very fast during the year I spent in that section, for besides acquiring the vices of the white people they had acquired also their diseases. The measles and the smallpox were both amazingly fatal. In their wild state, before the appearance of the white man among them, the principal complaints they were subject to were those produced by long involuntary fasting, violent exercise in pursuit of game and over-eating.

Instinct more than reason had taught them a remedy for these ills. It was the steam bath. Something like a bake-oven was built, large enough to admit a man lying down. Bushes were stuck in the ground in two rows about six feet long and some two or three feet apart; other bushes connected the rows at one end. The tops of the bushes were drawn together to interlace and confined in that position; the whole was then plastered over with wet clay until every opening was filled. Just inside the open end of the oven the floor was scooped out so as to make a hole that would hold a bucket or two of water. These ovens were always built on the banks of a stream, a big spring or pool of water.

When a patient required a bath, a fire was built near the oven and a pile of stones put upon it. The cavity at the front was then filled with water. When the stones were sufficiently heated, the patient would draw himself into the oven; a blanket would be thrown over the open end and hot stones put into the water until the patient could stand it no longer. He was then withdrawn from his steam bath and doused into the cold stream near by. This treatment may have answered with the early ailments of the Indians. With the measles or smallpox it would kill every time.

During my year on the Columbia River the smallpox exterminated one small remnant of a band of Indians entirely and reduced others materially. I do not think there was a case of recovery among them until the doctor with the Hudson's Bay Company took the matter in hand and established a hospital. Nearly every case he treated recovered. . . . The decimation among the Indians I knew of personally, and the hospital established for their benefit was a Hudson's Bay building not a stone's throw from my own quarters.

The death of Colonel Bliss of the Adjutant General's department, which occurred July 5th, 1853, promoted me to the captaincy of a company then stationed at Humboldt Bay, California. The notice reached me in September of the same year and I very soon started to join my new command.

From *Personal Memoirs of U.S. Grant*, Volume I. (New York: C. L. Webster and Company, 1885).

XXXIX

Chief Seattle

Boredom among the garrison at Fort Vancouver was soon found to be not entirely warranted. The truculence with which the original landlords of the Northwest had been treated by three generations of white intruders was at last backfiring upon a fourth. Tribesmen—what few of them remained—were once again voicing their resentment and reasserting their rights, preparing for a last stand. For them it was now or never.

The immediate cause of the resentment was a new insult from the white men. Behind closed doors it had been decided that they and the Indians could never live together in civilized amity; the red men, therefore, would have to be segregated, moved to huge concentration camps politely called "reservations." Neither the settlers in Washington Territory nor the lawmakers in Washington, D.C., had the effrontery to propose that the Indian lands be expropriated without compensation; no, they would buy them—for as much as seven cents an acre. For a grand total of $150,000 some two million acres would be purchased outright. However, the purchasers couldn't afford to pay cash, or even money; but over a period of twenty years the value of $150,000 would be distributed in "useful articles."

Being neither mathematicians nor economists, a large majority of the would-be beneficiaries interpreted the deal as a bargain, since they were not familiar with the principle of installment payment and assumed that $150,000 worth of goods would be parceled out among them annually for twenty years. None of the brokers bothered to point out that the largess each year would amount to approximately two dollars per individual.

The full implications of the offer seemed to be understood by only one Indian leader, Chief Seattle (c. 1786–1866), "a Titan among Lilliputians," standing "six feet full in his moccasins, broad shouldered, deep chested and finely proportioned," the chief who had recently succeeded in uniting most of the reduced and disparate coastal tribes, and who was to lend his name to the great city of the Northwest. Seattle was an intelligent man and an impressive orator, but even he assumed that George Washington was still the President of the United States, the durable Great White Father; that "George"—King George III—continued to reign in England; and that the newly appointed governor of Washington Territory was, of course, a son of the Great White Father.

In 1854 the new governor, West Point soldier and frontiersman Isaac I. Stevens, invited all the tribes in the Puget Sound area to a spectacular powwow to hear about the generous terms of the land purchase. Stevens made a speech of welcome, and in glowing terms outlined the magnanimity in the latest scheme for getting the Indians out of the way. Then it was Chief Seattle's turn to respond. He could remember back—or thought he could—to the coming of Vancouver's ships, the days of the early traders, of Lewis and Clark, Astoria, and the North West Company, and with this perspective had his say in one of the great political addresses of the century—though at least a little of the poetry and tempered cynicism in the speech may be attributed to Seattle linguist Dr. Henry A. Smith, who heard it and translated the sonorous Chinook oratory into English.

And Nothing to Gain

Yonder sky that has wept tears of compassion on our fathers for centuries untold, and which to us looks eternal, may change. Today it is fair, but tomorrow it may be overcast with clouds. My

words are like the stars that never set. What Seattle says, the great Chief Washington can rely upon with as much certainty as our pale-face brothers can rely upon the return of the seasons.
The son of the white chief says his father sends us greetings of friendship and good will. This is kind, for we know he has little need of our friendship in return, because his people are many. They are like the grass that covers the vast prairies, while my people are few and resemble the scattering trees of the storm-swept plain.

The great, and I presume also good, white chief sends us word that he wants to buy our lands, but is willing to allow us to reserve enough to live on comfortably. This indeed appears generous, for the red man no longer has rights that he need respect, and the offer may be wise also, for we are no longer in need of a great country.

There was a time when our people covered the whole land as the waves of a wind-ruffled sea cover its shell-paved floor. But that time has long since passed away, with the greatness of tribes now almost forgotten. I will not mourn over our untimely decay, nor reproach my pale-face brothers for hastening it, for we too may have been somewhat to blame. When our young men grow angry at some real or imaginary wrong, and disfigure their faces with black paint, their hearts also are disfigured and turn black, and then their cruelty is relentless and knows no bounds, and our old men are not able to restrain them.

But let us hope that hostilities between the red man and his pale-face brothers may never return. We would have everything to lose and nothing to gain. True it is, that revenge with our young braves is considered gain, even at the cost of their own lives, but old men who stay at home from times of war, and old women who have sons to lose, know better.

Our great father Washington—for I presume he is now our father as well as yours, since George has moved his boundaries to the north—our great and good father, I say, sends us word by his son, who, no doubt, is a great chief among his people, that if we do as he desires, he will protect us. His brave armies will be to us a bristling wall of strength, and his great ships of war will fill our harbors, so that our ancient enemies far to the northward, the

Simsiams and Hydas, will no longer frighten our women and old men. Then he will be our father and we will be his children.

But can this ever be? Your God loves your people and hates mine; he folds his strong arms lovingly about the pale-face and leads him as a father leads his infant son, but he has forsaken his red children. He makes your people wax strong every day, and soon they will fill the land, while my people are ebbing away like a fast-receding tide that will never flow again. The white man's God cannot love his red children or he would protect them. They seem to be orphans and can look somewhere for help. How then can we become brothers? How can your father become our father and bring us prosperity and awaken in us dreams of returning greatness?

Your God seems to us to be partial. He came to the white man. We never saw him, never even heard his voice; he gave the white man laws, but he had no word for his red children, whose teeming millions filled this vast continent as the stars fill the firmament. No, we are two distinct races and must ever remain so. There is little in common between us. The ashes of our ancestors are sacred and their final resting place is hallowed ground, while you wander away from the tombs of your fathers seemingly without regret.

Your religion was written on tables of stone by the iron finger of an angry God, lest you might forget it. The red man could never remember nor comprehend it. Our religion is the traditions of our ancestors, the dreams of our old men, given them by the Great Spirit, and the visions of our sachems, and is written in the hearts of our people.

Your dead cease to love you and the homes of their nativity as soon as they pass the portals of the tomb. They wander far off beyond the stars, are soon forgotten and never return. Our dead never forget the beautiful world that gave them being. They still love its winding rivers, its great mountains and its sequestered vales, and they ever yearn in tenderest affection over the lonely-hearted living, and often return to visit and comfort them.

Day and night cannot dwell together. The red man has ever fled the approach of the white man, as the changing mists on the mountainside flee before the blazing morning sun. However, your proposition seems a just one, and I think my folks will accept it and will retire to the reservation you offer them, and we will dwell apart and in peace, for the words of the great white chief seem to be the voice of nature speaking to my people out of the thick darkness that is fast gathering around them, like a dense fog floating inward from a midnight sea.

It matters but little where we pass the remainder of our days. They are not many. The Indian's night promises to be dark. No bright star hovers about the horizon. Sad-voiced winds moan in the distance. Some grim Nemesis of our race is on the red man's trail, and wherever he goes he will still hear the sure approaching footsteps of the fell destroyer and prepare to meet his doom, as does the wounded doe that hears the approaching footsteps of the hunter. A few more moons, a few more winters, and not one of all the mighty hosts that once filled this broad land, or that now roam in fragmentary bands through these vast solitudes will remain to weep over the tombs of a people once as powerful and as hopeful as your own.

But why should we repine? Why should I mourn for my people? Tribes are made up of individuals and therefore are no better than they. Men come and go like the waves of the sea. A tear, a *tomanawos*, a dirge, and they are gone from our longing eyes forever. Even the white man, whose God walked and talked with him as friend to friend, is not exempt from the common destiny. We *may* be brothers after all. We shall see.

We will ponder your proposition, and when we have decided we will tell you. But should we accept it, I here and now make this the first condition: that we will not be denied the privilege, without molestation, of visiting at will the graves of our ancestors and friends. Every part of this country is sacred to my people. Every hillside, every valley, every plain and grove has been hallowed by some fond memory or some sad experience of my tribe.

Even the rocks that seem to lie dumb as they swelter in the sun along the silent seashore in solemn grandeur thrill with memories of past events connected with the fate of my people, and the very dust under your feet responds more lovingly to our footsteps than to yours, because it is the ashes of our ancestors and our bare feet are conscious of the sympathetic touch, for the soil is rich with the life of our kindred.

The sable braves and fond mothers and glad-hearted maidens and the little children who lived and rejoiced here, and whose very names are now forgotten, still love these solitudes, and their deep fastnesses at eventide grow shadowy with the presence of dusky spirits. And when the last red man shall have perished from the earth and his memory among white men shall have become a myth, these shores shall swarm with the invisible men of my tribe, and when your children's children shall think themselves alone in the field, the store, the shop, upon the highway or in the silence of the woods, they will not be alone.

In all the earth there is no place dedicated to solitude. At night when the streets of your cities and villages shall be silent and you think them deserted, they will throng with the returning hosts that once filled and still love this beautiful land. The white man will never be alone. Let him be just and deal kindly with my people, for the dead are not altogether powerless.

From "Early Reminiscences," H. A. Smith. Seattle *Sunday Star,* November 5, 1887.

XL

Theodore Winthrop

Writers in Washington Territory took themselves and their troubles all too seriously. Few ever applied the light touch. In California, professional and amateur scribes were mining a wealth of fun and farce, along with the gold, but the Sierra jesters seemed to shy away from the more northerly terrain, or if one of them did appear in the Columbia or Puget Sound settlements, he at once became preoccupied with drafting preachment or formal documents rather than drollery.

Theodore Winthrop (1828–1861), a descendant of Governor John Winthrop of Massachusetts—and therefore a notable New England socialite—occasional poet and touted author of *Cecil Dreeme* and *John Brent,* was an exception. To fight off a physical ailment, he had taken a job with the Pacific Mail Company, sailed around the Horn to Vancouver Island for his employers, then crossed to Port Townsend, where he was to start a canoe-and-saddle trip overland to New York.

Though his account of Port Townsend in a state of inebriation pitifully demonstrated the level to which rum and civilization had reduced the Indians there, it was also one of the merriest pieces to come out of the region.

I Kicked a King

The Duke of York was ducally drunk. His brother, King George, was drunk—royally. Royalty may disdain public opinion and fall as low as it pleases. But a brother of the throne, leader of the opposition, possible Regent, possible King, must retain at least a swaying perpendicular. King George had kept his chair of state until an angular sitting position was impossible; then he subsided into a curvilinear droop, and at last fairly toppled over, and lay in his lodge limp and stertorous.

In his lodge lay Georgius Rex, in flabby insensibility. Dead to the duties of sovereignty was the King of the Klalams. Like other royal Georges in palaces more regal than this Port Townsend wigwam, in realms more civilized than here where the great tides of Puget's Sound rise and fall, this royal George had sunk in absolute wreck. Kings are but men. Several kings have thought themselves the god Bacchus. George of the Klalams had imbibed this ambitious error, and had proved himself very much lower than a god, much lower than a man, lower than any plebeian Klalam Indian—a drunken king.

In the great shed of slabs that served them for palace sat the Queen—sat the Queens—mild-eyed, melancholy, copper-colored persons, also, sad to say, not sober. Etiquette demanded inebriety. The stern rules of royal indecorum must be obeyed. The Queen Dowager had succumbed to ceremony; the Queen Consort was sinking; every lesser queen—the favorites for sympathy, the neglected for consolation—all had imitated their lord and master.

Courtiers had done likewise. Chamberlain Gold Stick, Black Rod, Garter King at Arms, a dozen high functionaries, were prostrate by the side of prostrate majesty. Courtiers grovelled with their sovereign. . . . King, royal household and court all were powerless, and I was suppliant here on the waters of the Pacific for means of commencing my homeward journey across the continent toward the Atlantic. I needed a bark from that fleet by which King George ruled the waves. I had . . . consumed invaluable hours in making a detour from my proper course to inspect the house, the sawmill, the bluff and the beach, called Port Townsend. These were the last days of August, 1853, I was to meet my overland comrades, a pair of roughs, at the Dalles of the Columbia on the first of September.

Between me and the rendezvous were the leagues of Puget's Sound, the preparation for an ultramontane trip, the passes of the Cascades, and all the dilatoriness and danger of Indian guidance. Moments now were worth days of common life. Therefore, as I saw those winged moments flit away unharnessed to my chariot of departure, I became wroth, and advancing where the king of all this region lay, limp, stertorous and futile, I kicked him liberally.

Yes! I have kicked a king!

Proudly I claim that I have outdone the most radical regicide. I have offered indignities to the person of royalty with a moccasined toe . . . and no scalping knife leaped from greasy seal-skin sheath to avenge the insult. One bottle-holder in waiting, upon whose head I had casually trodden, did indeed stagger to his seat and stammer truculently in Chinook jargon, "Potlatch lum!— Give me to drink," quoth he, and incontinently fell prone again, a poor, collapsed bottle-holder.

But kicking the insensible King of the Klalams, that dominant nation of the southern shores of Puget's Sound, did not procure me one of his canoes and a crew of his braves to paddle me to Nisqually, my next station, for a blanket apiece and gratuities of sundries. There was no help to be had from that smoky barn or its sorry inmates, so regally nicknamed by British voyagers. I left them upon their dirty mats, among their fishy baskets, and strode away, applying the salutary toe to each dignitary as I passed.

Fortunately, without, I found the Duke of York, only ducally drunk. The duke's share of the potables had added some degrees to the arc of vibration of his swagger, but had not sent it beyond equilibrium. He was a reversed pendulum, somewhat spasmodic in swing, and not constructed on the compensation principle— when one muscle relaxed, another did not tighten. However, the Duke was still sober enough to have speculation in his eyes, and as he was Regent now, and Lord High Admiral, I might still by his favor be expedited.

It was a chance festival that had intoxicated the Klalams, king and court. There had been a fraternization, a powwow, a wah-wah, a peace congress with some neighboring tribe . . . and just as the festival begun, there had come to Port Townsend . . . a devil-send of a lumber brig, with liquor of the fieriest. An orgy followed, a nation was prostrate.

The Duke was my only hope. Yet I must not betray eagerness. A dignitary among Indians does not like to be bored with energy. If I were too ardent, the Duke would grow coy. Prices would climb to the unapproachable. . . . My big talk with the Duke of York went on in a lingo somewhat as follows: "Pottlelum mitlite King Jawge—Drunk lieth King George," said I. "Cultus tyee ocook—a beggarly majesty that. Hyas tyee mika—a mighty prince art thou—pe kumtux skookoom mamook esick—and knowest how robustly to ply paddle. Nika tikky hyack klatawah copa Squally, copa canim—I would with speed canoe it to Squally. Hui pississy nika potlatch pe hui ikta—store of blankets will I give and plenteous sundries."

"Nawitka siks—yea, friend," responded the Duke, grasping my hand after two drunken clutches at empty air. "Klosche nika tum tum copa hyas Baasten tyee; tender is my heart toward thee, O great Yankee don. Yaka pottlelum—halo nika—wake cultus mann Dookeryawk—he indeed is drunk—not I—no loafer-man, the Duke of York. Mitlite canim; got canoe. Pe klosche nika tikky klatawah copa Squally—and heartily do I wish to go to Squally."

Had the Duke wavered still and been apathetic to temptation of blankets, and sympathetic toward the joys of continued satur-nalia, a new influence now brought to bear would have steadied him. One of his Duchesses, only duchessly intoxicated, came forth from the ducal lodge, and urged him to effort.

"Go, by all means, with the distinguished stranger, my love," said she, in Chinook, "and I will be the solace of thy voyage. Perchance, also, a string of beads and a pocket mirror shall be my meed from the Boston chief, a very generous man, I am sure."

Then she smiled enticingly, her flat-faced grace, and introduced herself as Jenny Lind, or as she called it, "Chin Lin."

Indianesque, not fully Indian, was her countenance. There was a trace of tin in her copper color, possibly a dash of Caucasian blood in her veins. Brazenness of hue was the result of this union, and a very pretty color it is with eloquent blushes mantling through it, as they do mantle in Indian cheeks. Her forehead was slightly and coquettishly flattened by art, as a woman's should be by nature, unless nature destines her for missions foreign to feminineness, and means that she shall be an intellectual round-head, and shall sternly keep a graceless school to irritate youthful cherubim into original sinners. . . .

At last persuaded by his own desires and the solicitations of his fair Duchess, the Duke determined to transport me. He pointed to a grand canoe on the beach. . . . "Hyas tyee Dookeryawk, wake pottlelum—kumtux skookoom mamook esick, pe tikky hyack klatawah copa Squally—mighty chief the Duke of York, not drunk, understand to ply paddle mightily and want to go fast to Squally." . . .

"And now," continued the Duke, drawing sundry greasy documents from the pocket of that shapeless draggle-coat of his, "mika tikky nanitch nika teapot—wilt thou inspect my certificates?"

I took the foul papers without a shudder. . . . There was nothing ambiguous in the wording of these "teapots." . . . The Duke's testimonials were signed by Yankee skippers, by British naval officers, by casual travelers—all unanimous in their opprobrium. He was called a drunken rascal, a shameless liar, a thief; called each of these in various idioms, with plentiful epithets thrown in. . . . Such certificates he presented gravely, and with tranquil pride. He deemed himself endorsed by civilization, not branded. Men do not always comprehend the world's cynical praise.

It seemed also that his Grace had once voyaged to San Francisco in what he called a "skookoom canim copa moxt stick—a colossal canoe with two masts." He did not state what part he played on board, whether cook, captain, stowaway, or Klalam plenipo to those within the Golden Gate. His photograph had been taken at San Francisco. This he also exhibited in a grandiose manner. . . .

Now it must not be supposed that the Duke was not still ducally drunk, or that it was easy to keep him steady in position or intention. . . . Our preparations went heavily enough. Sometimes the whole party would squat on the beach and jabber for ten minutes, ending always by demanding of me liquor or higher wages. But patience and purpose always prevail.

At last, by cool urgency, I got them on board and away. Adieu Port Townsend, then a town of one house on a grand bluff, and one sawmill in a black ravine. Adieu intoxicated lodges of Georgius Rex Klalamorum! Adieu Royalty! Remember my kick, and continue to be h'happy as you may.

From *The Canoe and the Saddle*, Theodore Winthrop (Boston: Ticknor and Fields, 1864).

XLI

James G. Swan

The high aims of the missionaries, both Protestant and Catholic, had fallen short of their mark, whether at Port Townsend or Walla Walla, on the Clearwater or on the Columbia. The red men—with the possible exception of the Nez Percés—just didn't seem to get the message. In appraising the accomplishment, no one would have been more considerate of all concerned than James G. Swan (1818–1900), like Winthrop a Bay Stater, and unlike Winthrop a man with a great respect for Indians anywhere. After living with them for many years in the Northwest, studying them, working with them, and teaching them, he felt compelled to admit that the missionaries had not been very successful.

Swan had started out as a Boston ship chandler, but his real interest was in the West. He joined the gold rush; tried chandlery and ship proprietorship on the Sacramento River; shifted residence to Willapa Bay, where he went into the oyster trade; was a collector for the Smithsonian Institution and a secret agent for the Northern Pacific Railroad, an Indian Agent and finally director of the Makah Indian School at Neah Bay. He became the foremost authority on Indian culture of western Washington and the Territory's greatest historian. For fifty years he studied Indians and concluded that they made pretty poor converts.

But Words of Foolishness

All the Indian fasts or observances I have witnessed bore no resemblance to any form which we denominate worship. . . . They have each a private *tomanawos,* or guardian spirit, to whom they make all their wants known, and that in the most private manner. It must not be supposed, however, that they have no religious sentiment. In fact, the Indian is at all times impressed with the sense of the actual presence of his *tomanawos;* and whatever he does, whether it be good or bad, stealing or helping, murdering or giving aid, he always looks for assistance from his *tomanawos.* The only outward demonstration of address to the spiritual world that I saw was during cases of sickness or when bewailing the dead.

All of them had a general idea of the Christian religion, but not one believed it, although several had been considered, during the residence of the priest at Chinook, as exemplary members of the church. But when the restrictions of the church were taken away by the absence of the priest, they all returned to their old heathenism again. They cannot strictly be termed idolators, for they do not worship the outward symbols of anything: that is directly opposed to their system of studiously concealing the name of their *tomanawos;* and if that *tomanawos* should chance to have been a bear or a salmon, by making an image of either and addressing it in terms of adoration or supplication, they would at once reveal the name and object of their secret worship.

The only way, in my opinion, in which an Indian can be thoroughly changed and Christianized is by either taking the child from its parents and bringing it up under Christian instruction, and away from tribal influences and prejudices, or by gradually civilizing the tribe and letting the rising generation

make the change. In all the accounts we have that are to be relied
upon, it will be seen that any and all Christian Indians are those
of a generation succeeding that to whom the missionaries first
addressed themselves; and all the missionaries who have really
and truly succeeded, have done so first by teaching the Indian the
manners of a civilized life and gradually, as he became accustomed to a change of life, they could teach him a change of
heart.

All other converts, or seeming converts, who have been suffered
to live in their primitive style, are sure at heart to retain their
ancient religion. Nor is this strange. From their earliest infancy
they have heard the legends and mythological tales told them
daily, and on every occasion, by the ancient people, by their own
parents, and repeated by their playfellows. These early impressions cannot easily be eradicated.

The same difficulties in approaching the Indian tribes was
experienced in the early settlement of the country. The missionaries are not always chosen from the right class of people; zealous
themselves, they press their zeal without knowledge and attempt
to make the Indians understand the mysterious doctrines of our
religion, when, in fact, the Indian is like an infant scarce able
either to talk or understand. . . .

One day a number of children were . . . very busy on the
beach where they seemed intently engaged in some very quiet
games. I went where they were seated and found they were
playing church, and were imitating the Catholic service that they
had seen at Chinook. One smart little fellow about fifteen years
old, named Quellahho, was officiating as priest, and had proceeded so far as the baptism, which at that time he was engaged
in, bestowing names on all the dolls belonging to the party.

He would rattle over the Latin, or what to him seemed as such,
giving the priest's intonations in a most astonishing manner, and
so nearly right that a person at a short distance might readily
suppose he was actually performing the Catholic service. As the
girls objected to his putting water on their babies, he was using
dry sand instead, and when it came the time to chant, they all
joined in as near an imitation as they could.

When I came up they did not observe me till I had watched them some time, when they all got into the greatest glee, thinking the whole subject a capital joke. *"Ensika mamoke heehee La Plate,"* or "We are playing priest," said they in answer to my inquiry on what they were doing. I told them it was not right for them to make fun of the priest, and they must not play priest any more. They promised that they would not—but insisted that their dolls should retain the names their priest had given them.

I afterward found that this was one of the favorite plays with the children; it showed how much value the ritual of the church had either in their eyes or in their parents', who used to encourage them to mimic the ceremonies that they had seen. . . .

The present state of the Indian population in Oregon and Washington does not reflect much credit on their Christian acquirements; and although in times of peace they are willing to flock round the missions and receive spiritual as well as temporal food, yet no sooner does an opportunity occur when they can raise the war-whoop than we find these Christian converts among the most ruthless of the savages in their horrid deeds of blood.

The Indians can see but little or no difference between their system of *tomanawos* and our own views as taught them. For instance, the *talipus,* or fox, is their emblem of the creative power; the *smispee,* or duck, that of wisdom. And they say that the Boston people, or Americans, have for their *tomanawos* the *wheark,* or eagle, and that the King George, or English people, have a lion for their *tomanawos.*

In matters of religion, as taught them by the priest, they have no idea of their spiritual signification. The emblem of the Holy Spirit is to them a simple pigeon, and the Agnus Dei but a sheep, *la mouton* being the only word which can be used to express the meaning of the emblem. Nor can they be made to understand or believe the miraculous history of our Savior's birth. The difficulty with these, as with all other savage tribes, is the want of suitable words to convey our ideas.

The Indian must first be taught the English language, and then he can understand what the English or Americans wish to teach them; for it is impossible in their barbarous jargon to convey any but the most commonplace ideas. . . . As the country becomes more thickly settled, and they are brought more in contact with civilization, their condition may improve, and they become able to understand what to them now are but words of foolishness.

From *The Northwest Coast,* James G. Swan (New York: Harper and Brothers, 1857).

XLII

Lawrence Kip

Most of the problems in Washington Territory were now Indian problems, which agents, appointed in the other Washington, were trying to settle at magnificent powwows. The conclave at which Chief Seattle delivered his epic address was a grand and glittering affair, but it could scarcely stand comparison with the far larger and more spectacular council that opened May 23, 1855, thirty miles east of Fort Walla Walla. Its purpose was the same as that of the Puget Sound assembly—to consider a treaty under which the Indians of the interior would evacuate their lands and withdraw to reservations.

Lawrence Kip (1836–1899), author of *Army Life on the Pacific*, an urbane, lighthearted lieutenant who was dispatched upriver from his station at Fort Vancouver with a company of forty men to serve as honor guard for Governor Stevens, made the most of his opportunity to describe the proceedings—probably the most picturesque council in the history of American-Indian relations. In all the flow of ambiguous oratory, the reversals of stand, the circumlocution and confusion of tongues, frequently no one knew what was going on; and only General Joel Palmer, then in charge of Indian Affairs in Oregon, appeared to have the slightest intimation of the peril to which a handful of white men were exposing themselves in the presence of five thousand largely hostile tribesmen of a half-dozen different nations.

Of More than One Heart

Wednesday, May 23rd [1855]. At two o'clock P.M. we arrived at the ground selected for the Council, . . . one of the most beautiful spots of the Walla Walla Valley, well wooded and with plenty of water. Ten miles distant is seen the range of the Blue Mountains, forming the southeast boundary of the great plains along the Columbia. . . . It stretches away along the horizon until it is lost in the dim distance, where the chain unites with the Snake River Mountains.

Here we found General [Joel] Palmer, the Indian Agent, and Governor Stevens, with their party, who had already pitched their tents. . . . As was proper for the highest dignitary on the ground, he had a dining room separate from his tent. An arbor had been erected near it, in which was placed a table, hastily constructed from split pine logs, smoothed off, but not very smooth. . . .

Thursday, May 24th.— . . . About 2500 of the Nez Percé tribe have arrived. It was our first specimen of this Prairie cavalry, and it certainly realized all our conceptions of these wild warriors of the plains. Their coming was announced about ten o'clock, and going out on the plain to where the flag staff had been erected, we saw them approaching on horseback in one long line. They were almost entirely naked, gaudily painted and decorated with their wild trappings. Their plumes fluttered above them, while below, skins and trinkets and all kinds of fantastic embellishments flaunted in the sunshine.

Trained from early childhood almost to live upon horseback, they sat upon their fine animals as if they were centaurs. Their horses, too, were arrayed in the most glaring finery. They were painted with such colors as formed the greatest contrast; the white being smeared with crimson in fantastic figures, and the dark colored streaked with white clay. Beads and fringes of gaudy colors were hanging from the bridles, while the plumes of eagle feathers interwoven with the mane and tail fluttered as the breeze swept over them, and completed their wild and fantastic appearance.

When about a mile distant, they halted and half a dozen chiefs rode forward and were presented to Governor Stevens and General Palmer in the order of their rank. On came the rest of the wild horsemen in single file, clashing their shields, singing and beating their drums as they marched past us. They formed a circle and dashed around us while our little group stood there, the center of their wild evolutions. They would gallop up as if about to make a charge, then wheel round and round, sounding their loud whoops until they had apparently worked themselves up into an intense excitement. Then some score or two dismounted, and forming a ring, danced for about twenty minutes while those surrounding them beat time on their drums.

After these performances, more than twenty of the chiefs went over to the tent of Governor Stevens, where they sat for some time smoking the "pipe of peace" in token of good fellowship, and then returned to their camping ground. The Nez Percés, or pierced-nose Indians . . . are the most friendly to the whites of any tribe in this region; they are at the same time one of the most numerous and powerful. . . . They hunt the elk, the white bear, the mountain sheep and the buffalo, while they trap the beaver to sell the skins to the whites. They are celebrated for their droves of horses. . . .

About seventy women were seen among the warriors, for their presence is necessary when the tribe is to be encamped for any length of time. They perform all the menial offices, arranging the lodge, cooking and bringing wood, for it would be a disgrace to their lords to be seen engaged in these things. . . . Everything but the perils of war and the chase are beneath their attention. When at home and not occupied in preparing their arms, or in feats of horsemanship, they are gambling, lounging in groups on the mounds of the prairie, or listening to some story-teller, who recounts the exploits of the old warriors of the tribe.

The Walla Wallas, another of the principal tribes present, is one much reduced in numbers and in importance since the pioneer trappers first came among them. They range through the valley for thirty miles to old Fort Walla Walla, once a central trading post of the Hudson Bay Company. . . . Towards evening the Cayuse tribe arrived, numbering about three hundred. They came in whooping and singing in the Indian fashion, and after riding around the camp of the Nez Percés two or three times, they retired to form their own at some little distance.

In a short time some of the principal chiefs paid their respects to Governor Stevens and then came down to look at our camp. It was not, as we had reason to believe afterwards, a friendly visit, but rather a reconnaissance to learn our numbers and estimate our powers of resistance. . . .

Sunday, May 27th.— . . . We went to the Nez Percé camp, where we found they were holding service in one of the largest lodges; two of the chiefs were officiating, one of them delivering an address—taking the Ten Commandments for his text—and at the end of each sentence the other chief would repeat it in a louder tone of voice. This is their invariable custom with all their speeches. Everything was conducted with the greatest propriety, and the singing, in which they all joined, had an exceedingly musical effect.

There is an odd mixture of this world and the next in some of the Nez Percés—an equal love for fighting and devotion—the wildest Indian traits with a strictness in some religious rites which might shame those "who profess and call themselves Christians." They have prayers in their lodges every morning and evening, service several times on Sunday—and nothing will induce them on that day to engage in any trading. . . .

After service we rode through the Cayuse camp, but saw no evidence of Sunday there. The young warriors were lounging about their lodges, preparing their arms or taking care of their horses to be ready for their evening races. The Christianity among these Indians, we suspect is confined to the Nez Percés.

Monday, May 28th.— . . . We spent the afternoon at the Nez Percé camp, where a band of some thirty warriors were engaged in dancing and singing. Their musical instruments are few in number and of the rudest kind. The singing is very harsh and to us . . . seemed utterly discordant. The songs are almost entirely extemporaneous, like the Improvisatore recitations of the Italians, a narrative of some past events, or perhaps suggested by the sight of persons present, or some trifling circumstances known to the audience. . . .

Today leading chiefs belonging to some of the most distant tribes, attended by their followers, have been coming into the camp, and most of those for which the Commissioners have been waiting are now represented. Their encampments and lodges are scattered over the valley for more than a mile, presenting a wild and fantastic appearance. . . .

Wednesday, May 30th.—At one o'clock this afternoon the Council met, and business seems to be really commencing. It was a striking scene. Directly in front of Governor Stevens' tent a small arbor had been erected, in which at a table sat several of his party taking notes of everything said. In front of the arbor on a bench sat Governor Stevens and General Palmer and before them in the open air, in concentric semicircles, were ranged the Indians, the chiefs in the front ranks, in order of their dignity, while the far background was filled with women and children. . . . There were probably a thousand present at the time. [The official count was nearer five thousand.]

After smoking for half an hour—a ceremony which with them precedes all business—the Council was opened by a short address from General Palmer. Governor Stevens then rose and made a long speech, setting forth the object of the Council, and what was desired of them, . . . explaining the benefits they would receive from signing a treaty, and the advantages which would result to them from their removal to the new lands offered in exchange for their present hunting grounds. . . . As he finished each sentence, the interpreters repeated it to two of the Indians, who announced it in a loud voice to the rest—one in the Nez Percé and the other in the Walla Walla language. This process necessarily causes business to move slowly. . . .

This evening we went as usual to the Nez Percé camp. There was a foot race, but the great events of the evening were the horse races. Each of the tribes now here possesses large numbers of horses, so that wherever they are, the prairies about them are covered with these animals roaming at large until wanted by their masters. . . . Living as they do on horseback, racing forms one of their greatest amusements. They will ride for miles, often having heavy bets depending on the result. On this occasion we saw nearly thirty Indians start at once and dash over the plain like the winds, sweeping round in a circle of several miles. . . .

Monday, June 4th. . . . The diplomatists met today at half-past one o'clock. After Governor Stevens' address, the old Nez Percé chief, Lawyer, spoke, which was the first time anything had been heard from the Nez Percés. Several of the other chiefs followed, and the Council finally adjourned at five o'clock without having yet made any sensible progress. The maxim that "Time is money," which prevails so extensively among the Anglo-Saxons, has not yet penetrated into the wilderness. . . . With the Indians "the next moon" will answer just as well as this month for any business that is to be transacted. I should think, however, that the Commissioners would have their patience utterly exhausted.

Until a late hour we heard from the Indian camps the sound of their singing and the beating of their drums, and could see the figures flit before the fires as the dancing went on.

Tuesday, June 5th. . . . The same routine of the Council: Governor Stevens at the opening gave them the most elaborate address he has yet made, explaining to the chiefs most definitely what lands he wished them to give up and what their "Great Father," (the President), would give them in return, together with the benefits they would derive from the exchange. General Palmer afterwards made a speech an hour long, in which he endeavored to illustrate to his audience the many advantages resulting from their being brought into contact with civilization.

His reasoning at one time led him to give an account of the Railroad and Telegraph. It was sufficiently amusing to listen to this scientific lecture "quaintly conceived and curiously pronounced, and to a well-chosen congregation," but it probably would have been much more diverting could we have known the precise impressions left upon the minds of his audience, or have heard them talk it over afterwards in their lodges. . . . There is evidently a more hostile feeling towards the whites getting up among some of the tribes. . . .

The races tonight were the most exciting we have seen, as the Indians had bet some sixteen or eighteen blankets—a great stake for them—on the result, and all the passions of their savage natures were called into play. . . . After the races were finished, I concluded to ride into the camp of our amiable friends, the Cayuses, to see how they felt this evening. There was no attempt to exclude us, though if savage and scowling looks could have killed, we should have ended our mortal career this evening in this Valley of the Walla Walla. . . .

Thursday, June 7th. . . . The Council met today at twelve, when I went into the arbor, and taking my seat at the reporters' table wrote . . . a few extracts to show the manner in which these wearisome debates were conducted day after day:

Governor Stevens. "My brothers! we expect to have your hearts today. Let us have your hearts straight out."

Lawyer, the old Nez Percé chief. (The first part of his speech was historical, relating the discovery of this country by the Spaniards, which is a favorite topic with the Indian orators. . . . He thus described the manner in which the tribes at the East receded at the approach of the whites.) "The red men traveled away farther, and from that time they kept traveling away farther, as the white people came up with them. And this man's people" (pointing to a Delaware Indian, who was one of the interpreters) "are from that people. They have come on from the Great Lake where the sun rises, until they are near to us now at the setting sun. And from that country, somewhere from the center, came Lewis and Clark, and that is the way the white people traveled and came on here to my forefathers. They passed through our country; they became acquainted with our country and all our streams, and our forefathers used them well, as well as they could, and from the time of Columbus, from the time of Lewis and Clark we have known you, my friends; we poor people have known you as brothers." (He concluded by expressing his approval of the treaty, only urging that the whites should act towards them in good faith.)

Governor Stevens. "We have now the hearts of the Nez Percés through their chief. Their hearts and our hearts are one. We want the hearts of the other tribes through their chiefs."

Young Chief of the Cayuses. (He was evidently opposed to the treaty. . . .) "I wonder if the ground has anything to say! . . . The ground says, 'It is the Great Spirit that placed me here. The Great Spirit tells me to take care of the Indians, to feed them aright.' The Great Spirit appointed the roots to feed the Indians on. The water says the same thing. The Great Spirit directs me, 'Feed the Indians well.' The grass says the same thing, 'Feed the horses and cattle.' The ground, water and grass say, 'The Great Spirit has given us our names. We have these names and hold these names. Neither the Indians nor the Whites have a right to change these names.' The ground says, 'The Great Spirit has placed me here to produce all that grows on me, trees and fruit.' The same way the ground says, 'It was from me man was made.' The Great Spirit in placing men on the earth desired them to take good care of the ground and to do each other no harm. The Great Spirit said, 'You Indians who take care of certain portions of the country should not trade it off except you get a fair price.' . . ."

General Palmer. "I would inquire whether Peu-peu-mox-mox or Young Chief has spoken for the Umatillas. I would wish to know farther whether the Umatillas are of the same heart.

Owhi, Umatilla Chief. "We are talking together, and the Great Spirit hears all that we say today. The Great Spirit gave us the land and measured the land to us. This is the reason I am afraid to say anything about this land. I am afraid of the laws of the Great Spirit. This is the reason of my heart being sad. This is the reason I cannot give you an answer. I am afraid of the Great Spirit. Shall I steal this land and sell it? Or what shall I do? This is the reason why my heart is sad. The Great Spirit made our friends, but the Great Spirit made *our* bodies from the earth, as if they were different from the whites. What shall I do? Shall I give the land which is part of my body and leave myself poor and destitute? Shall I say I will give you my land? I cannot say so. I am afraid of the Great Spirit. I love my life. The reason why I do not give my land away is that I am afraid I shall be sent to hell. I love my friends. I love my life. . . . This is the reason I cannot give you an answer. I show you my heart. This is all I have to say." . . .

General Palmer. "We have listened and heard our chiefs speak. . . . We were in hopes we should have had but one heart. Why should we have more than one heart? . . . Can we bring these saw mills and these grist mills on our backs to show these people? Can we bring these blacksmith shops, these wagons and tents on our backs to show them at this time? Can we cause fields of wheat and corn to spring up in a day that they may see them? Can we build these schoolhouses and these dwellings in a day? Can we bring all the money that these things will cost, that they may see it? It takes time to do these things. We come first to see you and make a bargain. We brought but a few goods with us. But whatever we promise to give you, you will get. . . . We do not come to steal your land. We pay you more than it is worth. . . . What is it worth to us? Not half what we have offered you for it. Why do we offer you so much? Because our Great Father has told us to take care of his red people. We come to you with his message, to try and do you good." Etc., etc. . . .

All but the Nez Percés were evidently disinclined to the treaty, and it was melancholy to see their reluctance to abandon the old hunting grounds of their fathers, and their impotent struggles against the overpowering influence of the whites. . . .

Friday, June 8th. . . . It seemed as if we were getting on charmingly and the end of all difficulties was at hand when suddenly a new explosive element dropped down into this little political caldron. Just before the Council adjourned, an Indian runner arrived with the news that Looking Glass, the war chief of the Nez Percés, was coming. Half an hour afterwards he with another chief and about twenty warriors came in. . . . Looking Glass, without dismounting from his horse, made a short and very violent speech, . . . an expression of his indignation at their selling the country. The Council then adjourned.

At the races this evening in the Nez Percés camp, we found ten of the young braves who came in that afternoon, basking in the enjoyment of their laurels. Dressed in buffalo skins, painted and decorated in the most fantastic style, they stood in a line on the side of the race ground exhibiting themselves as much as possible and singing songs in honor of their exploits. After the races we rode through the Cayuse camp. They seemed to be in commotion, apparently making preparation to depart.

Saturday, June 9th. . . . On the strength of the assent yesterday given by all the tribes except the Yakimas, the papers were drawn up and brought into the Council to be signed by the principal chiefs. Governor Stevens once more—for Looking Glass' benefit—explained the principal points of the treaty, and among other things told them there would be three Reservations—the Cayuses, the Walla Wallas and Umatillas to be placed upon one—the Nez Percés on another—and the Yakimas on the third, and that they were not to be removed to these Reservations for two or three years. Looking Glass then arose and made a strong speech against the treaty, which had such an effect that not only the Nez Percés but all the other tribes refused to sign it. . . .

The Council was obliged to adjourn until Monday. In the meanwhile, it is supposed that the Commissioners will bring some cogent arguments to bear upon Looking Glass and induce him to accede to the treaty. Near the race ground this evening we found the women collected in circles on the ground, gambling with the most intense earnestness. Like the men they will spend hours around the lodge fires staking everything they have on the changes and chances of the game. . . .

Monday, June 11th. . . . At ten o'clock the Council met. Governor Stevens opened it with a short speech, at the close of which he asked the chiefs to come forward and sign the papers. This they all did without the least opposition. What he has been doing with Looking Glass since last Saturday, we cannot imagine, but we suppose savage nature in the wilderness is the same as civilized nature was in England in Walpole's day and "every man has his price." After this was over, the presents which General Palmer had brought with him were distributed, and the Council, like other legislative bodies, adjourned *sine die*. . . .

We have now ended our connection with the Council and bid adieu to our Indian friends. . . . We subsequently discovered we had been all the while unconsciously treading on a mine.

Some of the friendly Indians afterwards disclosed to the traders that during the whole meeting of the Council active negotiations were on foot to cut off the whites. This plot originated with the Cayuses in their indignation at the prospect of being deprived of their lands.

Their program was first to massacre the escort, which could easily have been done. Fifty soldiers against three thousand Indian warriors out on the open plain made rather too great odds. We should have had time . . . to have delivered one fire and then the contest would have been over. Their next move was to surprise the post at the Dalles, which they could easily have done. . . . This would have been the beginning of their war of extermination upon the settlers.

The only thing which prevented the execution of this scheme was the refusal of the Nez Percés to accede to it, and as they were more powerful than the others united, it was impossible to make this outbreak without their concurrence. Constant negotiations were going on between the tribes, but without effect; nor was it discovered by the whites until after the Council had separated.

Condensed from *The Indian Council in the Valley of the Walla-Walla*, Lawrence Kip (San Francisco: Whitton, Towne and Co., 1855).

XLIII

David Lavender

From the Walla Walla council Governor Stevens pushed on to the more easterly limits of his vast Washington territorial realm, the wilds of Montana, for still further treaty-making assemblages of Indians. His energy was as boundless as his responsibilities and the lands he governed. Moreover, both he and his superiors kept adding to those responsibilities. He was a West Pointer, had been a Brevet-Major in the Army Engineer Corps, held an adjutancy of engineers in the Mexican War, and had served as executive assistant to the Chief of the U.S. Coast Guard Survey; then resigned his commission to accept the governorship of Washington Territory, a concurrent superintendency of Indian Affairs, and several other appointments that would have occupied anyone else full time.

Military man though he was, he had little reverence for Army regulations and the Army way of doing things. At heart he was as independent as a rebel and cherished his new civilian employment because of the freedom of action it gave him, yet he retained enough of his military indoctrination to delegate all manner of duties he hadn't time to carry out, expecting his subordinates to execute orders in every detail as only he would have executed them.

When he went off to Montana, he left at the new capital in

Olympia an inexperienced youngster in his early twenties named Charles Mason as acting governor in charge of all military and civil affairs. Stevens had thoroughly drilled into Mason his convictions on the relative superiority of volunteer recruits over regulation soldiery, in case any Indian uprising presented an emergency.

It was in Montana that Governor Stevens learned that his treaties had gone awry, that Indians all the way from Spokane to Seattle had indeed revolted, that the whole Territory was a tinderbox, and worst of all, that, though volunteers had been called up, the regular army had been obliged to step in. The governor was needed desperately in Olympia, but desperate as was that need, he could not possibly survive a crossing of those hundreds of miles of inflamed terrain, and was urgently advised not to try.

Stevens' journey home to his capital, and his contention with the generals who were usurping his military prerogatives, is recounted in that superb book of the Northwest *Land of Giants* by David Lavender (1910–   ), a son of the West, scholar, teacher, and historian with a rare aptitude for bringing the past to life.

The Short Way Home

As usual, the Americans misunderstood the workings of their own government. The treaties signed at Walla Walla by the Indians would not become operative until ratified by the United States Senate. But the Walla Walla council had scarcely adjourned when word spread that gold had been discovered near Fort Colville on the Columbia. Excited prospectors swarmed across the mountains. If they reflected at all about legal technicalities, they probably concluded that the signing of the treaties gave them every right to enter upon the "erstwhile" Indian lands.

The Yakimas fell upon the trespassers. There may have been outrages, as later charged—Indian women violated, Indian horses stolen. Or it may simply be that the restless savages found the small, ill-armed parties an irresistible temptation.

The survivors of one ambushed group fled back to Seattle with the alarm. Twenty-five-year-old Acting Governor Charles Mason . . . called for volunteers. At approximately the same time (mid-September, 1855) the Yakima agent, A. J. Bolen, determined to investigate. Reasoning that an escort of soldiers would attract rather than forestall resistance, he rode alone northward from the Dalles into the Yakima Valley. Three wild young braves slew him and tried to conceal the murder by burning his and his horse's bodies.

An Indian spy carried word of the killing to the Dalles. From the cantonment there, Major Granville Haller marched against the Indians with eighty-four men and a howitzer. Another fifty men under Lieutenant W. A. Slaughter were ordered to cross Naches Pass from Fort Steilacoom and join Haller. The would-be squeeze play almost turned into a debacle. Several hundred Yakima warriors under Kamiakin killed five of Haller's men, wounded seventeen, captured his mules and made him abandon his howitzer in a precipitate retreat. Warned in time, Lieutenant Slaughter escaped by a night march back across the mountains to Puget Sound.

Slaughter's retreat proved fortunate. Taking advantage of the dearth of troops in the Sound area, the local Indians late in October killed nine settlers along the White River above Seattle. The survivors fled into the town, whose citizens hastily threw up blockhouses and fenced themselves off from land attack by a stockade. Then Slaughter unexpectedly reappeared to discomfit the Indians, and what might have been a general uprising dwindled off into sporadic hit-and-run clashes. One of the victims was Slaughter himself, shot through the heart one evening when he injudiciously exposed himself beside a campfire.

Well before this, the Northwest had braced itself for a major campaign. Regular troops from Fort Vancouver began moving ponderously up the Columbia toward Yakima country. Both Mason of Washington and Governor George Curry of Oregon called for increased numbers of volunteers. . . . A messenger who overtook Governor Stevens in Montana [where he was negotiating other Indian treaties] gasped out an exaggerated account of as many of these details as he knew. He also added an urgent recommendation from officials in the settlements that Stevens not try to reach his office by riding west through hostile territory, but that he retreat instead down the Missouri and journey home by way of Panama.

Stevens refused. Physical fear was no part of his make-up. . . . Straight back through the enemy lands he dashed, over one pass so snowy that Indians crossing it a few days earlier had lost ten of their horses. Taking routes no one expected him to take, he caught first the Coeur d'Alenes and then the Spokanes by such surprise that they decided they had better not join the warring Indians after all.

Eighteen frightened miners had assembled for mutual protection not far from where Stevens held his conference with the Spokanes. He formed them into a militia company, complete with officers, called the Spokane Invincibles. Members of his own party organized under the name of the Stevens Guards. In retrospect it smacks of play acting, but at the time it was deadly serious. Plans were afoot, so the Spokanes warned, for the Yakimas and Walla Wallas to waylay the party; Peu-peu-mox-mox [Walla Walla chief] himself had boasted that he would personally take the governor's scalp. Against these hundreds, perhaps thousands, of embittered warriors, the Invincibles and the Guards could muster scarcely fifty rifles.

William Craig was sent ahead to Lapwai to assemble the Nez Percés. If the tribe was friendly, they could help cut a way through enemy territory. If not—well, perhaps boldness would neutralize them, as it had the Coeur d'Alenes and Spokanes. Stripping equipment and supplies to a minimum, Stevens prepared to follow Craig on a fast dash through the sodden sleet of early December.

To the party's relief and mystification, they did not see a single Indian along the way. At Lapwai they learned why. Regular Army troops and a sprinkling of volunteers under bumbling Major Gabriel Rains had invaded the Yakima country in a fruitless campaign. The Indians easily slid out of the major's inept traps, but at least the sport had kept them occupied.

Peu-peu-mox-mox and his warriors had fared less well. Finding the Hudson's Bay Company's Fort Walla Walla abandoned, the Indians had joyfully burned it—inglorious end to the fabled landmark which Donald McKenzie had erected nearly forty years before. Belatedly worried by what they had done, the Indians then withdrew to their old homelands on the Touchet River. . . . There Oregon volunteers commanded by James Kelley caught up with them.

Under a flag of truce Peu-peu-mox-mox and half a dozen chiefs rode out to talk peace. Kelley gave his terms. Peu-peu-mox-mox sent one of his men to the village to tell the tribe what they must do. The other negotiators were held as hostages—by their own consent. In spite of this, a great horde of Indians attacked. As the outnumbered volunteers edged away from the brushy defiles, the savages worked themselves into proper ecstasy by erecting on the hilltops tall poles bearing white scalps and dancing about them in a frenzy.

As the successive charges came, Peu-peu-mox-mox, though a hostage, howled exhortations to his warriors. During one desperate flurry Kelley ordered the Indian prisoners tied. Peu-peu-mox-mox protested: "No tie men; tie dogs and horses." The struggling savages were nevertheless dragged to the ground. When Peu-peu-mox-mox produced a hidden dagger, one of the volunteers hit him over the head with a gun barrel, killed him, and took his scalp—"a beauty," recalled one witness, "the hair about eighteen inches long, all braided in with beads and eagle feathers."

The battle, which ended in the defeat of the Indians, lasted four days. During that critical period, while every Indian in the vicinity was involved either as a spectator or a participant, Stevens crossed undetected to Lapwai.

Several hundred Nez Percés were assembled there. Most of them were friendly—or became so after learning of the Walla Wallas' defeat. Enrolling a gaily bedecked company as auxiliaries and appointing Craig their lieutenant colonel, Stevens hurried on to a temporary fort which the Oregon volunteers had established two miles above Whitman's old Waiilatpu mission. . . . There the governor was met with word that General Wool, in command of the Department of the Pacific, had appeared at Vancouver and was throwing more obstacles into the prosecution of the war—or at least the war as the settlers wanted it fought—than were the Indians.

John Ellis Wool was seventy-one years old. He had had a successful military career, beginning with the War of 1812. He was used to command and was solidified in the conviction that army methods were the only proper methods—an attitude almost certain to strike sparks from the equally flinty self-assurance of Isaac Stevens. The violent splinter wars of southern Oregon and northern California had persuaded Wool that the whites were often the chief aggressors and that the Indians needed the protection of his troops even more than did the settlers. He felt that the volunteer militia which the territorial governors threw into the field at the least sign of emergency were illegal and inefficient. He even believed that the emergencies were sometimes manufactured to provide pay checks for the volunteers and supply contracts for local merchants.

With these opinions firmly fixed, he set sail in November to see just what was happening in the Northwest. The trip northward from California did not improve his disposition. The weather was tempestuous. As the steamer was wallowing across the Columbia bar a boiler burst and the ship, laden with gunpowder, took fire. Fortunately a breaker hit the crippled vessel's stern and helped boost her over the bar into comparatively quiet water, where soldiers were able to extinguish the blaze.

At Vancouver, Wool learned that Governor Curry of Oregon, who knew the general's feelings about volunteers, had disobeyed regulations by refusing to put his home-mustered troops under command of the Regular Army officers. Infuriated, Wool ordered the Oregon volunteers disbanded. Curry declined. . . . Meanwhile some Washington volunteers had arrived at Vancouver for mustering in. Wool ordered them home. Included in the number was a company recruited by former Indian agent Benjamin Shaw . . . for the express purpose of rescuing Stevens. Nonsense, said Wool. Stevens should do as he had been told and come home via Panama.

All this was relayed to Stevens at the temporary fort on the Walla Walla by Shaw himself. For the time being, however, the governor swallowed his resentment. He had conceived a grandiose plan for a winter campaign, no small part of it based on the construction of a fleet of barges to master the Columbia's difficult supply routes. He dispatched a detailed outline of the scheme to Wool, but almost immediately an unprecedented cold wave turned the Columbia to ice as far as the mouth of the Willamette. Realizing his proposed operation would have to wait, Stevens started a chill ride for Olympia, intending to call on Wool en route. .

The general must have known he was coming, but urgent messages from California led Wool to sail the evening before Stevens arrived. Considering himself insulted once again, the governor crossed to Olympia. There he threw himself energetically into defense measures that included removing all friendly Indians to the west side of the Sound and erecting numerous blockhouses to ward off the unfriendly ones. The danger was acute. On January 26, 1856, Indians attacked Seattle itself, burning outlying houses but being driven off by cannon fire from a warship in the harbor and by the energetic presence of a company of marines.

In February, from California, Wool responded to Stevens' overexcited but now dormant plans for a winter campaign with unnecessary sarcasm. "You should have recollected," he wrote, "that I have neither the resources of a Territory nor the treasury of the United States at my command." Complacently he added, "Still . . . I think I shall be able to bring the war to a close in a few months, provided the extermination of the Indians, which I do not approve of, is not determined on, and private war prevented, and the volunteers withdrawn from the Walla Walla country." . . .

The letter and Wool's failure to call on him during a subsequent visit to the Sound roused Stevens to a furious reply. In 2500 words of sonorous euphemisms he charged Wool with imbecility, inefficiency, untruthfulness, and wanton neglect of duty, especially in failing to let Stevens be rescued by Shaw's volunteers. If any faint possibility of co-ordinating the services had still existed, that letter ended it.

Condensed from *Land of Giants,* David Lavender (Garden City, N.Y.: Doubleday and Company, Inc., 1958).

XLIV

Isaac I. Stevens

For four years the Indian Wars wore on sporadically, spilling over into Oregon and east toward the Rockies—wars with the "canoe" tribes of the coast and the "horse" tribes of the interior. The nature of the battles had much in common with those at the outbreak of hostilities; always the Indians held numerical advantage and usually strategic advantage, but sooner or later they were repulsed. No part of Washington Territory was entirely free of peril; there were major embroilments in Yakima Valley, in the Simcoe Mountains, at Rosalia, at Fort Walla Walla, at the Cascades.

The struggle between regulars and volunteers muddled along, too. Though regulars chalked up most of the major victories, the volunteers, who had fought Indians from covered wagons on the plains, ambushed them on beaver trails, taken pot shots at them from cabins and stockades, in the end won the respect of the professional soldiery.

Not until 1859, four years after Governor Stevens had negotiated his first regional treaties with the different tribes, did Congress get around to ratifying them, to give legal and logical reason for a cease-fire. Then at last the defeated redmen slowly began taking up residence in the reservations—a process that would require another fifty years.

The Indian wars did not yield many heroes worthy of a place in a national hall of fame. Governor Isaac I. Stevens (1818–1862), despite all the equivocation over his personality and policies, came as near to such merit as any. But before the termination of hostilities, he was released as governor to become Territorial delegate to Congress, where he could wage more effectively a propaganda war for Washington. Among the spare-time employments he had carried on while holding the title of Governor was making a survey for a northern railroad from the Mississippi to Seattle, at the request of the President. Incongruous as was the notion of running a railway across that Indian country, in the nation's capital the delegate argued influentially for acceptance of his survey—a major political feat, since no Southerner could see any advantage to the South in planting an expensive line so far north.

But visionary Stevens foresaw Puget Sound as a trade terminal that might outclass any other on the face of the globe, if the country would only build his railroad, and made progress at winning over the Southern dissenters by maintaining that even their cotton crops would eventually be shipped out of Seattle.

Direct Line to Shanghai

A question of the highest importance in connection with the proposed northern railroad is the effect which it will have in securing for this country the control of the Asiatic trade. . . . The position of this country, standing midway between the great centers of Asiatic and European population, indicates its future commercial greatness. Facing our Pacific possessions, and separated from them by the smooth Pacific, is a vast region covering an area of over twelve millions of square miles, and having a population of over six hundred millions, the outlets of whose commerce and productions are nearer . . . than to the ports of any European nation. . . .

The trade of this vast region, including China, Japan and the

Asiatic Archipelago, has been the great commercial prize in ancient and modern times. Persia, Assyria, Carthage and Rome each swayed the world, as it controlled the commerce of the East. Venice, Genoa, Lisbon, Amsterdam and London each in its turn attained commercial supremacy as it became the dispenser of eastern luxuries to the western world. . . .

An important fact bearing upon the feasibility of diverting the trade of Asia from the old channels is the comparative nearness of our Pacific possessions to the city of Shanghai, which is most favorably situated to become the future emporium of China, and the outlet of trade for over three hundred millions of people, who are just beginning to break away from that exclusive policy which has for so many centuries shut them out from the rest of the world. . . . Shanghai, which may be called the New Orleans of China, is distant only 5,000 miles from Puget Sound, and the route passes by Japan with its fifty millions of inhabitants—Jeddo being only 3,660 miles distant from Puget Sound.

Nature has clearly indicated the northern pathway for the commerce from the future mart of Asiatic trade to this country and Europe. The Great Lakes carry us water-borne halfway across the continent. The proposed road communicates on a direct line with the northern Lake trade—the most wonderful internal commerce the world has ever known—a traffic which is stated to have amounted in 1851 to $326,000,000, employing 74,000 tons of steam and 138,000 tons of sea vessels. It intersects the Mississippi River and thus communicates with the Southern States. It is on the line of the great wheat-producing region of America; and, above all, it is on the direct line of the shortest distance between the centers of European and Asiatic population.

The opening of this avenue is already eagerly sought by our own people to facilitate the exchange of their products with those of Asia. From New York to Shanghai, by way of Cape Horn and Lima, the sailing distance is 21,000 miles. By way of the Cape of Good Hope the distance is about 15,000 miles. From New York to Shanghai, by way of the proposed railroad and Puget Sound, the distance will be 7,800 to 8,000 miles. . . .

In predicting the future course of Asiatic trade, it is presumed that lines of steamships will be established between Shanghai and our Pacific possessions. The coal of Puget Sound, lying on the route from San Francisco to Shanghai, will furnish the necessary combustible. It is also presumed that the difficulty of carrying freight . . . will be greatly overcome by the increased size of vessels—steamships of even 10,000 tons burden being now in the course of construction—and also by mechanical inventions and improvements in motive power. . . . It may be safely assumed that by the time the proposed road is completed the average time on the Pacific, so much more favorable for steam voyages than the Atlantic, will exceed fifteen miles per hour.

When an uninterrupted line of steam communication is established, a portion of the European trade, and nearly all the travel to Asia, must take its course across our continent, and on the northern road as the shortest route. The present sailing distance from Liverpool to Shanghai is 14,400 miles. By way of Puget Sound the distance will be 10,800 miles, a difference equal to a voyage across the Atlantic. . . . The saving of time will carry European travel and mails, even as far as Calcutta . . . by the proposed route. . . . Travel from Shanghai to New York would be performed in eighteen days; from Shanghai to England in thirty days, being a saving of fifty-four days from New York and thirty days from England. . . .

The short route to China is of the utmost importance to this country to facilitate the exportation of goods manufactured from the great American staple. . . . There can be no reasonable doubt that, with the advantages of the rapidity of transit and shortness of distance, all our cotton fabrics . . . will be transported by rail to Puget Sound. It has been estimated that the supply necessary for these new markets will require an amount of cotton equal to the present "entire" crop of upland cotton of the United States. . . . The manufacturing skill and enterprise of the North and the resources of the South are adequate to meet the future demands of an unparalleled trade.

From *Reports of the Explorations and Surveys to Ascertain the Most Practicable and Economical Route for a Railroad from the Mississippi to the Pacific Ocean,* Volume 1. (Washington: Beverley Tucker, 1855) (33rd Congress, 2nd Session, Senate Ex. Doc. No. 78).

XLV

J. Ross Browne

The big talk about Puget Sound's becoming one of the major marts of the world was the more incongruous in view of the nature of the settlements along its shores. Few of the projected port cities were more than ramshackle villages with makeshift landings. Port Townsend was not too far-fetched an example. According to the settlers, great things were destined to happen there; it was going to be the "key city" of the Northwest; its location at the entrance to Puget Sound inevitably betokened that, and already, by virtue of its strategic setting, it was an official port of entry with a customhouse of the United States government.

But as late as 1852 the white population of Port Townsend consisted of exactly "three families and fifteen bachelors." As with most of the Puget Sound villages, during the wars and long afterward, forward-looking, industrious settlers were far outnumbered by loafing Indians, vagabonds, and hangers-on.

It was difficult for a casual visitor to take such a place seriously, and J. Ross Browne (1821–1875), the witty raconteur and satirist of the West, made no attempt to. He dropped in at Port Townsend in 1857, just four years after Theodore Winthrop had called there to cast aspersions on the bibulous habits of Indian royalty, and Browne found the Duke of York, his wives and courtiers in quite the same condition Winthrop had left them. Nor was the handful of white settlers unworthy of a little derision either; the whole town seemed to thrive on whiskey.

Browne was a son of Ireland who had migrated to Kentucky, and on two counts therefore was familiar with better brands of whiskey than those sold on the shores of Puget Sound. "Port Townsend whiskey," he alleged, "would kill the strongest man that ever lived, in less than six months, if he drank nothing else."

Chronically afflicted with wanderlust, Browne had drifted around much of the world, settled down briefly as a shorthand reporter in the chambers of the United States Senate, gone off on a whaling expedition, taken a fling at gold digging in California, and finally accepted a job with the federal Treasury Department in San Francisco. It was as an inspector for that Department that he came to Washington to investigate and curtail the forbidden sale of whiskey to Indians (as well as to make a belated investigation of the Whitman massacre), but he allowed himself to veer into his customary humor in reporting on Port Townsend.

The City Whiskey Built

Port Townsend is indeed a remarkable place. I am not acquainted with quite such another place in the whole world. It certainly possesses natural and artificial advantages over most of the cities of the Atlantic States or Europe. In front there is an extensive water privilege, embracing the various ramifications of Puget's Sound. Admiralty Inlet forms an outlet for the exports of the country and Hood's Canal is an excellent place for hoodwinking the revenue officers.

On the rear, extending to Dungeness Point, is a jungle of pine and matted brush through which neither man nor beast can penetrate without considerable effort. This will always be a secure place of retreat in case of an invasion from a war canoe manned by Northern Indians.

With regard to the town itself, it is singularly picturesque and diversified. The prevailing style of architecture is a mixed order of the Gothic, Doric, Ionic and Corinthian. The houses, of which there must be at least twenty in the city and suburbs, are built chiefly of pine boards, thatched with shingles, canvas and wooded slabs. The palace and outbuildings of the Duke of York are built of driftwood from the sawmills of Port Ludlow, and are eligibly located near the wharf so as to be convenient to the clams and oysters and afford his maids of honor an opportunity of indulging in frequent ablutions. There is somewhat of an ancient and fishlike odor about the premises of his highness, and it must be admitted that his chimneys smoke horribly, but still the artistic effect is very fine at a distance.

The streets of Port Townsend are paved with sand and the public squares are curiously ornamented with dead horses and the bones of many dead cows, upon the beef of which the inhabitants have partially subsisted since the foundation of the city. This, of course, gives a very original appearance to the public pleasure grounds and enables strangers to know when they arrive in the city, by reason of the peculiar odor, so that even admitting the absence of lamps, no person can fail to recognize Port Townsend in the darkest night. . . .

The principal luxuries afforded by the market of this delightful seaport are clams and the carcasses of dead whales that drift ashore, by reason of eating which the natives have clammy skins and are given to much spouting at public meetings. The prevailing languages spoken are the Clallam, Chinook, and Skookum-Chuck or Strong Water, with a mixture of broken English; and all the public notices are written on shingles with burnt sticks and nailed up over the door of the town hall.

A newspaper, issued here once every six months, is printed by means of wooden types whittled out of pine knots by the Indians and rubbed against the bottom of the editor's potato pot. The castoff shirts of the inhabitants answer for paper. For the preservation of public morals a jail has been constructed out of logs that drifted ashore in times past, in which noted criminals are put for safe-keeping.

The first and last prisoners ever incarcerated in that institution were eleven Northern Indians. . . . As the logs are laid upon sand to make the foundation secure, the Indians, while rooting for clams one night, happened to come up at the outside of the jail and finding the watchman who had been placed there by the citizens fast asleep with an empty whiskey bottle in the distance, they stole his blanket, hat, boots and pipe, and bade an affectionate farewell to Port Townsend.

The municipal affairs of the city are managed by a mayor and six councilmen who are elected to office in a very peculiar manner. On the day of election, notice having been previously given on the town shingles, all the candidates for corporate honors go up on the top of the hill back of the waterfront and play at pitch penny and quoits till a certain number are declared eligible, after which all the eligible candidates are required to climb a greased pole in the center of the main public square. The two best then become eligible for the mayoralty and the twelve next best for the common council. These fourteen candidates then get on the roof of the town hall and begin to yell like Indians. Whoever can yell the loudest is declared mayor and the six next loudest become the members of the common council for the ensuing year. . . .

The principal articles of commerce, I soon discovered, were whiskey, cotton handkerchiefs, tobacco and cigars, and the principal shops were devoted to billiards and the sale of grog. I was introduced by the Indian Agent to the Duke, who inhabited that region and still disputed the possession of the place with the white settlers. If the settlers paid him anything for the land upon which they built their shanties it must have been in whiskey, for the Duke was lying drunk in his wigwam at the time of my visit.

For the sake of morals, I regret to say that he had two wives, ambitiously named Queen Victoria and Jenny Lind, and for the good repute of Indian ladies of rank it grieves me to add that the Queen and Jenny were also very tipsy, if not quite drunk, when I called to pay my respects. The Duke was lying on a rough wooden bedstead with a bullock's hide stretched over it, enjoying his ease with the ladies of his household. When the agent informed him that a *Hyas Tyee,* or Big Chief, had called to see him with a message from the Great Chief of all the Indians, the Duke grunted significantly, as much as to say, "That's all right."

The Queen, who sat near him in the bed, gave him a few whacks to rouse him up, and by the aid of Jenny Lind succeeded after a while in getting him in an upright position. His costume consisted of a red shirt and nothing else, but neither of the royal ladies seemed at all put out by the scantiness of his wardrobe. There was something very amiable and jolly in the face of the old Duke, even stupefied as he was by whiskey. He took me by the hand in a friendly manner, and patting his stomach, remarked, "Duke York, belly good man!"

Of course, I complimented him upon his general reputation as a good man, and proceeded to make the usual speech, derived from the official formula, about the Great Chief in Washington, whose children were as numerous as the leaves on the trees and the grass on the plains.

"Oh, damn!" said the Duke impatiently, "him send any whiskey?"

No, on the contrary, the Great Chief had heard with profound regret that the Indians of Puget Sound were addicted to the evil practice of drinking whiskey, and it made his heart bleed to learn that it was killing them off rapidly, and was the principal cause of all their misery. It was very cruel and very wicked for white men to sell whiskey to the Indians, and it was his earnest wish that the law against this illicit traffic might be enforced and the offenders punished.

"Oh, damn!" said the Duke, turning over on his bed and contemptuously waving his hand in termination of the interview, "dis *Tyee* no count."

The following year I made bold to pay my old friends [another] visit. A delegation of the Common Council met me on the wharf. There were no hacks yet introduced, but any number of horses were placed at my disposal. The greeting was cordial and impressive. A most complimentary address was read to me by the mayor of the city. . . . These gratifying public demonstrations over, we adjourned to the nearest saloon and buried the hatchet forever in an ocean of the best Port Townsend whiskey. . . . At all events, I think it has been clearly demonstrated that whiskey built a great city.

From "The Great Port Townsend Controversy . . .", *Crusoe's Island*, J. Ross Browne (New York: Harper and Brothers, 1864).

XLVI

Loo-Wit Lat-Kla

The Territory had more than its share of disruptive influences crowded into the 1850s—the Indian wars, lingering disputes with Great Britain over border and island possessions, growing pains from too rapid emigration, regional contention over needed roads, schools, and government to cope with that emigration, flash-in-the-pan fantasies about rail connections with the East, goings and comings to and from the California gold fields; and not the least of the disruption came from little gold rushes of its own.

California gold fever was contagious: it stood to reason that if the precious metal was so liberally distributed through the uplands to the south, the northerly mountains should be equally providential. Substance was added to that fancy in 1855 when gold actually was discovered near the old Hudson's Bay Company post at Fort Colvile. A stampede not unlike those that took place out of Monterey or San Francisco immediately followed. But the Indians objected, and the takings soon proved to be far less rewarding than were similar placers of California.

That burst of enthusiasm faded only to be replaced by greater excitement over a succession of strikes at widely separated points, like the Similkameen River, Wenatchee, Conconully, Ruby Creek, Sultan Basin, Peshastin Creek, and the Swauk country under

Mount Stuart. Thousands of prospectors from far and near swept into those areas the moment word of a find leaked out.

Altogether considerable gold was recovered, but Washington never could work up a boom comparable to those in the Sierra foothills. A few prospectors did hit it rich—very few; the vast majority suffered agonies only to shuffle home fatigued, frustrated, and empty-handed. Most of Washington's real profits from gold mining were to come later from playing host to miners in Idaho, Canada, and Alaska, or from working its own lode deposits with heavy machinery.

Poor independent gold diggers in the Territory usually remained poor, and too embarrassed over their failures to tell their story; they preferred to remain silent and anonymous. However, one typical victim of defeat, with a glimmering sense of humor, hid his identity behind a pseudonym compounded from the Indian name for Mount St. Helens, Loo-Wit Lat-Kla, and told all. His was the tale of many.

Next-Week Gold

The good people of this settlement and vicinity have been subjected to periodical attacks of "gold fever," which has frequently prompted small companies and individuals to start out and spend days and weeks in prospecting the large and small sand bars of Lewis River and the deep gulches of its tributaries for the precious deposits which, to their excited imagination, lay hid but a little way beneath the surface. As these companies rarely failed to find the "color," their return created the most intense excitement. . . .

Each miner was beset with anxious inquirers, whose eyes dilated and sparkled with excitement while he unfolded the small particles of yellow glittering dust which he had carefully saved from his numerous "washings." Although these specimens would now be considered the reverse of encouraging, they were then received as incontestable evidences of immensely valuable "diggings"; and when the miner announced his determination to return "next week," a crowd of anxious men would rush in to inquire whether they, individually and collectively, might not form part of the escort. . . .

While all the explorers persisted in asserting their conviction that gold in immense quantities could be found at many points, which they named, and that with less than ordinary labor handsome fortunes might be realized, not a man, so far as I can ascertain, ever made a second trip to his new El Dorado! . . . Their failure to realize their "piles" was not owing to the scarcity of the precious deposit; but they failed because the season of their arrival was too early or too late; the river was too high or too low; it was too wet or too dry; too much or too little snow; or they could not find the spot after leaving it once; or the men failed from fatigue; their provisions failed because laboring men would eat; or they had no rocker, or tom, or pick, or spade. . . .

Sometime during the month of August, 1860, some six or eight gentlemen proposed to form a small party which would go out on the new trail to Kalima, rusticate awhile and hunt elk, which are said to abound in that vicinity. But before they put their purpose to practice, news of the rich, paying, and highly valuable mines on the North Fork and the Cascade streams reached them, in a manner more than ordinarily authentic.

The plan of the trip was, therefore, somewhat modified and enlarged so as to include both pleasure and, if possible, profit. The deep interest felt, and the anxiety evinced by everyone . . . induced this party to purchase a regular outfit of superior mining tools, an increased supply of provisions, and with a resolute determination to see the "elephant," trunk or no trunk, they directed their course towards the gold regions on the headwaters of Lewis River. . . .

Having completed the necessary preparations, the horses were packed, guns loaded, dogs tied, and about ten o'clock on the morning of the 19th of September, this new party of explorers started out to prospect the "new" mines. . . . We proceeded some four miles on the way when we came to the house of a gentleman, then absent, of which we took peaceable possession, and made ourselves very comfortable by confiscating a large share of provisions, melons, oats and onions. Next morning we were astir betimes, and by eight o'clock were on the trail leading to the Chalacha.

As only one of the party had ever been "from home" in that direction, we duly elected him to the very responsible office of "bell boy," which he accepted with becoming dignity and immediately entered upon the discharge of his onerous duties. . . . While there was but one road and, of course, no possible chance to be mistaken, no rivers to ford and no wolves howling around, our little bell boy rode ahead and conducted the train as well as a grownup man would, while merrily we traveled to the music of the horse bell. . . .

Half a day's travel brought us to Chalacha, a beautiful rolling plain, containing probably three thousand acres of land. Upon it are some improvements which were abandoned during the Indian War. Lately several families have settled upon some of the old claims and are busily engaged in cultivating and improving them. This prairie is surrounded by high mountains, which give it the appearance of great seclusion and loneliness. It really seemed farther from any place than any settlement I had ever visited; still the residents say it is pleasant enough. . . .

Our arrival on the Chalacha did not create the furor which such an expedition as ours would have called forth in the States, but we consoled ourselves with reflecting that the presence even of his Royal Highness could not possibly create a great excitement, there being not more than twenty persons old and young.

Shortly after our camp was pitched, we were visited by a miner who had just come in from the "diggings" above the Canyon. His report of the prospect in that vicinity was flattering; we therefore determined to establish our headquarters at this point, pack ourselves and start for the Canyon next morning.

Before starting, we concluded a bargain by which this miner was to become our guide, he being able, as he stated, to conduct us to the mines in four miles travel, whereas if we took the trail, we would be compelled to go nine miles over a bad road. At the time of our departure, however, he was not quite ready. We took the direction indicated and commenced what proved to be one of the most laborious, vexatious and unprofitable trips conceivable.

Our man did not overtake us as he promised, nor did we see him afterwards, but we learned that he took the other end of the road and made tracks for the settlements for the purpose of making the necessary arrangements to return "next week." We soon became entangled in the gigantic ferns, the thick brush and the swampy swails, so that to make the trip of four miles, we traveled all day.

On the morning of the 23rd we arose before the sun, full of hope and enthusiasm, for here, within three miles of us, according to the positive assurance of reliable men, from $5 to $10 a day could be made. After an early breakfast our company . . . set out prospecting in earnest. All the bars on the east side of the river for three miles from the Canyon were thoroughly examined, then the streams which came in on that side were prospected down to the bed rock.

In every panful of sand or dirt there was the "color," but it was so fine the naked eye could scarcely distinguish it. We bridged the river and passed over to the other side, down which we examined every sand bar and stream until we arrived at the "hole," from which a gentleman informed me he had taken $5 in a few hours. We *failed to get the color.* In order to get back to camp, we were compelled to build a raft, which came near swamping. With our enthusiasm somewhat cooled, weary and worn with fatigue, we reached the camp, no richer, but much wiser.

Two days spent in laborious explorations in and about the Big Canyon Creek and its tributaries convinced us that we were not in a gold region. Indeed, had it not been for the assurance of gentlemen—in whose integrity I have the utmost confidence—that the points to which our attention was particularly directed, would richly remunerate the laborer, we would not for a single moment have entertained the idea that gold could be found in that vicinity in sufficient quantity to pay, for neither its geological formation nor a comparison with other diggings on the Pacific slope and elsewhere, warrants the presumption that paying gold mines will ever be discovered in that portion of the Cascade Range.

Condensed from *Gold Hunting in the Cascade Mountains,* Loo-Wit Lat-Kla. (Vancouver, W.T.: Chronicle Office, 1861).

XLVII

Francis Henry

The general sentiment on Territorial mining voiced by Loo-Wit Lat-Kla was reiterated even more informally by Francis Henry (1827–1893) in a ballad that was to outlive him and become one of the most popular folk songs of the Northwest. The ballad was autobiographical, but an additional twenty stanzas would scarcely have hinted at all the vicissitudes of the ballader's career.

Henry, a native of Illinois and a fervent veteran of the Mexican War, turned up at Olympia in 1862 with the avowed purpose of rallying a troop of cavalry volunteers to fight in the Union cause. But as far as most Washingtonians were concerned, the Civil War might as well have been an engagement on another continent. It was too remote to excite very many patriots into marching all the way back East to participate in a fray no more glamorous than their own Indian wars. In fact, there were draft dodgers who journeyed cross-country to Puget Sound to avoid involvement. Henry met such indifference that he abandoned the undertaking, hung up his uniform, and settled down himself as a civilian surveyor and lawyer.

It was not his first trip to the West Coast. Between law study in Illinois, army service in Mexico, and employment as a deputy U.S. Marshal in Wisconsin, he had sandwiched in a period of gold digging on the Pacific slopes and seen enough of the country to have a hankering to take up residence there. After hanging out an attorney's shingle in Olympia, he entered politics, was repeatedly elected to the legislature, and spent his last years answering to the title of Judge.

His hobby, however, during all his years in Olympia, was dashing off rhymes and song lyrics for the amusement of brethren in the various fraternal lodges to which he belonged. Of all those compositions, the most durable one, adapted to the air of "Rosin the Bow," was his ballad "The Old Settler."

The Old Settler

I'd wandered all over the country,
　　Prospecting and digging for gold—
I'd tunneled, hydraulicked and cradled,
　　And I had been frequently sold.

　　Chorus—
　　　　And I had been frequently s-o-l-d,
　　　　And I had been frequently sold;
　　　　I'd tunneled, hydraulicked and cradled,
　　　　And I had been frequently sold.

For one who gets riches by mining,
　　Perceiving that hundreds grow poor,
I made up my mind to try farming—
　　The only pursuit that is sure.

So rolling my grub in my blankets,
　　I left all my tools on the ground,
And started one morning to shank it
　　For a country they call Puget Sound.

Arriving flat broke in mid-winter,
　　I found it enveloped in fog,
And covered all over with timber
　　Thick as hair on the back of a dog.

As I looked on a prospect so gloomy,
   The tears trickled over my face,
For I thought my travels had brought me
   To the edge of the jumping-off place.

I took up a claim in the forest
   And sat myself down to hard toil;
For two years I chopped and I niggered,
   But I never got down to the soil.

I tried to get out of the country,
   But poverty forced me to stay;
Until I became an old settler,
   Then nothing could drive me away.

And now that I'm used to the climate,
   I think that if man ever found
A spot to live easy and happy,
   That Eden is on Puget Sound.

No longer the slave of ambition,
   I laugh at the world and its shams,
As I think of my pleasant condition
   Surrounded by acres of clams.

From the *Washington Standard*, Olympia, April 11, 1877, with minor revisions given in the *Olympian-Tribune*, September 26, 1893.

XLVIII

Frances Fuller Victor

To prove that the Northwest could produce serious versification as well as doggerel of the Francis Henry variety, and to prove also that appraisals of the country did not have to be entirely in terms of future commerce, gold, timber, potatoes, and things material, along came Frances Fuller Victor (1826–1902) to compete with contemporary Victorian poets of the East and offer an appraisal of Washington in terms of aesthetics and poetic appreciation of setting.

Like most of the white population, she could not claim local nativity. At the age of fourteen she had moved with her family from Rome, New York, to Ohio, where she began her writing career. Her marriage to a naval engineer in 1863 took her to Oregon, where she resided until her husband was lost in a sea disaster twelve years later. After that, she turned to authorship full time, contributing to the San Francisco *Call-Bulletin*, to *Golden Era*, and to *Overland*. Besides poetry and short stories, she wrote two books that ranked for years as standard works on the Northwest: *The River of the West* and *All Over Oregon and Washington Territory*.

She was not only the first woman to be identified specifically as a professional writer of the Northwest, but also the first to proclaim the sheer beauties of the coast and size up the region as a recreational wonderland.

Sunset at the Mouth of the Columbia

There sinks the sun; like cavalier of old,
    Servant of crafty Spain,
He flaunts his banner, barred with blood and gold,
    Wide o'er the western main;
A thousand spear-heads glint beyond the trees
    In columns bright and long,
While kindling fancy hears upon the breeze
    The swell of shout and song.

And yet, not here Spain's gay, adventurous host
    Dipped sword or planted cross;
The treasures guarded by this rock-bound coast
    Counted them gain nor loss.
The blue Columbia, sired by the eternal hills,
    And wedded with the sea,
O'er golden sands, tithes from a thousand rills,
    Rolled in lone majesty—

Through deep ravine, through burning, barren plain,
    Through wild and rocky strait,
Through forests dark, and mountains rent in twain,
    Toward the sunset gate,
While curious eyes, keen with the lust of gold,
    Caught not the informing gleam,
These mighty breakers age on age have rolled
    To meet this mighty stream.

Age after age these noble hills have kept
    The same majestic lines:
Age after age the horizon's edge been swept
    By fringe of pointed pines.
Summers and Winters circling came and went,
    Bringing no change of scene;
Unresting, and unhasting, and unspent,
    Dwelt nature here serene,

Till God's own time to plant of Freedom's seed
  In this selected soil,
Denied forever unto blood and greed,
  But blest to honest toil.
There sinks the sun! Gay Cavalier no more,
  His banners trail the sea,
And all his legions shining on the shore
  Fade into mystery.

The swelling tide laps on the shingly beach,
  Like any starving thing,
And hungry breakers, white with wrath, upreach
  In a vain clamoring.
The shadows fall; just level with mine eye
  Sweet Hesper stands and shines,
And shines beneath an arc of golden sky,
  Pinked round with pointed pines.

A noble scene, all breadth, deep tone and power,
  Suggesting glorious themes,
Shaming the idler who would fill the hour
  With unsubstantial dreams.
Be mine the dreams prophetic, shadowing forth
  The things that yet shall be,
As through this gate the treasures of the North
  Flow outward to the sea.

From *Poems,* Frances Fuller Victor (Author's edition, 1900).

XLIX

Tom S. Hyland

In keeping with all its social, political, and economic changes, the cumbersome northwest cornerstone of the United States was gradually being cut up into parcels of manageable size. After Oregon was split off in 1853, Washington Territory was left still with more magnitude than could be handled effectively from Olympia. Then a decade later, it took on more reasonable proportions when Idaho and Montana were chipped off the eastern flank, and Washington was at last reduced to its final dimensions.

At the time of the first division, there were less than four thousand white residents in the whole sprawling empire; yet ten years later, despite the great territorial reduction of Washington proper, its population was more than three times that figure. The only serious criticism of those residents was their disproportionate allocation by sex. Nine-tenths were male. The recurrent Indian wars, the Whitman massacre, lawlessness, and the generally unsettled conditions had given the Territory a bad reputation as a habitat for women.

What Washington needed more than anything else was womanhood—eligible virgins, the feminine touch, maidens, girls, wives. And only a man with the fertile imagination of a professional booster or an eager bachelor could have thought up the practical, self-evident solution to the dilemma. Asa S. Mercer was both. Import them en masse, suggested Asa.

No sooner had he made the proposal than he went into action. Headlines across the country heralded every step in his recruitment:

HEGIRA OF SPINSTERS

PETTICOAT BRIGADE

CARGO OF HEIFERS

SEWING MACHINES

WIVES FOR THE WIFELESS

MERCER-NARY ADVENTURE

Mercer was blessed and roundly condemned for his wholesale roundup of adventuresses, but in Washington Territory his reward was mostly blessing.

The nation's press followed his every move, sometimes gallantly protective of American femininity, sometimes scandalously vilifying the promoter for his trafficking in womanhood, more often lampooning the whole idea. Labeling Asa "The Moses of this Exodus from New England to the West," an antifeminist writer for *Harper's Weekly* wryly commented: "We wish him success in his undertaking, hoping that this first Exodus may not be the last."

Scores of news stories, articles, and editorials passed judgment on Mercer's 1866 enterprise, and the romance of it all was never allowed to die. Three-quarters of a century after the girls set sail from New York, the facts and embellishments were raked over by a *Time* editor and free lance, Tom S. Hyland (1917–   ) for *American Mercury*.

Around the Horn to Matrimony

This is the chronicle of the Washington man-rush in 1866, a saga of three hundred women who sailed the grim passage around Cape Horn and dared the wrath of man and nature to meet total strangers, be wooed by them and bear their children in the frontier wilderness of Puget Sound. Asa Shinn Mercer, the leader of the expedition, promised only a splendid wilderness and thousands of brawny suitors. For his unusual humanitarianism he was rewarded by the eternal gratitude of numerous bridegrooms and a virtuous manhandling by press and public which left him a discredited bankrupt.

Mercer's epic began in 1861, when he left a small Ohio college and crossed the Great Plains, toiled over the Rockies and up into the chasmal valley of the Snake River and on down the timbered slopes of the Cascade Range to Puget Sound. There he became a leading figure in the small clearings of the vast Pacific forests. He was made President of the University of Washington and his first academic duties were to take up his ax and clear a site for the school, erect the buildings, tour the lumber camps for prospective students and teach all the classes.

Everywhere in the territory he found the same complaint and the same unrest: no women. Indian squaws were common as wives and mistresses of the settlers; their half-breed offspring carried the blood of men whose names are now historic. But this was only an aggravation of the problem. It was not alone a biologic lack: it was a lack of the homemaker, the mother, the companion. And the economic progress of the territory was blighted.

Young Mercer decided that women, not learning, was the first need of the frontier. He suggested that the state officially subsidize female immigration. The governor, the legislature and the voters were willing, to a man, but the public treasury was empty. Private contributors pitched in, however, and Mercer went to Boston, where he urged young women, orphaned or widowed by the Civil War, to accompany him to Puget Sound. Scores of girls volunteered to go, but at sailing time only eleven found courage to risk being transplanted. They arrived in Seattle via Panama on midnight of May 16, 1864.

This haul of only eleven girls made Mercer the most famous man in the Sound country. Within a few months all the girls were married. An election swept Mercer into the territorial legislature and the imaginative young man began to plot a tremendous raid on the marriageable females of the East. Late in 1865 he set out

again. "I had been taught to believe, and did believe," he observed nobly, "that practically all the goodness in the world came
from the influence of pure-minded women."

He planned to win President Lincoln's help. "Knowing the
goodness of his heart," said Mercer, "not a shadow of a doubt
existed in my mind as to the outcome." Arriving from Panama, he
found New York City hung with crepe: Lincoln had been shot the
night before. His plans, built wholly on his simple faith in
Lincoln's help, were shattered. Forlorn and bewildered, he
traveled to the nation's capital, where he found that President
Johnson, the Cabinet and many Senators favored sending wives to
the citizens of Puget Sound. But in spite of their unanimous
devotion to home and family, they were one and all unwilling to
give more than their blessing to the cause.

Luckily, Mercer found one backer who was indifferent to the
electorate. It was Ulysses Grant. From his service in the forts on
Puget Sound, General Grant had a vivid memory of loveless men,
sordid squaws and half-breed bratlings. He persuaded Johnson
and the Cabinet to donate a steamboat, but they insisted that any
blame was to be Grant's alone.

Half an hour after executive approval, Grant gave Mercer an
order on the quartermaster of the Army for a large steamship.
Mercer's faith in his vision soared again. Thinking the ship was as
good as his, he hurried off at once to fill it to the hatches with
unwed females. Speeches in Boston's churches and notices in
New York newspapers attracted five hundred women in no time.
Then he hurried back to Washington to claim his ship. But the
Army's quartermaster, in a peevish mood, held that Grant's order
was illegal and refused to honor it.

Mercer's plans again collapsed. He returned to New York to
gloom away several wintry weeks. Suddenly the quartermaster
retreated from his position and offered a new Army transport for
$80,000 cash—one-third its real value. But Mercer was broke.
Washington Territory, so the overland telegraph clicked, was also
broke. The money was nowhere in sight and young ladies with
carpetbags were pouring into New York to claim the promised sea-
borne voyage to matrimony.

At that point, Ben Holladay and two silk-hatted lawyers stepped into the drama. Holladay ran a coast-to-coast express line by stagecoach and ship. He proposed that Mercer allow him to snap up the bargain steamship, and in return, he would take five hundred ladies to Puget Sound at a very low price per head. Mercer signed on the dotted line.

Buoyant once more, Mercer prepared to embark with his husband-seekers when a new blow upset his plans. The New York *Herald* published lurid charges on its front page that the girls were really destined for brothels. Puget Sound's men were all debauched, the *Herald* said, and any female who cherished her virtue—or, less important, her life—should stay at home. The sensational attack was reprinted everywhere. Half of Mercer's gentle flock tearfully canceled their passages. The remainder doubted the sinfulness of Puget Sound—or else felt they were doubly needed to win its men from perdition.

Frantically Mercer printed his references and denials, then rushed to Holladay's office to plead for time to fill his ranks. The stagecoach magnate announced bluntly that the contract was off: it had called for no less than five hundred passengers in order to get cheap fares. He offered to carry the remainder, however, at regular fares. "Then," Mercer reported bitterly, "I saw the little joker in the contract." And before he left the office, Mercer also perceived that it was Holladay himself who had inspired the tales of brothels and rampant lechery. Holladay got a $240,000 vessel for $80,000; Mercer got nothing. Such were the business ethics of that era.

Asa Mercer heroically rallied his protégées, persuaded some to pay their own passages, borrowed money for others, and at last prepared to cast off in Ben Holladay's new *Continental,* with three hundred women. On January 6, 1866 a great crowd cheered the laden vessel out of New York harbor, but the clamor was dim in Mercer's ears. He was hiding in the coal bunkers. His many creditors in New York had begun to threaten and growl; Mercer alone saw that Puget Sound's need for women was more urgent than his creditors' need for silver. . . .

The *Continental* was no faery bark. By the time it reached the mouth of the Amazon, the first mate was in chains for the brutal murder of a seaman. Only a partial fumigation and the addition of an organ for evening hymns had converted the Army transport into a three months' dwelling for young ladies. Food was bad and scarce. Ben Holladay, from whom all blessings flowed, did not let gallantry trim his profits. Etiquette was abandoned as the girls stormed the tables each day to snatch a few bits of fried liver. For seventeen consecutive days the menu was boiled beans with salt-water tea. At the captain's table, however, the food was rich and plentiful. . . . The girls often joined the waiters in scavenging the remains of the captain's feast.

Romance outranked hymns as the chief shipboard diversion. . . . Even Mercer fell in love as soon as he emerged from the bunkers and looked over his cargo, but the lady rebuffed him. He transferred his affections to another belle and married her as soon as they reached California. . . . Ninety-six days out of New York, the *Continental* steamed into the Golden Gate. Mercer described the arrival graphically:

> As we sailed up along the wharves, a black surging mass crowded every avenue of approach for three or four miles. Even at a distance we could hear the mighty cheers that swept across the water. The anchor had not touched bottom before the sea was alive with hundreds of boats pushing out to us. The air was lively with songs and shouts. There was quite a rivalry among the boats to get along-side for a glimpse of my precious cargo. One man attempted to make it by climbing up the ship's side on a rope, but I stood by the railing and knocked him off. This action, noted by thousands of spectators, was greeted with cheers.

This furore was inspired, Mercer complained, by "evil-minded gossips who were at work spreading scandalous reports of the character of the women and the object of my mission." The New York *Herald* had won Mercer nationwide fame as a wholesale procurer, and pure or impure women were almost as rare in California as in Washington. Good folk came down to the ship to dissuade the girls from continuing their journey into sin. San Francisco's papers dinned warnings of the crudity and lust infesting Puget Sound, blandly ignoring the city's own iniquities.

As his own contribution to the Mercer girls' ruin, Ben Holladay refused to take the girls on to Puget Sound. Mercer spent his last two dollars on a desperate telegram to the governor of Washington. He received in reply (collect) a hundred words of congratulation and no mention of money. Somehow he arranged passage northward for his girls on lumber schooners and accompanied the first party of forty himself. . . .

As the schooner *Tanner* neared Seattle, the passengers heard rumors from port to port that the settlers were angry at the bad name Mercer had brought upon them. More important were Mercer's financial dealings. Friends and relatives in Washington had given him large sums for purchases and investments in the East. With that sublime faith in his visions which had already caused him so much trouble, he had diverted all these funds to his immigration project. A defrauded investor could scarcely attach two or three blooming virgins as security for his money. A kindly cleric advised Mercer to enter Seattle as he had left New York—deep in the hold.

But the grandeur of his efforts filled Mercer with daring. He ignored reports that his life was in danger. As the ship approached the crowded wharf, Mercer stood boldly on the prow and swung his hat, as he later recalled, "with something of a triumphant air." The men on the wharf broke into cheers and tossed their hats into the sky. Plans for a lynching were forgotten. . . . Within six months most of the girls were wooed and wedded. . . .

As for Mercer, he was weary and bankrupt, cold-shouldered by his former friends. He left Washington to its new devices and wandered through Oregon, Texas, Arizona and Wyoming, changing his business and his homes, but he always glowed with faith in his visions and the West. . . . He fostered hundreds of marriages, in an era when they were presumed to be made in Heaven, and he invigorated a great American state. His achievements were unique.

From "Around the Horn to Matrimony," Tom S. Hyland. *American Mercury,* October, 1942.

L

James F. Rusling

Mercer's damsels couldn't take all the credit for the new bloom of civilization that seemed to sweep over the Territory about the time they arrived. Men and events made their contributions, too. With the capitulation of the Indian tribes, old war paths were being turned into thoroughfares of progress; and with Hudson's Bay Company officials no longer dictating developments in commercial policy, Americans now felt freer to experiment with individual enterprise—open shipyards, plant ever larger wheatfields, start coachlines, try out irrigation schemes, erect sawmills.

The influx of Argonauts into California had created a mass market for housing—lumber, more lumber, incredible quantities of boards, timbers, shingles. Their own fir and redwood mills couldn't begin to fill the demand. The nearest inexhaustible source was on Puget Sound and the Columbia River. Fleets of freighters plied north to load lumber as fast as it came, green and warm, from the saws. The lumber boom was on.

Then the tide of gold seekers itself swung northward from California—100,000 strong—pushing through the Territory en route to strikes in Boise City, Clearwater, Oro Fino, Powder River, Coeur d'Alene. They demanded transportation up the Columbia, and they got it. Coasters turned into riverboats; side-wheelers and stern-wheelers brought shiploads of miners from the Sacramento and stayed on to ferry men and supplies up and down the big river and into its tributaries. Other vessels that had seen service on Eastern rivers took the precarious course around the Horn to join the Columbia fleet.

Far up the Columbia or the Snake, beyond falls and unnavigable white water, sprang up little temporary shipyards, where more boats were built to navigate shorter sections of the waterways. Horse-drawn or ox-drawn portages around cascades were replaced with makeshift rail lines. The Oregon Steamship Navigation Company was born, with an imposing monopoly of steamboats, such as the *Jason P. Flint, Carrie Ladd, Wasco,* and *Mountain Bird.* At the height of the mining rush, a prospector could board a steamer at Fort Vancouver, and with frequent changes of craft, travel by public conveyance all the way to Revelstoke, British Columbia, or east to Lewiston, Idaho. With or without women, the whole Territory had suddenly opened.

The year after Appomattox, one of the Union's lesser generals, James D. Rusling (1834–1918), a pre-war New Jersey lawyer, was given the assignment of inspecting all the army posts in the Military Division of the Pacific, a tour that was to take him overland from Kansas to San Francisco by way of Denver, Salt Lake, Boise City, and Fort Vancouver. His rank gave him considerable latitude on both his mode and rate of travel, and he elected to make the trip in as leisurely and luxurious a fashion as the nature of the expedition allowed, lining up a task force of army mule skinners, guards, cooks, and cavalry to do his bidding; and to cushion the jolts of the journey for himself, he requisitioned the plushest vehicle in the quartermaster's depot—an ambulance.

All these comforts and conveniences left him free to concentrate on his official inspection reports, and on a less official, amusing, and enlightening memoir of his experiences, *Across America.* His personal enjoyment of the jaunt, however, fell short of his expectations. "Jordan is a hard road to travel," he acknowledged, "and anything but romantic." He suffered through blistering heat waves, prairie storms, mountain blizzards, supply shortages, traffic congestion with other overlanders, and, at last, even a breakdown of his ambulance. His delight on reaching Umatilla on

the Columbia was unconfined. He boarded one of those diminutive riverboats, and on it catalogued a typical down-river cruise.

Back to Civilization

Good-bye, driver—Good-bye, mustangs and donkeys! Good-bye
stagecoaches and ambulances! Two thousand four hundred miles
of their drag and shake, of their rattle and bang, across the Plains
and over the mountains, had given us our fill of them. We had
had runaways, we had had breakdowns, and about every experience except a general upset, and how we happened to escape that
will always remain a mystery. . . . There before us now lay the
lordly Columbia, with visions of steamboats and locomotives.
And looking back on our long jaunt with all its discomforts and
dangers, it seemed for a moment as if nothing could induce us to
take it again. Hereafter, we felt assured, we should appreciate the
comfort and speed of eastern travel more, and pray for the
hastening of all our Pacific railroads. . . .

Ding! Dong! Puff! Puff! The steamer had come, and November
28th we at length embarked for down the Columbia. She was a
little stern-wheel boat, scarcely longer than your finger, called
Nez Percé Chief, Captain Stump, master. Her fare to Fort Vancouver or Portland, including railroad portages, was $18 in coin,
which at rates then current was equivalent to $25 in greenbacks.
Meals were extra, at a cost of $1.50 each, in currency, besides.
The distance to Portland was about 200 miles; to the mouth of the
Columbia, 100 or so more.

We found Captain Stump a very obliging Oregonian. . . . His
boat was part of a line belonging to the Oregon Steam Navigation
Company, a gigantic corporation that controlled all the navigable
waters of the Columbia, and with far-reaching enterprise was
now seeking to connect them with the headwaters of the Missouri. . . . These were weighty facts, marrying the Pacific to the
Atlantic; but Captain Stump thought the O.S.N. Company could
accomplish them, or anything else, indeed, it seriously under-

took . . . and he said it would beat the Northern Pacific Railroad yet. . . .

And so we were off down the Columbia at last. How exquisitely pleasant, how cosy and delightful, our little steamer seemed after 2,400 miles of jolting and banging by stagecoach and ambulance! The staterooms were clean and tidy, the meals well-cooked and excellent, and we went steaming down the Columbia without thought or care, as on "summer seas."

Occasionally rapids appeared, of a serious character; but as a rule the river was broad and deep, majestic in size and volume. On the banks were frequent Indian villages, with their hardy little ponies browsing around—apparently on nothing but sagebrush and cobblestones. . . . Past Owyhee rapids and the seething caldron of Hell-Gate, we reached Celilo, eighty-five miles from Umatilla, with its long warehouse (935 feet), and its mosquito fleet of five or six pigmy steamers that formed the up-river line.

Here we disembarked, and took the railroad around the "chutes" or rapids, some fourteen miles, to still water again below. The shrill whistle of the locomotive and the rattle of the cars were delightful sounds after our long exile from them, and soon convinced us we were on the right road to civilization again. This portage had formerly been made by pack-mules, and then by wagons; but recently a railroad had been constructed, after much hard blasting and costly wall work, and now "riding on a rail" there, with the Columbia boiling and roaring at your side, like the Rapids above Niagara, was exhilarating and superb.

At very high water these "chutes" or rapids somewhat disappear, though they still continue very dangerous. No attempt had been made to ascend them with a steamer; but the spring before, Captain Stump had safely descended them, much against his will. It was high water in the Columbia, with a strong current, and his boat drifting near the rapids was suddenly sucked in before he knew it. Clearly, escape was impossible; so he put on all steam to give her steerage way, and then headed down stream—neck or nothing. There was a good deal of bumping and thumping—it was a toss and a plunge for awhile—and everybody he feared was pretty badly scared; but his gallant little boat ran the rapids for all that, and reached still water below safely at last. . . .

The locomotive carried us to the Dalles at the foot of the rapids, a town of some two thousand inhabitants, with a maturer civilization than any we had seen since leaving Salt Lake. It was but five or six years old, yet it was already in its decrepitude. A rush of miners a few years before to alleged fine diggings near there, had suddenly elevated it from an obscure landing into quite a town; but the mines did not justify their promise, and the Dalles was now at a standstill, if not something worse . . . and her few merchants sat by their doors watching for customers in vain. . . .

Halting at the Dalles overnight, the next morning we took the sidewheel steamer *Idaho* and ran down to Upper Cascades, some fifty miles, through the heart of the Cascade Mountains. Here we took the railroad again for six miles, to flank more rapids, and at Lower Cascades embarked on the *W. G. Hunt*, a large and elegant sidewheel steamer that some years before had come round the Horn from New York. . . .

Our sail down the Columbia and through the Cascade Mountains altogether was a notable one, and surpassed everything in the way of wild and picturesque river scenery that we had seen yet. Some have compared the Columbia to the Hudson, but it is the Hudson many times magnified, and infinitely finer. It is the Hudson without its teeming travel, its towns and villas, its civilization and culture, but with many times its grandeur and sublimity. The noble Palisades, famed justly throughout the world, sink into insignificance before the stupendous walls of the Cascade Range. . . .

Piled along the sky on either side, up two or three thousand feet, for fifty miles at a stretch, with only a narrow gorge between, the Columbia whirls and boils along through this in supreme mightiness and power, while from the summit of the great walls little streams here and there topple over, run like lace for a time, then break into a million drops, and finally come sifting down as mist into the far depths below. Some of these tiny cascades streaked the cyclopean walls like threads of silver from top to bottom. Others seemed mere webs of gossamer, and these the wind at times caught up and swayed to and fro like veils fit for goddesses. . . . All along, the vast basaltic walls of the canyon are shaped and fashioned into domes and turrets, ramparts and battlements; and surely in point of picturesque grandeur and effect the Columbia would be hard to beat. . . .

Soon issuing from the mountains, it now became a broad and majestic river, with good depths of water to the ocean all the year round, and larger vessels even than the *W. G. Hunt* might readily ascend to Lower Cascades, if necessary. Our good boat, however, bore us bravely on to Fort Vancouver amidst multiplying signs of civilization again, and as we landed there, we realized another great link of our journey was over.

From *Across America: or The Great West and the Pacific Coast* (New York: Sheldon and Company, 1874).

LI

Caroline C. Leighton

Only the threat of competition from the railroad builders gave pause to the ambitions of the Oregon Steam Navigation Company to create a substitute for a Northwest Passage. In the 1860s, entrepreneurs of that company were talking seriously of carrying its riverboat line—supplemented by a great many portages—beyond the Columbia and Snake rivers to within some two hundred miles of Salt Lake; and it would be just a matter of time, and the construction of a major rail portage, before the Columbia boat system connected with steamers of the Missouri and Mississippi.

The boatmen refused to look at the insurmountable obstacles in their scheme quite as realistically as did Caroline C. Leighton, a revered and venturesome Washington penwoman of the period—who preferred to be secretive about details of her *vita*. With the spirit of a male pioneer, she boldly struck out into the half-explored regions of the interior, writing vividly of everything she saw, and in July, 1866, took passage on the *Forty-nine*, an exploratory steamer that was scheduled to penetrate the upper reaches of the Columbia, across the border into British Columbia.

She at least saw the impracticability of regular service on that stretch of river. "Some of the passengers," she remarked in whimsical understatement, "came to the conclusion that the river was never intended to be navigated in places the *Forty-nine* attempted to run through. . . . But the more opposition she meets with, and the more predictions there are against her success, the more resolute she is to go through."

The weather that July was particularly uncooperative. Unseasonable deluge followed cloudburst and incessant precipitation. An excursion that had been billed as a four-day sail extended into three weeks. The plucky *Forty-nine* at length reached the mouth of a narrow gorge, where the water upon occasion could suddenly rise "fifty, sixty, even seventy feet." The river rose. In a protected cove below the gorge, the skipper tied up his vessel and prepared to wait for a change in the weather and a subsidence in the current.

Between showers, he ferried the excursionists ashore, pitched a camp in the woods, and to contend with the boredom of waiting, resourcefully produced sketch pads and pencils and set up a class in landscape drawing. "The magnificence of the scenery made everyone an artist from the captain to the cook," asserted Miss Leighton.

For hours they patiently sketched and waited. But as the hours multiplied into days, creative art lost its appeal. A week passed, twelve days. Still the rains came intermittently and the surge of the river held. Patience and food supplies ran out, and the captain sensed that he had mutinous passengers on his hands. On the twelfth day he realized he could delay no longer; either he must proceed or retreat, and he was not one to retreat. Caroline Leighton saw something like a parable in this contest between the boatmen and the Columbia, a contest eventually won by the river—and the railroads.

In Defiance of the River Gods

At length one night the captain said he would try it the next morning, although he had never before been up when the water was so high. A heavy rain came on, lasting all night, so that it seemed rather desperate to attempt going through, if the river was too high the night before; and I could hardly believe it when I heard the engineer getting up the steam to start.

The wildest weather prevailed at this time. . . . As soon as we went on board the boat, in first starting, a violent thunderstorm came on, lightning, hail and rain; and a great pine tree came crashing down and fell across the bow of the boat. . . . There were most evident signs of disapproval all about us—the sky perfect gloom, and the river continually replenishing its resources from the pouring rain, and strengthening itself against us.

But we steamed up to the entrance of the canyon. Then the boat was fastened by three lines to the shore, and the men took out a cable six hundred feet in length, which they carried along the steep, slippery rocks and fastened to a great tree. One of the men rolled down fifty feet into the water, but was caught by his companions before he was whirled away. They then returned to the boat, let on all the steam, and began to wind up the cable on the capstan.

With the utmost power of the men and steam, it was sometimes impossible to see any progress. Finally, however, that line was wound up; and the boat was again secured to the bank, and the cable put out a second time. This part of the passage was still more difficult; and after the line was arranged, two men were left on shore with grappling irons to keep it off the rocks—a great, fine-looking one who appeared equal to any emergency, and a little, common one with sandy hair and a lobster-colored face and neck.

We watched them intently; and as we drew near, we saw that the line had caught on something beneath the surface of the water, so that they could not extricate it. The little man toiled vigorously at it, standing in the water nearly up to his head, but appeared to be feebly seconded by the big one, who remained on the rocks.

It seemed as if the line would part from the strain, or the boat strike the next moment. The mate shouted and gesticulated to them, but no voice could be heard above the raging water, and they either could not understand his motions, or could not do as

River Boat—multiplying signs of civilization

they were directed. The boat bore directly down upon them. Presently it seemed evident to us that the little man must sacrifice himself for the steamer, but I did not know how it looked to him. . . .

He stopped a second, then flung back his cap and pole, and threw himself under the boiling water. Up came the rope to the surface, but the man was gone. Instantly after, he scrambled up the bank; and the great magnificent man did nothing but clutch him on the back when he was safely out.

We had then wound up about two-thirds of the cable. Immediately . . . the great heavy line came wholly up out of the water. A bolt flew out of the capstan, which was a signal for the men who were at work on it to spring out of the way. The captain shouted, "Cut the rope!", but that instant the iron capstan was torn out of the deck and jumped overboard with the cable attached to it. I felt thankful for it, for I knew it was the only thing that could put an end to our presumptuous attempt. . . . Three of our four rudders were broken; but the remaining one enabled us to get into an eddy that carried us to a little cove, where we stopped to repair damages sufficiently to come down the river.

All day, the rain had never ceased; and the river had seemed to me like some of those Greek streams that Homer tells of, which had so much personal feeling against individuals. I felt as if we were going to be punished for an audacious attempt instead of rewarded for what might otherwise have been considered a brave one. When the capstan disappeared, it was just as if some great river god, with a whiff of his breath or a snap of his fingers, had tossed it contemptuously aside.

So we turned back defeated. . . . With Nature so vigorous and unsubdued about us, all conventionalities seemed swept away; and something fresh and strong awoke in us, as if it had long slumbered until the presence of its kindred in these mountain streams called it to consciousness—something of the force and freedom of these wild, tireless Titans that poured down their white floods to the sea.

From *Life at Puget Sound*, Caroline C. Leighton (Boston: Lee and Shepard, 1884).

LII

Samuel Bowles

It was a water-oriented society. Even settlers who came from riverless farm country of the Midwest took naturally to water transportation in Washington, whether the craft was a canoe or a magnificent side-wheeler. Roads were of secondary importance. Wild schemes were being trumped up for boat transportation from Cape Disappointment into the heart of the continent before there existed anywhere a single respectable highway from one town to the next, not even between the capital and the Columbia, where nature and common sense decreed there had to be one to link Puget Sound with the big river.

Samuel Bowles (1826–1878) of Springfield, Massachusetts, learned this the hard way—in attempting to reach Olympia by wagon coach—and Bowles was one of the last Americans anyone cared to leave with an unfavorable impression. He was editor of the Springfield *Republican,* which was then among the half-dozen top-ranking newspapers of the country, nationally influential, the newspaper that had been largely instrumental in the creation of the Republican Party.

Bowles prided himself in keeping abreast of the times by watching events firsthand, and wanted to weigh for himself the full significance of the "westward movement." With the Honorable Schuyler Colfax, Speaker of the House of Representatives, he had traveled across the continent "simply to see the country, to study its resources, to learn its people and wants," though everywhere they put in an appearance, they had difficulty convincing people that they hadn't come "at least to speculate in mines and buy corner lots." After roaming through California, Bowles could not resist the temptation of taking a look at the new Washington Territory, particularly its transportation facilities.

They Called It a Highway

We unrolled our maps and looked up towards the North Pole. So near the northwestern limit of the Republic and not to touch it; so close to John Bull and not to shake his grim paw and ask him what he thinks of the preposterous Yankees since they have re-established and re-invigorated the Republic by war and freedom; so near to that rarely beautiful sheet of water, Puget Sound, and not to sail through it, and know its commercial capacities and feel its natural attractions—it would never do.

So we put out of Portland, steamed down the Columbia for fifty miles, and up its Cowlitz branch for two miles (all that is now navigable) and landed on the Washington Territory side, at two houses and a state wagon, bearing the classic name of Monticello. Mr. Jefferson of Virginia was not at home; but in his place was the everlasting and all-subduing Massachusetts Yankee, testifying, like all the rest of these border settlers away from schools and churches and society that there was no such other country anywhere, and that you could not drive them back to the snows and cold winters of "the States."

The next question was how to put eleven passengers in an open wagon that only held seven, for a ninety-mile and two-day drive across the Territory. It was successfully achieved by putting three of them on saddle horses and the other extra one in somebody's lap; and off we bounced into the woods at the rate of three or four miles an hour. . . . The road was rough beyond description; during the winter rains it is just impassable, and is abandoned; for miles it is over trees and sticks laid down roughly in swamps; and for the rest—ungraded, and simply a path cut through the dense forest—the height and depth are fully equal to the length of it. Those who worked their passage by whipping lazy mules whose backs they strode, and paid twenty dollars for the privilege, made the best time, and had the easiest experience. Yet for days afterwards I observed that, with tender memories of hard saddles, they preferred to "stand and wait" to sitting upon wooden chairs.

But the majestic beauty of the fir and cedar forests through which we rode almost continuously for the day and a half that the road stretched out was compensation for much discomfort. These were the finest forests of all we had traversed or beheld—the trees larger and taller and standing thicker, so thick and tall that the ground they occupy could not hold them cut and corded as wood; and the undergrowth of shrub and flower and vine and fern almost tropical in its luxuriance and impenetrable for its closeness. Washington Territory must have more timber and ferns and blackberries and snakes to the square mile than any other state or territory of the Union.

We occasionally struck a narrow prairie or threadlike valley—perhaps once in ten miles a clearing of an acre or two, rugged and rough in its half-redemption from primitive forest, but for the most part it was a continuous ride through forests so high and thick that the sun could not reach the road, so unpeopled and untouched that the very spirit of solitude reigned supreme and made us feel its presence as never upon ocean or plain. The ferns were delicious, little and big—more of them and larger than can be seen in any of the eastern states—and spread with beautiful shapes on every hand. But the settlers apply adjectives less complimentary to them, for they vindicate their right to the soil, in plain as well as forest, with most tenacious obstinacy, and to root them out is a long and difficult job for the farmer.

We dined on the second day at Skookem Chuck (which is Indian for "big water") and came at night to the head of Puget Sound, which kindly shortens the land passage across the Terri-

tory one-half, and were ushered into Olympia, the capital, amid
the roar of cannon, the din of brass band and the waving of
banners by its patriotic and enthusiastic citizens. It lies charmingly under the hill by the waterside; counts its inhabitants by
the hundreds, though still the largest town of the Territory, save
the mining center of Wallula, away down in the southeast towards Idaho; numbers more stumps than houses within its city
limits; but is the social and political center for a large extent of
country; puts on the airs and holds many of the materials of fine
society; and entertained us at a most comfortable little inn, whose
presiding genius, a fat and fair African of fifty years and three
hundred pounds, robed in spotless white, welcomed us with the
grace and dignity of a queen, and fed us as if we were in training
for a cannibal's table.

If there is one thing, indeed, more than another among the
facts of civilization which the Pacific Coast organizes most
quickly and completely, it is good eating. From the Occidental at
San Francisco to the loneliest of ranches on the most wilderness
of weekly stage routes, a "good square meal" is the rule; while
every village of five hundred inhabitants has its restaurants and
French or Italian cooks. I say this with the near experience and
the lively recollection of one or two most illustrious exceptions,
where the meals consisted of coarse bacon, ancient beans and
villainous mustard, and where o' nights the beds could e'en rise
and walk with fleas and bedbugs.

When the Puritans settled New England their first public duty
was to build a church with thrifty thought for their souls. Out
here their degenerate sons begin with organizing a restaurant and
supplying Hostetter's stomachic bitters and a European or Asiatic cook. So the seat of empire in its travel westward changes its
base from soul to stomach, from brains to bowels. Perhaps it is
only in obedience to that delicate law of our later civilization,
which forbids us to enjoy our religion unless we have already
enjoyed our victual, and which sends a dyspeptic to hell by an
eternal regard to the fitness of things. And certainly the piety that
ascends from a grateful and gratified stomach is as likely to be
worthy of that fitfully fructified by Brandreth's pills.

Is it not a little singular that only our forty-oddth state should bear the name of Washington? that it is left to this day and to this far away corner Territory to enroll his name among the stars of the Republic's banner? Washington Territory is the upper half of old Oregon, divided by the Columbia River and the fortieth parallel for the southern boundary, and extending up to the forty-ninth, to which, under the reaction from the unmartial Polk's "fifty-four-forty or fight" pretentions, our northern line was ig-nominiously limited to.

Its population is small, not more than twenty thousand, and not likely to grow fast, or make it a state for some years to come, unless the chance, not probable, of rich gold and silver mines within its lines should flood it with a rapid immigration. But it holds sure wealth and a large future through its certain illimit-able forests and its probable immense coal deposits. Of all its surface, west of the Cascade or Sierra Nevada Mountains, not more than one-eighth is prairie or open land; the rest is covered by a growth of timber such as, both in density and in size, no other like space on the earth's surface can boast of.

Beyond the mountains to the east the country partakes of the same characteristics as that below it: hilly, barren of trees, un-fruitful, whose chief promises and possibilities are in the cattle and sheep line. Its arable land this side the mountains, where the forests are cleared or interrupted, is less fertile than that of Oregon and California, but it sufficeth for its present population and even admits of considerable exports of grain and meat for the mining populations of British Columbia, and will grow in extent and productiveness probably as fast as the necessities of the Ter-ritory require.

We were a full day and night in passing down through Puget Sound to British Columbia on the steamer from Olympia, loiter-ing along at the villages on its either shore, and studying the already considerable development of its lumber interests, as well as regaling ourselves with the beauty of its waters and its richly-stored forest shores. Only the upper section of the southern branch of these grand series of inland seas and rivers that sweep into the continent here and make Vancouver's Island, and open

up a vast region of interior country to the ocean, is now called
Puget Sound—only forty miles or so from Olympia north.

Formerly the whole confines went by that name, and rightfully
it should remain to all which runs up into Washington Territory
from out the Strait of San Juan de Fuca, for this has a unity and
serves a similar purpose. For beauty and for use this is, indeed,
one of the water wonders of the world; curiosity and commerce
will give it year by year increase of fame and visitors. It narrows
to a river's width; it circles and swoops into the land with
coquettish freedom; and then it widens into miles of breadth,
carrying the largest of ships anywhere on its surface, even close to
the forests' edge, free of rocks, safe from wind and wave, the
home of all craft, clear, blue and fathomless.

It is the great lumber market of all the Pacific Coast. Already
over a dozen sawmills are located on its shores; one which we
visited was three hundred and thirty-six feet long and turns out
one hundred thousand feet of lumber daily; three ships and two
barks of five hundred to one thousand tons each were loading
with the product direct from the mill; and the present entire
export of the Sound, in prepared lumber and masts and spars,
reaches nearly to one hundred millions of feet yearly, and yields
at the average price of ten dollars a thousand about one million
of dollars.

San Francisco is the largest customer, but the Sandwich Islands, China, all the Pacific American ports, south and north, and
even Buenos Aires around on the Atlantic, come hither for building materials, and France finds here her cheapest and best spars
and masts. Much of the shipping employed in the business is
owned on the Sound; one mill company has twelve vessels of from
three hundred to one thousand tons each. . . .

The size of these Washington Territory trees was rather overpowering—for we had not then seen the Big Trees of California—
and not daring to trust unaccustomed eyes, we resorted to the
statistics of the lumbermen. Trees, six to seven feet in diameter
and two hundred to two hundred and fifty feet high, are very
common, perhaps rarely out of sight in the forest; eight feet in
diameter and three hundred feet high are rarer, but still not at all

uncommon. . . . A monster tree that had fallen—the forests are full of fallen trees—measured three hundred and twenty-five feet long; and another tree, at the distance of ninety feet from its root, was seven feet in diameter! Masts for ships are readily procurable, straight as an arrow and without a knot for one hundred feet, and forty inches in diameter at thirty feet from the base. . . .

The business is but in its very infancy; it will grow with the growth of the whole Pacific Coast, and with the increasing dearth of fine ship timber in other parts of the world, for it is impossible to calculate the time when, cut and saw as we may, all these forests shall be used up and the supply become exhausted.

From *Our New West*, Samuel Bowles (Hartford: Hartford Publishing Company, 1869).

LIII

Hazard Stevens

The acquisition of Alaska in 1867 nudged Washington half a continent nearer to civilization; that Territory was no longer thought of as the outpost of a nation; Chinook land was close at hand compared to the land of the Esquimeaux. Puget Sound was so much nearer the Potomac that legislators in Olympia were flirting with Congress over the prospect of statehood. They had a transcontinental telegraph line. Steamboats plying the Columbia and its tributaries linked settlements of the far interior with coastal ports. People were now talking up construction of highways more serviceable than those over which Samuel Bowles had jolted. And railroads from the outside world were creeping nearer.

Still, there were areas within the Territory that were not yet even explored. Among them was the most conspicuous elevation in the Northwest—Mount Rainier, as Seattle residents called it; Mount Tacoma or Takhoma, as it was known to settlers a little farther south. Though the mountain had been on the map for almost two centuries, no white man had yet reached its summit, and the few who had attempted an ascent had stumbled back with the affirmation that it was "utterly insurmountable."

Hazard Stevens (1842–1914), son of the Territorial governor, a mountaineer who had repeatedly tramped over inaccessible passes in the Rockies, and a Civil War veteran who had distinguished himself as the Union's youngest general, knew that the mountain could be climbed. To prove it, early in the summer of 1870 he started assembling a team: a strapping unemployed miner, Philomon Beecher Van Trump, and an English landscape artist and erstwhile Alpinist, Edward T. Coleman.

With a minimum of equipment, the trio set out for the white heights, hoping to recruit others on the way. On the southern flank at Yelm Prairie they persuaded a farmer named James Longmire to guide them over some sixty circuitous miles of forest wilderness to Bear Prairie at an altitude of 2630 feet. And at Bear Prairie they talked a nomad Indian resident, Sluiskin, the real authority on Mount Rainier, into agreeing to conduct them to the summit.

Indians, in general, were dead set against permitting anyone to ascend their mountain: it was sacred; it was haunted; and the native deity who tenanted the summit was a vengeful being bound to bring death or disaster to any trespassers. Nevertheless, the renegade Sluiskin promised to accompany them.

Before the party reached Bear Prairie, all were exhausted from almost a week of rough tramping. They had frequently been lost, had been dunked in rampageous streams, narrowly missed being crushed when a giant pine toppled on their encampment, and beside the expected suffering from thirst, painful blisters, and trail bruises, they were on short rations from failure to find the game on which they had counted for food. They were almost convinced that there was more than myth in the tale of that Indian devil that ruled the mountain. And the real hardships were just beginning.

The first day out from Bear Prairie, they were deserted by Coleman, who had lagged behind and reached a point on a sheer precipice where he could neither ascend nor descend with his forty-pound pack. So it was jettisoned over the cliff and irretrievably lost. It happened to contain their bacon and most of the food reserves. Denounced by Sluiskin as *cultus* King George Man," Coleman retreated to the base camp. The trio—Stevens, Van Trump, and Sluiskin—pushed on, without the Britisher and the bacon. Two days later came the real challenge. The towering white peak confronted them.

Leviathan of Mountains

Directly in front and apparently not over two miles distant—although really twenty—old Takhoma loomed up more gigantic than ever. We were far above the level of the lower snow line on Takhoma. The high peak upon which we clung seemed the central core or focus of all the mountains around, and on every side we looked down vertically thousands of feet, deep down into vast, terrible defiles, black and fir-clothed, which stretched away until lost in the distance and smoke.

Between them, separating one from another, the mountain walls rose precipitously and terminated in bare, columnar peaks of black basaltic or volcanic rock as sharp as needles. It seemed incredible that any human foot could have followed out the course we came, as we looked back upon it.

After a few hours more of this climbing, we stood upon the summit of the last mountain ridge that separated us from Takhoma. We were in a saddle of the ridge; a lofty peak rose on either side. Below us extended a long, steep hollow or gulch filled with snow, the farther extremity of which seemed to crop off perpendicularly into a deep valley or basin. Across this valley, directly in front, filling up the whole horizon, a view with an indescribable aspect of magnitude and grandeur, stood the old leviathan of mountains. The broad, snowy dome rose far among and above the clouds. The sides fell off in vertical steeps and fearful black walls of rock for a third of its altitude; lower down, vast, broad, gently sloping snow fields surrounded the mountain and were broken here and there by ledges or masses of the dark basaltic rock protruding above them.

Long, green ridges projected from this snow belt at intervals, radiating from the mountain and extending many miles until lost in the distant forests. Deep valleys lay between these ridges. Each at its upper end formed the bed of a glacier, which closed and filled it up with solid ice. Below the snow line bright green grass with countless flowers, whose vivid scarlet, blue and purple formed bodies of color in the distance, clothed the whole region of ridges and valleys for a breadth of five miles. The beautiful balsam firs, about thirty feet in height, and of a purple, dark green color, stood scattered over the landscape, now singly, now in groves, and now in long lines, as though planted in some well-kept park.

Farther down, an unbroken fir forest surrounded the mountain and clad the lower portions of the ridges and valleys. In every sheltered depression or hollow lay beds of snow with tiny brooks and rivulets flowing from them. The glaciers terminated not gradually, but abruptly, with a wall of ice from one to five hundred feet high, from beneath which yeasty torrents burst forth and rushed roaring and tumbling down the valleys. The principal of these, far away on our left front, could be seen plunging over two considerable falls, half hidden in the forest, while the roar of the waters was distinctly audible.

At length we cautiously descended the snow bed, and climbing at least fifteen hundred feet down a steep but ancient landslide by means of the bushes growing among the loose rocks, reached the valley and encountered a beautiful, peaceful, limpid creek. . . . After an hour's rest and a hearty repast, we resumed our packs, despite Sluiskin's protests, who seemed tired out with his arduous day's toil and pleaded hard against traveling further. Crossing the stream, we walked through several grassy glades or meadows, alternating with open woods.

We soon came to the foot of one of the long ridges, and ascending it, followed it for several miles through open woods until we emerged upon the enchanting emerald and flowery meads which clothe these upper regions. . . . A little to the left we beheld a beautiful lake. . . . It was at once evident that the lake was upon a summit or divide between the waters of the Nisqually and Cowlitz rivers. . . .

We camped, as the twilight fell upon us, in an aromatic grove of balsam firs. A grouse, the fruit of Sluiskin's rifle, broiled before the fire and impartially divided, gave a relish to the dry bread and coffee. After supper we reclined upon our blankets in front of the bright, blazing fire, well satisfied. The Indian, when starting from Bear Prairie, had evidently deemed our intention of ascending Takhoma too absurd to deserve notice . . . but his views had undergone a change with the day's march. The affair began to look serious to him, and now in Chinook, interspersed with a few words of broken English and many signs and gesticulations, he began a solemn exhortation and warning against our rash project.

Takhoma, he said, was an enchanted mountain, inhabited by an evil spirit who dwelt in a fiery lake on its summit. No human being could ascend it or even attempt its ascent and survive. At first, indeed, the way was easy. The broad snow fields, over which he had so often hunted the mountain goat, interposed no obstacle, but above them the rash adventurer would be compelled to climb up steeps of loose, rolling rocks, which would turn beneath his feet and cast him headlong into the deep abyss below.

The upper snow slopes, too, were so steep that not even a goat, far less a man, could get over them. And he would have to pass below lofty walls and precipices whence avalanches of snow and vast masses of rock were continually falling; and these would inevitably bury the intruder beneath their ruins. Moreover, a furious tempest continually swept the crown of the mountain, and the luckless adventurer, even if he wonderfully escaped the perils below, would be torn from the mountain and whirled through the air by this fearful blast.

And the awful being upon the summit, who would surely punish the sacrilegious attempt to invade his sanctuary—who could hope to escape his vengeance? Many years ago, he continued, his grandfather, a great chief and warrior, and a mighty hunter, had ascended part way up the mountain, and had encountered some of these dangers, but he fortunately turned back in time to escape destruction; and no other Indian had ever gone so far.

Finding that his words did not produce the desired effect, he assured us that, if we persisted in attempting the ascent, he would wait three days for our return, and would then proceed to Olympia and inform our friends of our death; and he begged us to give him a paper (a written note) to take to them, so that they might believe his story.

Sluiskin's manner during this harangue was earnest in the

extreme, and he was undoubtedly sincere in his forebodings. After we had retired to rest he kept up a most dismal chant or dirge until late in the night. A dim, white, spectral mass towering so near, the roar of the torrents below us and the occasional thunder of avalanches, several of which fell during the night, added to the weird effect of Sluiskin's song.

The next morning we moved two miles farther up the ridge and made camp in the last clump of trees, quite within the limit of perpetual snow. Thence, with snow spikes upon our feet and Alpine staff in hand, we went up the snow fields to reconnoitre the best line of ascent. We spent four hours, walking fast, in reaching the foot of the steep, abrupt part of the mountain. After carefully scanning the southern approaches, we decided to ascend on the morrow by a steep, rocky ridge that seemed to lead up to the snowy crown.

Our camp was pitched on a high knoll crowned by a grove of balsam firs, near a turbulent glacial torrent. About nine o'clock, after we had lain down for the night, the firs round our camp took fire and suddenly burst out in a vivid conflagration. The night was dark and windy, and the scene—the vast, dim outlines of Takhoma, the white snow fields, the roaring torrent, the crackling blaze of the burning trees—was strikingly wild and picturesque. . . .

Before daylight the next morning, Wednesday, August 17, 1870, we were up and had breakfasted, and at six o'clock we started to ascend Takhoma. Besides our Alpine staffs and creepers, we carried a long rope, an ice ax, a brass plate inscribed with our names, our flags, a large canteen and some luncheon. . . . Being satisfied from our late reconnaissance that we could reach the summit and return on the same day, we left behind our coats and blankets.

In three hours of fast walking we reached the highest point of the preceding day's trip and commenced the ascent by the steep, rocky ridge . . . reaching up to the snowy dome. We found it to be a very narrow, steep, irregular backbone, composed of crumbling basaltic conglomerate, the top only being solid rock, while the sides were composed of loose broken rocks and debris. Up this ridge, keeping upon the spine when possible, and sometimes forced to pick our way over the loose and broken rocks at the sides, around columnar masses which we could not directly climb over, we toiled for five hundred yards, ascending at an angle of nearly forty-five degrees.

Here the ridge connected, by a narrow neck or saddle, with a vast square rock, whose huge and distinct outline can be clearly perceived from a distance of twenty-five miles. This, like the ridge, is a conglomerate of basalt and trap . . . rapidly disintegrating and continually falling in showers and even masses of rocks and rubbish, under the action of frost by night and melting snow by day. It lies embedded in the side of the mountain . . . and overhanging deep, terrible gorges. . . . Crossing by the saddle from the ridge, despite a strong wind that swept across it, we gained a narrow ledge . . . and creeping along it, hugging close to the main rock on our right, laboriously and cautiously continued the ascent.

The wind was blowing violently. We were now crawling along the face of the precipice almost in mid-air. On the right the rock towered far above us perpendicularly. On the left it fell sheer off two thousand feet into a vast abyss. A great glacier filled its bed and stretched away for several miles, all seamed or wrinkled across with countless crevasses. We crept up and along a ledge, not of solid, sure rock, but one obstructed with the loose stones and debris which were continually falling from above, and we trod on the upper edge of a steep slope of this rubbish, sending the stones at every step rolling and bounding into the depths below.

Several times during our progress showers of rocks fell from the precipice above across our path, and rolled into the abyss, but fortunately none struck us. Four hundred yards of this progress brought us to where the rock joined the overhanging edge of the vast *névé* or snow field that descended from the dome of the mountain and was from time to time breaking off in immense masses, which fell with the noise of thunder into the great canyon on our left side.

The junction of rock and ice afforded our only line of ascent. It was an almost perpendicular gutter, but here our ice ax came into play, and by cutting steps in the ice and availing ourselves of every crevice or projecting point of the rock, we slowly worked our way up two hundred yards higher. Falling stones were continually coming down. Mr. Van Trump was hit by a small one, and another struck his staff from his hands. Abandoning the rock, then, at the earliest practical point, we ascended directly up the ice, cutting steps for a short distance, until we reached ice so corrugated as to afford a foothold.

These folds or pinnacles were about two or three feet high. . . . Up this safe footing we climbed rapidly, the side of the mountain becoming less and less steep, and the ice waves smaller and more regular, and after ascending about three hundred yards, stood fairly upon the broad dome of mighty Takhoma. It rose before us like a broad, gently swelling headland of dazzling white, topped with black. . . .

Ascending diagonally towards the left, we continued our course. The snow was hard and firm under foot . . . intersected by a number of crevasses which we crossed at narrow places without difficulty. About half way up the slope we encountered one from eight to twenty feet wide and of profound depth. The most beautiful vivid emerald-green color seemed to fill the abyss. . . . Throwing a bight of the rope around a projecting pinnacle on the upper side, we climbed up, hand over hand, and thus effected a crossing.

We were now obliged to travel slowly, with frequent rests. In that rare atmosphere, after taking seventy or eighty steps, our breath would be gone, our muscles grew tired and strained, and we experienced all the sensations of extreme fatigue. An instant's pause, however, was sufficient to recover strength and breath, and we would start again. The wind, which we had not felt while climbing the steepest part of the mountain, now again blew furiously, and we began to suffer from the cold.

Our course—directed still diagonally towards the left— brought us first to the southwest peak. This is a long, exceedingly sharp, narrow ridge springing out from the main dome for a mile into mid-air. The ridge affords not over ten or twelve feet of foothold on top, and the sides descend almost vertically. On the

right side the snow lay firm and smooth for a few feet on top, and
then descended in a steep, unbroken sheet, like an immense,
flowing curtain, into the tremendous basin which lies on the west
side of the mountain. . . . The left side, too steep for the snow to
lie on, was vertical bare rock.

The wind blew so violently that we were obliged to brace ourselves with our Alpine staffs and use great caution to guard
against being swept off the ridge. We threw ourselves behind the
pinnacles or into the cracks every seventy steps, for rest and
shelter against the bitter, piercing wind.

Hastening forward in this way along the dizzy, narrow and
precarious ridge, we reached at length the highest point. Sheltered behind a pinnacle of ice we rested a moment, took out our
flags and fastened them upon the Alpine staffs, and then, standing
erect in the furious blast, waved them in triumph with three
cheers.

From "The Ascent of Takhoma," Hazard Stevens. *Atlantic Monthly,* November,
1876.

LIV

Charles M. Scammon

Less sporting than the conquest of Washington's peaks, but no less laborious or intriguing, was the slow conquest of the forest that rimmed their bases. This, too, was a job for men with a taste for struggle.

In addition to the prairie-schooner emigrants and their nautically inclined cousins who came around the Horn, was an entirely different breed who took a more northerly course across the continent, traveling the most circuitous, hardest route of all. They came through the forests, chopping trees as they advanced, and taking so long on the journey that many who started out as youngsters were middle-aged or old men when they reached Puget Sound.

The nucleus of this wave of emigrants originated in the state of Maine, where they were known simply as woodsmen or loggers. After thinning out the great pine forests there, they moved slowly westward, to the uplands of the Connecticut River Valley, to upstate New York and Pennsylvania, on to the Great Lakes forests of Michigan, Wisconsin, and Minnesota, and finally to the big-tree country of California, Oregon, and Washington.

With them, over a distance of at least four thousand miles, they carried their Maine traditions, lingo, and lumbering techniques, Maine axes, Maine peaveys, Maine baked beans, and a rich Maine glossary of profanity. Along the way they picked up and helped indoctrinate recruits of a dozen nationalities, but mostly Scandinavian, German, and French-Canadian. And by the time they reached the West Coast, they were all known professionally as lumberjacks.

Not until they reached the Pacific shores was the Maine system of lumbering altered appreciably. There the trees were so enormous that they were obliged to work out innovations in felling and hauling, and somewhere en route they lost the familiar Yankee woodsmen's warning yell of "TimBER!" sounded as a tree was about to fall; in Washington it was translated into "UnDER! UnDER!"

Captain Charles M. Scammon (b. 1825) did not accompany the woodsmen across the country, but he was born in Pittston, Maine, and was familiar with logging there. He took to the sea instead of the woods, first sailed to the Pacific in 1850, joined the whaling fleet, scoured the seas for years in search of whales, and was the discoverer of the haunts of the gray whale on the California coast.

Then when the whaling trade petered out during the Civil War, he turned to service as commander of a U.S. revenue cutter—and to authorship—writing, most notably, a definitive treatise on "Marine Mammals of the Northwestern Coast." But as a Maine man brought up in an earlier lumbering country, he felt under compulsion to record also his observations on the big, colorful timbering operations that were now attracting attention in Washington Territory.

Lumber—Clear or Cultus

When sailing along those deep inland waters, which are generally known among lumbermen and coasters as Puget Sound . . . the whole wooded landscape is of such grand proportions that one looks upon the millions of broad acres covered with tall firs as a vast field of waving shrubbery; and not until he beholds the *modus operandi* of converting the leviathan trees into the lumber of commerce, does he get a faint idea of their mammoth proportions . . . or the background for establishing a camp of loggers. It all starts with the locating of a "chance."

A good "chance" having been chosen by the explorer—who oftentimes is the "boss"—the logging crew commence their operations. A camp is built of "*cultus* lumber," about thirty feet long by eighteen wide, with a partition through the middle, which divides it into two rooms—one for the cook and the other a sleeping apartment for the men. The latter is fitted up with bunks, similar to those on shipboard, and a space near the center of the room, raised just above the rough board floor, composed of a concrete of rock and earth, serves as a fireplace; a wooden chimney, flaring at the bottom and appearing as if suspended from the ridgepole, conducts the smoke upward to wreathe through the tree tops.

The apartment is lighted by day by a window or two, and by night by a blazing fire, beside which the men, of almost every nation and caste, amuse themselves in reading, smoking and talking, and in playing their everlasting games of cards. The cook's apartment is furnished with a huge stove and an ample table, the latter surrounded with seats or benches to accommodate the hungry company who thrice a day gather around the homely board.

A small but convenient shanty is usually built for the boss, separate from the main camp, where he ensconces himself apart from the force under his charge. Then there is a "hovel," the sides of which are built of logs, and the roof covered with a species of long shingles called "shakes," where the oxen are housed and their provender of hay and grain is stored.

Shelter and subsistence for both man and beast having been provided, the whole encampment is speedily awake to the varied and laborious duties. First comes the boss, who takes the general superintendence of the whole establishment, selects and purchases the oxen for the teams, "keeps the men's time" and gives orders for their pay, and like a careful commanding officer especially looks after the cook to see that meals are properly prepared and served promptly at the appointed hours.

Skid Road—with a shout and a spur, the team all pulls together

Next comes the teamster, whose only business is to drive the team and take care of it. Then comes the chopper, whose work is to chop down the trees. The fourth man is the "hook-tender," whose duties are to wait on the team and "snipe the logs" [round off log ends to which drawing chains are attached]. Then there are two sawyers, who saw the trees, after being felled, into suitable lengths for logs. Two men called "swampers" make the roads under the direction of the boss. Another called the "skidder" skids the road; and two others called "barkers" chip the bark from the logs on the "riding side," or when the sap runs, the bark is peeled off with a "barking iron." The cook, who is the most important man of the whole gang, cuts his own wood and attends to preparing and cooking the meals, which are always ready at the regular mealtime

At the morning hour the day's work begins. The cook turns out at four o'clock and has breakfast ready at twenty minutes before six. At about twenty minutes past five he walks to the door, puts a bullock's horn to his mouth and blows repeated loud blasts to arouse the sleepers, who quickly wash and dress for their morning meal. At twenty minutes to six he gives one blast from his horn, when the whole crew sit down to breakfast, which consists of boiled corned beef, potatoes, baked beans, hash, hot griddle cakes, biscuits, butter and coffee. About the same bill of fare is served for dinner and supper.

The morning repast being over, each one goes to his work. . . . The mere felling of a tree, as generally understood by woodmen, is but a simple matter of labor, but in the forests of Washington Territory it is quite a novel undertaking. The tree being extremely large at its base, with immense, outspreading roots, and frequently "shaky," or perhaps a little decayed at the butt, it is found to be a saving of labor to cut it sometimes as high up as fifteen feet from the ground.

To do this, the chopper makes a square notch into it, as high up as practicable, and inserts the end of his board—which is about five feet long and eight or nine inches wide, furnished with an iron "lip" at the end, which catches in the upper side of the notch in the tree, preventing it from slipping out when the man is standing on it; he then leaps upon the board, cuts another notch as high up as he can reach, strikes his ax into the trunk above his head, holding on to the helve with one hand, sticks his toes into the notch below, and then removes the board from it to the notch above; while half jumping and climbing, he mounts his board again.

If high enough up, he chips off the bark with his heavier ax and with his thin, sharp one cuts a broad scarf into the heart of the tree on the side he desires it to fall; then, chopping the other side till the tree is about to come down, he calls out "Under! under!" as a warning signal. A few more strokes with the keen ax and the leviathan of the forest begins to bow its towering top. When sure of its falling, the chopper flings his axes at a distance to the ground, quickly removes his board to the notch below; and . . . jumps to the ground, while the tree comes down with a crashing noise that is heard for miles distant.

The two sawyers then mount the fallen tree, and the chief, with an eight-foot pole, measures off the length of each log, according as they will cut to the best advantage. Twenty-four-foot lengths predominate. . . . Then come the swampers, who, under the direction of the boss, clear the roads, and the skidder with ax, mattock, crowbar and shovel, who prepares and places the skids. A tall, slender sapling is selected for the purpose, felled and cut into nine-foot lengths. These skids are placed across the road about seven feet apart, and with as much precision as the ties of a railroad; the bark is chipped off on the upper side after the skid is laid in order that the logs may glide glibly over the ribbed road, and when the skids become dry, they are moistened with oil.

The logs having been duly prepared by the barkers, next comes the teamster with his team of eight oxen. . . . With a shout and a spur, the team all pull together, and the log is soon hauled to the "rolling tier." . . . The road may wind along the side of a mountain, or down an abrupt declivity. . . . Sometimes ten or a dozen logs are coupled together by short chains. Their appearance when worming down the well-skidded, meandering trail is not unlike an immense, jointed serpent winding its way to the valley below.

These logs frequently run one after another so rapidly, when descending the steep, that the team is unable to keep ahead, and it occasionally happens that oxen are seriously injured or killed outright. At other times they glide smoothly along till they come to rising ground on the road, when the ends come in contact one after another with a report like the rapid firing of distant artillery. They are then uncoupled and hauled singly or in pairs to the bank, and when the rolling tier is full, the stoppers are removed and the logs are rolled or tumbled over long stringers into the water . . . to rebound to the surface in every fantastic fashion.

Sufficient logs having been collected in the boom, which receives them from the bank, they are then made into a raft . . . for transportation to the mill. . . . From three to four hundred thousand feet of logs generally constitute a "round" boom, while in a "square" or "heater" there is usually not less than five hundred thousand feet. . . . All being in readiness, the tug boat comes and tows it to the mill.

A steamer towing a boom of logs is an odd sight to the stranger, who sees the craft at a distance, puffing under a full head of steam, but appearing to make but little way through the water. . . . These rafts or booms cannot be towed more than two miles an hour without danger of breaking up; and occasionally when there is a heavy breeze and an adverse tide, the Sound becomes so rough that the raft does break up and all is lost, except the boom sticks, which are shackled together by the massive chains. Many millions of feet of lumber have been lost by the breaking up of these rafts, although under ordinary circumstances there is no difficulty in towing rafts in any part of the inlets and Sound. Once at the mill, the logs are deposited in the boom adjoining, and the steamer returns to camp for another tow. . . .

At the mills all is hurry and excitement. Coasting and foreign vessels are lying at the wharves, some discharging freight or ballast, while others are loading with the manufactured lumber, which varies from the heavy square timber a hundred and thirty feet in length, down to laths, which require a hundred to make up a bunch. The principal mills upon the Sound are on an extensive scale. Of these, that at Port Madison is one of the best, sawing a hundred thousand feet of lumber daily. . . .

A slip runs from the upper floor of the main building to the water, where the logs are floated. A chain with dog hooks is fastened to the log, which is hauled up the slip by steam power into the mill. It is then rolled upon the "carriage," and a sawyer forwards it toward the immense circular saw, which quickly runs through it, cutting a slab from one side; and the carriage instantly runs back; the log is quickly turned by machinery on its flat side and is set in motion again, the saw ripping it into planks of a thickness required. . . . The massive planks in a body are transported again by machinery to the edging table, where they are sawed into boards. . . . From the edger the lumber is passed to another table, where whirls another saw, called the trimmer. Here the ends of each board or plank are clipped off squarely, which finishes it for market, and it is then run out of the mill to the wharf to be embarked on board ship.

All the mills are run by steam power, the fuel used being nothing but sawdust, although but half the quantity made by the saws is required for the furnaces. In order to get rid of the surplus dust, edgings and the general debris, it is found necessary to burn them. . . . Strange as it may seem, these fires, once kindled, have been kept constantly going for years. . . . It will be readily seen that if no vessels are at the mill loading, the manufactured materials of all descriptions accumulate rapidly. Such instances happen occasionally, by reason of dense fogs or headwinds delaying the ships. The wharves creak under their bulky weight, and those interested look anxiously for the tardy vessels.

At last the white sails are seen through the trees, or the long-looked-for messenger bursts instantly upon their view from behind a bold headland and comes dashing up to the anchorage. Down go the sails, and down goes the anchor; lines are run to the buoys and to the shore; the vessel is hauled head-on to the wharf . . . and the work of loading commences. . . . Such carriers as the barks *North-West, Tidal Wave* and the brig *Deacon* have their deck loads piled so high when fully laden that instead of showing their symmetrical hulls, little else is seen but the huge

piles of lumber and the vessel's spars peering above them. . . .
They set sail for domestic ports both on the Pacific and Atlantic
coasts, or to Australia, England, France, China, the East Indies,
South America, the Sandwich Islands, and various others in
Oceanica. . . .

When considering the heavily timbered region that is of so
great an extent, the rapid growth of the forest, the unparalleled
facilities for interior navigation leading in every direction . . . it
is possible that the lumbering business of Puget Sound will long
continue, as it now is, the great source of wealth of Washington
Territory.

From "Lumbering in Washington Territory," Captain C. M. Scammon. *Overland Monthly,* July, 1870.

LV

Charles Nordhoff

Next to lumbering, the occupation that was bringing in the steadiest cash returns year after year in western Washington was salmon fishing—an industrial development that had been foreseen by the earliest river explorers when they witnessed what the Indians were doing with their phenomenal catches. With an eye on Atlantic markets, enterprising pioneers had improved on native techniques; they had experimented with drying salmon for shipment, with salting, smoking, pickling, barreling, even sealing boiled salmon in glass jars.

Toward the middle of the century, the invention of the "stamp can" began to revolutionize the process of food preservation everywhere. Putting up cooked fish in hermetically sealed cans had been given a more or less successful trial on the Maine coast. And as with Maine's lumbering methods, Washingtonians freely cribbed the canning idea from the Yankee Down Easters, and by the 1870s salmon marketing had developed into a big business—a drab, smelly business to most viewers, but not to Charles Nordhoff (1830–1901), connoisseur of American vacation spots, past editor of the New York *Evening Post,* and grandsire of the *Bounty* trilogy co-creator. Along with lumbering and all the other uncommon attractions of the Columbia and Puget Sound regions, he envisioned the canneries as a sight worthy of major tourist appeal.

A dozen years earlier it would have been thoroughly bizarre for one to suggest that Washington had any practical virtues as a tourist destination, comparable to those of Switzerland, the Adirondacks, Italy, Norway, or the New England coast, yet now a recognized arbiter and guide to fashionable resorts was promoting that Territory in the far-away Northwest as an ideal tourist mecca. His testimony was the opening bid for Washington tourists, and on his list of starred attractions were the salmon canneries, which he was sure any gourmet who had ever pried open a ten-cent can of the pink flesh would be thrilled to inspect.

Two Million Tin Cans

In less than forty-eight hours after you leave San Francisco you find yourself crossing the bar which lies at the mouth of the Columbia River. . . . I don't know where I got the belief that the Columbia was a second-rate river. There must have been some blunder in the geographies out of which I got my lessons and my notions of the Northwest coast at school. Possibly, too, the knowledge that navigation is interrupted by rapids at the Cascades and Dalles contributed to form an impression conspicuously wrong. In fact, the Columbia is one of the great rivers of the world.

It seems to me larger, as it is infinitely grander, than the Mississippi. Between Astoria and the junction of the Willamette its breadth, its depth, its rapid current, and the vast body of water it carries to sea reminded me of descriptions I had read of the Amazon; and I suspect the Columbia would rank with that stream, were it not for the unlucky obstructions at the Cascades and Dalles, which divide the stream into two unequal parts.

For ten miles above Astoria the river is so wide that it forms really a vast bay. Then it narrows somewhat and the channel approaches now one and then the other of its bold, picturesque shores, which often for miles resemble the Palisades of the Hudson in steepness, and exceed them in height. But even after it becomes narrower, the river frequently widens into broad, open, lake-like expanses, which are studded with lovely islands, and wherever the shore lowers, you see, beyond, grand mountain ranges snow-clad and amazingly fine.

The banks are precipitous nearly all the way to the junction of the Willamette, and . . . along this part of the river are the "salmon factories," whence come the Oregon salmon which, put up in cans, are now to be bought not only in our Eastern states but all over the world. The fish are caught in weirs, in gill nets, as shad are caught on the Hudson, and this is the only part of the labor performed by white men. The fishermen carry the salmon in boats to the factory—usually a large frame building erected on piles over the water—and here they fall into the hands of Chinese, who get for their labor a dollar a day and their food.

The salmon are flung up on a stage, where they lie in heaps of a thousand at a time, a surprising sight to an Eastern person, for in such a pile you may see many fish weighing from thirty to sixty pounds. The work of preparing them for the cans is conducted with exact method and great cleanliness, water being abundant. One Chinaman seizes a fish and cuts off his head; the next slashes off the fins and disembowels the fish; it then falls into a large vat where the blood soaks out—a salmon bleeds like a bull—and after soaking and repeated washing in different vats, it falls at last into the hands of one of a gang of Chinese whose business it is, with heavy knives, to chop the fish into chunks of suitable size for the tins.

These pieces are plunged into brine, and presently stuffed into cans, it being the object to fill each can as full as possible with fish, the bone being excluded. The top of the can, which has a small hole pierced in it, is then soldered on, and five hundred tins set on a form are lowered into a huge kettle of boiling water, where they remain until the heat has expelled all the air.

Then a Chinaman neatly drops a little solder over each pinhole, and after another boiling, the object of which is to make sure that the cans are hermetically sealed, the process is complete, and the salmon are ready to take a journey longer and more remarkable even than that which their progenitors took when, seized with the curious rage of spawning, they ascended the Columbia to deposit their eggs in its headwaters, near the center of the continent.

I was assured by the fishermen that the salmon do not decrease in numbers or in size, yet in this year, 1873, more than two millions of pounds were put up in tin cans on the Lower Columbia alone, besides fifteen or twenty thousand barrels of salted salmon.

From *Northern California, Oregon and the Sandwich Islands,* Charles Nordhoff (New York: Harper and Brothers, 1874).

LVI

George Henry Atkinson

Most Washington emigrants had traveled on trains before they left the East; they had at least been awed by the luxurious cars and the mechanical monster rumbling through crossings; they knew what a railroad could do for rural country, and hoped and fervently prayed that one day they would see this same symbol of modern civilization roaring through their wilderness. But the cars were slow in coming, despite the convincing pleas of Isaac Stevens.

The first improvisation of a railroad in the Territory was the by-pass at the Cascades, a single flatcar drawn by two mules over a mile-and-a-half stretch of wooden rails between upper and lower boat landings. The line was laid in 1851, and over a period of a dozen years carried thousands of passengers and many thousands of freight tons over the route of the older pedestrian portage.

In 1863 the mules were replaced by a real steam engine and the rails followed a less steep six-mile route around the portage. It was the pride of the river region, but still a poor sample of the rail service opened that same year to Sacramento, California, by the Union-Central Pacific.

While waiting for a spur of that southern track, or a Northern Pacific line of their own during the next two decades, scattered towns pooled their resources and laid tracks between the settlements, anticipating the day when they might connect with much longer lines. There was the Kalama-Tacoma, for example, and the narrow-guage Walla Walla and Wallula; optimistically Seattle interests started laying ties and rails in the direction of Walla Walla, but funds ran out after twenty miles of it were completed, and the promoters gave up. During all those years the nearest railroad station where one could entrain for the outside world was at Kelton, Utah, and that could be reached only by stage-coach.

The delay in the railroad's getting to Washington, however, could never be attributed to lack of oratory in its support. Everyone was talking up railroads, and the most vociferous spokesman of all was the Reverend George Henry Atkinson (1819–1889), who for most of his life slighted the pulpit to boost the cause of a rail line to the Northwest. His appeals were plaintive, naïve, incessant; his was the voice of the people. From one end of the country to the other he lectured on the dire need for a Northern Pacific Railroad, and supplemented the addresses with pamphlets and books. He was also an agitator on subjects as diverse as wheat growing and public education in Washington, but his most fanatical eloquence, salted with wearisome statistics, quaint sophistry, and not always credible logic, was reserved for a rail line over that route surveyed by Governor Stevens way back in 1853.

The Only Answer Is a Railroad

The route of the North Pacific Railroad is through a good belt of country. Its capacities for pasturage, for the cereal, for vegetables and fruits have been proved. Soil and climate invite settlers. But these products cannot be transported to the markets of the world. It is useless to raise any for export. The lands lie idle, as they have for a thousand years. The lumber of the mountains falls and decays or is burned up. The coal beds are untouched. The minerals cannot be brought into use. The lands must remain unsold or unsurveyed for want of buyers.

Complete the road from the Columbia to the Missouri and this strip, eighty miles wide and two thousand long, of 160,000 square miles or 102,400,000 acres, will acquire a real worth—at one dollar per acre of $102,400,000; at two dollars per acre it will be worth $204,800,000; at the government price for even sections, $2.50 per acre, the whole amount will be worth $256,000,000, of which the government will receive half, and the builders of the road the other half. That new value will be created by the road, and will become steadily available to the government and people. Without the road it cannot exist; without the road it never will exist. . . .

Railroads give actual value to lands. Even where fares and freights equal the old coach and wagon rates, the time saved is money to the farmer and the merchant. A trip of six days for a man and team would be required to take a ton of wheat (33 bushels) one hundred miles, at a cost of not less than $12, or $2 per day, which is equal to thirty-six cents per bushel. The car will put that wheat into market in half a day and leave man and team home to work.

Six days of work on, say, six acres are worth $12, which sum is added to the value of the land. This sum is equal to $2 per acre per year, or the interest of $20 per acre. If the land is worth $5 per acre without the railroad, it is worth $25 with it, counting merely the time saved. But if the railroad rate is one-half or one-third the wagon rate, as is usually the case, it will save enough to add 100 per cent more to the original value of the land. . . .

The power of transportation is a definite commercial value created by the railroad. It is a commodity produced where none existed before, as really as the product of new grain fields or new manufactories. The only question is whether such wealth producers are needed or are in excess. When the New York Central Railroad was first proposed, farmers objected to the project as an injury to the freight business by wagons, and, in fact, to the business of raising horses. The one answer to all such objections is that two, perhaps three, broad belts of the continent within our national limits can be traversed by *new railroads,* and resources developed by them, and *in no other way can this ever be done.*

The North Pacific Railroad is as truly a military necessity in this section as the Union Pacific or Central Pacific railroads were in their sections. It will annually save millions of dollars to the government in freights alone. It will quell Indian outbreaks so quickly and effectually that they will be less and less likely to occur. Such outbreaks do not happen as formerly in Nebraska, Wyoming, Utah, and Nevada. Had the North Pacific Railroad been completed, the Black Hills War would have been speedily closed, and with less sacrifice of life. The present war with Chief Joseph's band of Nez Percés could have been nipped in the bud if the North Pacific had been built.

The one Pacific railroad is now developing a central tier of states across the continent. . . . It is the part of good statesmanship to provide for the future welfare of our country, so it would seem a present duty to establish a tier of states on our northern border from the lakes to the Pacific. In order to do this, every hand and every voice ought to help on the building of this road. . . . Wilderness regions along that belt of country will become rich states by thus opening the highway of commerce. . . . The iron, the coal, the manufactories, the skilled and unskilled labor of the country wait to be employed on such national enterprises.

In the problem of a nation's life, easy intercommunication is found to be an essential factor. Already our nation feels the vital force of the Union and Central Pacific. The heterogeneous population that presses into new regions, especially those rich in the precious metals and in mineral and agricultural resources, as the electric chain, needs that constant connection with the whole body politic. Interlace the continent with railroads and you ensure the unity of the people by the community of interest which must and will be quickly felt. No power acts with such force now to harmonize the North and the South, the East and the West. This force is needed along the northern and southern belts from the Atlantic to the Pacific.

Dakota, Montana, Idaho, Washington and Oregon wait for this road. It will stimulate all their energies. It will establish vigorous settlements. It will open new regions. It will unfold the hidden treasures of the soil, the mines, the forests, the river, the lakes and the ocean. It will hasten the immigrations by giving confidence to the people that their labors and enterprise shall be rewarded.

From *The Northwest Coast,* George H. Atkinson (Portland: A. G. Walling, 1878).

LVII

Randall V. Mills

While other towns were talking extravagantly about the railroad they would one day have, Walla Wallans did something about it. Theirs wasn't much of a town as yet. It consisted principally of the battered walls of the old Hudson's Bay Company fort, a hotel and barroom—the civic center for the place—and a nearby saw-mill with a collection of rough buildings, a store, and a black-smith, all built of slabs and called Slabtown.

On the outskirts of Walla Walla, however, farmers were just beginning to sow wheat in quantity. Prodigious crops could be harvested, but the grain simply couldn't be shipped out by team economically. If the town was to prosper, they had to have a railroad to Wallula on the Columbia. Their future depended on it, and by good fortune, they had in their local physician, Dr. Dorsey Baker—who had already opened at Walla Walla the first bank in the Territory—an enterprising magnate ready to take on the project.

Baker gradually assembled a group of stockholders for the rail-road; improvised a locomotive of sorts, topped with a conspicuous stack and spark catcher; and imported wheels and iron parts on which carpenters were set to work constructing boxcars, coaches, flatcars, and a cab for the engineer. But capital ran out before the rails were laid. Equal to any challenge, Baker ordered that pine two-by-fours be substituted for iron, and on these wooden rails the Walla Walla and Columbia Railroad went into operation late in 1872—with a terminal six miles from town: there weren't funds to lay even wooden rails over that last six miles.

The two-by-fours, of course, began to splinter and break up under the weight of the locomotive in a matter of days. Baker solved that setback by ordering rolls of iron strapping, and had that tacked onto the top of the rails. For a time it worked, but from start to finish, the line was an extemporization, and about it soon accumulated a wealth of drollery, myth, and half-truth. In his enlightening and highly entertaining volume, *Railroads Down the Valleys*, Randall V. Mills (1908–1952), professor of English at the University of Oregon, avid antiquarian and collector of folklore, and first president of the Oregon Folklore Society, presented the most acceptable assortment of fact and fiction about the line.

No, Thank You, Doctor, I'm in a Hurry

Building a railroad, even one like the Walla Walla and Columbia River, took money; Baker had money, and so did his friends, but not enough to handle the job. One by one the stockholders lost faith and sold their stock—to Baker. A mortgage failed to be negotiated. It was an old western saying that it takes a gold mine to support a silver mine, and this was a potential silver mine that was going to take a whole lot of assessments before the lode opened up. . . . Baker had a railroad, hardly a first-class one, and to keep it alive and operating he was forced to use stringent economies—a nice phrase for makeshift methods.

That the Walla Walla and Columbia River lacked certain of the conveniences for smooth running could not be denied. It was about twenty miles long, but it had no turntables, and it had no water tanks. When the little engines needed water, the engineer stopped on a bridge or by a creek, and the fireman took a bucket tied to a rope and dipped up water, pouring it by bucketfuls into the tank until it had enough. . . . Regular bearing oil was expensive, but hog lard, made locally, would do, and so hog lard, poured out of another tin can, lubricated the locomotives and cars. . . .

Once running regularly, the little engines on the strap rail did not turn in a spectacular performance. Hitched to a string of homemade flat or boxcars, they huffed and wheezed their way back and forth, now and then tearing along at four or five miles an hour, for ten miles an hour was their best speed—downgrade and running light. . . .

The strap iron had a nasty habit of working loose under the train and rising up until it poked its way through the floor of a car, forming the familiar snakehead, known on eastern roads thirty years before. When a long strip of iron came prodding through a car, it was time for the passengers to scatter. . . . Then the train stopped—it had to, for the snakehead simply pinned the whole outfit to the track—and the crew went for the blockade with sledge hammers and cold chisels. It was only a hazard of travel, and passengers watched the floor rather than the scenery. . . .

One otherwise trustworthy narrator, . . . warned that he would be safer riding a flatcar than a coach, . . . climbed onto a flatcar and waited for the train to leave Wallula. Eventually the conductor came by and told the engineer to go ahead, that the conductor had some business at hand but would catch up with them before too long. The little engine gasped, clattered and shuddered; the whistle bleated in pain, and the trip started. Within a short time the whole shebang was rocketing along at a steady two miles an hour, swaying and jolting on the uncertain track "like a canoe in a cross sea," a plaintive pling-pling-pling coming from the strap iron under the wheels. . . .

Within an hour the conductor came sauntering up the track, passed his laboring train and nodded to the engineer. But did he get aboard? Certainly not. It was easier to walk, and besides, how could a conductor maintain dignity while hanging onto that rocking, teetering contraption? Soberly, calmly, he walked by his train, like the captain of an overland caravan, guiding and soothing, and paying no attention to the ribaldries of teamsters driving their ox-teams along the dusty paralleling road to Walla Walla. Scornfully he ignored their challenges to race. Their taunts fell on deaf ears and they got no satisfaction. Besides, in a race, the oxen probably would have won. . . .

One day a freight train to Walla Walla jumped the track, as it frequently did—when Dr. Baker was along. While the crew was at work chivvying the cars back onto the rails, a pedestrian sauntered up, saw what was happening, and amiably skinned off his coat to help. When the train was ready to go again, the Doctor thanked the stranger for his aid and invited him aboard to ride the rest of the way. The stranger was polite. "No, thank you, Doctor," he said. "I'm in a hurry."

As the twenty miles often required seven hours of riding, the stranger had an argument, but now and then a lightning express made the whole run in three hours and scared everybody to death. Trains might be freight or mixed or passenger, but . . . they were all accommodations. If a farmer had freight to load, the train stopped at his farm and loaded it. If someone wanted to ride the train, he stood by the track, and the train stopped for him. If he happened already to be aboard and wanted to get off, he yelled at the engineer, who stopped the train—and waited. . . .

At the end of the train rambled the passenger equipment, either coach, or both of them, though usually one was quite enough. . . . Inside were wooden seats running lengthwise of the car, so that passengers were ranged along the sides, facing each other. . . . Mainly women and children rode the coaches; the men preferred airy perches on the flatcars or the roofs of the boxcars. . . .

At Wallula was a sort of hotel . . . with a roaring saloon where, rather than risk the hardships and livestock of the hotel beds, the men collected to pass the hours [while waiting for the train], soaking up red-eye and figuring chances on poker. By morning the passengers were a bit bleary, some with eyes that were red, others, who had opinions they expressed too loudly, with eyes that were black. Uncertainly all made their way to the train and limply poured themselves aboard. . . . [One morning following] a particularly lively night at Wallula, the passengers were suffering the torments of glorious hangovers. As the train chugged up the valley, few watched the scenery, such as it was.

Then a woman asked the conductor how she might get a drink of water for her little girl. The coach, she pointed out, lacked certain facilities, like a water tank and a tin dipper on a chain. The conductor, always ready to help, waved at the engineer and the train stopped. A quarter of a mile away was a spring, and he would fetch some water, he assured the lady. Then taking a bucket, he started back down the track. The gentlemen passengers watched him leave and fell in behind, an uncertain procession, looking for water. In an hour they were back, heads dripping, but not aching so much; the conductor brought in the bucket, improvised a cup, and the baby had a drink. Then the train started again its slow journey toward Walla Walla, the baby asleep, the hangovers abated, the little engine refreshed. Service—that was the motto of the Walla Walla flyer. . . .

Somehow the strap-iron railroad became, in the telling, the rawhide railway, with the story that the rails were covered by strips of rawhide that dries and becomes hard as iron. Next came the story, by logical progression, that during a famous hard winter, hungry wolves came down from the hills and ate the rawhide, thereby tying up the line. . . . In the Far West rawhide was used for everything. It held together timbers in buildings when no nails were available; . . . it patched wagons and went into harness; . . . rawhide was usually cut into straps, and since the railroad had straps on the top of its wooden rails, the identity could be made.

But rawhide had some other meanings. . . . From its widespread use to patch, fix and improvise anything, it came to mean *makeshift,* so that a rawhide outfit meant *cheap* or *improvised,* much as haywire, from its equal availability to repair anything, came to be used. A rawhide railroad was a road that depended on cheap substitutes or extreme economies, just as a haywire outfit was one that had inadequate equipment. And no one would deny that the Walla Walla road could qualify as a rawhide rail-road. . . .

Rawhide or not, the Walla Walla was serving its purpose. . . . [It] carried the wheat from the valley to the river cheaper and faster than the freighting wagons could do it. . . . Very early in its operations the railroad showed that it could make wheat in the valley a practical and profitable crop. . . . But the terminal, six miles from Walla Walla, also handicapped the railroad; it was a little too far from town and the center of the valley to be con-venient, and Dr. Baker knew that he had to do something about it.

After a season or two of operations, the road could afford to extend its line and refurbish its equipment, and the Doctor set about preparing the way. First, recognizing that the wooden rails were steadily giving out in spite of the strap iron, and that the threat of snakeheads kept the operations slow and expensive, Baker ordered enough iron rail from Wales to re-lay the track and build on to Walla Walla. . . .

By the fall of 1875 the rail arrived, and quickly the old wooden track was taken up and the new rail laid. The strap iron had served three years, long enough to establish a tradition. Walla Walla, too, thought better of the railroad and subscribed enough money and donated enough land to permit Baker to extend the road. So at last the Walla Wallans got their railroad.

Condensed from *Railroads Down the Valleys*, Randall V. Mills (Palo Alto: Pacific Books, 1950).

LVIII

The New York Times

Of all the struggles in the Northwest, the bitterest and the most prolonged was over its railroad connection with the East. It went on for more than three decades. The Walla Walla sideshow was only a comic diversion compared to the epoch-making spectacle under rehearsal by the great Northern Pacific Company.

That company had been chartered in 1857, four years after the completion of Stevens' survey, but work on the eastern end had scarcely commenced when the Civil War intervened. In 1870 financier Jay Cooke, who had marketed the huge Civil War loans for the federal government, turned to railroad bonds and undertook to raise $100,000,000 for Northern Pacific construction. His capital took the line to Bismarck, North Dakota, but the financial strain was too great. Jay Cooke and Company collapsed in 1873, precipitating in large measure the national panic of that year.

A German journalist and professional promoter, Henry Villard, came to the rescue, turned financial agent for holders of Western railroad securities, and by 1881 held a controlling interest in the Northern Pacific, stepped into its presidency, and though the effort was to bankrupt him temporarily, he at last completed the line to Tacoma two years later.

September 8, 1883, was a red-letter day not only in the Northwest but also on the other side of the continent, where most of the funds had been garnered. It was the date on which the eastern and western ends of the road were finally linked at Golden Spike, Montana, an historic occasion, for which carloads of international bigwigs were transported from the East, free of charge, and several more carloads transported from the West as special guests of President Villard. The event called for national celebrating.

Far from the scene, *The New York Times* triumphed—with a little tongue-in-cheek sympathy, but with almost as much pride and zest as the press in Washington Territory: "The last spike of the Northern Pacific Road was driven this afternoon on the Pacific slope of the Rocky Mountains, 2,500 miles from the Atlantic Ocean and 800 miles from the Pacific—and 91 years after the idea of a highway from the Lakes to the Pacific was first suggested by Thomas Jefferson. . . . Three thousand people, besides the 400 distinguished guests who came with Mr. Villard stood on the grassy meadow overlooked on the east by the main range of the Rocky Mountains. . . . The valley is so civilized that the inhabitants have not for five years had to run from the Indians. . . ."

At the scene, the men of the hour were Villard and the country's foremost lawyer-orator, ex-U.S. Attorney General and ex-U.S. Secretary of State William M. Evarts. President Villard welcomed the guests to the celebration, sketched the history of the construction, supervised the driving of the last spike, and proclaimed the official opening of "a new highway between Europe, America, and Asia."

But he left the real oratory to guest-speaker Evarts, who declared grandiloquently: "The Northern Pacific thus completed forms one more portage for the water-borne commerce which plies between Europe and Asia. It brings new fields of tillage adequate to feed tens of millions, under whose healthful and happy toil their seedtime and harvest shall never fail, and tens of thousands more, less fortunate, who crowd the workshops and the factories, the cities and the mines of Europe and America in this age of industry. It will help to assuage inequalities of nature and disparities of fortune among our own people, and to spread peace, plenty and prosperity to all nations."

The press from Golden Spike to Seattle was too exuberant, too exhilarated with anticipation of what the coming of the cars would bring to its domain to give the event realistic appraisal. It took an editorial writer of the remote *New York Times* to put the occasion into global perspective with its heavy, authoritative prose.

Manifest Destiny

It has been said that it requires a more active imagination to be *touched* in America than in Europe, for the reason that the most characteristic sights of Europe are memorials to what is past, while the most characteristic sights of this country are but vague prefigurements of what is coming. There has not often been an occasion better adapted to bring this truth to mind than the simple ceremony with which the Northern Pacific Railroad was yesterday dedicated to the public use.

The excursionists found a scene which had been robbed of its primeval impressiveness by touches of man's handiwork, that only sufficed to make it look raw and crude, without giving it in the least the aspect of settlement or of civilization. It is only through the transfiguring power of the imagination that the actual opening of the new transcontinental thoroughfare can have been made to seem as momentous an event in the history of this country as assuredly it is, and even in the history of the world, if we adopt the description, than which it would be hard to find a better, of the history of civilization as the history of roads.

But it must have been a very dull spirit that was not quickened, not indeed by the somewhat perfunctory oratory of the occasion, but by the thought of the "manifest destiny" of the enormous tract of country which the opening of this road opens to the use of mankind. The ultimate destiny of the Northwest was as plain when Jay Cooke prematurely undertook to enter in and possess the land as it is now that this project has become an accomplished fact.

We may make a considerable abatement from the accounts of the productiveness and extent of the Northern wheat belt, which is neither unnatural nor discreditable that the sanguine promoters of the road should give out, and which have the disadvantage of being in the nature of a prospectus rather than of a retrospect. And we may perhaps safely tone down with gray the rose-color with which the enthusiasm of the occasion will invest the newly opened region in the eyes of Mr. Villard's guests.

But after all possible abatements, it will remain true that the wilderness now open to civilization is adequate to support in comfort the surplus population of all Europe, while there is every prospect that the pressure put upon the agriculture of Europe by the competition of this vast area of arable land, of which the fee simple costs less per acre than the yearly rent of arable land in Europe, will within a few years work economic and social changes of which what has already happened in Great Britain is but a faint and far-off hint.

And when we consider that there are now men living who were living before the first white pioneer had penetrated the region now opened for human conquest, the contrast becomes vivid between the creeping steps by which material civilization advanced before James Watt's time and the leaps and bounds with which it is advancing in our day.

From "The Northern Pacific," an editorial in *The New York Times*, September 8, 1883.

Railroad down the River

LIX

Ernest Ingersoll

The railroad sparked an economic revolution in Washington Territory, but to the little settlements along the tracks it did not bring urbanity with quite the "leaps and bounds" suggested by *The New York Times*. Ernest Ingersoll (1852–1946), gifted naturalist and one of the extremely popular travel commentators of his generation, passed through the dry country east of the Cascade Mountains the year after the line was completed and noted, with slight exaggeration, that "there is no station better than a switch and telegraph office for two hundred and fifty miles, or all the way from the Dalles to the Spokane Valley." He picked out Cheney as a sample boom town created by the Northern Pacific—"the most active village in eastern Washington"—and paused there for a night on the town.

Metropolis of the Region

My first impression of the town of Cheney was that it was the scene of a military funeral. Getting nearer, the truth appeared. The nucleus of a band was playing before a theatre door, the brazen character of the performance appearing more in the tem-

erity of the musicians than in the nature of their instruments. To
make up for this deficiency, tones of thunder were being struck
from a big bass drum by a sad-spirited German, and it was this I
had mistaken for the minute-guns of my funeral.

Several times the music seemed about to break down, and the
musicians to turn and flee; but the big drum kept thundering on
to keep their courage up, and the little snare drum trotted bravely
along at the heels of the humming and banging as a sort of rear
guard to force into the thin ranks any cowardly or straggling
notes that might fall behind.

I thought the deepest misery of tavern life had been sounded at
Walla Walla and Palouse City; but, bless you! I was inexperienced. The "gentlemanly clerk" of the Cheney Hotel was a homi-
cide, not only under conviction, but actually undergoing a year's
sentence, and he went up to the jail to sleep every night, carrying
the key to his cell in his pocket.

The crockery was the most valuable of bric-a-brac, if cracks are
a criterion. The waiters were assorted into three nationalities and
two colors, to suit every taste, and were obliging enough to sit
beside you at the table and entertain you with enlivening conversation if their duties were slack for a moment. The bill of fare was
gorgeously adorned with Egyptian scenery, composed by the job
printer out of material kindly furnished by the type foundry, and
contained line after line of French dishes that complimented the
erudition of the coolie cook far more than his ability when they
presented themselves.

"Beef à la mode!" one traveler was heard to exclaim. "I suppose
that means 'after a fashion.' "

A very bad fashion.

When I wanted to go to bed I was conducted to a house some
distance away, and shown a little doorless cell upstairs, built of
new lumber out of which the resin was exuding in big drops and
trickling streams. The total furniture consisted of three nails, a tin
candlestick and a rough bedstead, on which was laid an inch or so
of hay in a sack, and two army blankets. A series of these
balsamic cells was occupied at a dollar a night each by men very
glad to get any place to lie down.

A pair of stentor-voiced minstrels going through a long reper-
tory for the benefit of a contiguous beer saloon, in which "Rock of
Ages" came next to "Patrick, Mind the Baby," and "Annie Laurie"
found herself in close pursuit of "Biddy McGee," made no hurtful
impression upon my drowsy ears. It did wake me up, however,
when at midnight one lodger, who had left his bed for five
minutes in search of a drink—of water, he said, but that is doubtful—came back to find a stranger between his warm blankets.

Naturally a row ensued, but nobody was killed; and presently
the sunshine of another day came streaming through the horizontal cracks in the wall and the vertical cracks in the partition,
dividing the gloom of my cell into hundreds of cubes of gleaming
dust-motes.

Cheney possesses several hundred people, all of whom are
enterprising and busy. Two years ago there was not a vestige of a
town. Now it is the chief place for business "in the upper country," except Spokane Falls; is building brick stores, churches, a big
new hotel, has a large academy, and is selling town lots at big
prices. That it will have long and steady life, I have no doubt;
whether its ambition of becoming the metropolis of the region is
to be realized, remains to be seen. As yet it is new and rough to
the last degree.

From "Wheat Fields of the Columbia," Ernest Ingersoll. *Harper's* Magazine,
September, 1884.

LX

Myron Eells

With unsparing generosity credit was now lavished upon the builders of the Northern Pacific as the real benefactors and saviors of Washington Territory. But there were broader-sighted individualists, notably adherents of the missions and churches founded by pioneer clerics, who maintained that the Almighty had also shown a powerful hand in the process. Despite their being far outnumbered by commercial-minded latecomers, these God-fearing men and women still exerted a dynamic influence; during the last decades of the century the religious persuasion in church-oriented communities continued to reflect the Puritanical doctrine brought by missionaries from New England and the Midwest.

Myron Eells (1843–1907), son of pioneer missionary Cushing Eells, himself a missionary at the Skokomish Reservation and a recognized authority on Pacific Northwest Indians, voiced that Puritan carryover in a commencement address at Whitman College in 1888. It was a very long declamation, echoing the essence of Jonathan Edwards' philosophy of predestination, buttressed with many scriptural quotations and further supported by citations from eminent statesmen and political writers. He left no doubt about whose the guiding hand had been.

To help preserve some sense of the flow and flavor of the

address, ellipses are omitted from the brief excerpts presented here.

The Hand of God

I wish to speak of the hand of Providence in the history of this Pacific Coast, and to show how that hand has guided us so that we have become what we are. It is plain that this coast has been more highly developed by us, under the Providence of God, than it would have been under any other nation. Much has been said and written in regard to what missions have done to save this coast to the nation. That is how God honored the missions in making them instrumental in this great work, but not only has God done this, He has done more: He has also overruled many other events in which missions had nothing to do, in order to accomplish this.

How this all occurred, however, is not attributed to one great event of Providence like a single great battle, so much as to a series of Providences of which God is the author. True, if the United States had bent every energy to acquire this northwest coast, and had been successful, God's hand would still have been in it. But it is very interesting to note how, when the United States did not do so, the Most High still ruled in the kingdoms of men, and gave them to whomsoever He would.

It is acknowledged without dispute that Great Britain wanted the Oregon of 1838, not to develop its resources, but to keep it simply as it was, a fur producing country for the benefit of the Hudson's Bay Company. It is just as plainly acknowledged that under the United States it has been developed far more than it would have been, had Great Britain obtained it.

In 1788 the English Lieutenant Meares, having heard a report that there was a great river on this coast, had tried to find it, but God blinded his eyes so that after looking carefully past the place where it is, he had declared that no such river existed. Vancouver was sent out about the same time as Gray to the region on a voyage of discovery, but God also blinded his eyes, so that he, after a careful search, likewise said that there was no such river. And then the same God opened the eyes of Captain Gray and sent him into the river only fourteen days after Vancouver had passed it. The discovery of the Columbia rendered most desirable, if not necessary, the Louisiana Purchase, and led to the Lewis and Clarke expedition, and those subsequent acts by which Oregon became a part of the United States.

Do you suppose that when LaSalle went from Lake Ontario through unknown forests to the Mississippi, and from thence to its mouth, and the French settled Louisiana, they had any idea of helping to build up an American nation on this coast? No, but God did. They intended to rival Great Britain and Spain with a New France. But He who seeth the end from the beginning foresaw that France would sell Louisiana and all her contiguous territory to the United States, and that this would help us in our claim to the country.

Can anyone believe that the Hudson's Bay Company, when they came here, intended to help the United States to acquire Oregon? No. They intended precisely the opposite—to help Great Britain to obtain the country so that it might be made over to them as a hunting ground for beaver. But God intended that they should take some note of the Sabbath, as the Bible requires, and talk some about God, and arouse a desire in the hearts of a few Indians to know more about Him. God also wanted the Hudson's Bay Company here to take care of the missionaries, without whose protection and support it would have been impracticable for them to have been sustained here.

Did the Indians who went to St. Louis in 1832 for the missionaries wish to make a link in the chain which would give Oregon to the United States? That was farthest from their thoughts. God did, however, and the result was that the pioneers of pioneer settlers came.

Another thing was needed here. It was Christian homes and proof that the trip across the continent could be made by woman. This was the work for Mrs. Whitman and Mrs. Spalding to do in 1836 and others in 1838. It was not their intention thus to open a road for families and homes. No, for when they were across, Mr. Spalding wrote to his home Board of Missions: "Never send another white woman over these mountains, if you have any regard for human life." But the deed was done. It was too late to stop the stone rolling down hill, for God was behind it and pushing it.

The emigrants came. Why did they do so? To save Oregon to the United States? A very few have said that was in their mind, but the great majority say no. What was it, then, that brought them here? The same persons give the following answers: unknown adventure; to better their fortunes; to escape the fever and ague; to secure 640 acres of land or even 320; to escape from a land of slavery; to find new fields for politics; to help establish churches, schools, temperance, virtue and morals; "Ask the bird, goose or salmon emigrant—ask them why they go"; "Because it has been tramp, tramp, tramp from the Garden of Eden until now"; "Because the thing was not fenced in and nobody dared keep him off." But God overruled all these motives to bring them here, and when here He very naturally used them to possess the country.

What has God meant by doing all this? Does He mean to make us a great nation, so that we can say, "See how great we are!" No, indeed. Or has He done it so that we may have a large population, a great empire, with its transcontinental lines of railroads, its extensive mines of gold, silver, coal, and the like, with its vast agricultural resources and its commerce across the Pacific? Yes. This and something more: that we may use it for Christ and our country. This is the work for us, the successors of those old pioneers.

From "The Hand of God in the History of the Pacific Coast," Myron Eells. (Address at Whitman College, June 1, 1888).

LXI

John Muir

John Muir (1838–1914) observed the designs of the hand of God in an entirely different light. He was the realistic naturalist of the West who for years had been making himself conspicuous in California with his preachment that invading mankind was doing its best to ruin the original works of the Creator. He had been remarkably successful in focusing attention on natural wonders that others seemed to be overlooking, and was making a great many exploiters of those wonders uncomfortable through his irrepressible conservation talk.

Muir was California's man-of-the-Sierra, an upland explorer and maverick philosopher whose prose often read like poetry. Washington Territory would benefit in large measure from an endorsement of its setting by this Scottish critic of nature.

He made his first visit there in 1879 on his way to Alaska, and saw Puget Sound only in passing, but he was enthralled; the white peaks of the Cascade Range beckoned to him seductively, and since his itinerary was "without any definite plan," he was almost persuaded to postpone the Alaska trip. But instead of following Hazard Stevens up Mount Rainier, he sailed on north to discover, among other Arctic landmarks, magnificent Muir Glacier.

That tantalizing preview of Washington, however, was just

enough to whet his appetite, and he was soon back to investigate the Olympics, inspect the shore line of Puget Sound more carefully, climb Mount Rainier, catalogue the kind of people who had been attracted to the region, and report his findings. They were favorable. Though he was wont to castigate anyone guilty of disrupting nature in the raw, he graciously accepted everything the lumbermen and pioneer industrialists were doing along the sound, acknowledged that they had made scarcely a visible dent in the wilderness scenery, referred to the woodchoppers amiably, and treated the bustling businessmen of Seattle and Tacoma with his gentlest satire.

The Mediterranean of America

Puget Sound, so justly famous the world over for the surpassing size and excellence and abundance of its timber, is a long, many-fingered arm of the sea reaching southward from the head of the Strait of Juan de Fuca into the heart of the grand forests of the western portions of Washington, between the Cascade Range and the mountains of the coast. It is less than a hundred miles in length, but so numerous are the branches into which it divides, and so many its bays, harbors and islands that its entire shore line is said to measure more than 1800 miles. Throughout its whole vast extent ships move in safety, and find shelter from every wind that blows, the entire mountain-girt sea forming one grand unrivaled harbor and center for commerce.

The forest trees press forward to the water around all the windings of the shores in most imposing array, as if they were courting their fate, coming down from the mountains far and near to offer themselves to the axe, thus making the place a perfect paradise for the lumberman. To the lover of nature the scene is enchanting. Water and sky, mountain and forest, clad in sunshine and clouds, are composed in landscapes sublime in magnitude, yet exquisitely fine and fresh, and full of glad rejoicing life. . . .

All the way from the Strait of Juan de Fuca up to Olympia, a hopeful town situated at the head of one of the farthest-reaching of the fingers of the sound, we are so completely inland and surrounded by mountains, that it is hard to realize that we are sailing on a branch of the salt sea. We are constantly reminded of Lake Tahoe. . . . There is the same clearness of water in calm weather, without any trace of the ocean swell; the same picturesque winding and sculpture of the shore line and flowery, leafy luxuriance; only here the trees are taller, and stand much closer together; and the backgrounds are higher and far more extensive. . . .

The handsome little town of Port Townsend [is] situated at the mouth of Puget Sound on the west side. . . . This being the port of entry, all vessels have to stop here, and they make a lively show about the wharves and in the bay. The winds stir the flags of every civilized nation, while the Indians in their long-beaked canoes glide about from ship to ship, satisfying their curiosity or trading with the crews. Keen traders these Indians are, and few indeed of the sailors or merchants from any country ever get the better of them in bargains.

Curious groups of people may often be seen in the streets and stores, made up of English, French, Spanish, Portuguese, Scandinavians, Germans, Greeks, Moors, Japanese and Chinese of every rank and station and style of dress and behavior; settlers from many a nook and bay and island up and down the coast; hunters from the wilderness; tourists on their way home by the sound and the Columbia River or to Alaska or California. . . .

Leaving Port Townsend for Seattle and Tacoma, we enter the sound and sail down into the heart of the green aspiring forests, and find—look where you may—beauty ever changing in lavish profusion. Puget Sound, "The Mediterranean of America," as it is sometimes called, is in many respects one of the most remarkable bodies of water in the world. . . .

The towns of the sound are of a very lively, progressive and aspiring kind, fortunately with abundance of substance about them to warrant their ambition and make them grow. Like young sapling sequoias, they are sending out their roots far and near for nourishment, counting confidently on longevity and grandeur of stature. Seattle and Tacoma are at present far in the lead of all the others in the race for supremacy, and these two are keen, active rivals, to all appearances well matched. Tacoma . . . calls itself the "City of Destiny"; Seattle . . . the "Queen City of the Sound" and the "Metropolis of Washington."

What the populations of these towns number I am not able to say with anything like exactness. They are probably about the same size and they each claim to have about twenty thousand people; but the figures are so rapidly changing, and so often mixed up with counts that refer to the future that exact measurements of either of these places are about as hard to obtain as measurements of the clouds of a growing storm. Their edges run back for miles into the woods among the trees and stumps and brush which hide a good many of the houses and the stakes which mark the lots, so that, without being as yet very large towns, they seem to fade away in the distance.

But though young and loose-jointed, they are fast taking on the forms and manners of old cities, putting on airs, as some would say, like boys in haste to be men. They are already towns "with all modern improvements, first-class in every particular," as is said of hotels. They have electric motors and lights, paved broadways and boulevards, substantial business blocks, schools, churches, factories, and foundries. The lusty, titanic clang of boiler-making may be heard there, and plenty of the languid music of pianos mingling with the babel noises of commerce carried on in a hundred tongues.

The main streets are crowded with bright, wide-awake lawyers, ministers, merchants, agents for everything under the sun; ox-drivers and loggers in stiff, gummy overalls; back-slanting dudes, well-tailored and shiny; and fashions and bonnets of every feather and color bloom gayly in the noisy throng and advertise London and Paris. Vigorous life and strife are to be seen everywhere. The spirit of progress is in the air. Still it is hard to realize how much good work is being done here of a kind that makes for civilization—the enthusiastic, exulting energy displayed in the building of new towns, railroads and mills, in the opening of mines of coal and iron and the development of natural resources in general.

To many, especially in the Atlantic States, Washington is hardly known at all. It is regarded as being yet a far wild west—a dim, nebulous expanse of woods—by those who do not know that railroads and steamers have brought the country out of the wilderness and abolished the old distances. It is now near to all the world and is in possession of a share of the best of all that civilization has to offer, while on some of the lines of advancement it is at the front.

Notwithstanding the sharp rivalry between different sections and towns, the leading men mostly pull together for the general good and glory—building, buying, borrowing to push the country to its place; keeping arithmetic busy in counting population present and to come, ships, towns, factories, tons of coal and iron, feet of lumber, miles of railroad—Americans, Scandinavians, Irish, Scotch and Germans being joined together in the white heat of work, like religious crowds in time of revival who have forgotten sectarianism. It is a fine thing to see people in hot earnest about anything; therefore, however extravagant and high the brag ascending from Puget Sound, in most cases, it is likely to appear pardonable and more. . . .

In spite of the tremendous energy displayed in lumbering and the grand scale on which it is being carried on, and the number of settlers pushing into every opening in search of farmlands, the woods of Washington are still almost entirely virgin and wild, without trace of human touch, savage or civilized. . . . With the exception of the bottom lands around the sound and on the lower reaches of the rivers, there are comparatively few spots of cultivation in western Washington.

On every meadow or opening of any kind someone will be found keeping cattle, planting hop vines or raising hay, vegetables, and patches of grain. All the large spaces available . . . were occupied long ago. The newcomers, building their cabins where the beavers once built theirs, keep a few cows and industriously seek to enlarge their small meadow patches by chopping, girdling and burning the edge of the encircling forest, gnawing like beavers, and scratching for a living among the blackened stumps and logs, regarding the trees as their greatest enemies—a sort of larger pernicious weed immensely difficult to get rid of.

But all these are as yet mere spots, making no visible scar in the distance and leaving the grand stretches of the forest as wild as they were before the discovery of the continent. For many years the axe has been busy around the shores of the sound and chips have been falling in perpetual storm like flakes of snow. The best of the timber has been cut for a distance of eight or ten miles from the water, and to a much greater distance along the streams deep enough to float the logs. Railroads, too, have been built to fetch in the logs from the best bodies of timber otherwise inaccessible except at great cost. None of the ground, however, has been completely denuded.

Most of the young trees have been left, together with the hemlocks and other trees undesirable in kind or in some way defective, so that the neighboring trees appear to have closed over the gaps made by the removal of the larger and better ones, maintaining the general continuity of the forest and leaving no sign on the sylvan sea, at least as seen from a distance. . . .

The mills of Puget Sound and those of the redwood region of California are said to be the largest and most effective lumbermakers in the world. Tacoma alone claims to have eleven sawmills, and Seattle about as many, while at many other points on the sound, where the conditions are particularly favorable, there are immense lumbering establishments, as at Ports Blakely, Madison, Discovery, Gamble, Ludlow, etc., with a capacity altogether of over three million feet a day.

Nevertheless, the observer coming up the sound sees not nor hears anything of this fierce storm of steel that is devouring the forests, save perhaps the shriek of some whistle or the columns of smoke that mark the position of the mills. All else seems as serene and unscathed as the silent watching mountains.

From "Washington and Puget Sound," John Muir, in *Picturesque California and the Region West of the Rocky Mountains from Alaska to Mexico,* Volume VI, edited by John Muir (San Francisco and New York: J. Dewing Company, 1888).

LXII

Edmond S. Meany

Periodically for more than twenty years the legislature had been petitioning Congress for admission of the Territory to statehood. A new constitution was at last adopted in October, 1889, and six weeks later President Harrison welcomed the forty-second state into the Union.

Washingtonians liked to think their commonwealth had come of age. It had a population of over 330,000. For six years it had possessed a railroad connection with the East, via the Columbia River, and now a slightly shorter route to Tacoma via Stampede Tunnel in the Cascades. The sawmill cities on Puget Sound were booming; mines were producing a wealth of ore; wheat fields and apple orchards east of the mountains were flourishing and expanding; the state had a university at Seattle and private Whitman College at Walla Walla; it had a commendable system of steamboat transportation on Puget Sound and the Columbia, a few stretches of macadam highway, good public schools and churches, well-ordered government, excellent newspapers, and— some thought—a leaning toward cultural and literary pursuits.

But that latter claim was hotly contested by Edmond S. Meany (1862–1935), alumnus of the Territorial university—class of 1885 —and professor of history at his alma mater. The dissenter was convinced that there were few regions in the United States where literature was so conspicuously neglected. Later he was to become an honored legislator and state historian, active nationally in a movement to memorialize distinguished Americans with appropriate statues and monuments, and a leader in the formation of historical societies; but in the year that Washington attained its statehood, he charged his fellow citizens with what some of them considered an unjust, ill-timed, disloyal accusation that they had utterly failed to produce any semblance of a distinctive literature.

Has Puget Sound a Literature?

No, Puget Sound has no literature. But this region has plenty of real estate, timber, coal, iron and fish, and at present the inhabitants are scrambling over each other in their efforts to become rich out of these natural wealths of the land. There is no time to devote to the production or the appreciation of a distinctive literature.

There is nothing that can drive the thoughts of literature from a man's mind so completely as the impetuous, eager, absorbing chase for gold. Look about you. There are not many you can point to who have produced any work of a true and lasting literary character. Cast your eyes backward over the broad field and you will find but few lonely looking figures standing distinctly outlined on the horizon. Many men have risen, grown great and fallen, and then risen again in the fields of lumber making, coal mining, land buying and fish catching, but in pure literary work all are yet pioneers and you can nearly count them on your fingers.

Not another section of the nation is thus bare of literary representation, and few others offer more interesting phases of life for character sketching. What an abundance of useful material could an author find among the Puget Sound Indians, the pioneers, the original trappers and hunters, the early missionaries, the typical woodsmen, besides the frontier surveyors and railroad makers.

Why has such material been lying dormant so long? Men are too busy. Women are too few. They have no literary societies. They encourage no literary entertainments. They buy and sell too eagerly. Literature will be fostered by and by. . . .

See what Howells and Burroughs are doing for New England, and what George W. Cable and Charles Egbert Craddock are doing for the South; what Eggleston is doing for the Middle States; Bret Harte, Joaquin Miller and the late Helen Hunt Jackson for California and neighboring states. Puget Sound has a life and an atmosphere just as peculiarly its own as the like elements in any of those other districts.

Why should not characters drawn from Puget Sound life grace the pages of the novelists, poets, historians and scientists? Must we wait till the novelists, poets and scientists make their way up this far? But we have waited, and we have been passed by. . . . This hurly-burly rush for gold has covered over whatever taste for literature may have existed here or may have been imported; it has caused a lack of literary appreciation and a consequent lack of encouragement for literary effort; it has placed a premium on hurried and unfinished work in the newspapers. The wonder is that we can boast of even a remnant of a literature.

From "Has Puget Sound a Literature?", Edmond S. Meany. *Washington Magazine*, September, 1889.

LXIII

Owen Wister

Just the kind of litterateur that Professor Meany was calling for to celebrate Washington's "peculiar life and atmosphere" did appear on the other side of the Cascade Mountains three years later in Owen Wister (1860–1938), the urbane Philadelphian and Harvardian, gifted musician, lawyer, and world traveler, intimate of Theodore Roosevelt, William Dean Howells, Henry James, Rudyard Kipling, and Oliver Wendell Holmes. However, the creator of the classic Western *The Virginian* had come only for a short visit, and little that he had to say about Meany's state was flattering to it. To Wister eastern Washington was a crossroads of desolation, a barren, dismal, sorrowful region that reminded him of the line from Stevenson: "The most distressful country that ever yet was seen."

Since 1885 Wister had been spending summers in Wyoming, collecting material for his stories; he was drawn a little farther West in the fall of 1892 to look up a Harvard classmate turned pioneer who was operating a general store in the remote Methow River valley. But he was also on the prowl for Washington story material and found it in plenty, as exemplified in "The Promised Land."

That short story was essentially a tale of the devotion of a father to his demented son, but it was filled out with emigrants and Indians, hard riding and hard drinking, blood and bullets, all set on the southern edge of the Colville Indian Reservation. An emigrant family from Iowa—John and Elizabeth Clallam, their teen-age son, Mart, and a younger daughter, Nancy—en route to a homestead in the Methow Valley region, accept the overnight hospitality and offer of ferry services from an amiable store-keeper, Wild-Goose Jake, at a ford of the Okanogan River, only to discover that he is an outlaw selling contraband liquor to the Siwashes.

Back at his home in Canaan, Connecticut, Jake was a pretty civilized character, but he suffered reverses of fortune there, fathered a half-wit son, Andy, and following the death of his wife migrated West to shelter the boy from ridicule and earn the wherewithal to have him cured by competent doctors. In his rude cabin, which doubles as his store and saloon, he has become more and more degraded and demoralized, lives with a common squaw, and dispenses spirits profitably to Indians. But he still retains enough of his former respectability to treat the Clallams cour-teously, sets a good dinner for them, tidies up his bedroom next to the bar for Mrs. Clallam and Nancy, and shows John and Mart to the only other accommodations, the haystack.

But the Clallams happen to arrive on a day of crisis when the Indians have been doled out too great an abundance of whiskey —*piah-chuck*—and no sooner do mother and daughter retire than already drunken Siwashes return for more *piah-chuck*. Affairs get rapidly out of hand, and Jake is now accused by his customers of double-crossing them in offering to ferry the emigrants across the river; by previous agreement this remunerative employment had become an Indian prerogative. Tragedy ensues, but in the spirit that was later to characterize all good Westerns, the law steps in at the proper moment and the foul guy gets his due.

Following publication of *The Virginian* in 1902, Wister was lauded for his translation of the tradition of the ancient Knight of the Round Table into the heroic American cowboy. While in Washington he was evolving the Western, and "The Promised Land," despite its tone of moral indignation and heavy seasoning of Victorian sentimentality, was a good precursor of the saddle-and-dead-shot prototypes to come.

Piah-Chuck! Skookum!

Most white men know when they have had enough whiskey. Most Indians do not. This is the difference between the races of which government has taken notice. Government says that "no ardent spirits shall be introduced under any pretense into the Indian country." It also says that the white man who attempts to break the law "shall be punished by imprisonment for not more than two years and by a fine of not more than three hundred dollars."

It further says that if any superintendent of Indian affairs has reason to suspect a man, he may cause the "boats, stores, packages, wagons, sleds and places of deposit" of such person to be searched, and if ardent spirits be found, it shall be forfeit, together with the boats and all other substances with it connected, one half to the informer and the other half to the use of the United States.

The courts and all legal machines necessary for trial and punishment of offenders are oiled and ready; two years is a long while in jail; three hundred dollars and confiscation sounds heavy; altogether the penalty looks severe on the printed page—and all the while there's no brisker success in our far West than selling whiskey to Indians.

Very few people know what the whiskey is made of, and the Indian does not care. He drinks till he drops senseless. If he has killed nobody and nobody him during the process, it is a good thing, for then the matter ends with his getting sober and going home to his tent till such happy time when he can put his hand on some further possession to trade away. The white offender is caught now and then; but Okanogan County lies pretty snug from the arm of the law. It's against Canada to the north, and the empty county of Stevens to the east; south of it rushes the

Columbia, with the naked horrible Big Bend beyond, and to its west rises a domain of unfooted mountains. There is law up in the top of it at Conconully sometimes, but not much even today, for that it is still a new country, where flow the Methow, the Ashinola and the Similikameen.

Consequently a cabin like Wild-Goose Jake's was a holiday place. The blanketed denizens of the Colville Reservation crossed to it, and the citizens who had neighboring cabins along the trail repaired here to spend what money they had. As Mrs. Clallam lay in her bed, she heard customers arrive. Two or three loud voices spoke in English, and several Indians and squaws seemed to be with the party, bantering in Chinook. The visitors were in too strong force for Jake's word about coming some other night to be of any avail.

"Open your cellar and quit your talk," Elizabeth heard; and next she heard some door that stuck pulled open with a shriek of the warped timber. Next they were gambling, and made not much noise over it at first. But the Indians in due time began to lose to the soberer whites, becoming quarrelsome, and raising a clumsy disturbance, though it was plain the whites had their own way and were feared.

The voices rose, and soon there was no moment that several were not shouting curses at once, till Mrs. Clallam stopped her ears. She was still for a time, hearing only in a muffled way, when all at once the smell of drink and tobacco that had sifted only a little through the cracks, grew heavy in the room, and she felt Nancy shrink close to her side. "Mother, mother," the child whispered, "what's that?"

It had gone beyond card playing with the company in the saloon; they seem now to be having a savage horseplay, those on their feet tramping in their scuffles upon others on the floor, who bellowed incoherently. Elizabeth Clallam took Nancy in her arms and told her that nobody would come where they were. But the child was shaking. "Yes, they will," she whispered in terror. "They are!" And she began a tearless sobbing, holding her mother with her whole strength.

A little sound came close by the bed. . . . Something was moving over the floor. It came quite near, but turned, and its slight rustle crawled away toward the window.

"Who is that?" demanded Mrs. Clallam, sitting up.

There was no answer, but the slow creeping continued, always close along the floor, like the folds of stuff rubbing, and hands feeling their way in short slides against the boards. She had no way to find where her husband was sleeping, and while she thought of this and whether or not to rush at the door, the table was gently shaken; there was a drawer opened, and some object fell.

"Only a thief," she said to herself, and in a sort of sharp joy cried out her question again.

The singular broken voice of a woman answered, seemingly in fear. "Match-es," it said; and "Match-es," said a second voice, pronouncing with difficulty like the first. She knew it was some of the squaws and sprang from the bed, asking what they were doing there. "Match-es," they murmured; and when she had struck a light she saw how the two were cringing, their blankets huddled around them. Their motionless black eyes looked up at her from the floor where they lay sprawled, making no offer to get up.

It was clear to her from the pleading fear in the one word they answered to whatever she said that they had come here to hide from the fury in the next room; and as she stood listening to that, she would have let them remain, but their escape had been noticed. A man burst into the room, and at sight of her and Nancy stopped, and was blundering excuses, when Jake caught his arm and had dragged him almost out. But he saw the two on the floor. At this, getting himself free, he half swept the crouching figures with his boot as they fled out of the room, and the door was swung shut.

Mrs. Clallam heard his violent words to the squaws for daring to disturb the strangers, and there followed the heavy lashing of a quirt, with screams and lamenting. No trouble came from the Indian husbands, for they were stupefied on the ground, and when their intelligences quickened enough for them to move, the

punishment was long over and no one in the house awake but
Elizabeth and Nancy, seated together in bed watching for the
day.

Mother and daughter heard them rise and go out one by one,
and the horses grew distant up and down the river. As the
rustling trees lighted and turned transparent in the rising sun,
Jake roused those that remained and got them away. Later he
knocked at the door. "I hev a little raft fixed this morning," said
he, "and I guess we can swim the wagon."

"Whatever's quickest to take us from this place," Elizabeth
answered. . . . If selling whiskey led to such things in this
country, the man who sold it was much worse than any mere
lawbreaker. . . .

"Breakfast'll be ready, ma'am, whenever you say."

"I am ready now. I shall want to start ferrying our things——
Where's Mr. Clallam? Tell him to come here."

"I will, ma'am. I'm sorry——"

"Tell Mr. Clallam to come here, please."

John had slept sound in his haystack, and heard nothing.

"Now," said Jake to Clallam, "they ain't gone." . . . The noise
and flight of riders descended along the river bank. They went in
a circle, with hoarse shouts round the cabin. . . . The Indians
tied their horses and rambled into the cabin. . . . "They're after
your contract," said Jake quietly. They say they're going to have
the job of taking your stuff acrosst the Okanogan. . . . Me and
them, ye see, ma'am, we hev a sort of bargain they're to get certain ferryin'. I can't make 'em savvy how I took charge of you. If
you want them——" He paused.

"We want them!" exclaimed Elizabeth. "If you're joking, its a
poor joke."

"It ain't no joke at all, ma'am." Jake's face grew brooding. "Of
course, folks kin say who they'll be ferried by. And you may
believe I'd rather do it. I didn't look for just this complication;
but maybe I kin steer through; and it's myself I've got to thank.
Of course, if them Siwashes did git your job, they'd sober up
gittin' ready. And——"

The emigrants waited, but he did not go on with what was in his mind. "It's all right," said he in a brisk tone. "Whatever's a-comin's a-comin'." He turned abruptly toward the door. "Keep yerselves away jest now," he added and went inside.

The parents sought their children, finding Mart had concealed Nancy in the haystack. They put Mrs. Clallam also in a protected place, as a loud altercation seemed to be rising in the cabin. This grew as they listened, and Jake's squaw came running to hide herself. . . . She touched John's rifle, signing to know if it were loaded, and was greatly relieved when he showed her the magazine full of cartridges. The quarreling had fallen silent, but rose to a new gust of fierceness. . . . John risked a survey. . . . "Stay with the children, Liza."

"You're never going into that cabin," she said.

"It's a scrape, mother." John started away heedless of his wife's despair. At his coming the Indians shouted and surrounded him, while he heard Jake say, "Drop your gun and drink with them."

"Drink!" said Andy, laughing with a screech. . . . "We're all going to Canaan, Connecticut."

Each Indian held a tin cup, and at the instant these were emptied, they were thrust toward Jake, who filled them again. . . . Once he was not quick and an Indian drunkenly dashed it on Jake's head. Jake laughed good-humoredly and filled the cup.

"It's our one chance," said he to John as the Indian, propping himself by a hand on the wall, offered the whiskey to Clallam.

"We cross you Okanogan," he said. "What yes?"

"Maybe you say no?" said another, pressing the emigrant to the wall. A third interfered. . . . They talked a moment with threatening rage till suddenly all drew pistols and a shot went through the roof. Jake was there in one step with a keg. "Piah-chuck!" yelled the Indians, scarcely able to stand. All other thought had left them. . . . They held their tin cups in the left hand and pistols in the right, pushing so it was a slow matter to get the keg opened. They were fast nearing the sodden stage, and one sank to the floor.

Jake glanced in at the door behind him and filled the cups once again. While all were drinking he went in the storeroom and set more liquor open, beckoning them to come as they looked up from the rims where their lips had been glued. They moved round behind the table, grasping it to keep on their feet, with the one on the floor crawling among the legs of the rest. When they were all inside, Jake leaped out and locked the door. "They kin sleep now," said he. "Gunpowder won't be needed. Keep wide away from in front."

There was a minute of stillness within, and then a groveling noise and struggle. A couple of bullets came harmless through the door. Those inside fought together as well as they could, while those outside listened as it grew less, the bodies falling stupefied without further sound of rising. One or two, still active, began striking at the boards with what heavy thing they could find, until suddenly the blade of an axe crashed through.

"Keep away!" cried Jake. But Andy had leaped insanely in front of the door, and fell dead with a bullet through him. With a terrible scream Jake flung himself at the place and poured six shots through the panel; then, as Clallam caught him, wrenched at the lock, and they saw inside. Whiskey and blood dripped together, and no one was moving there. It was liquor with some and death with others, and all of it lay on the guilty soul of Jake.

"You deserve killing yourself," said Clallam.

"That's been attended to," replied Jake, and he reeled, for during his fire the Indian shot once more.

Clallam supported him to the room where his wife and Nancy had passed the night and laid him on the bed. "I'll get Mrs. Clallam," said he.

"If she'd be willing to see me," said the wounded man humbly.

She came, dazed beyond feeling any horror, or even any joy, and she did what she could.

"It was seein' 'em hit Andy," said Jake. "Is Andy gone? Yes, I kin tell he's gone from your face." He shut his eyes and lay still so long a time that they thought he might be dying now; but he moved at length and looked slowly round the wall till he saw the print of the village among the elms and the covered bridge. His hand lifted to show them this. "That's the road," said he. "Andy

and me used to go fishin' acrosst that bridge. . . . We've fished a
lot there. Cornwall, Connecticut. The hills are pretty there. Then
Andy got worse. . . . We knowed he weren't—weren't goin' to
grow up like the other boys he played with.

"So after a while, when she was gone, I got ashamed seein'
Andy's friends makin' their way when he couldn't seem to, and so
I took him away where nobody hed ever been acquainted with us.
I was layin' money by to git him the best doctor in Europe. I 'ain't
been a good man."

. . . They came and went quietly, and Jake seemed in a
deepening torpor, once only rousing suddenly to call his son's
name, and then, upon looking from one to the other, he recollected, and his eyes closed again. His mind wandered, but very
little, for torpor seemed to be overcoming him. The squaw had
stolen in, and sat cowering and useless.

Towards sunset John's heart sickened at the sound of more
horsemen; but it was only two white men, a sheriff and his
deputy.

"Go easy," said John. "He's not going to resist."

"What's up here, anyway? Who are you?"

Clallam explained and was evidently not so much as half
believed.

"If there are Indians killed," said the sheriff, "there's still another matter for the law to settle with him. We're sent to search
for whiskey. The county's about tired of him."

"You'll find him pretty sick," said John.

"People I find always are pretty sick," said the sheriff, and
pushed his way in, stopping at sight of Mrs. Clallam and the
figure on the bed. "I'm arresting that man, madam," he said, with
a shade of apology. "The county court wants him."

Jake sat up and knew the sheriff. "You're a little late, Proctor,"
said he. "The Supreme Court's a-goin' to call my case." Then he
fell back, for his case had been called.

From "The Promised Land," Owen Wister. *Harper's New Monthly Magazine*,
April, 1894.

LXIV

Kirk Munroe

The drab desolation and the endless miles of sagebush in eastern Washington, which had depressed Owen Wister, were already interrupted here and there by conspicuous patches of lush greenery. Yakima was one of these oases.

During its early settlement days everyone had assumed that only cattle ranchers could make a living off the parched terrain. Then it had been discovered that the soil was really volcanic ash, rich and deep. All it needed was moisture. Back in 1852 the Catholic padres at St. Joseph's Mission had first demonstrated that wonderful crops could be grown in that soil by conducting a trickle of water into the fields from the Yakima River. Twenty years later three enterprising settlers had expanded upon the idea and dug a ditch into the town. The result was miraculous. Suddenly irrigation became the major interest in the whole region.

Cattlemen sold off their herds and reemployed themselves as orchardists and gardeners. By 1883 the settlement had several stores, a hotel, two newspapers, and a population of four hundred, so it was incorporated as a city. Prosperity was around the corner.

But just when the future appeared brightest, the Northern Pacific came through, skirted the town widely, planted a station four miles to the northwest and labeled it North Yakima. Yakima proper was doomed. Yet the city fathers quickly rose to the challenge and averted disaster by moving the city to the railroad station. During the winter of 1884 the entire metropolis of some hundred buildings was trundled on rollers and skids four miles northwest, the stores and hotel continuing in business as they rolled along. At its new location, Yakima—which soon dropped the "North"—boomed.

Into the revitalized city in 1894 dropped the adventurous Kirk Munroe (1850–1930), first editor of *Harper's* "Round Table," editor of *Eminent Men of Our Times* and author of two score books for boys. Munroe had a great fondness for the Northwest, acquired while helping to plot a route for the Northern Pacific, and from a close friendship with Kit Carson and Buffalo Bill. He gave expression to it in a succession of articles on Washington. Though he was prejudiced against the dry lands east of the Cascades, he quickly recognized the miracle that had been wrought at Yakima.

The Miracle of Yakima

Previous to entering the state of Washington, the traveler journeying westward over the Northern Pacific in the summertime becomes so weary of dust and alkali, suffocating heat, scorching winds and the blinding glare from ever-lengthening miles of sand and sagebrush that he mentally, if not audibly, reviles the parched aridity of the land and declares the term "Great American Desert," once applied to the entire region bounded by the Rockies and the Sierra, to be the only one that fully describes the country. Alternated with his fretful complainings is a longing to reach the Washington boundary and cross the line that he fancies must be one of the sharpest demarcation, separating Idaho from the "Evergreen State." . . .

But for dust, glare, heat and dreary monotony of scenery, a midsummer ride through that section of eastern Washington traversed by the Northern Pacific is unsurpassed by any other portion of the Great American Desert. . . . Our traveler, fretting under manifold discomforts, cannot find words strong enough to express his disgust and disappointment. Even an approach to the majestic Columbia brings no relief, for its low banks are verdureless to the water's edge. After it has been crossed and left behind, there is no apparent change for the better in the succeeding hundred miles.

To be sure, there is another river to be seen after a while, and the dust-enveloped train seems to be following its course, but the glare and heat are unabated, while on both sides the sagebrush still flaunts its ashen-hued mockery of foliage. Under these conditions it is so irritating to hear some fellow-sufferer declare this valley of the Yakima to be one of the most fertile sections of the state, and the surrounding wastes to be the coming hopyard of the world, that one is moved to make retort and deride a proposition of such manifest absurdity. . . . When I was finally persuaded to stop off at North Yakima to see for myself, it was rather with a view to confounding this particular bit of braggadocio by its own testimony than with the hope of being shown anything worthy of attention.

The bus ride from station to hotel revealed nothing of special interest, except that the street was very wide and that its dust had been thoroughly laid by a copious watering; but on leaving the vehicle I must confess to a feeling of amazement at my surroundings. Barren hills and sagebrush were still to be seen on the outskirts of the little city, but only by glimpses through a grateful screen of rustling foliage. The ripple of running waters was in the air, and it came from clear streams that lined both sides of every street between roadway and sidewalk. The same streets were filled with shade from end to end, for though the city is very young, the growth of its shade trees, whose roots have never known thirst, has been rapid beyond belief.

This pleasant bordering of the thoroughfares is completed by bands of verdant sward. Every house in town stands by itself, embowered by fruit trees, in yards green with grass or gay with a riotous growth of roses. Every street rivulet is a miniature irrigating canal, from which a little lateral reaches to each garden or

dooryard, and every householder may use as much water as he
pleases. . . .

While the North Yakima of today, containing a population of
4000 souls, is thus a place of abundant waters, grass, trees, flowers
and pleasant houses, only eight years have elapsed since its site
was as barren a bit of sagebrush desert as existed in eastern
Washington. The region of which it formed a part was a poor
grazing country, in which often more cattle were starved to death
than grew fat, and for agricultural purposes it was considered
worthless. Its lands could hardly be given away, and few persons
were found so poor as to be willing to accept them. The valley of
the Yakima was considered to be cursed by the hottest of suns,
the bluest of skies, and a drought rarely broken between April
and November.

In 1885 the Northern Pacific dragged its dusty length through
this despised desert and a station was established at North Yakima. About the railroad tanks, the scattered dwellings, or wherever there was water, seeds dropped by chance or planted with
faint hopes that they would germinate, sprang up with the vigor
and rapidity of Jack's beanstalk. Thus did the land of the Yakima
seize every opportunity for redeeming its name from the universal
obloquy attached to it.

Very soon chemists began to analyze the powdery soil and
found it to be a volcanic deposit containing every element of
fertility. Artesian wells were sunk into it and through it. Some of
them yielded water, while others did not, but all showed the soil
to be of inexhaustible depth, ranging from twenty to one hundred
feet, and irrigation was declared to be the thing needful for transforming the Yakima Valley from a desert into one of the garden
spots of the earth.

There was slender capital available for such a purpose; but
with such as could be secured, irrigation was undertaken, at first
by means of water wheels established on the river banks and
discharging into pipes or rude troughs that led to the narrow
fields. Then came such short canals as small companies of the
interested land owners could afford to dig and maintain. Finally,

and so recently that it is not yet finished, came the great artificial waterway known as the Sunnyside Canal, one of the most extensive irrigating propositions in the West.

This canal, which has its head-gates a few miles below the city on the east bank of the Yakima, from which it takes its water, is two miles long, 60 feet wide on top and 32 at the bottom, is eight feet deep and carries 700 cubic feet of water per second. At the close of the irrigating season of 1893, 48 miles of the main canal, 14 miles of the branch canals, and over 200 miles of the laterals were in active operation. This single enterprise is converting . . . about 75,000 acres of absolutely barren and unproductive desert into as valuable an agricultural area as can be found in the United States. . . . Lands already within reach of the life-giving waters, and which need but the opening of a floodgate to render them incredibly prolific, are sold at from $40 to as high as $150 per acre. . . . In addition to the purchase money, all land "under the canal" is taxed with an annual maintenance fee of one dollar per acre.

Twenty dollars per acre will clear the land of sagebrush, its only wild growth, and provide it with irrigation ditches, when it is at once ready for cultivation, and it will begin to yield an income within two months if planted in vegetables or alfalfa. If set out with hop vines, these will yield 1000 pounds to the acre at the end of the first season, and 1800 to 2000 the second year, and after that from 2000 to 2400, which readily bring from 18 to 22 cents per pound. . . .

With irrigation an accomplished fact, the very heat, the unbroken droughts and cloudless skies that prevail east of the Cascade Mountains, and once combined to make the desert a desert, have become most potent agents of prosperity. Owing to them, forage crops may be cured at any time in the open air with absolute certainty. Grain knows neither blight, rust nor mildew. Melons and small fruits attain a luscious maturity rivaling that of California.

Peach trees are laden with perfect sun-kissed fruit at the end of their second year. Prunes come into bearing in three years; apples and pears in from three to five years, and grapes at the end of a single season. The growth of alfalfa, the great forage crop of the West, is so rapid . . . that five crops may be cut from the same piece of land during a six months' season. . . .

With all its diversity of generous yields, the glory of this reclaimed section of the great desert lies in its hops. Nowhere else, save in the Sonoma district of California, are hops grown to such size and perfection. . . . Yakima can already boast of the largest single hopyard in the world. It contains 600 acres. . . .

After being provided with a voluminous dust coat, which is as indispensable during the summer of that region as is an overcoat in winter, I was taken on a comprehensive tour of the surrounding country. The moment we left the watered streets of the town the dust clouds of our own raising became gigantic and overwhelming. Irrigation is kind to the Yakima country, but it has never undertaken to rule the highways, in which dust, choking, penetrating and suffocating, reigns triumphant.

The wearing of a particular outer garment is a farce, for the Yakima dust not only penetrates its every fold, but sifts through it at will. The impalpable chocolate-colored powder of the roadway was about six inches deep, and was lifted by and poured from the wagon spokes like water by a mill-wheel. The fresh morning breeze whirled it aloft in such a manner that our enveloping cloud would have proved an ample guide by day for the Children of Israel.

While the vehicle was in motion it was seldom that we on its seat could catch a glimpse of our horses' heads. Not being an agriculturist gone daft over the glories of Yakima, I said unpleasant things about the dust as often as I dared open my mouth, but my companion, who owned an immensely profitable hop ranch in that vicinity, only noticed it by remarking, "How's that for soil?"

Everything was all right—whenever we halted and gave the dust clouds a chance to settle or slowly drive away, when, as by the uplifting of a curtain, were disclosed broad fields of alfalfa, in which sleek cattle stood knee-deep, and areas of golden-crowned hop vines, tall, thick-set, and forming jungles in which one might become lost and wander for hours without discovering an exit.

Vineyards of a lusty growth, not higher than a man's knee, but heavily laden with ripening fruit, stretched away in parallel rows until merged by perspective into solid beds of green. Thrifty orchards of young trees shaded pleasant cottage houses, very humble in most cases, but surrounded by unmistakable evidences of comfort and plenty. . . .

Birds sang and flowers bloomed on all sides. Everywhere were the ripple and glimmer of water. The roadside canals and lateral ditches were brimming full, and it gurgled merrily through little floodgates, giving access to the green fields wherever it found them open. Save for the occasional intrusion of narrow belts of unwatered sand and melancholy sage, it would have been beyond belief that this smiling landscape could have ever formed part of the Great American Desert. These evidences were, however, irrefutable, and in contrasting them with their environment, one could not but marvel at the miracle.

From "Eastern Washington and the Water Miracle of Yakima," Kirk Munroe. *Harper's Weekly,* May 19, 1894.

LXV

Archie Binns

Miracles being wrought in the desert by irrigation had stolen the Washington show. The apples and grapes and hops and alfalfa flourishing in that worthless sagebrush country caught the imagination of Easterners with an eye on the West. Even when the Great Northern had engineered a competing rail line across the state and established a terminal at Seattle, the cities of Puget Sound were less exciting to outsiders than the drama of transforming waterless land into an Eden.

Besides, Seattle still wasn't a very important West Coast port, despite its Chamber-of-Commerce boasting; it had just about everything that could make it important—the continental rail terminal, a waterfront inviting to Pacific commerce, lumbering, and other growing industries to feed it commerce—but as a great, sophisticated city and shipping center, it hadn't really arrived. In lighter moments its most ardent boosters gently slurred it with the declaration: "Sure, the largest city in the world—for its age." That was undoubtedly true.

Then the spotlight suddenly swung back to Puget Sound. On the afternoon of July 15, 1897, a new age dawned for Seattle. Archie Binns (1899–   ), native of Port Ludlow, one of the state's foremost journalists, editor, former Washington correspondent, and author of half a dozen of the best books on his native state, reconstructed the events of that notable day and its aftermath.

Gateway to Gold

The sentiment is this: you live only once at most, and if you are poor, only part of once. If you are comfortably fixed, there is still inefficiency and loss, and this life is never wholly satisfactory. You live in the sometimes dull house, in the dull street, reconciled and sometimes compensated, and yet—part of you still waits for something great and splendid to happen. Part of you still listens for the blare of the master calliope and the roll of chariots that are not gilded but gold. Part of you still waits for some spark to fall and ignite this sodden life.

In the depression years . . . Seattle was the dull house on the dull street. The house and the street had grown tremendously—so had the dissatisfaction with life. Those who had something were afraid of losing it, and those who had nothing were afraid of having even less; and great and splendid things were the impossible dreams of youth.

On July fifteenth, 1897, people in thousands of depressed towns heard the unexpected blare of the master calliope and the roll of golden chariots. The steamship *Excelsior* had reached San Francisco with prospectors from the Yukon; among them they had a fortune in gold from the new Golconda on Klondike Creek. A blacksmith had brought back $115,000; a fruit grower had $130,-000, and he was offered $2,000,000 for his claim; a Y.M.C.A. secretary had cleaned up $85,000 in two months; another man had brought $96,000.

Two days afterward there was even greater news from Seattle. The steamer *Portland* had arrived with a ton and a half of gold, and she was racing back for more. Her prospectors had only a sample of the incredibly rich ore of the Klondike. A servant girl had cleaned up $50,000 in one week; a man had panned $24,000 on Bonanza Creek in one day; $800 in gold had been washed out of one pan of gravel; a man from Michigan had taken out $100,000 in the first half of the summer and then sold half his claim for $1,300,000. The placer gold of the Klondike was not the

usual difficult dust; it was coarse gold and nuggets, easily picked
up. Expeditions were already fitting out in Seattle, which was the
jumping-off place for the new Eldorado.

In dull streets all over the United States, and farther away, men
heard the blaring of the master calliope and the roll of golden
chariots. The great parade was happening at last and it was
forming in Seattle; for those who joined it there was escape from
all the ills that poverty and moderate circumstance are heir to.
The chance for wealth had come, and for life without inefficiency
and loss.

Schoolteachers drew their savings from the bank and farmers
left their farms; dry-goods clerks in New York pooled their
savings and drew lots to choose the fortunate one who would go
to the Klondike and bring back fortunes for them all; tin-horn
gamblers packed their bags with sure-thing games; and ministers
left their flocks. And all the time news dispatches and articles
fanned the excitement and most of them spoke of Seattle as the
fitting-out point. Some of them said, indignantly, that the fitting-
out point was San Francisco, or Portland, or Tacoma, or Victoria,
or Vancouver—but those did not ring true. The majority of dispatches came from Seattle, and they agreed overwhelmingly that
Seattle was the place.

On every project as delicate as acquiring great and sudden
wealth you can't afford not to be superstitious. If you fitted out at
Portland or Tacoma, how could you be sure of finding the gold of
the Seattle dispatches?

The gold rush made up in Seattle. Gold seekers tumbled out of
every Northern Pacific and Great Northern train and out of every
Sound steamer: pale bookkeepers and brown farm hands and
pursy businessmen; self-conscious young men with determined
young wives who believed that wealth is as much a woman's
business as a man's; unsuccessful lawyers, undertakers and prosti-
tutes; boys who had never been away from home and men in their
seventies—all with the gleam of gold-getting in their eyes. There
were also miners among them.

They arrived by the thousand. Hotels put up extra cots in
rooms and in the corridors. Livery stables rented sleeping space,

and strange bedfellows woke in the hay and looked at one another; then they remembered about the gold in the Yukon and they brushed off the hayseeds and began another day preparatory to glory.

The depression was over for Seattle. Swelling crowds squeezed through narrowing alleyways between store fronts and piled-up goods waiting for drays. Cooper and Levy were the biggest Alaska outfitters. They advertised: *The bigger the party, the better,* and outfits they had sold were stacked up like cordwood for two blocks along First Avenue. The swelling parade to fortune buffeted between mountains of goods and the doors of restaurants and saloons that roared as unceasingly as waterfalls.

Emancipated dry-goods clerks and Sunday-school superintendents and housewives fitted themselves out for the land of gold, and thereby scattered nuggets where they were. Newspapers and outfitters printed lists of necessities, which started with food and supplies for a year and a dog team. Single entrepreneurs invented and sold devices which they hoped would assist the innocents' gold gathering—or their own. Two brothers, susceptible to advice, spent ten thousand dollars outfitting themselves. New buildings went up in the city growing overnight. . . .

The city roared, and the water front roared. Every day good steamers and schooners and barkentines, and doubtful ones and deathtraps, sailed with their overloads of men and women and dogs and freight. And after each crowded sailing there were more passengers and freight than before. Vessels were on their way round the Horn from New York; and along the beach amateurs were building boats, syndicates were slapping steamers together, and the Moran Brothers shipyard, awakened from depression, was turning out an even dozen of identical stern-wheelers for the Yukon River. Dawson was the capital of the Yukon gold country, and Dawson was the goal. . . .

There the road to the gold seekers' Calvary was strewn with discarded six-shooters in new holsters, shotguns, fishing rods, gold-locating devices and preparations to drive away Artic mosquitoes. Overloaded men fell exhausted on the trail; determined young wives sat in the snow and cried; some of the tenderfeet started back; the litter of discarded equipment kept growing, and hardly anyone increased his burden from the free supply. Only now and then a broken and despairing gold seeker picked up a discarded revolver and shot himself. . . .

But there was gold in the Yukon, and in the States the fever went up, and in Seattle the rush grew. Even after the last ice-scarred steamer from St. Michael limped into Elliott Bay, the gold seekers kept pouring into Seattle to get outfitted and be ready for the opening of shipping. Enterprising men started schools of mining, with real sluice boxes and gold pans, and experienced miners for professors; and there were dog sleds, which the pupils learned to drive, although the mild winter of Seattle brought more rain than snow.

Those stirring times were an athletic field for popular emotion. . . . The gold rush of 1897 had its embarrassing moments, and its cost in suffering and loss, and loss of life. It also proved that there was gold in the Yukon, and in the spring of 1898 the blare of the golden calliope was louder in the land. A war with Spain was going on, but it did not get in the way of the gold rush. In the Seattle papers even the news of Dewey's victory at Manila was somewhat cramped by Alaska steamship advertisements that shared the front page. . . . With gold and war and sailings, the newspapers were as full of life. And to make it fuller there were ads for ladies' complete Alaska outfits, including furs, and persistent ads for the restoration of manhood.

Gold seekers poured silver and currency into Seattle, and the city roared and grew as they passed through the mill and went north. . . . That was the big year of the Klondike rush, and before the end of spring forty-five thousand men had disembarked at the head of Lynn Canal. All of them were heading for Klondike Creek, which was not one of the great rivers of the earth, and the size of the gold field was limited. But the golden tide had started, and the tide was fed. The last steamer out of St. Michael in the fall brought the news of the strike at Nome. . . .

Gold prospecting has its romance, but if you are interested in the gold itself the best chance is to let it alone and keep a store.

Seattle kept store for Yukon and Alaska gold fields, and Seattle prospered. In 1898 a Government assay office was opened, and in the first ten years the purchase of bullion was more than $174,-000,000. A generous share of that amount was spent near by. On First Avenue the Horseshoe Saloon opened with the mahogany bar and fixtures that had won first prize at the Centennial Exposition, and its sign was a solid silver horseshoe with nails and calks of gold. One bawdy house spent two hundred thousand dollars for tapestries and plush. . . .

Northern gold did not build Seattle, which already had the facilities of greatness, but it was profitable grist for the city's big, waiting mill. It gave Seattle some of its activity and color . . . : the big Alaska steamship piers, with their weekly sailings; the Alaska outfitters who still hold forth on the older, southern coast of the city; and the tradition of a totem pole in Pioneer Square.

Condensed from *Northwest Gateway*, Archie Binns (New York: Doubleday, Doran & Company, 1941).

LXVI

William Denison Lyman

A score of outspoken prophets, from George Vancouver and Robert Gray down to Samuel Bowles and George Atkinson, had foreseen great promise for the ports of Puget Sound, but it took the gold of the Yukon pouring into Seattle to convince skeptics. Now sober projectors, who thought they had a global outlook, were certain that the earlier prophets, if anything, had understated the case: Seattle was going to outrank New York, London, Hamburg, Shanghai, Rio, Calcutta, and, of course, sisterly San Francisco.

As William Denison Lyman (1852–1920) sized up geography, Puget Sound wasn't going to stop at being a mere American Mediterranean; it was destined to become "the hub of Pacific coast trade," indeed, "the natural exchange point of all lands." And Lyman was a prophet worth heeding. He was an energetic professor who alternated between chairs in English Literature, History, and Economics, first at Pacific University and later at Whitman, regional historian, nationally known advocate of river and harbor improvements, author of *The Columbia River*, thrice a delegate to the prestigious Rivers and Harbors Congress in Washington, D.C., and in spare time an avid mountaineer and photographer. Even though it sounded expansive, what Professor Lyman had to say about the future of Puget Sound couldn't be taken lightly.

Hub of the Pacific

With respect to the productive capacity of Washington, accounts so glowing as to excite incredulity have sometimes found their way into the Eastern press. Yet, in truth, the "frozen facts" are more and more enlisting the interest and the industry of shrewd and far-seeing men. The state is not a paradise, and it has its drawbacks, but the consensus of capable observers is that it is conspicuous among American states for ability to supply all the needs of civilized man.

The great fact is its variety of resources. Substantially every industry possible to a temperate climate is represented here, either actually or potentially. Lumbering, shipbuilding, fishing, dairying, mining of every sort, agriculture, horticulture, fruit-raising, stock-raising of all kinds, manufacturing of every manner of fabrics, utensils and structures—all these industries not only have every natural facility but exist in such relation to each other as to give the utmost variety and fullness of development. . . .

But great as is the sum of the commerce already reached here, it sinks into insignificance compared with the prospective trans-continental and oceanic business that is heading for Puget Sound. Note the position that this body of water occupies with respect to the world. It sounds extravagant now, but sober and cool-headed businessmen, familiar with the facts, believe that Washington holds the key to the future commerce of the world. She stands at the crossroads of the nations, at the confluence of the commodities of the four quarters of the globe.

She is the successor of Phoenicia, Carthage, Italy and England as the natural exchange point of all lands. Europe and the United States are at her back, Alaska and British Columbia at her right hand, the tropics at her left, and the Orient with half the population of the world in front. Formerly California was supposed to be the natural center of our western frontage. We cannot discredit the magnificent location and resources of that state, but it is true that Washington is gaining on California by leaps and bounds.

This is due to three causes: first, Washington has five transcontinental railways in reach, California is under the despotism of one; second, the vast developments of Alaska and British Columbia have made Puget Sound the hub of Pacific coast trade; third, and most important, the route to the Orient, owing to the rotundity of the earth, is materially shorter by Puget Sound than by the Golden Gate.

The epic of Washington is going to involve the nations of the earth. The great fact of the twentieth century will undoubtedly be the commerce of the Pacific Ocean and the disposition of the Orient. And at what point is that mighty commerce first to touch the American continent? A student of maps, history and contemporary trade can hardly doubt that Puget Sound is to be the place of destiny, the great wharf of the continent.

And not alone are Occident and Orient about to clasp hands over the "Mediterranean of the Pacific," but Alaska rises from her boreal mists to join with tropic islands in a grasp of this handle of the world's trade. Latitudes and longitudes are merging along these fair archipelagoes which the mythical old Greek pilot of Cephalonia, Juan de Fuca, imagined to link Atlantic and Pacific. The genius of this railroad age has created a substitute for the fabled Strait of Anian. That dream of the older navigators has been realized, though it lies between lines of steel instead of headlands of the sea.

From "The State of Washington," W. D. Lyman. *The Atlantic Monthly,* April, 1901.

LXVII

Seattle Times

A state brimming with such abundant natural resources could also be subject to monumental catastrophe. And time and again it came—most notably in the form of stupendous forest fires, infernos in which it would appear that everything from the Cascades to the Pacific was in flames. Casual observers from John Meares to John Muir had commented on the "inexhaustible" forests; when day was turned into night by the smudge of a dozen fires sweeping simultaneously across mountains and valleys, even the optimists voiced doubts about the inexhaustibility.

In December, 1902, Dr. Henry Gannett of the U.S. Geological Survey asserted that "in less than a generation two-fifths of the standing timber has been destroyed in one of the richest timber regions of the continent. . . . Not less than $30,000,000 worth has gone up in smoke, a dead loss to the people of the state."

Dr. Gannett was making note of the most recent holocaust, the great Yacolt Fire of the previous summer. "AS DARK AS NIGHT," clarioned the Seattle *Daily Times* on September 12, 1902, in a banner headline of seventy-two-point type. "Awful Forest Fires in Oregon and Washington Destroy Property and Stop Business—Tacoma, Portland and Olympia Shrouded in Gloom of Midnight—Shades of Evening at Seattle—Millions of Dollars Worth of Timber Being Burned in Two States, and Mills and Farm

[398]

Property Going Down Before Relentless Sweep of Clouds of Fire." The entire front page of the *Times* and much of the Vancouver *Columbian* were devoted to the incredible devastation.

Black Pathway Across the Hills

What was a week ago the beautiful and fertile valley of the Lewis is now a hot and silent valley of death, covered promiscuously with the blackened bodies of both man and beast. . . .

Reports from the fire-stricken districts of Lewis River continue to grow worse. The charred and lifeless bodies of thirty-eight people have already been found, and all believe that there will be more to follow. Many settlers and an unknown number of campers from outside points are missing.

The burned district was settled by perhaps five hundred people, most of whom were prosperous, while many were well-to-do. Nearly all of the farmers had good buildings, their barns filled with hay, and their pastures well stocked with cattle. . . .

At one place the irons of a burned wagon, the roasted remains of a team of horses and the dead bodies of nine people tell the tale of an unsuccessful attempt of a party of pleasure seekers to escape. While fleeing from the flames, they were stopped by a big log that had fallen across the road. The team was burned on the spot, and so fierce was the fire that none of the nine persons was able to get more than a few steps from the wagon.

Many people saved their lives by jumping into the Lewis River, the water of which in some places was warm from the intense heat of the surrounding flames. About sixty people who were camping at Trout Lake, near the base of Mount St. Helens, were saved by taking to the water on improvised rafts of poles and logs.

About one hundred and forty sections of the finest timber land in Cowlitz County have been burned over, and much of it destroyed completely. It is estimated that the property loss in this county will not be less that $1,000,000. Three hundred people have been left destitute and homeless.

Dense clouds of smoke overhang the entire western slope of Washington and Oregon from the Cascades to the sea. Forest fires without number are burning fiercely in the mountains and foothills and a hundred villages and towns are threatened with total destruction. Seattle is almost cut off from telegraphic and telephone communication with the outside world. The situation is the worst in the annals of the great Pacific Northwest. Hundreds of lives may have been sacrificed to the greed of the fire demon . . . which, aided by dry underbrush, unmoistened for days past by rain, is marking a black pathway of destruction across the hills and mountains of western Washington.

At Portland and Tacoma black clouds of smoke obscure the sun and both cities are in almost total darkness. Olympia is as badly off. In Seattle at high noon the light was little better than that which prevails an hour after sunset. Lights were burned in all stores and in many offices. By four o'clock lights were universally in use throughout the city.

Mariners on Puget Sound are faring badly. The Sound is overhung with smoke and many of the steamers are forced to run at half speed. Landmarks, by the aid of which the captains guide their vessels, are entirely hidden by the universal smoke. . . .

Seattle, while not suffering directly from the forest fires, or being at any time in danger, nevertheless awaits anxiously for definite news from the towns that are in danger. . . . At Olympia this morning the stores were closed and business of all kinds was suspended. . . . At noon the darkness lightened a little and there was a peculiar red glow in the atmosphere, but it was still so dark that it was impossible to see further than across the street. At noon the power which supplies the electric light failed entirely and the town was in total darkness. . . . A large camp meeting of Seventh Day Adventists, in session a half-mile from town . . . added not a little to the general excitement by loudly proclaiming the present condition as due to the prophecies as to the near approach of the end of the world. . . .

Tacoma lies under a heavy blanket of smoke, which hangs high in the heavens, giving no odor, but admitting very little light. . . . From five o'clock this morning until seven o'clock the entire sky was blood red, with no signs of sunrise. The smoke is so high that many people refuse to believe that the phenomenon results from forest fires and many of them are congregated on street corners predicting dire disaster. . . .

At nine o'clock all wires to the great Gray's Harbor timber country went down and no word can be had from Elma or Aberdeen. At eleven o'clock a telegram reported Enumclaw, in King County on the main line of the Northern Pacific east, in great danger. The town appeals for a fire engine and hose, but as many small brush fires are burning on Tacoma's outskirts, none can be spared.

The town of Bucoda, in Thurston County, forty-five miles south of here, was in inky darkness at eleven o'clock and the people were obliged to go about with lanterns. . . .

A man has just arrived on horseback from Elma and states that the fire has again broken out in that section, and Allen and White's shingle mill, the Star Shingle Mill and Ravel's Shingle Mill and store have been entirely consumed, and the settlers are all out fighting the fire desperately. An old settler named Mays, four miles this side of Elma, has had his ranch and all his effects destroyed by the fire and the family were forced to flee for their lives. . . .

A high east wind favors the fire, and its roar, like the sound of the sea as it comes over the bar, can be heard for miles. The flames, leaping from top to top among the tall fir and cedar trees, makes a sight of wonderful sublimity, while the continuous thunderous crack of falling trees is appalling. . . . Horses are running and neighing with fright; chickens are going to their roosts and crowing, owing to the darkness caused by the smoke. Ashes are falling like a skirmish before a snowstorm; leaves burned to a crisp and half-burned ferns are floating over Elma. . . .

The danger in Mason County is very grave. The reports are to the effect that almost every portion of that county is in flames with the exception of the town of Shelton. . . .

The fire is raging now in the Washougal country. People are deserting their homes and fleeing for their lives. Great damage is done in the extensive mining camp of Ladd and Boune, where the powder houses at the Last Chance and Skamania mines exploded. The buildings were burned and much valuable machinery recently installed is believed to be ruined. The properties are at present deserted.

The fire is now rapidly nearing the outskirts of Vancouver. . . . Vancouver is under a mantle of ashes. The sun is almost obscured by a dense stifling smoke. One Eureka farmer says at one o'clock Thursday afternoon he had to light a match to see what time it was. . . .

Skamania County is passing through the ordeal of the greatest forest conflagration she has ever known. Not only does it involve great areas of valuable timber, but settlers are losing their homes and improvements in the general devastation. . . . Napoleon at Waterloo prayed for night or Blucher. We in Skamania County have likewise a prayer . . . for rain or a cessation of the winds.

The fire which has caused the greatest havoc started in the neighborhood of Chenowith from a lightning bolt in the storm of six weeks ago and has been gradually eating its way to the westward, until it has now reached the upper part of the Wind River Valley, its path marked for fifteen miles by a bed of ashes and partly consumed timber. At night the skies are aglow with the saffron-colored hues made by flames afar. . . . The force of the advancing forest fire, driven by heavy winds is prodigious. The heated air seems to neutralize the force of gravitation, so that heavy pieces of burning bark or wood are lifted and carried for long distances. Fire has been known to jump for half a mile and commence burning in a new place.

The origin of the fires is unknown in general. A few brush fires were lost control of, while campers in some sections let their fires get away. But to describe the situation as expressed by many who escaped with their lives, the fires seemed to start in almost every part of the vast burned area at about the same time. It is believed by some that an eruption somewhere between Mounts Hood and St. Helens started the big fires. Fires were known to be burning in scattered spots, but were not deemed sufficient even under a high wind to work the resultant damage. The spread has been phenomenal and the rapidity with which the flames spread over the whole country almost surpasses belief. . . .

In several instances wild beasts, deer, bear and coyotes took common refuge, together with people and domestic animals, apparently oblivious to one another's presence in their endeavor to seek protection from the terrific clouds of flames that swept everything in their path. On the Little Washougal wild rabbits ran unharmed among the domestic animals and dogs unmolested, so great was the danger and fright. . . .

The burned section extends from Etna on the North Fork of Lewis River to the summit of the Cascades on the east, and embraces nearly all the country between there and the Columbia River, running as far west as Vancouver. But few spots escaped. The great belt of big timber lying between the North Fork of Lewis River and the Columbia has been destroyed and its value runs into millions of dollars. . . . Old timers say the denseness of the smoke at the present time has not been equalled since 1883, when a gloom hung over the country from June to September.

From news stories in the Seattle *Daily Times,* September 12, 1902, and the Vancouver *Columbian,* September 18, 1902.

LXVIII

Ray Stannard Baker

But no forest conflagration could dim a vision of greatness. In little more than a settlers' generation, Washington and Washingtonians had acquired a distinctive character as different as that of Vermont from Virginia, Kansas from Connecticut. Ray Stannard Baker (1870–1946) spotted it almost as soon as he crossed the border. Though he was just beginning his career as a writer, he was already an astute observer and shrewd analyst— qualities that were later to give him a foremost place among the editors and critics of his time, as editor of the *American Magazine,* one of the original "muckrakers," creator of the David Grayson series, and author of the Pulitzer Prize-winning biography of Woodrow Wilson.

Let's Grow

When the new settler crosses the Rockies, the altitude, or the rarefied atmosphere, or some vapor of the West yet unnamed by science, seems to endow him with the roseate vision, so that ever afterward all that he beholds is good and beautiful—and bigger than anywhere else. There is something refreshing and edifying in the way the Northwesterner shows off his town to the stranger: his boundless admiration for the new Episcopal church; his pride in the paving of Main Street; his brotherly interest in the development of the First National Bank; the imagination with which he prophesies the glorious future of the place, and exhibits the acres and acres of desert and hillside which the town is presently to populate. It is an adamantine visitor indeed who goes away without taking a deed or two for hopeful corner lots in the residential district.

I recall a little town in western Washington where the train stopped for a twenty-minute breakfast—a dusty road, and a distant spire rising above a row of dry cottonwoods. Fate had set the town back from the railroad, where its charms were invisible from passing trains; but the people, proud of their place, were not to be outdone. Close to the platform, where it could not escape attention, they had set up an enormous frame hung with photographic views of the town: the Cascade Hotel with a row of armchairs in front, the residence of Hon. John Smith, the interior of Roe's hardware store, prize apples raised by Joseph Jones, Esq., and so on. In the corner they had placed a little pocketful of circulars labeled, "Take one."

I took one. It gave a beguiling picture of the hopes of this new, struggling, ambitious, engaging town. I wish now that I had stopped and walked up the dusty road . . . I should have felt, at least, the irresistible spirit of these towns—youth, enthusiasm, health, hospitality. You never go amiss for a friend in a Western town.

Seattle, Tacoma, Spokane throb with enterprise and rivalry. . . . There is something immensely attractive in the pugnacity with which Seattle advances her fine new shipyard, while Tacoma counters with a low death rate and enormous wheat shipments. . . . With what enthusiasm Spokane, acquiring a new flour mill, hurls it, figuratively, in the teeth of her rivals! Fairhaven offers battle with its salmon industry, and no one who visits Washington can escape the belligerent banner of Everett—the smoke from her manufacturing chimneys. Every city on the coast has made up its mind firmly, if not quietly, to become the metropolis of the West.

Oftentimes the rivalry has its humorous side. While in Seattle I heard much of Mount Rainier. . . . The people of Seattle are proud of Mount Rainier; they regard it as a special Seattle attraction and have even named a certain brew of beer after the mountain. When I reached Tacoma one of the first things to which my attention was called was Mount Tacoma, rising gloriously in the southeast. It struck me that it bore a singular resemblance to Mount Rainier, and I said as much. "It *is* sometimes called Mount Rainier," said my informant; "but if you call it anything but Mount Tacoma over here, you can't get anything to eat." And so the mountain is the dear scenic possession, under separate names, of two cities.

Here in the Northwest one encounters the living representation of the strenuous life. Here men work together in a way unknown anywhere else. The East is insular, every man for himself. The Northwest—indeed, the whole West—has learned the value of cooperation and community interest. Migrating to a new country with difficulties and dangers on every hand, the people have been forced to combine and stand with solid front to the world. As a result, innumerable organizations have sprung up having for their purpose the advancement of some community interest.

Here the Chamber of Commerce is seen in its true glory—an organization of the leading businessmen of the town, supported by voluntary but liberal contributions, the object being to "boom" the city. A Western town that begrudges an appropriation of a hundred dollars for repairing the pavement of the main street will cheerfully empty its pockets of a thousand dollars for heralding the glories of the place. Let's grow, they say; never mind the patches—a youthfulness that we can't help liking.

So the Chamber circulates broadcast advertising matter showing the superiority of its town over all rivals, the purity of its waters, the sweetness of its air, its unequaled business opportunities, until the fluttering visitor, dazzled by this display of charms, casts here his fortunes. And it is the curious and wonderful property of this expansiveness that, once within its spell, the unwary one remains bedazzled forever and ever, so that he sees no longer wood and stone, but marble and gold and precious stones.

The Chamber of Commerce engages itself in gathering plums. A plum in the Western sense is a new railroad, a new coaling station, a new manufacturing plant; it falls to the most energetic shaking. Behold then these associations bringing down plums to the right joyous cheering of their respective constituencies, and you will appreciate one factor at least in the Western joy of life. And then there are numberless lesser organizations—to advance Oriental trade, to secure wheat shipments, to boom the mines of a certain county, to prevent the shipment of poor fruit, to kill jack rabbits. . . . A whole farming community may turn out at a day's notice to help kill jack rabbits or catch grasshoppers, and with a zest and hilarity that would astonish an Eastern farmer. . . .

As a result of this spirit, it requires only a breath to raise a crowd in a Western town, whether for a wedding, a barn-raising or a lynching. An Eastern village may continue a century without being stirred with a moment of crowd enthusiasm, but the people of the Northwestern town are constantly rising and doing things, sometimes amusing, sometimes serious, always interesting. People work together naturally.

An expression of this social helpfulness is manifested by the prevalence of the secret society. In the hotel at Tacoma I met a jovial man with a double chin, who had a singularly hearty way of shaking hands. He asked me at once in a big husky voice if I was an Eagle. I was not. "Then perhaps you are a Concatenated Hoo-Hoo?" I was not a Hoo Hoo, and there was real anxiety in his voice when he inquired further as to whether I was an Elk, a Mason, a Forester or a Knight of Pythias. "If you stay long in the West," he said, "you'll have to join something or other."

Indeed, nearly every man in the Northwest wears the badge of some order, often several of them. In one extreme case I counted six badges on one person, four on the coat lapels, one pendent from the watch charm, and one worn as the seal setting for a ring. Imagine this man going about with his grips and passwords; he could not long escape brothers in any direction in which fate led him. . . . The importance of the place which these societies occupy in the life of the country is indicated by frequent and often gorgeous parades, street fairs, carnivals, balls. . . . Combined with their social features, these organizations usually possess a distinct benevolent purpose—the relief of unfortunate members and their families. In short, they express one of the most engaging characteristics of the country in Western parlance, its "good-heartedness," its "good-fellowship," its willingness to help and be friendly. . . .

In the Northwest everything seems to have happened within the last ten years; events which would be of epoch-making importance in any country at any time have here crowded one upon another with wanton prodigality. . . . Think of this march of events! It was barely eight years ago that the gold fields of the Klondike were brought to the knowledge of the world, causing a rush of Americans to the Northwest. . . . Following the Klondike excitement, came the various Alaska discoveries and Seattle and Tacoma were and are the natural headquarters for most of the supplies shipped northward. . . . Hardly had the gold excitement calmed to the paces of a steady business enterprise when the Spanish War broke out, and these Pacific cities were thrown into the turmoil of visiting battleships and of provisioning and transporting the army of the Philippines.

Then came the opening trade with the new insular possessions in the Pacific, the Chinese War and its call for equipment and its stir of soldiery and transports, followed by the recent commercial expansion of Japan, with its trade demands. And now an element has just entered into the calculations of the coast—the construction of the Panama Canal—which will revolutionize whole departments of the world's trade and exercise a profound influence for good or evil on the cities of the Northwestern coast. While these world events were crowding upon one another, the development of the country tributary to the coast, upon which the solid

Wheat—twenty-five million bushels

progress of the cities must ultimately rest, was going forward with unprecedented rapidity. . . .

One finds it difficult to tell of the wonders of the coastal Northwest without in some degree sharing the enthusiasm of the American of Puget Sound. . . . No visitor can fail to be impressed with the luxuriance of the trees, shrubs, crops. Here the dandelion grows in thick clumps as high as one's waist; the dogwood is here a large and beautiful tree; clover grows rank beyond belief. Here are the greatest and most valuable forests on the continent, if not in the world, an apparently inexhaustible supply of timber. . . . The product of the mills is shipped to New York and even to Maine. . . .

In Washington the decay of centuries of rich vegetation has left in some of the heavily forested districts a singularly deep and productive soil, so that farmers have come in and planted apple trees and clover among the stumps. These little farms are a constant marvel to the visitor: a little log house, hardly larger than many of the great stumps, sometimes even built against a stump, a rude barn, a fence and a rich green field. In many places where the great trees stand close above ground, coal deposits have been discovered underneath—the remains of the forests of an earlier day. At one favored spot I saw land which had yielded a large return in lumber, was then being farmed on the surface, while a coal mine was in process of development underneath—a sort of threefold increment. . . .

Twenty years ago Washington produced no wheat worth mentioning; in 1900 the crop of the state was over twenty-five million bushels. . . . Hop culture on a large scale is also assuming great importance. . . . The salmon fisheries of Puget Sound and the Columbia River must now be numbered among the great fishing industries of the world. . . . In 1901, a phenomenal year, Washington packed over seven million dollars' worth of fish. . . . Fruit raising is also becoming yearly a more valuable resource of the arid land. Nothing can exceed the beauty of the orchards and fields of such irrigated valleys as the Yakima in Washington. . . .

But the sea, and not its fisheries—nor even the wonderful resources of the soil, nor mines, nor lumber—is the great hope and opportunity of the Pacific Northwest. Here is the Gateway of Empire. . . . As an enthusiastic Westerner has asserted, "The development of the United States began at the back door"— meaning the Atlantic Coast; "you will see one day what the front door is like."

Condensed from "The Great Northwest," Ray Stannard Baker. *Century Magazine,* March, 1903.

LXIX

Harper's Weekly

Ray Stannard Baker might have guessed it. Within months after he had categorized the men of Washington as exemplary promoters, Chamber of Commerce votaries, classic American go-getters, they came up with a sparkling new idea for boosting their state.

It was little short of preposterous for a city as youthful as Seattle to offer its candidacy as site for a World's Fair; such honors went to cities of renown, or wealth, or antiquity—London, Paris, Vienna, Philadelphia, New Orleans, Chicago—cities that had at least a centennial to celebrate. Not even San Francisco, most famed of West-coast cities, yet had the audacity to propose seriously that an international exposition be held there. But Washington publicists were not inclined to be intimidated by precedent.

Someone prudently suggested that Seattle be subordinated at least in the name of the fair, that they focus on Baker's idea of Puget Sound as a "front door" for the nation but give equal play to American possessions and trade routes in the Pacific, stretching in a wide arc from Alaska in the north to the Philippines in the south. It took a few years for the scheme to catch on, but it did catch on, in Washington, D.C., as well as Washington State.

By dint of persuasive argument, hard work, and federal subsidy, an impressive complex of exposition buildings rose on the outskirts of Seattle during the winter of 1908–09, and by spring the gates of the Alaska-Yukon-Pacific Exposition were ready for the formal opening. In a colorful spread, the editors of *Harper's Weekly* heralded the preparations and helped lure the 3,750,000 visitors that thronged to the site.

Nothing to Commemorate

A deal has been said of the "faith" that inspired the early settlers in New England, but in some lights it seems a weak and wavering thing, contrasted with the spirit that in less than fifty years has built the modern cities of the Northwest in what was only yesterday a green fir forest clothing bleak hillside above a storm-labored coast. . . . In 1860 Seattle had 3,533 inhabitants. In 1887 the first train reached Puget Sound over the Northern Pacific, and ten years later Seattle had grown to a population of 42,857. In 1900 it had some 80,000 inhabitants of all sorts, and eight years later this census had been more than trebled. In the story of civilization there is probably no record of more astonishing growth. . . .

The Alaska-Yukon-Pacific Exposition to be held in Seattle this year, . . . unlike most of its predecessors, has little or nothing to commemorate. Its history reaches back only a half-century or so. Other world's fairs have been held to mark anniversaries of momentous events in history. They have been milestones down the long journey from the past. The fundamental purpose of the Seattle Exposition is, rather, to establish a new point of departure for the future. The section of country which this exposition will reveal to hitherto uninformed people, as well as the population who have in hand its making, are distinctly the apostles of the new.

In its essence, this exhibition, upon which $10,000,000 is being expended, is purely educational. . . . There is force in the contention of the coast country that in the natural course of human destiny, the Pacific, so lately discovered, is to be the scene of the most important world movements during the centuries just now to come. . . . Its importance to the destiny of the United States seems to be the keynote of the undertaking.

Of course, there are narrow souls in Seattle and elsewhere who look on it merely as an opportunity to pick up a few desultory dollars. This is the small and sordid view. This exposition, if its promise be fulfilled, will bring the unknown to the known. . . . With governmental assistance, which is being so lavishly lent, it will give to Americans generally a clear comprehension, which they never have had, of the American domain that lies beyond the tide line of the Pacific Coast. It will bring Hawaii, the Philippines and Alaska under the educational stereoscope. What has hitherto been lamely or one-sidedly presented to the American people in print, will be shown in actuality. . . .

In every possible way, the entire Pacific Northwest hopes and intends to make this Fair a demonstration of its growth and possibility, to exploit thereby its land, its waters, its forests, its irrigation, its astounding volume of water power, its agriculture, its fisheries, its lumber, its industry and progressiveness, and its promise as a field for the investment of capital.

But beyond and beneath all these, the exposition has a mission and a meaning. It is to be to all the United States a lesson in magnified commerce. It is to show forth the huge volume of trade which it is possible for this country to carry on with the lands that border the Pacific—lands with eighteen millions of square miles of area, a billion of population, two billion dollars annually of exports and an equal amount of imports. . . .

Men familiar with similar expositions that have been held in the past declare that from an educational point of view . . . the range and extent of the exhibits which are to be displayed in the divers buildings scattered over the 250 acres of exposition grounds . . . will be unprecedented and the Alaska-Yukon-Pacific Exposition unique.

From "The Wonderful Northwest," *Harper's Weekly,* April 3, 1909.

LXX

James Stevens

The World's Fair at Seattle did help bring in new capital, new settlers, and new enterprises, but lumbering was still the most conspicuous industry along the shore lands and watershed of the state, as only a Christmas celebration in one of the mill towns could demonstrate. From lumber camps and lumber yards the men poured in to drown their sorrows, avenge their grievances, and "perform." They took over a town like Aberdeen, and the town always capitulated for the occasion.

James Stevens (1892–) described such a holiday conquest in his superb little book *Homer in the Sagebrush,* which makes as lively reading today as it did when it first appeared more than forty years ago. A Washington authority on lumbering and lumbermen, and the world authority on the Paul Bunyan legend, Stevens wrote half a dozen high-spirited volumes on his field, and for a quarter of a century served also as public relations counsel for the West Coast Lumbermen's Association.

Merry Christmas in Aberdeen

All the loggers from the Wishkah camp were on the road the day before Christmas. . . . The December wind was still on a rampage, blowing in a drizzle from Gray's Harbor. Heron Street was veiled in the foggy rain. Lights were shining through the windows of stores, restaurants, dance halls and saloons. The calked boots of a thousand loggers scrunched the wet boards of sidewalks as the bearded and mustached men in mackinaws and stagged pants roved from one saloon to the other. They straggled across the planks of the street to meet friends on the other side. Gangs gathered, whoops and laughs filled the air, bottles were passed around. Shingle-weavers, mill hands, fishermen and sailors stood aside for the men of the woods. Hard-looking customers eased among the gangs, searching for those who might be relieved of their rolls without too much trouble. . . .

In the first blocks from the left bank of the Wishkah the saloons packed Heron and Hume streets—the Humboldt, the Mug, the Whale, the Eagle, the Combination, the Gem, the North Pole, the Blazer, the Circle, and many more. Square-fronted one- and two-story buildings of wood in rusty paint, all resting on piling or on ground made by the fill of sawdust and edgings.

The best bars, such as the Humboldt and Blazer, had new floors, but already these were freckled and splotched from the calks of the loggers' boots. Twice a year these popular saloons had to lay new floors. Such tough joints as the Circle had iron-bound bars and sawdust floors. The sidewalks had slivery hollows, except where new planks had been nailed down. Aberdeen was still a rough-hewn frontier town. . . .

Two thousand men from the bullteam camps, the lumber and shingle mills, the ships and the fisheries were ready [to celebrate Christmas]. In the Blazer four aproned bartenders rushed and sweated between spigots, bar and till. Big Al, the thick-necked, fierce-eyed owner, who prided himself on running the squarest place in town and on having the muscles to keep it square and peaceable, was cashing check after check and banking for most of the loggers. His safe held twenty thousand dollars before midnight.

The loggers were six-deep before the bar. The bottles and glasses were skidded through splashes of beer and furrows of foam. The bartenders picked up wet dollars and half-dollars and the loggers picked up wet quarters and dimes of change. The rush was so heavy that the bartenders had no time to swab off the bar. The fog was thickening outside and the saloon lamps threw a richer glow over the scene. The splattered and foamy top of the bar shone. The mirrors back of it reflected light into the drinkers' faces, making them appear handsome and bright.

The rumble of talk and the clink of glasses quickened; shouted jokes and bawls of laughter sounded; all of a sudden there was a blast of hot argument, a hard tramp of feet, a thud, a grunt—and Big Al swung around the bar. He pried the two battlers apart, made them feel the power of his grip, then brought them to the bar.

"Drink together on the house," ordered Big Al. "Then keep the peace, or I'll work you both down with a bungstarter. This ain't no knock-down-and-drag-out joint, my lads."

Somebody smacked a twenty-dollar gold piece on the bar. "Set up the whisky! Everybody drink on a Michigan man!"

Big Al grinned and helped with the setting-up himself. The loggers were starting now, starting to blow 'er hard and fast.

The doors never stopped swinging. Loggers tramped in and loggers tramped out. Few were staggering any yet; the night was hardly born. But the street was darkening fast and few gangs were lingering outside now. It was ramble from one saloon to the other; at suppertime head for porkchops and eggs; then to the dance halls and the dance hall girls when the pianos began to thump and the fiddles to squeak foot-teasing tunes. Dance and drink until midnight. . . .

Hey, lad, it's a bum dancer you are, in logger boots, heavy and calked! No chance to slick and slide around in a fancy style. No chance to give the girls a treat with a nifty dancing show. But what the hell, Bill, what the hell! You're only a lousy timber beast anyway, here to blow in with the dance hall women! You're a camp man, old settler, a man who has to live away from women most of his days and get the timber out. Religious women look at you like a rabbit looks at a wolf. You've been "timber beast" to the good folks since a way back. So that's how you are what you are. That's why you perform. You got to get your high and mighty times any way you can. Well, lad, here's the fixings for you, here in your roaring old timber town! Redeye to uplift your Jeezus-jimmed soul, booze-mooching whores to ease your heart! Yea, lad, you know they'd spit in your eye if it wasn't for your silver and gold! Love—love hell! . . .

At two o'clock . . . the Blazer was jammed with a roaring mob. Six bartenders were handling the rush. The glasses of beer and whisky were passed back from hand to hand. The shrill voices of dance hall girls sounded among the chesty rumble of logger talk. Above the drab shades of the hanging coal oil lamps a drift of blue smoke hid the ceiling. On kegs and in chairs men who had drunk themselves off their feet lolled and snored. Big Al stood at the end of the bar, grinning from the corner of his mouth whenever a joke was shouted at him from the crowd, keeping his eyes peeled for pimps and stickup men. His was a logger's saloon and he protected his trade.

A young logger staggered up to him, seized one of Al's suspenders to steady himself, and asked for fifty dollars from the safe.

"You'll get nothin' till in the mornin', you polluted Siwash!" growled Big Al, and pushed him away.

The young logger weaved through the crowd, looking for sympathy. "Won't give me my own money, the suhvabish! Call' me p'luted Siwash!". . .

So it was in the timber country. . . . Tomorrow was Christmas—hell, it was Christmas already! Christmas, logger, Christmas! Blow in! Blow in! Booze up and battle and get a woman for yourself! That was Christmas for a logger—have a high and mighty time until his silver and gold are gone. That was it for a logger, bully one or not. Just a time in town, then out to the timber, eleven-hour labor, salt pork, tough beans and sourdough bread to eat, a stinking bunk shanty to sleep in, and lousy blankets for a lonesome sleep. Back to the life of a timber beast!

But what the hell, Bill, what the hell! A pocketful of gold, and it's time to perform! Come on, Babe. . . .

The wind never rested on Christmas day, and there was always rain in the hard wind. The restaurants had their turn at the loggers' stakes between noon and night. "Roast turkey with dressing and cranberry sauce. Home-made mince pies." In the hotel dining room there were white cloths on the tables. And the diners were served with wines. Calk boots, stagged pants and mackinaws were not wanted there. But the loggers didn't care a damn. To hell with the highfalutin stuff!

At the hotel bar you could have Tom and Jerrys and eggnog, drinks hot and rich. But to hell with that too. Redeye was good enough. Redeye in a joint where a man can whoop and sing and perform—come on, bullies, to the Blazer! We've got our money in Big Al's safe!

All of Christmas day loggers streamed through Heron Street, flowed in and out of the saloons. The Christmas blow-in reached its high tide at night. Big Al had kept the peace in the Blazer, but in the joints it had been a different story. In one a logger had taken a swing at a crooked faro dealer and got a bullet in the groin in return. He was in the hospital now, the bullet still in him. A doctor had probed for it for an hour, and then given it up. Probably he'd die.

Two brothers were looking for their younger one. Last anybody'd seen of him was in the Eagle. Probably he'd been slipped some knockout drops, rolled, then eased through a trapdoor into the river. Yep, prob'ly. That was the way she went. A pore damn logger certainly had to look out for himself in this tough town.

But most of the talk along the bar of the Blazer was roared boasts of performances of the night before and promises of the performances that were to come tonight. It was Christmas, the great day of the blow-in. Tomorrow the loggers would calm down and talk logging as they lined the bars. But today they had to perform.

Condensed from *Homer in the Sagebrush*, James Stevens (New York: Alfred A. Knopf, 1928).

LXXI

Ella Higginson

In entertainment establishments more decorous than those of Aberdeen, audiences of thousands in the early 1900s cheered the rendition of songs programmed as "The Lamp in the West," "Hey, Alder, Hang Thy Tassels Out," "Four-Leaf Clover." The voices that brought the applause were those of great opera stars like Emma Calvé, Enrico Caruso, and John McCormack, but the words they sang were those of Ella Higginson (1862–1940). The most widespread acclaim ever to greet any lyrics written in Washington were hers. They may be outmoded now, but so esteemed was Ella Higginson's poetry among an earlier generation that no less than fifty composers vied with one another to set it to music, and her work was praised by literary lights as brilliant as Sarah Orne Jewett, William Allen White, James Whitcomb Riley, and William Dean Howells, who regarded her as a peer.

Washingtonians revered her, for they knew that the sea and the seasons, the moss and mountains of which she wrote belonged to their state. It was her home and the things about her were her favorite subjects. Nor did she limit her creativity to poetry. She also penned short stories, essays and, in 1914, a novel, *Mariella: of Out-West*—and that was perhaps a mistake. It brought her more embarrassment than encomium; angry Bellingham neighbors thought they saw themselves revealed injudiciously on her pages and deluged her with vituperative letters. But over the years that indiscretion was forgiven and the Washington Federation of Women's Clubs elected her State Poet Laureate.

The Lamp in the West

Venus has lit her silver lamp,
    Low in the purple West,
Breathing a soft and mellow light
    Upon the sea's full breast;
It is the hour when velvet winds
    Tremble the alder's crest.

Far out, far out, the restless bar
    Starts from a troubled sleep,
Where roaring thro' the narrow straits
    The meeting waters leap.
But still that shining pathway leads
    Across the lonely deep.

When I sail out the narrow straits,
    Where unknown dangers be,
And cross the troubled, moaning bar,
    To the mysterious sea,
Dear God, wilt Thou not set a lamp
    Low in the West for me?

March

Hey, alder, hang thy tassels out
    This blue and golden morn;
And willow, show thy silver plush,
    Wild grape, thy scarlet thorn!

And velvet moss about the trees,
    Lift every russet cup;

The dew is coming down this way,
    With pearls to fill them up.

And birds, why tarry so a-South?
    Spent is the bitter rain!
With messages of love and cheer
    Come North, come North, again.

Four-Leaf Clover

I know a place where the sun is like gold,
    And cherry blossoms burst with snow,
And down underneath is the loveliest nook
    Where the four-leaf clovers grow.

    One leaf is for hope, and one is for faith,
        And one is for love, you know,
    And God put another in for luck—
        If you search, you will find where they grow.

But you must have hope, and you must have faith,
    You must love and be strong—and so—
If you work, if you wait, you will find the place
    Where the four-leaf clovers grow.

The Solemn Night

All through the tender, pulsing Summer night,
    The mellow-throated frogs steal through my dream;
A thousand tones of softness, blending, seem,
    Like one harmonious, choired whole; pale light
Shifts earthward from a million eyes and bright,
    While the violet vaults of heaven teem.
Dreaming, I lie; one restful, soft moonbeam
    Slants through my room athwart the dim twilight,

And rests my sleep-filled eyes. I seem to hear—
  So hushed the mystic night—the earth's pulse-beat,
Solemn, measured and full; faint, far, yet clear,
  Comes up the swelling murmur of the sea;
Winds fresh from piney forests, spiced, sweet,
  Breathing of mountain saps, steal in to me.

From *Ella Higginson: A Tribute* (Washington State Federation of Women's Clubs, 1941).

LXXII

Murray C. Morgan

Logging, as it came from Maine, was a hale, happy-go-lucky, picturesque occupation, but on the West coast it lost much of its old character when it grew into a major industry—when skid road was converted into a narrow-gauge rail line, when the ox team was replaced by a locomotive or a "donkey" engine, when all manner of mechanical equipment began to take the place of hand tools.

Into the 1880s lumbering in Washington remained a relatively small operation, carried on by many little companies and little close-knit gangs with strong loyalties to the boss. Altogether the tally of loggers wasn't over two thousand. Then came a rapid change. Great companies with substantial outside capital moved in. The Northern Pacific, which had won title to hundreds of thousands of forest acres as its bonus for construction of the line, started selling off holdings in enormous chunks to big lumber dealers.

In the early 1900s lumber production leaped to four billion feet a year, and the work force to some thirty-five thousand, but the men were losing their sense of participation in a small endeavor; they were being demoted to laborers in a huge impersonalized establishment, and were no longer content to put in a ten- or twelve-hour day in arduous, dangerous work for wages of $1.00,

$1.50, or even $2.00. They knew they were not getting their share of the profits.

Clouds were gathering for one of the dark episodes in Washington annals. Actually the labor situation in the Northwest was not very different from what it was in other parts of the country, but there was an esprit de corps among loggers in general that existed in few other employments; they were more closely united, more direct in their demands, more impatient for immediate action and, being a little nearer in time and distance to the frontier, they were ready to use more rugged methods in making their convictions known.

In *The Last Wilderness* Murray C. Morgan (1916–), who has distinguished himself as author of half a dozen lively books on the state, traced the complicated background of the labor disputes and reported in retrospect the sequential developments.

The Grinning Cat on a Wooden Shoe

One day at Port Ludlow in the late 1890's when a loading car slipped partly off an overhead track, Cyrus Walker dispatched a workman to chain the lumber on the car and save it from sliding off and getting bruised. The lumber slipped anyway, and the man was crushed. A foreman passed the hat among the employees and collected for the funeral expenses. Then he added something new. He held out the hat to Walker, who said, "I would like to help that poor woman and her children. But I can give nothing. If I did, it would set an unfortunate precedent and give the impression that an employer has responsibilities to his employees."

That was the standard-brand attitude. Walker was not a harsh man; by the standards of the day, Pope and Talbot was a good place to work. But the attitude remained: If you don't like it, draw your pay; nobody says you've got to stay; it's a free country.

Hence the unions. On the peninsula the first unions in the lumber industry were organized among the workers in the shingle mills, whose occupation was particularly hazardous. A reporter who visited a shingle mill in the first decade of the twentieth century has left this description:

> Shingle-weaving is not a trade, it is a battle. For ten hours a day the the sawyer faces two teethed steel disks whirling around 200 times a minute. To the one on the left he feeds the heavy blocks of cedar, reaching over with his left hand to remove the heavy shingles it rips out.
>
> Hour after hour the shingle-weaver's hands and arms, plain unarmored flesh and blood, are staked against the screeching steel that cares not what it severs. Hour after hour the steel sings its crescendo note as it bites into the wood, the sawdust thickens, the wet sponge under the sawyer's nose fills with fine particles. If "cedar asthma," the shingle-weaver's occupational disease, does not get him, the steel will. Sooner or later he reaches over a little too far, the whirling blade tosses drops of deep red into the air, a finger, a hand, or part of an arm comes sliding down the slick chute.

Shingle-weavers' locals flared up by spontaneous combustion in all the lumber towns around the peninsula and sound in 1900 and 1901. The necessary elements were all present: danger, poor pay, job insecurity, a feeling of craft solidarity among men who lived close together, and the need of the operators for workers with some skill. In 1903 delegates met in Everett to form the International Shingle Weavers Union of America. The same year sawmill workers started to organize. In 1905 the International Brotherhood of Woodsmen and Sawmill Workers was chartered by the American Federation of Labor.

The operators were outraged. They were individualistic men, accustomed to making their own decisions. Their feeling of responsibility toward their men was at best paternalistic. Not infrequently an operator would drop around to give an old hand who had joined a union some sincere and fatherly advice: "Don't get mixed up with those wild men; we'd hate to have to let you go."

Many of the employers were sincerely convinced that most of the men in the mills and woods *liked* taking risks and working long hours. "Gives 'em a feeling of independence. Makes 'em know they're men. I know how they feel, dammit. I started there myself."

After 1900 all the employers were caught in the bind between rising prices for raw materials and declining prices for the finished product due to increased production. The operators formed associations of their own to limit output and regulate prices and achieve a standard grading system for lumber, but they were too individualistic for their own good. W. B. Mack, an Aberdeen operator, told a meeting of the Pacific Lumber Manufacturers Association in 1911, "I don't see a ray of hope. . . . Every time a price is given, some other fellow cuts it. Everybody seems to be fighting everybody else."

There was a welter of strikes. They boiled up in Hoquiam, were settled, then erupted in Raymond and Aberdeen, Cosmopolis and Port Ludlow; then back to Hoquiam, where at one stage union men were loaded into boxcars for deportation to nobody knew where, but the mayor declared himself out of sympathy with the project, and railroad men refused to move the train.

These first strikes, though violent and productive of deep bitterness on both sides, were strikes for such limited objectives as a larger share of the profits and a safer place to work. They were intended not to change the world but only to change conditions in a given plant. Then along came the Industrial Workers of the World, born of a meeting of forty-three unions in Chicago in 1905.

The I.W.W., or Wobblies, as they soon came to be called, didn't ask for a larger slice of the economic melon; they wanted the whole thing, flesh, rind and pits, and they wanted it right away. The Wobblies believed in world revolution, not in distant future but today. The Red Dawn would not be tomorrow but had come yesterday, and the Wobblies were at war with society. They claimed no common ground with the employer except the industrial battlefield. They considered the craft unions, even the militant shingle-weavers, to be merely creatures of the employers, nursemaids of reaction, traitors to the working class. They quoted Mark Hanna on "the labor lieutenants of the captains of industry," but they didn't mean this as a compliment.

The Wobblies considered themselves soldiers in a battle already joined. They were brave, unreasonable, ingenious, cantankerous, violent. To the rootless men in the forest camps they offered an outlet for frustration more exciting than a brothel. The I.W.W. appealed to idealists who wanted a better world and to outsized juvenile delinquents in corked boots who wanted to smash back at a world they never made. The Wobs were every bit as rough as the conditions that spawned them.

There were Wobbly halls in all the lumber towns, usually somewhere along the skid road, preferably near the "slave markets," as the employment agencies were known. These headquarters were bare beat-up buildings, furnished with battered chairs and decorated with pictures of Joe Hill, the romantic radical poet who was executed by a firing squad in Utah for a holdup he perhaps did not commit and thereby became for the Wobblies that martyr without whom no cause can be complete.

These halls were raided diligently by town police, and also by such elements of the outraged citizenry as the employers—now suffering from the Wobbly Horrors—could organize and arm. But the hall was always just a rented hall; and if some of the men who packed the rigging—that is, gave signed-up members their red cards and passed out the gaudy propaganda broadsides and the Wobbly song books—were driven out of town in various conditions of disrepair, there were sure to be more fellow workers swinging down from the freight cars a few days later.

The Wobs brought to near perfection a technique later employed by Gandhi. When their right to harangue the stiffs on some lumbertown skid road was denied, they swarmed into the town and started talking at every street corner, inviting arrest. When the jail got too full (in one strike in Spokane the demonstrators filled the city jail, the county jail, a deserted schoolhouse and an M.P. barracks) and the cost of feeding the prisoners began to damage the city budget, the authorities usually backed down. But not always.

Up in Everett in the spring of 1916 the Wobbly speakers moved in when the town was already made tense by strikes of longshoremen, tugboat crews and shingle-weavers. The first Wobbly organizer to hit town, one James Rowan, almost immediately got into a street-corner argument with a craft-union organizer and was vagged out of town by the police. Soon another Wobbly showed up, and the police chased him out of town along with thirty-five sympathizers. This kept up through the summer. In the fall, with the strike still dragging on, a party of forty Wobblies arrived on a passenger steamer from Seattle for a free-speech demonstration. They were captured by deputized vigilantes, taken to the edge of town, stripped, and made to run a gantlet of men armed with clubs and with branches of devil's club, a prickly brush. All survived, but some were hospitalized.

A few days later the Wobblies, at the suggestion of a Seattle clergyman, the Reverend Oscar McGill, announced that they would hold a mass meeting on Sunday afternoon, November 6, in Everett. The idea was that the vigilantes would not resort to violence in public.

That Sunday 250 Wobblies left Seattle for Everett on the regular passenger steamer *Verona*, and another fifty left on the *Calista*, which was chartered. The *Verona* got there first. As she tied up at the dock the Wobblies were singing:

> We meet today in Freedom's cause,
> And raise our voices high;
> We'll join our hands in union strong,
> To battle or to die. . . .

From the dock the sheriff shouted, "Who is your leader?"
"We're all leaders."
"Don't try to land here."
Some Wobblies rushed the gangplank. Vigilantes concealed in the warehouse started shooting. Eleven of the Wobblies died, along with two deputy sheriffs; thirty men on the boat and fifteen on the dock were wounded before a Wobbly with a revolver forced the *Verona*'s engineer to reverse the engines. The towline snapped, and the steamer wallowed away. No one took the wheel until she was almost out of range from shore.

The police were waiting when the *Verona* docked in Seattle. Seventy-four men were arrested and charged with first-degree murder. One of them, Thomas H. Tracy, was tried and found not guilty. The charges against the others were eventually dropped.

The Wobblies had won their greatest legal victory, but on the morning that Tracy's attorney, George F. Vanderveer, rose in superior court in Seattle to open the case for the defense, President Woodrow Wilson stood before a joint session of Congress in Washington to ask that war be declared on Germany. The war made the Wobblies more unpopular than ever.

In the spring of 1917 both the craft unions and the I.W.W. asked lumber operators for an eight-hour day, at three dollars, in the mills and either an eight-hour day or a nine-hour day, at $3.50, in the camps. The operators refused the demands and turned down government requests that they arbitrate; instead they formed the Lumberman's Protective Association, which was empowered to fine any member five hundred dollars a day for operating less than ten hours per shift. In July men walked out of nearly every mill and camp in the state. It was the biggest strike the Far West had known.

After six weeks the men went back to work, their demands unmet. The craft unions authorized their men to return to the job, although they were to remain technically on strike until the eight-hour day was granted. The Wobblies also went back, but not exactly to work; they appeared in mill and camp, but practiced what they called "conscientious withdrawal of efficiency"—the slowdown.

The ingenious Wobblies, long adept at sabotage, could think of a lot of ways to botch a job. For instance, they could work eight hours and then quit. If they were fired, the next crew was unlikely to be better. They were accused of driving spikes in logs to break saws in the mills—a really terrible thing to do, since a saw that hit metal filled the mill with flying steel. The Wobblies denied doing this, but they did not deny that they were striking on the job. Signs of the grinning cat perched on the wooden shoe—the symbol of sabotage—leered from the windows of Wobbly halls.

Lumber production got into such a snarl that the War Department dispatched Colonel Bryce P. Disque to see what could be done to get fir and hemlock and pine, and especially spruce, moving out of the woods. Spruce was the glamour wood; it went into airplanes. As a result of the colonel's visit two strange new organizations appeared in the woods: the Loyal Legion of Loggers and Lumbermen, and the Spruce Production Division.

The 4-L, as the Loyal Legion came to be called, was called a "fifty-fifty outfit: half employer, half employee, and half you-know-what." All real power centered in the Army in the person of Colonel Disque. Each 4-L member, boss or worker, had to sign a pledge to help the war effort, "to stamp out any sedition or acts of hostility against the United States which may come to their knowledge. . . ."

Though the craft unions and the Wobblies expressed loud doubts about the impartiality of the War Department in any labor-management dispute . . . Colonel Disque became convinced that most of the union demands would have to be met if lumber was to be cut. He finally ordered the operators to cut shifts to eight hours and pay time-and-a-half for overtime; shortly after, he ruled that employees must furnish bunkhouses with clean bedding and change the sheets and pillow cases weekly. . . .

It took some time to get things untangled in the tall timber after the outbreak of peace. . . . The Loyal Legion of Loggers and Lumbermen came unstuck when the glue of patriotism and wartime profits was removed. . . . The A.F. of L. mill and camp unions tried to fill the vacuum left by the Loyal Legion. They failed. . . . That left the woods to the Wobblies.

They carried on the fight as before, and again they were met with violence, the worst of it in Centralia, a lumber and farm town fifty miles up the Chehalis River from Aberdeen. There on Armistice Day, 1919, an American Legion parade unit paused before the Wobbly hall. . . . For days there had been rumors that the hall was to be raided. The Wobblies had even appealed to their old enemies, the police and the governor, for protection. Their lawyer had advised them that they had a right to protect themselves if attacked. Inside the hall were armed men; other Wobblies with rifles were stationed in a hotel across the street and on a nearby hill. So when the Legionnaires stopped in front of the hall on that chill, bitter day, the whole town seemed to hold its breath.

It has never been determined whether the shooting started before the Legionnaires charged the door. But when the ugly business was over three young Legionnaires were dead, and so was a fourth veteran, Wesley Everest, who had been inside the building, and who had killed at least two of the others. Everest had been chased through town by the mob. They caught him on the bank of the Chehalis. He was taken to the city jail, but that night he was lynched. The mob . . . hanged him from the bridge, and while he was hanging they shot him.

The trial of the Wobblies for the murder of the Legionnaires was held in Montesano, the county seat of Grays Harbor. Ten men were charged with murder. . . . Seven were found guilty of second-degree murder and sent to prison for terms of twenty-five to forty years. . . .

The Wobblies had a new set of martyrs to set up alongside Joe Hill. They used them with skill. But things were different, somehow. The stiffs in the woods were sorry about Wesley Everest and the other guys, but hell! that's how things are. What do you expect me to do about it?

"Revolt," said the Wobblies. "Throw off your chains."

But the loggers didn't want a revolution. Better pay, shorter hours. Revolution, no.

The era of raw violence had ended. As we look back, it seems probable that it ended on the day when Colonel Disque ordered the eight-hour day and the sheets changed every week, for then the timber beast became an industrial worker.

From *The Last Wilderness*, Murray Morgan (New York: Viking Press, 1955).

LXXIII

Anna Louise Strong

From the lumber industry, unrest among labor spread to other employments. Apprehension with regard to the "bolshevik menace" was creeping across the United States, and Seattle, one of the last spots that alarmists had flagged for a dangerous outcropping of red infection, suddenly was drawing bold headlines. Newspapers from Boston to Bellingham were trumping up "Red Seattle." Nine months before the Centralia tragedy on Armistice Day of 1919, occurred the first general strike that had ever been called in an American city. It was to go down in history as "The Seattle Revolution."

The inside story of that "Revolution" from the worker's point of view was forthrightly related by a left-wing participant in the day-to-day organization of the strike, Anna Louise Strong (1885–), who had received her undergraduate education at conservative Bryn Mawr and Oberlin, earned her Ph.D. at the University of Chicago, become a practicing sociologist and welfare worker, then had taken a sharp turn to the left and made a stand as outspoken champion of the labor movement.

Before the war she had come to Washington to organize "Know Your City" institutes in Seattle, Walla Walla, and Spokane. She knew the state intimately, was a member of the Seattle School Board, feature editor for the *Seattle Union Record,* a syndicated state correspondent. And already she was writing impressive social studies, later epitomized in such widely read books as *China's Millions, This Soviet World, Spain in Arms, I Change Worlds.* In 1930 she organized the first English newspaper in Russia, *The Moscow Daily News,* and for most of her adult life has been near the core of world-shaking social movements. She was on the train returning to Seattle from a labor conference in Chicago when she first heard about the impending general strike.

Red in the Ranks

From coast to coast in January 1919 went the report that revolution was imminent in Seattle. A general strike had been called in sympathy with the shipyard workers and nobody knew how it might end. Government officials in Washington announced that Bolshevism had made its appearance in the northwest of the United States.

The tension in Seattle before the strike is difficult to exaggerate. Businessmen took out riot insurance and purchased guns. Citizens laid in supplies for a long siege; kerosene lamps were dragged from storage to sell at high prices in case the strike should involve City Light. Some of the wealthy families took trips to Portland to be out of the upheaval. The press appealed to strikers not to ruin their home city. Later they changed their tone and demanded threateningly: "Which flag are you under? . . . if under the American flag then put down Bolshevism in your midst."

Ours was the first general strike, involving all the workers in a city, that ever took place on the North American continent. For years the I.W.W. had talked of the general strike, declaring that the power of the workers' folded arms would bring the collapse of capitalism. Few of them claimed to know concretely what would happen when such a strike started. It was like pulling the trigger of a gun without knowing with what ammunition it was loaded. Government officials and local business men said it was loaded with revolution. All our labor leaders busily denied this.

The strike would probably not have occurred at all if the "labor leaders" had been in town. . . . They were terrified when they heard that a general strike had been voted. They discussed it on the train on the way back to Seattle. . . . To what were they returning? I also was on that train from Chicago to Seattle. I rated now as a leader of Seattle workers. Within that movement I was considered one of the "progressives," which meant that I stood for industrial unionism (to be attained through a process of federating the craft unions), for political action by labor (we were developing a farmer-labor party against the reactionaries of the American Federation of Labor), and for eventual rule of the world by its workers, without specifying how and when.

From the day when I had walked into the offices of the *Call* to offer my services as writer, I had found both comradeship and freedom so naturally mingled that I never analyzed these blessings till long after they had gone. . . . My writing was winning reputation outside Seattle in the labor and socialist press of America. . . . We seem to have seen world revolution as a sealed packet which God, or the inevitable laws of human progress, would give us, a marching into a golden West which nobody could foreshadow. We passionately believed that a Great Change was coming, but when or how we did not know.

And now, when we faced on the train from Chicago to Seattle the first signs of actual change, we were frankly frightened. A general strike was unleashed power. It might easily smash something—us perhaps, our well-organized labor movement. Yet we could not repudiate action taken by sixty thousand workers. The cynical reactionaries of the American Federation of Labor often repudiated rank and file action, but we left-wing idealists stuck with the workers. Having no theory or plan for handling a general strike . . . the leaders wavered between an open support of the strike and an unadmitted wish to stop it.

The general strike thus thrust upon unwilling leaders grew out of a strike of thirty-five thousand shipyard workers for wage adjustments. Throughout the war, wages had been fixed by government boards in consultation with national presidents of craft unions. They bribed the highly skilled workers and cut the pay of the unskilled. . . . Discontent smoldered for a year and a half of war-time, ready to burst into flame when restraints should be removed.

Double dealing by the head of the Emergency Fleet Corporation supplied the torch for the bonfire. His frequent public statements that our workers had the right to bargain directly with their employers during war-time, were undermined by his private telegrams to the shipyard owners threatening to cut off the supply of steel or to cancel contracts if they changed the wage scales. Through the "mistake" of a messenger boy, one of these telegrams was delivered not to the Metal Trades Association (the employers) but to the Metal Trades Council (the workers). The anger of the shipyard workers was thus directed against Washington; they struck and asked all unions of the city to support them by a general strike. Such a strike—as a political protest—was against the policy of the American Federation of Labor.

Yet swiftly union after union violated its constitution, flouted its national officers and sacrificed hard-won agreements to join the strike. The conservative typographical union, the property-holding carpenters union, the weak hotel-maids union, the staid musicians, the fighting longshoremen and teamsters—swung united into line. . . . So did I.W.W. organizations. . . .

The General Strike Committee, composed of more than three hundred delegates from one hundred and ten unions, met all day Sunday, February 2, 1919. They faced and disregarded the national officers of craft unions who were telegraphing orders from the East. . . . They rejected as strike slogan the motto "We have nothing to lose but our chains and a whole world to gain," in favor of "Together WE Win." For they reasoned that they had a great deal to lose—jobs at good wages with which they were buying silk shirts, pianos and homes. They wanted solidarity but not class war. Then so little did they realize the problems before them that they fixed the strike for the following Thursday at 10 A.M. and adjourned to meet on Thursday evening after the strike should have started, meantime referring any new problems that might arise to a rather hastily elected "Committe of Fifteen."

This Committee of Fifteen became by the next morning the unintentional but actual rulers of Seattle. They were not organized for power; they strove to evade power; but power was thrust upon them. To "walk off the job" was not simple when it involved all activities of a city. Should streets be plunged into darkness? Should water-works stop? How would three hundred thousand people eat? . . .

"On Thursday at 10 A.M." sixty thousand workers went off their jobs in Seattle. The organized life of the city fell into their hands. They themselves hardly knew it; the sense of power was merely an extra fillip to the joyous solidarity felt among the workers. They laughed: "Our first vacation in three years." The union leaders bragged: "Sixty thousand out and not even a fist fight." They were proud of their pacifism and self-control. With smiling words the labor guards dispersed all crowds that gathered, lest someone provoke a riot.

Strike bulletins urged workers to stay off the streets, to patronize libraries and dig in home gardens to "make the most of your leisure," as this is "fine weather for vacation." The feeding of down-town workers was done by the provision trades, in twenty-one special dining rooms opened for the duration of the strike. By the end of the strike they were serving thirty thousand meals a day. Thus the fighting solidarity of Seattle's workers was carefully shepherded into a demonstration of law and order. . . . The ordinary police court arrests sank far below the average, so careful were the workers to avoid all fights.

In spite of this pacific attitude of the workers, the businessmen . . . knew that power had slipped from their hands into the keeping of these new, unconscious men. Their exasperation grew hourly; it became wrath and thirst for blood. They pressed upon the mayor, upon Washington; they bought guns from hardware stores and demanded rights as deputies. Two thousand four hundred "citizens," not workers, thus received the stars and guns which labor guards had refused. Troops from Camp Lewis were marched into the city and stationed in the armory to be "ready for trouble."

Ole Hanson, real estate promoter by profession and mayor of Seattle at the time, was an amiable politician and a good bluffer, as both his trade and his avocation demanded. When the strike was announced he took some of the labor leaders to lunch in Rippe's cafe and pled with them: "Boys, I want my street lights and water supply and hospitals. I don't care if you shut down all the rest of the city." . . .

Ole was no revolution-buster in those days; he was trying to conciliate the revolution. He was a small town politician, all things to all comers, a weathercock in the wind. Yet by such weathercocks one may tell whence wind is blowing. When Ole turned against us on the second day of the general strike, we should have guessed that he had discovered our weakness. When he began to mail hundreds of copies of his own photographs to newspapers all over the United States as the man who smashed the revolution in Seattle, we should have known that we had lost the battle.

Ole didn't dare make that announcement in Seattle. When word came back to us from other cities that Ole called our strike an attempted revolution which he had already put down, Seattle workers laughed. Not a union had gone back to work at Hanson's orders. . . . But suddenly on the fourth morning the strike was called off by a resolution which declared that there had been no defeat, but that everyone should return to work on the following day. It was a muddled resolution in which the only thing that was clear was that the strike was over, and that nobody could tell exactly why. . . .

Shall one blame the yellow leaders who sabotaged the strike and wished to end it? Such a charge is easy to make—and true. But it is more to the point to ask why it happened that as soon as any worker was made a leader he wanted to end that strike. A score of times in those five days I saw it happen. Workers in the ranks felt the thrill of massed power which they trusted their leaders to carry to victory. But as soon as one of those workers was put on a responsible committee, he also wished to stop "before there is riot and blood."

The strike could produce no leaders willing to keep it going. All of us were red in the ranks and yellow as leaders. For we lacked all intention of real battle; we expected to drift into power. We loved the emotion of a better world coming, but all of our leaders and not a few of our rank and file had much to lose in the old world. The general strike put into our hands the organized life of the city—all except the guns. We could last only until they started shooting; we were one gigantic bluff. . . .

Even when the strike was over, we would not admit it lost. . . . We bluffed ourselves and the workers with phrases of victory. We had "shown the strength of labor. . . . We had "learned more about the administration of a city than any workers in America knew before. . . ." We had "come close to the problems of management." We persuaded ourselves that this was what the strike had been for. And the workers believed us, or half-believed us, and went back to work with a sense of having gained something, they were not sure just what.

With determined optimism and almost mystical idealism, I was writing editorials which declared: "If by revolution is meant violence, forcible taking of property, killing of men, surely none of our workers dreamed of such action. But if by revolution is meant that a Great Change is coming over the face of the world which will transform our methods of carrying on industry—then we do believe in such a Great Change and that our general strike was one step towards it."

Condensed from *I Change Worlds*, Anna Louise Strong (New York: Henry Holt and Company, 1935).

LXXIV

Glenn Arthur Hughes

The ugliness of strikes and violence in the streets of Seattle represented only one phase of occurrences in Washington. Behind the
scenes of disorder, life in intellectual circles went on about as
usual. It was exemplified by Glenn Arthur Hughes (1894–1964),
professor of English at the University of Washington, director of
its school of drama, playwright, drama critic, student of imagist
poetry, and a poet of rank himself. While the struggle for fairer
distribution of worldly wealth and authority was waging, he was
content to stand apart and record in his verses some hint of the
more permanent natural wealth of the state.

To a Lonely Island

I know a lonely island
Beside a northern shore,
Where wind and rain and beating wave
Have ruled for evermore.

Here do the sea-birds clamor
In gray-white, whirling flocks;

Over the surf, over the sand,
Over the naked rocks.

In pools of dark sea-water,
Left by the ebbing tide,
The starfish and the shining crab
Lie stranded, side by side.

A curving line of driftwood
Marks where the sea can reach,
And stringy heaps of drying kelp
Litter the even beach.

Back from the sea's dominion
Are wind-blown clumps of pine,
Grown thick with moss and tangled brake
And wild blackberry vine.

Here in the humid darkness
A bird sings, unafraid,
Sings to the drearest solitude,
And yet is undismayed.

O lonely, lonely island
Beside a northern shore,
May wind and rain and beating wave
Rule thee forevermore!

December Clouds

Across the house-tops, piled with white,
Across the sea, all gray and dark,
In winter's robes of sallow light,
Slowly the tireless clouds embark.

They hang above the water's edge
In stern and ordered dignity;
They break and form an upper ledge
More sombre still. Between we see

The still and veiled white of space,
The pallid radiance of the sun
Whose glory lingers, though its face
Points to new worlds, now the day's done.

Clouds drift, and crumble, turn to gray,
Then gather into black once more;
A tender creeping-arm of day,
Saffron and pink, starts from the shore

To climb the ominous, wind-torn walls,
But it touches the first too timidly,
And lacking the strength, wavers and falls
From the ragged ramparts, into the sea.

Clouds drifting in the winter light,
Drifting into havens of mist,
Drifting into havens of night
Where winds are born, and stars have kissed.

At the Fair Grounds

Blue streaks hissing in the air,
Bursts of red fire on the ground;
Zing! of a hurtling rocket,
Plop! when it showers fire.
Whirl of green and yellow lights
In a dazzling framework spelling WELCOME.
And everywhere on the dusty field,
Scuffling amid the peanuts and confetti,
People, open-mouthed, with eyes uplifted
To the miracle of gaudy pyrotechnics.

Later, with the rockets lying dead
Upon the prairie, and the grounds
Left littered and unpeopled, lo! the stars!
The calm, eternal stars, set in the black vault
Of midnight, gazing down in pity and great wonder.

Nocturne

There is no need of making songs tonight,
For lovelier than song is that pure light
That lays a shimmering path across the sea,
And tips the darkening islands silverly.

Along the white-flecked margin of the shore
The rippling waves with cadenced sweetness pour,
And here beneath the moon of our delight
There is no need of making songs tonight.

From *Broken Lights*, Glenn Hughes (Seattle: University of Washington Department of Printing, 1920).

LXXV

Stoddard King

For a decade between the last years of World War I and the early days of the Depression, the most popular columnist in the state was a staff member of the Spokane *Spokesman-Review*, Stoddard King (1889–1933). He commented wittily on current events, on people, places, institutions, American mores—anything that came into his head—and invariably capped his column with a few impeccable rhymes in light verse on any theme that might have been slighted in the prose commentary.

It was the verse mostly that brought King his widespread popularity. The stanzas were quoted across the land, and re-quoted in a succession of four little volumes. His close friend Vachel Lindsay lauded his efforts; William Lyon Phelps vouched that his "light verse is not only unexcelled in America, but is unexcelled in the English-speaking world."

King's literary career started early; the *Spokesman-Review* took him on as roving journalist upon his graduation from high school, and he continued sending in contributions after he left Spokane to enter Yale. But in New Haven he first tasted failure: he wrote a sentimental ditty about a long winding trail; a fellow student wrote music for it; and the combination was sent off to Tin Pan Alley, where it was quickly rejected, though one music publisher did consent to retain it in his files.

From Yale King went on to Oxford in 1913 for graduate work; and one weekend down in London his ears perked up to hear a band playing a very familiar tune, his song, "There's a Long, Long Trail A-Winding." It was the first intimation he had that the composition had been published, and it was a hit. During the first World War it became the marching song for hundreds of thousands of British and Canadian troops, and was soon just as popular among Yankee legions and as an American theme song for all the Liberty Drives. King was famous.

The fame helped him get a job back in New York as associate editor of *Harper's Weekly*. Then came another reverse. He had hardly assumed his new post when the *Weekly* was merged with the *Independent*, and the new employee lost his editorship in the ensuing shuffle. But there was still a vacant desk back at the office of the *Spokesman-Review*. He returned to it and kept it the rest of his life. It was the fount of his verse—satiric, whimsical, genial, and always engaging.

Étude Géographique

Out West, they say, a man's a man; the legend still persists
That he is handy with a gun, and careless with his fists.
The fact is, though, you may not hear a stronger word than "Gosh!"
From Saskatoon, Saskatchewan, to Walla Walla, Wash.

In western towns 'tis many years since it was last the rage
For men to earn their daily bread by holding up the stage,
Yet story writers still ascribe such wild and wooly bosh
To Saskatoon, Saskatchewan, and Walla Walla, Wash.

The gents who roam the West today are manicured and meek,
They shave their features daily and they bathe three times a week.
They tote the tame umbrella and they wear the mild galosh
From Saskatoon, Saskatchewan, to Walla Walla, Wash.

But though the West has frowned upon its old nefarious games,
It still embellishes the map with sweet, melodious names,
Which grow in lush profusion like the apple and the squash
From Saskatoon, Saskatchewan, to Walla Walla, Wash.

Elegy Written in a Tourist Camping Ground

The klaxon sounds the knell of parting day,
Some late arrivals through the dustclouds creep,
And three hours after we have hit the hay
The noise calms down so we can get to sleep.

Save where, from yonder pennant-clad sedan,
A radio set emits its raucous squeal,
And, underneath a nearby light, a man
Pounds until daylight on a busted wheel.

Beneath those tattered tops, those patent tents,
Where falls the dust into each sunburned pore,
Each on his folding bed of slight expense,
The rude explorers of the highway snore.

Let not ambition mock their creaky cars,
Their khaki clothes, of vintages obscure,
Nor grandeur view, with hauteur like a czar's,
The short and simple flivers of the poor.

The boast of shiny paint, the pomp of power,
And all that charms the motoristic fop,
Await alike the inevitable hour—
The paths of touring lead but to the shop.

Can streamline hood or silver-plated hubs
Back to its mansion call the missing spark?
Can plush upholstery foil the clumsy dubs
Who bang into your fenders in the dark?

Full many a boob of purest ray serene
Succumbs each summer to the touring itch;
Full many a car is doomed to blush unseen,
And waste its sweetness in a western ditch.

The Old Settler Reports

When I came West in Nineteen-Two
(A parlous time ago!)
The cowboys were a dingy crew,
Their taste in dress was low.
But now, my dear, you'd simply love them!
They've learned what is expected of them.

When I came West in Nineteen-Two
(An age remote and dim)
The only Indian I knew
Was known as Dirty Jim.
Now he is Chief Ten-Dogs-Who-Bark,
And runs a "tribe" in Glacier Park.

When I came West in Nineteen-Two
No neighbor far or near
Had ever seen a buckaroo
Caress a longhorn steer;
But now the neighbors, one and all,
Attend our Round-up every fall.

The West has changed since Nineteen-Two
It's wilder now by far;
And let us give the films their due—
They've made us what we are.
Observe how Nature copies Art—
The West has learned to dress the part.

From *What the Queen Said and Further Facetious Fragments,* Stoddard King (New York: George H. Doran Company, 1923, 1924).

LXXVI

Betty MacDonald

Only a few years earlier, the avowed purpose of most Washington settlers had been to help convert a wilderness into a civilized, peopled country. Now it was all being reversed, and a new kind of emigrant was occasionally coming to the state in search of a hideaway, in search of a refuge from the encroachment of populous civilization, in search of the very setting that earlier families had been deliberately trying to destroy. In Washington there were still many such primeval locations, particularly on the Olympic Peninsula, and that was the chosen destination of Betty MacDonald (1908–1958) and her husband during the last of the Depression.

Leaving behind the cultivated Seattle society to which she had grown accustomed during her late teens—a society complete with "singing, piano, folk dancing, ballet, French and dramatic lessons," and three years of college—she set out with her husband for the Olympic backwoods, "the most untamed corner of the United States," "the most rugged, most westerly, greatest, deepest, largest, wildest, gamiest, richest, most fertile, loneliest and most desolate country in all the world," to eke out a living on a chicken ranch of their own creation. In the rollicking best seller *The Egg and I* Betty MacDonald told their story.

Into the Lap of the Olympics

The unconquerable forests thundered down at us from the hills. "This land resents civilization and it isn't a little futile stick-out-the-tongue kind of resentment, but a great big smashing resentment that is backed by all the forces of nature," I thought, huddling down into my coat and hoping we'd soon come to a town.

We did, and it boasted the mad confusion of four enterprises—a hotel, a barbershop, a gas station and a country store and post office. In addition there was a dear little graveyard and an imposing brick schoolhouse. Five roads led away from this small town but Bob didn't hesitate. He chose one pointing southwest toward the frosty Olympic Mountains.

For the next several hours we saw no more towns, only crossroads stores; rich valleys separated by heavily wooded hills; herds of cattle and widely spaced farm houses. We had nosed our way into the foothills of the Olympics while we were still in the farming country and it wasn't until I looked from the car window and saw, far below the road, a frustrated little mountain stream banging its head against immense canyon walls that I realized we were in the mountains proper.

Yellow highway signs announcing WINDING ROAD appeared at intervals and Bob put the car in second and then low gear as we spiraled forward and upward. We were climbing but seemed to be getting nowhere, for we were walled in on all sides by the robust green mountainsides, and only by sticking my head clear out of the window was I able to peer up and see the sky. Two or three hundred million board feet of Douglas fir. Later, we turned off the main highway onto a dirt road and jounced and skidded our way at last to the "little place."

On first sight it looked distressingly forlorn, huddled there in the laps of the great Olympics, the buildings grayed with weather, the orchard overgrown with second-growth firs, the fences collapsing, the windows sagging. It was the little old deserted farm that people point at from car windows, saying, "Look at that picturesque old place!" then quickly drive by toward something not quite so picturesque, but warmer and nearer to civilization.

Bob halted the car to take down the rails of the gate and I looked morosely around at the mountains so imminent they gave me a feeling of someone reading over my shoulder, and at the terrific virility of the forests, and I thought, "Good heavens, those mountains could flick us off this place like a fly off their skirts, rearrange their trees a little and no one would ever be the wiser."

It was not a comforting thought, and the driveway, which proved to be a rather inadequate tunnel under the linked arms of two rows of giant trees, did nothing to dispel it. Heavy green branches lashed the top of the car and smaller twigs clawed at the windows, and the car wheels churned and complained on the slick dry needles. We drove for perhaps a quarter of a mile like this and then abruptly the trees stopped and we were in the dooryard of the farm, where a great-grandfather of a cherry tree, hoary with bloom, stood guard over the huddled buildings.

I'm not sure whether it was the cherry tree or the purple carpet of sweet violets flanking the funny silvery woodshed, or the fact that the place was so clean, not a scrap of rubbish, not a single tin can, but it suddenly lost its sinister deserted look and began to appear lonely but eager to make friends. A responsive little farm that with a few kindnesses in the way of windows and paint and clearing might soon be licking our hands.

While I stood in the doorway "feeling" the place, Bob was bounding around with a hammer, pounding the walls and calling happily, "Look, Betty, hand-hewn-out-of-cedar logs, and sound as a nut." The hand-hewn cedar shakes which covered the sides and roof had worked loose in several places and Bob pulled them off to show me the cedar logs and the ax marks.

The house, evidently begun as a log cabin about twenty feet by twenty and added on to at either end, was beautifully situated on a small rise of ground from which an old orchard, peering out from the second-growth fir, sloped gently down to a small lake or large pond. The original cabin was the living room with windows on the north and south sides and a thin rickety porch across the front. It faced south, across the orchard, to the pond and, of course, the mountains. The mountains were everywhere—I'd start to turn around, come up against something large and solid, and wham! there was a mountain icily ignoring me.

Opening off the living room on the right, with windows north, west and south, we found a bedroom with roses and honeysuckle vines in heaps on the floor below the windows, as though they had climbed up to peek in and had fallen over the sills. Down three steps and to the left of the living room were an enormous square kitchen with windows east and north and a pantry the size of our apartment in town, with three windows facing east. Jutting off the kitchen toward the front was a bedroom with windows looking east and south. Up a creepy flight of stairs from the living room were two tiny slope-ceilinged bedrooms. Under the front porch we discovered a bat-hung cellar, and to one side of the kitchen, forming an ell with the living room, an entryway and wood room.

A very large, very surly and slightly rusty range was backed defiantly against the north wall of the kitchen—otherwise the place was empty. The floors were warped and splintery—the walls were covered with carefully tacked newspapers dated 1885.

At first glance the outbuildings seemed frail and useless, but closer examination revealed fine bone structure in the way of uprights, beams and stringers, and so we were able to include in the assets of the place, a very large barn, two small chicken houses, a woodshed and an outhouse. The assets also included ten acres of land showing evidences of having once been cleared, and thirty acres of virgin timber, cedar, fir and hemlock—some of it seven feet and more in diameter.

Scattered over the ten cleared acres, like figures in a tableau, were the dearest, fattest, most perfectly shaped Christmas trees I have ever seen. Each one was round and full at the bottom and

exquisitely trimmed with brown cones. I was caressing and exclaiming over these when Bob told me that such little jewels of
trees are cut by the hundreds of thousands by Christmas tree
dealers, who pay the farmers two cents each for them. Incredible
that anyone who professed a love of the soil would sanction such
vandalism and for such a paltry fee. . . .

We threaded our way through the orchard and found slender
fruit trees bravely blossoming with frail hands pushing futilely
against the dark green hairy chests of the invading firs. The firs
were everywhere, big and virile, with their strong roots pulling
all of the vitality out of the soil and leaving the poor little fruit
trees only enough food and light to keep an occasional branch
alive. These were no kin to the neatly spaced little Christmas tree
ladies of the back pasture. These were fierce invaders. Pillagers
and rapers.

The more we walked around, the stronger became my feeling
that we should hurry and move in so that we could help this little
farm in its fight against the wilderness. Bob was overjoyed when I
told him of this feeling and so we decided to buy it at once.

For the forty acres, the six-room log house, the barn, two small
chicken houses, woodshed, outhouse and the sulky stove, the
mortgage company was asking $450. Between us and by pooling
all savings accounts, weddings presents, birthday presents and by
drawing on a small legacy which I was to get when I became
twenty-one, we had $1500.

We sat in the sunny dooryard under the cherry tree, used a
blue carpenter's pencil and shingle and decided that we would
pay cash for the farm; put seven hundred dollars in the bank to
be used to buy, feed and raise three hundred and fifty pullets; and
we would use the rest to fix up the buildings. Fuel and water
were free and we'd have a large vegetable garden, a pig to eat
leavings, a few chickens for immediate eggs, and Bob would work
occasionally in one of the sawmills to eke out until the chickens
started to lay. Written out in blue pencil on the weathered
shingle, it was the simplest, most delightful design for living ever
devised for two people.

We left then and hurried home to put our plans into action.

The next morning Bob paid the $450 and brought home the deed.
The following week we borrowed a truck, loaded on everything
we possessed and left for the mountains to dive headfirst into the
chicken business.

From *The Egg and I*, Betty MacDonald (Philadelphia and New York: J. B.
Lippincott Company, 1945).

LXXVII

Audrey May Wurdemann

"Literature will be fostered by and by," a distressed Edmond Meany had prophesied hopefully to his generation. And now the prophecy was gaining fulfillment. To be sure, Washington could boast of no Longfellow, Whittier, Dr. Holmes, or modern Robert Frost, but in the 1930s it could claim at last a native poetess who had achieved national recognition—Audrey May Wurdemann (1911–1960).

As a young child in Seattle, Audrey had started penning verses for publication, and at fourteen she won the admiration of California's poet laureate, George Sterling, who at once adopted her as his protégée. She continued writing poetry during her attendance at the University of Washington and during youthful travels through the United States, Hawaii, and the Orient, habitually expressing in verse her reactions to places she visited and people she met.

Her lyrics were praised and published in such magazines as *Forum, The Bookman, Scribner's, Poetry,* and *The New Yorker,* and at the age of twenty-three—just before her marriage to another notable poet, Joseph Auslander—she was awarded the Pulitzer Prize for her first volume, *Bright Ambush.* Although specific places were rarely mentioned in her lines, it was the familiar country of her native state about which she most often wrote.

Spring Song

The sweet wild dogwood wears its flowers
Through silent shadow-patterned hours,
And ivory cream-cups make a star
Where robin and wake-robin are.
The judas-trees let crimson drip
From each spire-pointed fingertip,
And bishop's croziers unfold
To dust the ginger-root with gold.
Then, gathering all her loveliness,
Spring goes, and leaves us no address.

The Loneliness of Autumn

I exorcise myself of this September,
Of frost and falling leaves and harvest done;
I will not keep their annals, nor remember
The loneliness of autumn in the sun.

If I had but the linnet's little singing,
The small brave sparrow's copper bell gone still,
I could forget September, and the ringing
Low melancholy quail beyond the hill.

I exorcise myself; I have forbidden
The blue winds sighing now when sighing's done,
But I am frost-bewildered and witch-ridden
At seeing autumn lonely in the sun.

From *Bright Ambush*, Audrey Wurdemann (New York: A John Day Book, Reynal and Hitchcock, 1935).

LXXVIII

Franklin D. Roosevelt

There were men of practical affairs, as well as poets, grown so fond of Washington just as Nature had formed it with all its grandeur and all its deficiencies, that they vociferously objected to any man-made alterations. But they were a minority, and were being overruled by those who were confident they could improve upon Nature, and in the process do away with some of the deficiencies.

As early as 1905 the U.S. Reclamation Service took over the complex irrigation project at Sunnyside and prepared the way for converting more than a hundred thousand acres into richly productive farmland. Other federal projects followed: Kittitas Valley, Wapato, Tieton, Benton, Roza, and Rathdrum near Spokane. They brought into cultivation many more vast tracts that would be county-sized in any Eastern state, and helped taxpayers of Washington get used to the largess of the United States Government.

But when the great Bonneville Dam Project came along in the 1930s, drowning the famed, treacherous Cascades, an entirely new element was introduced. This was an undertaking so enormous that its benefits would extend beyond the bounds of the two states it connected, and Uncle Sam as benefactor demanded the right to dictate some of the terms under which the benefits would be administered. And so Washington was flung into the midst of a magnificent national controversy over the concept of expanding federal authority to effect regional welfare.

President Franklin D. Roosevelt (1882–1945) was on hand to defend his convictions at the dedication of the big dam on September 28, 1937—and incidentally to remind disputatious officials and businessmen in cities nearest to Bonneville that they were not entitled to the lower electric rates they wanted by virtue of their proximity to the turbines.

For the Benefit of the Many

The more we study the water resources of the nation, the more we accept the fact that their use is a matter of national concern, and that in our plans for their use, our line of thinking must include great regions as well as narrower localities.

If, for example, we had known as much and acted as effectively twenty and thirty and forty years ago as we do today in the development of the use of land in that great semi-arid strip in the center of the country, which runs from the Canadian border to Texas, we could have prevented in great part the abandonment of thousands and thousands of farms in portions of ten states, and thus prevented the migration of thousands of destitute families from these areas into the states of Washington and Oregon and California.

Some of my friends who talk glibly of the right of any individual to do anything he wants with any of his property take the point of view that it is not the concern of federal or state or local government to interfere with what they miscall "the liberty of the individual." With them I do not agree and never have agreed, because, unlike them, I am thinking of the future of the United States. My conception of liberty does not permit an individual citizen or group of citizens to commit acts of depredation against nature in such a way as to harm their neighbors. . . .

The watershed of the Columbia River . . . covers the greater part of the states of Oregon, Washington, Idaho and a part of Montana. It is increasingly important that we think of that region as a unit and especially in terms of the whole population of that area as it is today and as we expect it will be fifty and even a hundred years from now. . . .

That is why in developing electricity from the Bonneville Dam, from the Coulee Dam and from other dams to be built on the Columbia and its tributaries, the policy of the wisest use ought to prevail. The transmission of electricity is making such scientific strides today that we can well visualize a date, not far distant, when every community in this great area will be wholly electrified.

It is because I am thinking of the nation and the region fifty years from now that I venture the further prophecy that as time passes, we will do everything in our power to encourage the building up of the smaller communities of the United States. Today many people are beginning to realize that there is inherent weakness in cities which become too large and inherent strength in a wider geographical distribution of population. An overlarge city inevitably meets problems caused by oversize. . . .

There is doubtless a reasonable balance in all of this and it is a balance which ought to be given more and more study. No one would suggest, for example, that the great cities of Portland, Tacoma and Seattle and Spokane should stop their growth, but it is a fact that they could grow unhealthily at the expense of all the smaller communities of which they form logical centers. Their healthiest growth actually depends on the simultaneous healthy growth of every smaller community within a radius of hundreds of miles.

Your situation in the Northwest is in this respect no different from the situation in the other great regions of the nation. That is why it has been proposed in the Congress that regional planning boards be set up for the purpose of coordinating the planning for the future in seven or eight natural geographical regions.

You have read here as elsewhere many misleading and utterly untrue statements . . . that this proposed legislation would set up all-powerful authorities which would destroy state lines, take away local government and make what people call a totalitarian or authoritarian or some other kind of a dangerous national centralized control.

Most people realize that the exact opposite is the truth. . . . The responsibility of the federal government for the welfare of its citizens will not come from the top in the form of unplanned, hit-or-miss appropriations of money, but will progress to the national capital from the ground up—from the communities and counties and states which lie within each of the logical geographical areas. . . .

The Bonneville Dam on the Columbia River . . . with Oregon on the south side of the river and Washington on the north, is one of the major power and navigation projects undertaken since 1933. It is 170 feet high and 1,250 feet long. It has been built by the corps of engineers of the War Department, and when fully completed, with part of its power installations, will cost fifty-one million dollars.

Its locks will enable shipping to use this great waterway much farther inland than at present, and give an outlet to the enormously valuable agricultural and mineral products of Oregon and Washington and Idaho. Its generators will ultimately produce 580,000 horsepower of electricity.

Truly, in the construction of this dam we have had our eyes on the future of the nation. Its cost will be returned to the people of the United States many times over in the improvement of navigation and transportation, the cheapening of electric power, and the distribution of the power to hundreds of small communities within a great radius.

As I look upon Bonneville Dam today, I cannot help the thought that instead of spending, as some nations do, half their national income in piling up armaments and more armaments for purposes of war, we in America are wiser in using our wealth on projects like this which will give us more wealth, better living and greater happiness for our children.

From the text of President Roosevelt's address, Seattle *Post-Intelligencer,* September 29, 1937.

LXXIX

Richard L. Neuberger

After Bonneville came the even grander Coulee Dam, and to herald the coming rose its fluent advocate, Richard L. Neuberger (1912–1960). Politically Neuberger was an Oregonian. He was born in Portland, attended the University of Oregon, served in Oregon for many years as correspondent for *The New York Times*, was a state senator in Oregon and a U.S. Senator from Oregon. But in his exposition he freely crossed state lines, wrote almost as appreciatively of Washington as of his home state, drafted half a dozen books on the Northwest, and as long as that "most massive concrete escarpment in the world," the Grand Coulee Dam, was in the talking stage, the planning stage, the building stage, and finally in the productive stage, he was its volunteer press agent, turning out article after article on its wonders: "Miracle in Concrete," "Man's Greatest Structure," "Mightiest Man-Made Thing."

This Makes Sense

The morning fog lifts like a curtain in the granite canyon of the Columbia River and reveals the most massive concrete escarpment in the world, stretching from cliff to cliff. It is nearly a mile long and as thick as two city blocks at the base. Already it towers thirty stories above bedrock, and soon it will be higher. Its bulk is three times that of the Great Pyramid; it contains enough concrete to pave a roadway around the globe. Behind it there is filling up an enormous reservoir that will be almost as long as Lake Ontario.

This is the Grand Coulee Dam, started in 1934 and to be finished by the end of this year [1940] . . . . Grand Coulee will irrigate and reclaim 1,200,000 acres of land. This is an area equal in size to the whole state of Delaware. It is not much less than the acreage of all the farms in New Jersey. . . .

Twenty-five years ago George W. Norris, Senator from Nebraska, stood beside a little creek cascading to the Columbia and asked a native of a nearby village why the power was not used. The reply came with finality: "Jim Hill owns all the power sites. We don't have much to say about 'em." No railway magnate owns all the power sites now. Soon, over the brink of the Grand Coulee spillway will crash a sheet of water with five times the volume and nearly three times the height of Niagara Falls.

This shattering drop in the nation's second largest river will generate annually 10,708,000,000 kilowatt-hours of power, an amount equal to one-fourth of all the hydroelectric power produced in the United States in 1938. So much "juice" will be turned out that the twin powerhouses, each as big as a skyscraper and packing more than twice the force of Muscle Shoals, will have to be run by remote control, lest the operators be electrocuted.

Ranchers and settlers on the dry mesas are wiring their houses and cabins; they will be able to buy electricity for $2.50 a hundred kilowatt-hours. New industries, desperately needed in a frontier region that imports 75 per cent of its manufactured goods, are also expected to take advantage of the lowest commercial power rates in America. Already aluminum and steel factories are being built along the Columbia near Bonneville. Seattle and Portland businessmen, who regularly denounce the President, admit that his dams are saving the Northwest, and will give it an industrial foundation to replace the lumber industry.

Grand Coulee—most massive concrete escarpment in the world

Not all Grand Coulee's fabulous supply of power will brighten farmhouses and move the wheels of factories. Five of the eighteen generators will operate a dozen stupendous pumps, one of which could pump enough water for New York City. Each pump can lift fifty tons of water a second. And here is what the pumps will do. Grand Coulee Dam will raise the level of the Columbia River approximately 355 feet. The pumps will hoist part of the river another 250 feet, through great tunnels and conduits, from which it will flow into a deep chasm a mile wide and from twenty-five to thirty miles in length. This chasm, with walls as precipitous as the front of a safe, is the Grand Coulee of the Columbia River. It was carved ages ago when the river was diverted from its course by the Pleistocene ice sheet. The dam and pumps will duplicate the job the ice sheet did.

From the Grand Coulee the water will be coasted on to 1,200,-000 acres of land which needs only irrigation to grow peas, beans, pears, prunes, potatoes, celery, onions, alfalfa, and the other crops that mantle the green valleys of the Northwest. This land will not be monopolized by great corporate farms such as dominate agriculture in California, nor will it be scarred by the feudalism of tenant farming. It will be tilled by families working their own land, for Congress has passed a new law limiting land ownership at Grand Coulee to eighty acres a family; a single man can retain only half that much. The considerable portion of the region now held by private owners and in old Northern Pacific land grants will have to be sold at the price fixed by government appraisers. Any land held beyond the amount allowed will not be cut in on the irrigation system and will stay in its present virtually worthless condition. . . .

The surveys are under way now. Every foot of the 1,200,000 acres is being classified as to contour, value, ownership, soil content and crop possibilities. It is the most extensive land survey ever undertaken. President Roosevelt has made up his mind that the Coulee area, which he considers a "Promised Land," shall not be colonized carelessly. The National Resources Committee is at work studying where schools, hospitals, sewer systems, railroad yards and warehouses should be located.

Twenty-five thousand families cultivating fertile soil can support a large urban population. The towns near Grand Coulee will expand; other towns will spring up. The Resources Committee is trying to find out the opportunities for people with special training and abilities—doctors, nurses, schoolteachers, printers, lawyers, ministers, electricians, mechanics. Perhaps in this modern Canaan in the Northwest some of the highly skilled refugees from Europe may get a chance to participate in American life. . . . The total cost of the Grand Coulee project will be $394,500,-000. . . .

Despite all doubts and reservations, men of many faiths have stood on the granite crags above the huge dam and said, "This makes sense." The Pacific Northwest is the final frontier, the last refuge for people now living on exhausted soil in the Middle West, for men and women crowded in the tenements of the Atlantic coast. Major Roy Bessey of the Northwest Regional Planning Commission says that "with a reasonable development program from 1,000,000 to 2,500,000 additional people could readily be absorbed in the region within a generation. Migration toward the region during recent years seems to indicate that the population increase may approach the higher figure."

Of no other part of continental United States may this be said, and Grand Coulee is the principal feature of "the reasonable development program." The Columbia has three times as much potential hydroelectric power as any other river in America. Above its swift reaches is a great sweep of land that needs only water to replace sagebrush with orchards. The river twists through the Cascade Range and into the core of the Inland Empire. With dams and locks it could become a navigable waterway instead of a rapid-studded chute. Why not develop all these resources for men and women who must find a place to go! . . .

Dusk settles on the Columbia like a curtain dropping back. The tumble-down farmhouses which the settlers abandoned long ago lose shape in the twilight. But at the great dam ten thousand lights are turned on. Work goes forward night and day. This is a defense of democracy, too—as important as new destroyers and bombing planes. . . . That jackhammer man down in the chasm, wiping his forehead in the glare of the searchlights as he drills a tunnel through the cliffs for the water that will make a million acres bloom—perhaps he is doing more to protect America from foreign ideologies than the man who rivets a dreadnought's mast or prepares a torpedo for the open sea.

From "Miracle in Concrete," Richard L. Neuberger. *The Nation,* June 1, 1940.

LXXX

Frederick Simpich, Sr.

Grand Coulee Dam went into operation on the very eve of Pearl Harbor, as though its completion had been planned to meet the demands of World War II. With something like clairvoyance, Senator Neuberger had forecast that the dam would be as important to defense as new destroyers and bombing planes. It proved more important, for the power from Grand Coulee and Bonneville went not only into the construction of ships and bombers but into a thousand other wartime essentials.

The dams, the industry and general productivity of the state, the naval and army bases located there, and the geographical location in the northwest corner of the country all worked together to give Washington a frontier position in a national struggle. World War II came about as near to Puget Sound as it did to any segment of the United States. Residents of the coastal cities or in the shadow of sprawling, camouflaged factories considered it all too close for comfort.

The state was dotted with targets attractive to an enemy: huge industrial complexes, shipyards, airplane factories and fields, concentrations of shipping, key hydroelectric plants, the vast Puget Sound Navy Yard—the site for which, ironically, had been platted and sold to the United States Government by a German developer. Destruction of any one of these vulnerable centers could be very damaging to the war effort.

Frederick Simpich, Sr. (1878–1950), who had spent most of his life roving over the globe, making regional assessments for the State Department, the Army, *National Geographic* and other periodicals, drafting intelligence reports, and composing news stories and articles for leading American magazines, visited the Northwest early in the war to take inventory.

Too Near to Tokyo

Here are vast soldier cities that shelter 50,000 men. Here, too, are lonely island posts manned by veterans of another war, veterans with tattooed arms, gold teeth and rheumatism. Cheerfully and lively, they scan the sea and sky for advancing enemies, betimes playing bagpipes or throwing rocks at wild bears that rob camp kitchens. . . . This Pacific Northwest, by the Great Circle route through the Aleutians, is only about 4,700 miles from Tokyo. Its army posts, naval bases, docks, airplane factories, ship and lumber yards, mines and forests, railway terminals and fishing fleets are all possible objects of enemy attacks.

After the Aleutian thrust, Japanese U-boat shelling of Vancouver and Oregon coasts was no surprise. Portland, Seattle, Tacoma, Vancouver are all exposed to the risk of air raids. But now their all-out defense works, and grim evidence of aggressive warfare meets you at every turn. Great rifles and antiaircraft guns point their deadly snouts from coastal groves and hidden nooks. Destroyers, mine layers, sweepers, submarines and patrol bombers depart on mysterious missions. Soldiers afoot and in trucks patrol the roads and beaches. . . . Barrage balloon crews shield . . . an air base by flying scores of elephantine gasbags at the end of long cables. . . . Barbed wire and guards hold the inquisitive public far back from busy waterfronts, where blacked-out troop trains discharge men and where Army transports load on dark, rainy nights for "some northern port. . . ."

Mountain-high on the docks are piled the things campaigning armies use: engines, planes, extra wings, soap, flashlights, iron pipe, typewriters, kitchen ranges, tubs, pots, pans, bales of blankets, candy, cigarettes, rolls of camouflage material, big steel mats for making airplane landing floors on sandy beaches or rough fields, tents, tools, mattresses, even dog harness; food, too, shiploads of it. "How much grub is here?" I asked a quartermaster colonel. "Millions of rations," he said. "Perhaps enough to keep one soldier fat for 260,000 years."

Even Russian freighters are in this port—which must be nameless—loading lard. . . . Guns were being mounted now on these Russian ships, and bullet-proof cement walls are being built about their bridges. . . .

In cities war has vastly changed every-day life. One big shop that used to make railroad cars and buses now makes only welded tanks, vicious fire-vomiting monsters. Shops that made bathing suits and sport sweaters now make blankets and mittens for soldiers. Solemn, silent, mysterious as a pagan cemetery is one big, tree-covered hill. Tomblike powder magazines line its steep, crooked trails. Here are stored such potential volcanoes of explosive power that, were they all fired at once, they would blow navies of all the world sky-high. You stand a half-mile off and look, and you might say, "What a serene little mountain!" . . . And over all is the hush of censorship.

Monumental new aluminum, magnesium and alloy plants may in part answer the worker who asks, "Where can I get a job when the fighting stops?" Colossal fresh hydroelectric power from Grand Coulee and Bonneville dams in the Columbia River may help change many of these wartime mushroom plants into permanent industries. . . . Columbia River is now America's greatest power stream. . . .

New bombers, pursuit planes, merchant ships, long barges for landing invasion troops, mine sweepers and mine layers; destroyers, seaplane tenders, crash boats, carriers and transports made by converting freighters; uniforms, sleeping bags by the thousands, knockdown houses for use in Alaska; skis, dog sleds and dog harness; gas-mask fillers, incendiary bomb casings; cartridge clips, preserved foods, propellers, marine steering engines by hundreds—these are but a few of the things now made here. At one city are ocean piers two and a half miles long, among the world's largest. Graving docks are the largest in Allied hands on the whole Pacific. . . . From enormous plants in this Pacific Northwest come ever-increasing numbers of flying artillery, shuttling quickly away to distant battlefields. . . .

Today this fairly new country that used to thrive on fish, fruit and fresh-cut lumber sees its former ways of life utterly upset. By tens of thousands men have quit what they were doing yesterday and now hold jobs in the new mushroom wartime shops. . . . For Seattle, the Klondike gold rush itself was a quiet, sleepy event compared with today's unparalleled excitement.

From "Wartime in the Pacific Northwest," Frederick Simpich, Sr. *The National Geographic Magazine*, October, 1942.

LXXXI

Donald Culross Peattie

Wartime coast guardsmen appraised the Olympic Peninsula in terms of its isolation and the long, winding miles to Aberdeen, Port Angeles, or Port Townsend for an overnight leave; lumbermen sized it up in terms of board feet; fishermen concerned themselves with its onerous weather, the tides, and the possibility of an offshore catch; ranchers assessed the moisture and the soil fertility of the Peninsula; Betty MacDonald rated it in terms of the asocial environs and the foes of chickens and children; botanist Donald Culross Peattie (1898–1964), author of three dozen or more popular and technical volumes on the plant kingdom, saw the Peninsula as only a worshiper of the wild could see it. With his young family he visited "the land of Humptulips and Dosewallips and Duckabush" for the first time in the early 1940s and reported his reactions with the same vividness and excitement of discovery that he employed to bring to students of natural environment fresh awareness of scores of beauty spots from the Carolinas to California.

Like a Fairy-Tale Forest

The Olympic Peninsula is about the size of Connecticut, but you must imagine the Nutmeg State dominated by a range of eternally snow-clad mountains, and covered from timberline to tidewater with a dark canopy of virgin conifers.

And what conifers! There are endless miles of dark Sitka spruces, pencil-slim, some of them up to 200 feet high, that seem to have marched down from the fjords of maritime Alaska. Exquisite western hemlocks, tall as the spruces, the king of all the tribe of hemlock, spread their ferny gracious foliage, giving the forest a peculiarly light and airy cool charm, in contrast with the dark titanic features of the Douglas firs.

Douglas fir, second only to the sequoias as the most majestic of conifers in the world, reaches on the Olympic Peninsula a height of 300 feet, and a circumference of 25 feet above the butt. The serrated spires of Douglas fir stand shoulder to shoulder; they have covered the peninsula with their compact Gothic growth; they look as noble as they are somber; they are fertile as they are strong; the harvest of their cones is scattered in untold millions on the ancient forest mold.

For contrast you have the canoe cedar, that same arbor-vitae out of which the Northwest Indians carve their totem poles, and of whose wood, so durable in water, they make their dugouts from a single log, capable of carrying forty warriors. With its ruddy trunks, combining tensile strength with fluted grace, its flat sprays of softly gleaming foliage, this tree runs up to heights of 175 feet, and wherever it occurs it makes you think of something classic and lasting. The boles look Doric; the foliage ought to adorn a victor's brow.

. . . There are the true firs, known to lumbermen rather poetically by the names of amiable fir, noble fir and grand fir. And grand they all are, with their clean gleaming boles, their pagoda-like whorls of boughs and incense-bearing foliage. And I mustn't forget the little yew trees, or the Nootka cypress which looks like a Christmas tree after it is trimmed; I mean that the downsweeping boughs look weighted, and the foliage seems to drip with streamers of wiry light. Indeed the whole forest is made up of "Christmas trees," because these are conifers-other-than-pine.

The Olympic forests are what you imagined virgin forests were when you were a child. They are tall as trees of fairy tale, and dense as that. They are set deep, deep in ancient moss, damp, feathery sphagnum that looks as if it went back to the beginning of time. . . . If this is primeval forest, then nothing I ever saw before remotely deserves the name.

Perhaps the aboriginal eastern forests looked this way—they *sound* so, in the first-hand accounts of Wilson and Audubon and Michaux, and in the imagination of Longfellow and Fenimore Cooper. But could they have been? No such height or girth has ever been claimed for any eastern trees, nor so dense a timber stand. No such rainfall is or was present in the East to make such sheer woody bulk possible. . . .

Never in my life did I think to get enough of trees, but this time I did. Tearing along the highway at fifty and sixty per, we went for hour after hour without seeing a single house, farm or clearing. The road was a narrow trough at the bottom of a layer of planetary vegetation too deep, too extensive for the mind to grasp.

Go look at the tallest tree in the East; imagine it three times as tall. Imagine that all about you are trees like that with their crowns interlocking till they shut out the sky. Imagine their trunks so close together that one cannot see more than a few rods into the forest, even though there is almost no high undergrowth. Imagine this forest going on, across bog, over mountains, crowding to the banks of rivers, unbroken over a stretch of about two hundred thousand acres.

But you can't imagine this. We couldn't imagine it even when we were seeing it. The adults in our party would look after a couple of hours into each other's eyes, searching there to see if into the other the same awe had entered, and it had. The children, usually romping and chattering, could not find their voices.

Sometimes a deep breath was drawn, and let out in a sigh—the deep sigh of human humility that I had never heard given before except by people who have thought too long about the stars, and the space between them.

From "The Nature of Things," Donald Culross Peattie. *Audubon Magazine,* September-October, 1941.

LXXXII

Stewart H. Holbrook

Whether the forest was on the Pacific side of the Olympic Peninsula, on Puget Sound, or high in the Cascades, revolution in the process of logging was now total. By mid-century lumbering was completely industrialized, mechanized, and modernized. It was an industry still colored with glamor and grandeur, but its soul was gone.

Stewart H. Holbrook (1893–1964), the born lumberjack who followed the steps in the revolution all the way from northern Vermont to the Northwest, and en route exchanged his ax for a typewriter to become the literary authority on lumbering, editor of *Lumber News*, and a witty, wise, and live-wire author of books like *Holy Old Mackinaw, Yankee Exodus, Yankee Loggers, The Columbia, Far Corner* and *Burning an Empire,* was the man most capable of composing a suitable requiem to the passing of an era.

Last of the Hellbent Loggers

When this writer quit working in the timber, back in the early 1920's, steam-logging had reached its peak. So had the footloose logger. Now I am an old settler, a man out of Genesis, for I can recall when Northwestern loggers preferred Copenhagen snuff to cigarettes, when fallers and buckers used crosscut saws, when steam donkeys did the yarding and loading, and logs came down the mountain behind a puffing Shay that rocked and rattled and had a voice to frighten a cougar on the last Forty of the most remote quarter section. I thought then it was a great and wonderful era. Thirty-odd years later I know it was.

I don't mean that its social consciousness was other than medieval. It was wasteful of timber. It was dangerous to human life. It was thoughtless and careless, breeding hatred and Wobblies, spawning fires that left uncounted acres a desolate waste. The whole ripsnorting shebang was inane, often cruel, always costly from the viewpoint of society. I loved every last bit of it, not for anything it accomplished, but because it was the greatest industrial show in North America.

That era has now passed. The logging railroads were the first to go. I have ridden the locomotives or the cars of 290-odd privately owned logging railroads in four states and one province. How many remain I do not know, but they cannot number more than half a dozen for the whole area. Trucks did away with them.

The great pounding steam donkeys, too, were driven out by the internal combustion engine fed on gasoline or diesel oils. When the old-time whistle punk yanked his signal wire, the steam donkey responded with a startled cry of a quality to alert the most sluggish mind. And when it was running, it emitted sound and smoke and steam and cinders in satisfying profusion. Small, smooth quiet diesel engines did away with the donkeys.

As late as the early 1940's trees were felled by muscular men who stood on springboards notched in the trunks and pulled the long glittering blade of a crosscut. They were mostly of Scandinavian origin—big blond men with sweeping mustaches who worked by the bushel, inch or mile, as piecework was called. Perfection of the power chainsaw drove the big Scandies from the woods. Either that, or they learned to operate a chainsaw, a rig that will down a giant in less time than it took to set a springboard for handwork.

Almost simultaneously with the chainsaw came a far more

important revolutionary change. I mean the coming in numbers of the private or company forester. He began to appear on rare occasions in the 1920's. To most logging bosses he was no more welcome than a union organizer. He knew a whole raft of fancy names for fir, pine, cedar and hemlock. He held dangerous theories among which was the proposition that, given a chance, a forest would renew itself. For a long time the forester was merely tolerated. The production man was the hero of the logging woods.

But time has taken its toll of the old-style operators, men of whom a standing, living tree was revolting evidence that their employees had failed to let all available daylight into the swamp. They died, and with them died the chief resistance to forestry. The forestry schools meanwhile went about their work more subtly: they started turning out graduates who were not only foresters but production men too. One by one these young men got jobs. Their number is now imposing. So is evidence of their influence. They are bringing to fruition the hopes of generations of honest conservationists, many of whom could not understand that sound forestry, if ever it came, was to be based less on the emotions expressed by only-God-can-make-a-tree than on hard economics.

Thus it came to pass that instead of letting his cut-over lands revert to the state for taxes, the logging operator was urged by his forester to retain the land, to protect it from fire, disease and pests; and to plant and thin where necessary, all with the idea that timber is a crop to be harvested over and over like wheat and potatoes, though naturally in widely spaced cycles. Even so, these tree farms, millions of acres of which have been registered in an association, could never have come into being without the radical modifications that have taken place in the idiotic and confiscatory tax structure which for more than a century had bedeviled American timberlands.

Another thing is that the lumber industry which for three centuries was predicated on boards and timbers made from old-growth forests has changed into a forest-products industry. Fibre products and plastics numbered by the hundreds; the marvelous new plywoods; and finally the impreg and compreg woods—as tough as mild steel, fire resistant, decay resistant—these and other new products of the forest have taken their place along with conventional boards and timbers and shingles.

It is all good. One can welcome the many things that changed a notoriously cut-out-and-get-out industry into a stable and permanent one. At the same time, one can regret that the logging camp will presently be a thing of the past. Yet I imagine that few of today's loggers, now thoroughly and perhaps happily domesticated, regret its passing.

Here and there, possibly, is one whose memory will conjure up a dawn when the sun came over the mountain to slant through the swirling mist, while the bullcook beat rhythmically on the gong and two hundred young men came stomping down the camp walks, their sharp calks clicking in the planks, heading for an incredible breakfast, a box of Copenhagen, then the thundering ride behind the Shay to where the spar-tree reared high above the big round stuff lying between the stumps. It was a great era. It already seems almost as remote as that of the stern-wheelers, or even of the Covered Wagons.

From *The Columbia,* Stewart H. Holbrook (New York: Rinehart and Company, 1956).

LXXXIII

Gary Snyder

By mechanizing the tools for producing two-by-fours, shingles, and plywood, the lumbermen had solved problems of meeting quantitative demands, but they still had human problems to solve recurrently; those who performed the physical labor of lumber production insisted on receiving perquisites and compensation consistent with the grand profits of the industry. And again in the summer of 1954 the sawmills of the Northwest were silenced when over a hundred thousand CIO and AFL workers walked off the job, cutting production almost in half.

The shutdown was memorialized by the vocal young poet Gary Snyder (1930–), who could be personally sympathetic with the strikers, for after leaving the home farm north of Seattle where he had been brought up, he had served a long stint in the forests of Washington, Oregon, and northern California. Then turning from forestry to poetry, he had helped Allen Ginsberg and Jack Kerouac introduce the "beat" movement into Western literature. That new beat and the free lingo of the laborer are present in his lines whether his theme is the seasons or salmon fishing, Indians or contemporary ideology.

The Late Snow & Lumber Strike
of the Summer of Fifty-Four

Whole towns shut down
    hitching the Coast road, only gypos
Running their beat trucks, no logs on
Gave me rides. Loggers all gone fishing
Chainsaws in a pool of cold oil
On back porches of ten thousand
Split-shake houses, quiet in summer rain.
Hitched north all of Washington
Crossing and re-crossing the passes
Blown like dust, no place to work.

Climbing the steep ridge below Shuksan
    clumps of pine
      float out the fog
No place to think or work
    drifting.

On Mt. Baker, alone
In a gully of blazing snow:
Cities down the long valleys west
Thinking of work, but here,
Burning in sun-glare
Below a wet cliff, above a frozen lake,
The whole Northwest on strike
Black burners cold,
The green-chain still,
I must turn and go back:
    caught on a snowpeak
    between heaven and earth
And stand in lines in Seattle.
Looking for work.

From *A Range of Poems*, Gary Snyder (London: Fulcrum Press, 1966).

LXXXIV

Hanson W. Baldwin

"Looking for work" was far less restrictive than it had once been. Competing with the sawmills now were expansive temples of industry dedicated to production of a sweeping assortment of wares and up-dated fabrications. Nor were the temples to be found only in older communities and high-production centers; they sprang up even in once-remote desert areas, to be surrounded immediately by spanking new municipalities.

Frederick Simpich's forecast that wartime factories would graduate into permanent peacetime industries materialized in a larger way than he predicted. Hanford offered a fair example. The censors declined to permit his mentioning the activities being carried on there under a shroud of secrecy during his visit to the state. Before the war Hanford had been an inconspicuous spot on the map hidden behind Yakima Ridge, the Saddle Mountains, the Rattlesnake Hills, and the elevated Horse Heaven country, and distinguished principally for its apples, cottontails, jackrabbits and elusive sage hens. Then came industry.

The story of Hanford's escape from oblivion was narrated by Hanson W. Baldwin (1903–   ), military editor of *The New York Times*, 1942 recipient of the Pulitzer Prize in journalism, author of *The Price of Power, The Great Arms Race*, and many other books and articles on military affairs.

A-Bomb Boom Town

The story of Hanford is largely the story of plutonium and the A-bomb. In 1942, the Manhattan District—predecessor of the Atomic Energy Commission—selected the general Hanford area as the site of its great piles. Isolation and the abundance of power and cold water from the Columbia River, both essential for operations of the piles, determined the selection of the sites.

At its peak in 1944 Hanford—the "tarpaper metropolis"—numbered 51,000 rough and ready inhabitants, who drank more beer in eight hours than Seattle, eight times as big, consumed in a day. They were not particular in those war days. There was no time for thorough F.B.I. checks, and men of dubious pasts rubbed elbows with the physicist and engineer. There was not much recreation for the workers; the beer joints were so popular that men used to sell their seats (under Washington State law a man must be seated if he is to be served liquor) for high prices to latecomers. Betting was a major pastime; men with easy money used to wager $10 or $20 on which of two flies would move first.

Hanford was first known as the White Bluffs Military Project, from the name of another small town absorbed by the plutonium works; then the name was changed to the Hanford Engineer Works, and today the official title of the largest plutonium production plant in the world is U.S. Atomic Energy Commission, Hanford Operations Office, Richland, Washington.

The old Hanford boomed during the period when construction workers lived in temporary hutments, connected by miles of hardtop macadam roads. Some 13,500 people lived in trailers. Today, all of the "tarpaper metropolis" is gone, and of the old Hanford of the peaceful farms and little orchards, only a few decaying and abandoned structures remain.

By spring of 1945, the permanent employees of the Hanford project were living in Richland, and a year later a wrecking company demolished the vast "tarpaper metropolis," which had cost at least $17,000,000 to build, for a bid of slightly more than

$100,000. Today the boom town is just a jumbled collection of a few of old Hanford's houses, some used for storage, some still earmarked for eventual removal.

The number of workers is expected to increase to between 10,000 and 13,000 toward the end of the year. Most of these temporary construction workers, who are building vast new piles and plutonium processing plants, are housed in a barracks and trailer city at North Richland, a short distance outside the security area. Barracks from the wartime Hanford were moved to North Richland, and two-story Navy barracks from the abandoned naval air station at Pasco were floated up the Columbia on barges.

North Richland has none of the rip-roaring qualities of the wartime Hanford. The peacetime construction workers are quite a different breed from the men who moved mountains when Hanford was being built. Most of them are F.B.I.-checked, and they are family men; the demands are for schools, and beer consumption has fallen off.

Richland itself, an "open town" since it lies outside the closely guarded manufacturing area, houses most of the 8,000 permanent employees. They are under the direction of the General Electric Company, the operator-manager for the A.E.C., which runs the piles and processing plants.

A major expansion program to increase the Government's investment to at least $700,000,000 when completed in June, 1952, will probably double plutonium production. But unless the A.E.C. chooses to reveal its secrets, no one is going to be able to tell easily just how much fissionable material Hanford is producing or what new methods it is using.

The plants at Hanford are more closely guarded than the Government gold in the vaults of Fort Knox. All roads and railroads leading to the security reservation pass through a guarded perimeter fence. Inside the reservation, the piles and processing plants are for both safety and security reasons widely scattered, and each is surrounded by a series of inner and outer fences manned by watch towers, guards and mechanical and electrical alarm systems. The General Electric Company maintains a specially trained security and police and guard force of 565 men (in addition to the Richland "city police force" of eighty–five men). These men are responsible for guarding a tract of land almost two-thirds the size of Rhode Island.

The ground security force is aided by an aircraft patrol maintained by the Atomic Energy Commission. One of the air patrol's three cub planes is aloft almost constantly during daylight hours, and the last aerial patrol just before nightfall covers a perimeter of about 1,000 square miles and looks particularly for any unusual concentration of people or vehicles on approaches leading to the area.

The local security force is responsible primarily for anti-sabotage guard, and for local defense protection. When the finished plutonium is ready to leave the Hanford area, it is turned over to a shipment security section of seventy-two men of the Atomic Energy Commission, who guard the plutonium while it is en route to its destination.

The security forces at the Hanford works can also count upon almost instant support from the Air Force and the Army in case of need. Fast jet interceptors are based at near-by Moses Lake Air Force Base, and Army antiaircraft units are at Richland, with the Second Division over the mountains at Fort Lewis, Washington. At the A.E.C.'s little local airport, a twenty-four-hour local radio and telephone hookup is maintained with the Army, the Air Force and the West Coast radar network.

The safety precautions at Hanford are just about as stringent and compelling as the security guard. It is Hanford's boast that it never has had an injury attributable to radiation . . . : "The Hanford operation is potentially the world's most hazardous industry, yet it is ten times as safe to work at Hanford as in an average chemical plant."

Part of this safety record is attributable to the care with which the piles and processing plants were built and to all sorts of safety devices incorporated in them. Massive concrete walls and other shielding protect the workers; remote control machinery handles the dangerous radioactive elements, and workers most exposed wear masks and protective clothing, and carry or wear film pack badges, or pocket ionization chambers which indicate the amount of radiation to which they are exposed. Sometimes safety precautions result in embarrassment; once, a visitor had to sacrifice his trousers; the cautious radiation monitors felt the trousers had picked up too much radiation during a special inspection tour.

. . . The health physicists take continual samplings of land, air and water to detect the presence of any serious contamination; vegetation and cattle near by are sampled, and twenty-nine "vacuum cleaners" around the reservation suck in air samples for inspection.

The wide dispersion of the plants, . . . the distance of the Tri-Cities on the edge of the reservation from the nearest plant, and the otherwise sparse population of the area are other inherent safety features. Nevertheless, in the unlikely event of a major accident in one of the plants, the Hanford Works have a well-prepared disaster plan.

The days of the sleepy little fruit and farming village of Hanford are gone forever, and the Hanford Works—one of the new capitals of the atomic age—epitomizes the American quest for security.

From "New Atomic Capital," Hanson W. Baldwin. *New York Times Magazine*, July 30, 1950.

LXXXV

Richard F. Hugo

The cadence of current poetry was changing in keeping with the new rhythm of industry and the times. But poems of place were still appropriate. No contemporary poet of the Northwest possesses a stronger sense of locale than Richard F. Hugo (1923–   ), native of Seattle, alumnus of the University of Washington—and of the Boeing Company—who crossed the mountains to join the English faculty of Montana State University. In his native state he found lyricism in settings like Snoqualmie, Hoh, Skagit, Kapowsin, and Duwamish, but whether he was recounting the living grandeur of a place or the decay of another, his lines inevitably evoked a universality.

A Map of the Peninsula

See this arm, the rivers have good names—
Dosewallips, Sol Duc, Bogachiel.
This map is right, they pioneer from hills
but at this bend and this, the boom
of cornered water kills the cry
of sea-run cutthroats and the hammering
lost cedars pouring to the sea.

Paint it grand with mountains, but the scrub
some gypo left, the one-o-one in ruts
from constant rain, shabby meadows
elk create, fog that fakes the ocean's
outer rim will smear your canvas, turn
your art as savage as the Indian
who bums you for a muscatel in Forks.

What is harsh is the bone-infecting,
sound-deranging, forest-brooding damp;
moss that hangs on maples like disease.
And there is drama in the annual run
of kings, though recently some bones
were left to testify they spawned
while we were tracing glaciers on the map.

These contour lines and layered browns
are mountains, this cartographic line
of blue that picks up thin blue streams,
a river dying in the ocean's far
too democratic green. Soak the map
in rain and when this cheap dye runs
only glaciers and the river names remain.

From *A Run of Jacks*, Richard F. Hugo (Minneapolis: University of Minnesota Press, 1961).

LXXXVI

William O. Douglas

Generations of home seekers had come to Washington dedicated to the proposition of civilizing a wilderness, and, alas, their success was so notable that voices were being raised to decry their accomplishment. People still searched for a place of escape, a natural retreat where they could find the blessings of solitude; but too many people were looking for the same thing; they reached their sanctuary only to find it crowded, and desecrated with facilities for crowd accommodation. Lamented William O. Douglas (1898–), associate justice of the Supreme Court: "The passion to bring 'civilization' into our wilderness areas is one sign that we Americans are getting soft."

The Justice, of course, was referring to remnants of wilderness, which he felt must be preserved if for no other reason than to furnish civilized man with a place to test his physical and moral stamina against a harsh natural environment. Bird Creek Meadows on Mount Adams was a case in point: an automobile road had replaced the rough old trail.

Douglas' lament was partly nostalgic. He had spent much of his youth in sight of the mountain, and taught school at Yakima for two years after his graduation from Whitman. Then he went East for his law degree and to start a career in law school teaching and government service that led to a seat on the highest bench of the nation. But the haunts of his younger years were never forgotten: he returned to them at every opportunity, and in many articles and chapters testified to his great affection for the state.

Lost Sanctuary

This Adams country is an old familiar friend. I hiked most of it as a boy, carrying a pack. I have fished its high lakes, slept on its shoulders, eaten its lush blueberries, stalked its deer, sampled its grouse, and listened to the music of its conifers. . . .

I climb it from the south side and learn that it, too, is fragile and fleeting. This great basalt uplift is crumbling and the rate must be fast, geologically speaking, for it is noticeable in my life span. Whole slopes on Mount Adams are made up of pyroclastics —ashes, cinders, pumice and bombs produced by an extinct volcano. Some of these rocks are filled with air holes, and are so light they will float for awhile in water. All of them make treacherous underfooting. They travel like shale, new pieces being constantly added to the descending rocks through the operation of frost, snow and ice.

When I was a boy I could see Mount Adams from our front porch in Yakima. Nowadays I can see it from my home in Glenwood. It is snow-capped the year round and shows various moods depending on the weather. On the clear days of summer it is resplendent in the bright rays of morning. Before a storm moves in from the west, the mountain seems to tower in dark rage. The fires that come when the humidity drops and the forests dry out sometimes cast a pall of smoke over the land. Then Mount Adams has softer lines and is distant and indistinct, a mountain of mystery. If the sun sets clear, there is a moment before the mountain is swallowed up by darkness when it is brightly luminous, incandescent, a startling ball of cold light. When the full moon rises, the distant snow fields dimly reflect a golden glow. Then the mountain seems so far, so remote, as to belong to another world.

My home is at 2000 feet elevation. Mount Adams is 12,307 feet. Though it towers nearly two miles above me, I may not see it for hours on end as I travel this mountain area, for the trail is usually beneath a ridge. Yet when I travel there I almost feel the presence of the mountain. I am filled with the expectancy of seeing it from every height of land, at every opening of a canyon. And the sight of its black basalt cliffs crowned with white snow, both set against a blue sky, is enough to make a man stop in wonderment. Sometimes as I travel around Mount Adams counterclockwise from the south I will be in the canyon of the Klickitat River for twenty miles or more. As the dirt road crosses a shoulder of a ridge, I may get a fleeting glimpse of Mount Adams—perhaps only a view of its rounded dome. But even that is enough to lift the heart.

The view of Adams best known is from the south, for the main arteries of travel are there. It was from that direction that Lewis and Clark saw it, calling it a "high humped" mountain. It does have a setback below the summit which to a climber creates the impression of a false top. The view I like most is the less familiar one from the north. From that angle Adams is black rock draped with glaciers, capped with snow, and set against a deep blue sky.

I like to take the dirt road out of Glenwood and travel the canyon of the Klickitat about twenty miles to Soda Springs Creek that comes in from the west. The road is far above the Klickitat River, so far as to catch none of its roar. But its white waters can be seen now and then a thousand feet or more down steep slopes. Glenwood is spotted with ponderosa pine, the yellow-bellied beauty that the lumbermen like. But one headed up the Klickitat canyon soon leaves the yellow pine behind and reaches the firs.

I park the jeep under the huge Douglas fir on Soda Springs Creek and take the steep trail to Mount Adams Lake. While the trail travels about four miles northwest, it climbs one-half mile or more. Almost every step is up. There is open shade under the conifers that cover the slopes. This is the eastern side of the Cascades. The western slopes catch most of the moisture that drips from the clouds drifting in from the Pacific. Their undergrowth is thick. But the forests on the eastern slopes have an open effect. The trees, except for occasional thick stands of spindly lodgepole pine, are scattered. Pine grass grows in between. This grass, which is not very nutritious to grazing animals, is tall, broad leaved, and slick to walk on. . . .

After one clears the ridge and just before he reaches Mount Adams Lake, he comes to a meadow where a spring offers clear, ice-cold water. We are now over 4500 feet high. Yet if one comes in August, the grass has begun to turn brown; and there's so much grazing by sheep that it's easy to stir up dust.

One comes to the lake quickly and without warning. It is like walking suddenly into the presence of something infinitely precious and beautiful. Several hundred acres of water are deep blue against the somber setting of conifers. Towering over it from the southwest is the mountain that Indian legend says was once a god named Klickitat. When the wind is down and the lake calm, the image of the mountain is in the lake. The reflection is so clear, the details so precise, that the image seems real. I have sat for hours in the shade of alpine fir at Mount Adams Lake watching the mountain in the lake. On the darkest, dreariest days of winter the picture comes back to me. . . .

Bird Creek Meadows lies about a mile high on the southeast shoulder of Mount Adams. It's not a single meadow but a series of alcoves that run nearly a mile along the southern rim of the peak. And above each alcove is a series of benches, one higher than the other. Bird Creek is a stream so small at this point one can step across it. Alpine fir and white bark pine fringe these meadows. The highest bench above one of these meadows looks down on Hellroaring Creek and up at Mount Adams, which now seems so close as to be in touching distance.

At this point I always feel as if I am standing on the threshold of another world. Mazama Glacier and Klickitat Glacier that feed Hellroaring Creek with milky water are dazzling in the brilliant July sun. Mount Adams is so high and massive it makes me shrink to the pint of ashes that man represents in the terrestrial scheme. The roar of the river comes faintly up the canyon. Above the roar can be heard the whine of the wind. All else is quiet. A golden eagle soars high in the void, catching a wind current. Nothing else moves.

Most glacial peaks exude an atmosphere of mystery. There is wonderment at the forces that created it. The sheer beauty of basalt cliffs, glacial ice, snow-crowned summits and blue sky is tranquilizing. The clash and turmoil of civilization are far behind. Now one faces the elemental forces—those that produced the great mountain, those that are in process of leveling it. The Buddhist monasteries in Asia are usually built on sites which command great views. There is good reason for it. The wonders of nature lessen tensions and create relaxing moods. They seem to put one in touch with the infinite. All man-made sounds, all distractions, all complexities of life are left behind. Man on the edge of Bird Creek Meadows is alone with himself and with God. This is a place of wonderment and of worship. Men and their quarrels and jealousies are blown away into the void. The individual stands in awe before his Creator. The high meadow at Bird Creek is more wonderful than any man-made cathedral. . . .

When I first traveled Mount Adams, as a boy, all its alpine meadows had pristine beauty. But today one who takes the circle trip finds at the northwest corner of the mountain exquisite meadows practically ruined by sheep. Dust has taken the place of bunch grass; pounding hoofs have torn up protective root systems; the slopes, heavy with the smell of sheep scat, promise to become an awful dust bowl, where spring runoffs create ugly gullies. This northwest corner is in the public domain. The north and east belong to the Indians, who exploit it greatly by allowing the white man to graze sheep and cattle there. Both areas are severely pounded, robbing this Mount Adams country, that was almost sacred to me, of much of its great glory.

A similar fate threatens Bird Creek Meadows. In the old days there were two routes there. . . . Whichever way we came, Bird Creek Meadows seemed a bit of paradise. Its alpine meadows are a mass of color during the first two months of summer. Great blankets of white and pink phlox cover the slopes. Spring beauty and monkey flowers decorate the creek. Indian paintbrush fills every field. There is purple fireweed too—fireweed that is knee-high. Pussypaws show streaks of white on the drier slopes—the plant whose tiny black seeds the chipmunks love. The more delicate alpine pussytoes are there, too, making up extensive mats.

The Monterey mariposa nods gracefully in the creek bed, its lilac petals dainty and translucent in the bright sun. Ground damp from recent high water is thick with Honenmann's willow-herb that shows tiny purplish flowers. The tiny alpine speedwell turns whole hillsides azure blue. Streaks of yellow hackweed cut through them.

I know of no alpine meadow more rewarding after a stiff climb. It is especially attractive on the bright days of July and August. Then the sky is a deep azure, the air cool and refreshing, Mount Adams splendid in its isolation. These high meadows even have charms when thunder echoes off the basalt cliffs of the mountain and the clouds close in. Then this high shoulder of the Cascades becomes a remote place, wrapped in fog and apart from this earth. The mist that settles down gives familiar objects a strange appearance; everything is blurred and out of focus. Mount Adams can produce weather peculiarly its own. While the sun is shining at Glenwood, the clouds around the mountain can spit sleet or spray ice-cold water. Local storms come and go during a night when no rain drops in the valley and he who planned to sleep out under the stars gets drenched.

I had not seen Bird Creek Meadows for over thirty years. I left Glenwood by jeep, planning to park it at road's end and hike in, as I used to do. As the jeep climbed on and on, I discovered to my dismay that the good dirt road went all the way. When I arrived, I counted twenty-seven cars ahead of me. My heart sank. An alpine meadow that I used to reach only after days of hiking was now accessible to everyone without effort. It had been desecrated by the automobile. This high shoulder of Mount Adams now had all the amenities of Rock Creek Park in Washington, D.C., and Central Park in New York City.

. . . I was greatly depressed by this transformation of Bird

Creek Meadows. Potbellied men, smoking black cigars, who never could climb a hundred feet, were now in the sacred precincts of a great mountain. Part of the charm of Bird Creek Meadows had been their remoteness and the struggle to reach them. Their romantic nature had been diluted. The mountain was still as magnificent as ever; the sky as blue; the fireweed as brilliant. But the meadows were no longer a sanctuary. They had become merely another spot on a busy highway, where the quiet was broken by the roar of motors and the sound of spinning tires. People crowded here as they do at Coney Island. There was no escape for man. The auto was claiming even the remote refuges and converting them into public squares.

The loss of Bird Creek Meadows to the wilderness is symptomatic of the transformation going on in most of our far-western forest areas. I have seen in my lifetime a wilderness of trails remade into a maze of roads. . . . The network of roads is so vast and intricate that almost every wilderness area is threatened. . . .

Man must be able to escape civilization if he is to survive. Some of his greatest needs are for refuges and retreats where he can recapture for a day or a week the primitive conditions of life. . . . The loggers and road builders look at every lovely ridge or basin for quick profits. They take heavily from the forests, sometimes destroying everything. There are others who take nothing from the forest except inspiration and high purpose. Their lives and character are indeed shaped by it. . . .

I realized from my day's journey how badly we need high alpine meadows which can only be reached on foot, how badly we need peaks which can only be conquered by daring. The passion to bring "civilization" into our wilderness areas is one sign that we Americans are getting soft and flabby. We want everything made easy. Yet success is worth having only when it comes through great effort and hazardous exertion.

The logistics of abundance call for mass production. This means the ascendency of the machine. The risk of man's becoming subservient to it are great. The struggle of our time is to maintain an economy of plenty and yet keep man's freedom intact. Roadless areas are one pledge to freedom. With them intact, man need not become an automaton. There he can escape the machine and become once more a vital individual. If these inner sanctuaries are invaded by the machine, there is no escape. For man and civilization will be molded by mass compulsions. If our wilderness areas are preserved, every person will have a better chance to maintain his freedom by allowing his idiosyncrasies to flower under the influence of the wonders of the wilderness.

These were my thoughts that night as I sat on my lawn watching the last glow of the sun leave the high snow fields of Mount Adams.

Condensed from "Mount Adams," in *My Wilderness: The Pacific West*, William O. Douglas (Garden City, N.Y.: Doubleday and Co., 1960).

LXXXVII

Lincoln Kirstein

To proclaim the virtues of its natural setting, its growing commerce and industrial prospects, Washington had put on a fair show fifty years earlier in the Alaska-Yukon-Pacific Exposition, and made a good accounting of itself. Perhaps it was time for a repeat performance. Only this time, reasoned the projectors, why not give emphasis to another side of the state's character—its less-known cultural development, the interests and achievements of its artists, architects, musicians, dramatis personae and literati? In these fields the state now had something to be proud of and to brag about—but keep the whole thing modest and low key; let the good works speak for themselves; avoid the splashy spectacle and refrain from any attempt to outdo in bigness and brilliance outsized fairs like those of New York, Nagoya, Chicago, Zurich, San Francisco, or Brussels. As world's fairs went, it would be conservative, refined, a little sophisticated; and most important of all, the buildings erected would not be extravagant, temporary structures, to stand for a few months and be demolished: they would be built as the nucleus of a permanent cultural center.

And so "Century 21," the Seattle World's Fair of 1962, accenting the creativity of the Northwest and setting forth its conception of "The World of Tomorrow," was born. Lincoln Kirstein (1907–   ), distinguished cultural critic, founder and director of

the New York City Ballet Company, author of many articles and
books on art, theater, and the dance, was so impressed with the
novelty of the plan that he made a special trip to Seattle to study
the architecture and draft a preview of the fair.

Accent on Culture

We now have many projects for "culture centers" all over the
country, from Lincoln Center in New York . . . to those projected for Los Angeles, Pittsburgh and Washington, D.C. But
next October, at the end of its World's Fair, Seattle will be in
possession of a vast civic improvement which will offer a complex
of facilities on a scale of practical generosity not even anticipated
by any other community. This center will contain an opera house-
concert hall, a small theater, a science pavilion, a sports arena and
an outdoor stadium, an exhibit hall and a coliseum. . . .

Lincoln Center will finally cost the federal, state and city governments, various foundations and individuals in the neighborhood of $200 million, while Seattle has completed its plan with
about $85 million. However, Manhattan is an island, and its costs
in land and labor are the nation's peaks. . . . Manhattan has not
been a frontier town for two centuries; in many ways, Seattle still
is. . . . The more one studies the organization of the Seattle
plan, the more one doubts it could have been effected on such a
scale in any other part of the country. . . .

From the outset, there has been a determined effort to maintain
a unit which contains an elastic interior vitality and variety,
presenting a unified, light, elegant stylistic whole. Unlike many
previous fairs, one's first impression is not of any startling ec-
centricity in a few arrogant and insistent profiles, but rather of a
more or less delicate fantasy within a compact plan. It sacrifices
no gaiety or playfulness, but it is designed as an integrated
precinct, rather than as a loose collection of temporary structures.

And unlike other world fairs, past and future, there was a root
necessity for the Seattle exposition, beyond the compulsive ex-

uberance of an energetic park commissioner, or the usual enthusiasm of a Chamber of Commerce. This necessity was the many-
sided and long-acknowledged demand for a center for industrial
shows, cultural activities, sports events and entertainment, serving not alone a large city but a whole region. . . . A concept of
permanence and continuous use was paramount from inception in
Seattle, and hence its integration, the ordering of its facilities, its
accessibility to the heart of the city, as well as the adjacent
growing outskirts were always considered. . . .

Having grown from its first notions of a state fair, to a regional
exposition, Century 21 sent Joseph Gandy, the energetic president
of the Fair and a local Ford dealer, to Paris, where he obtained
from the Bureau of International Expositions an authorization as
a legitimate world's fair. This recognition automatically allied
thirty member nations with the project. . . .

Beginning five years ago, a small key group of the busiest men
in the Northwest met on Fair business weekly, later twice a week,
from seven o'clock in the morning until their own offices opened.
It took three years of tactical maneuvering to clear the way for
actual construction. But the fact remains that for the last three
years, the Fair has enjoyed the strongest volunteer program both
in quality of leadership and dollars of underwriting, for any
public purpose in the history of the Seattle region. . . .

In order to accommodate diversity within a unified whole, a
repetitive module was established for much of the shelter skirting
the Fair walls. Tall, delicate, square, black-steel columns at
regular intervals support a more or less continuous colonnade,
facing the interior of the Fair grounds. . . . Local architects
have inserted a very handsome and capacious opera house seating
3,100 persons, with a huge and well-equipped stage and a luxurious lobby in rose marble, within the shell of the old civic
auditorium. Apart from serving the Seattle Symphony annually, it
can accommodate the San Francisco and Metropolitan operas, on
tour, in facilities as good as, or even better than, their own homes.
The Fair has taken similar advantage of other existing and adjacent structures. The sports arena, seating 5,500, has been hand-

somely refaced in brick; the large state stadium, seating 12,000, has been beautifully replanted. . . .

The Federal Science Pavilion, the single most ambitious complex at the Fair . . . has three large rectilinear structures around a water court; very tall pre-cast concrete columns in the center form an airy skeletal pavilion, capped with a lacy articulation of tracery and concrete spider-webbing which is almost late Gothic in feeling, and also recalls the construction of crystals. It is a masterpiece. . . .

The theme building of London's 1851 International Exhibition was Paxton's Crystal Palace. The fourth international French fair was adorned by Eiffel's tower which, until the present, has surpassed all other theme structures, including the Trylon and Perisphere of New York in 1939 and the atomic globes of Brussels in 1958. . . . What has become the Seattle Fair's theme building . . . the Space Tower . . . is far handsomer than early models. . . . In certain lights it seems entirely improbable, for its central service shaft disappears, and one sees only the slim profiles of the bundle of steel-and-concrete rods which support its diadem, 600 feet in the air. . . .

It would be good to think that what Seattle has been able to do about getting a culture center as the residual endowment from a world's fair could be done by half a dozen other American communities in the next thirty years. Boston, Atlanta, Chicago and Los Angeles naturally spring to mind. All have large and growing urban and suburban areas and are regional centers as well. The manner in which Seattle has responded to its necessity, its combination of salvage and courage, is certainly a model and an incitement.

From "Letter from Seattle," Lincoln Kirstein. *The Nation,* April 7, 1962.

Seattle—a model and an incitement

LXXXVIII

Nelson Bentley

With its accent on culture the state could now draw men of letters from other parts of the nation as well as produce them. Nelson Bentley (1918–   ) was lured from Michigan in 1952 to teach American Literature, modern poetry, and verse writing at the University of Washington. He adopted the state as enthusiastically as it adopted him, and began weaving the local scene into his own poetry with the familiarity of a native—seals, gulls, ferry boats, white-topped mountains, sand dunes, clams, ocean cliffs, pines, crows, the tides. In spare time he also took on the editorship of *Poetry Northwest* and the direction of the Northwest Poets Reading Series sponsored by the Seattle Public Library.

Phases of Rainier

Ghost
Afloat
In the most lost
Time: omitted remote
Acts of love: unaccounted cost:
Old thinking cap: pearl-sailed, swan-swaddled boat:
Egret of plunge and plume: scarred, flaw-flushed, embossed

Cone
That points
All the undone:
Antithesis of haunts:
Slopes reuniting the alone:
Manito the beaded moccasin tints:
Tangible trace: inestimable potlatch: bone,

Tooth
And shell
Sewn to our youth
To ornament the will:
White counterpoise to a brief breath:
Ancient refrain, wings of the syllable:
Cold, clear, intense ascent, asking neither or both.

Pine

Two pine trees made a ritual of rain.
Fragrant needles repairing a rent sky
Cradled in their sinews hyaline
All ancient tears' habitual embassy.
To pine, to pine,
Is properly to yearn to illumine.

Well up in the Cascade Range a cataract
In a world of pine makes a quadruple plunge
Whose white tumult is a changeless pact.
Green awes of childhood awake awash,
Well up, well up,
And, poised by pine, unite all start and stop.

Cannon Beach

Who love these rocks have studied to endure.
The tall waves roar
And break their whitest on those basalt snags:

Foam mounts like wings
Out of a sound unchanged since Genesis.

The ocean heaves the weight of time ashore:
The rocks stand sheer.
White seafowl slowly skim immobile nests.
Fish blue with warts,
Eyes glazed by water, swim under the blue surface.

Where one black monolith makes immortal thrust
And waves smash most,
Light like a halo holds the primitive tip.
From cape to cape
That rigid word orders the surge of chaos.

From *Sea Lion Caves and Other Poems,* Nelson Bentley (Denver: Alan Swallow, 1966).

LXXXIX

Time

Big industry that found sanctuary in once-remote areas like Hanford and Grand Coulee could be relatively inconspicuous: if the plants failed to melt into the dreary landscape, they at least enlivened it. But on the coast it was different. There industry streamed in with all its appurtenances like the invasion of an alien order, complete with gargantuan factories, sprawling housing developments, and a nervous vehicle or two to go with every lodging. Altogether it was anything but inconspicuous.

For its accommodation ribbons of freeway were necessary; it brought traffic congestion, overconcentration of population, noise, fumes, restiveness. Cities spread out to converge with expanding towns; little towns grew into little cities, and these reached out tentacles toward municipalities stretching from other directions. Two decades had introduced to the shores of Puget Sound the kind of congestion that had taken crowded regions of the Atlantic seaboard a century to acquire.

In the clipped journalese that belonged to the movement, *Time* reported a typical moment in the surging out of this new "Puget-opolis."

Pugetopolis

Along March Point on Washington's Fidalgo Island, where three generations of the March family let their sheep out to graze on bucolic farm land, there are now Shell and Texaco refineries and there will soon be a $15 million Lone Star Cement plant. Near by, at sleepy Port Townsend, Crown Zellerbach has built a pulp mill.

Throughout the entire Puget Sound area, stretching 140 miles from Tacoma through Seattle, Everett and Bellingham to the Canadian border, the land where settlers thought they had found a paradise, with sheltered waterways on the front step and mountains in the backyard, is bursting with new industry. Already, natives are dubbing it Pugetopolis. Said Washington Governor Daniel Evans last week: "In our state's history, the present expansion is second in significance only to that during the gold rush of 1898."

On the coast north of Bellingham, the first molten aluminum was tapped last week from the pots of the new $135 million Intalco plant, which will be the third biggest aluminum-producing plant in the world when its three potlines are on stream. The owners of Intalco—American Metal Climax, Howmet and France's Pechiney Co.—were attracted by cheap abundant power from the Bonneville grid, cheap land, sheltered deep water and fine living for employees.

Farther south, around Seattle, Boeing's huge $3 million backlog of orders means a $250 million expansion this year and 35,000 new jobs.

Intalco and Boeing are only two of the manifestations of Pugetopolis—and many Pugetopolitans are now worried about whether, in the process of industrialization, their paradise will be lost."How can our state grow with grace?" asks Governor Evans. "We have been the beneficiaries of time and space. We have not suffered the silt and smoke of overindustrialization—yet. We have not succeeded in completely obliterating the beauty of our countryside or polluting our waters—yet. But time, which has been on our side, is rapidly running out."

Some of the companies creating Pugetopolis are showing considerable conscience. On its 1,200 acres, Intalco has planted bird cover, posted the lands for hunting, leased ground cheaply to neighboring farmers and, where possible, kept the cherished fruit orchards. Its buildings are painted an inconspicuous earthy green and buff. Near Intalco, at a $50 million refinery, Mobil has built in a system for the bacteriological destruction of poisonous phenols, so that wastes discharged into Georgia Strait are not harmful to sea life. Every year Mobil surveys alternately the health of sea and plant life and the health of oyster and clam beds in tidal waters.

Governor Evans has created Design for Washington, Inc., to find ways of preventing the inevitable growth from botching up the landscape. An agency called Seattle Metro has been most successful in checking water pollution around Seattle. But Washington's laws on the whole are not yet ready for the boom. Around Bellingham there are no zoning or pollution regulations. Whether or not the coast remains a paradise is, for the moment at least, up to the esthetic sense of industry.

From "The Northwest—Pugetopolis," *Time*, May 27, 1966.

XC

Theodore Roethke

As a balance for its distinctive industrial character, Washington at last had a "distinctive literature," and one of those who helped bring it to full fruition was poet Theodore Roethke (1908–1963). He was late in reaching Washington—did not arrive until after World War II, and that left him little more than fifteen years in which to give song to what he found there. But in those few years he became recognized nationally as the great poet of Puget Sound, and as the leader of a group that called themselves "Poets of the Northwest." In *The New Yorker*, in *Poetry, Saturday Review, The Atlantic*, and a long list of other leading magazines were first published the lyrics his adopted state inspired—though the Oyster River "meditation" may have occurred at a vantage point north of Juan de Fuca Strait.

Meditation at Oyster River

1.

Over the low, barnacled, elephant-colored rocks,
Come the first tide-ripples, moving, almost without sound toward
    me,

Running along the narrow furrows of the shore, the rows of dead
    clam shells;
Then a runnel behind me, creeping closer,
Alive with tiny striped fish, and young crabs climbing in and out
    of the water.

No sound from the bay. No violence.
Even the gulls quiet on the far rocks,
Silent, in the deepening light,
Their cat-mewing over,
Their child-whimpering.

At last one long undulant ripple,
Blue-black from where I am sitting,
Makes almost a wave over a barrier of small stones,
Slapping lightly against a sunken log.
I dabble my toes in the brackish foam sliding forward,
Then retire to a rock higher up on the cliff-side.
The wind slackens, light as a moth fanning a stone:
A twilight wind, light as a child's breath
Turning not a leaf, not a ripple.
The dew revives on the beach-grass;
The salt-soaked wood of a fire crackles;
A fish raven turns on its perch (a dead tree in the rivermouth),
Its wings catching a last glint of the reflected sunlight.

2.

The self persists like a dying star,
In sleep, afraid. Death's face rises afresh,
Among the shy beasts, the deer at the salt-lick,
The doe with its sloped shoulders loping across the highway,
The young snake, poised in green leaves, waiting for its fly,
The hummingbird, whirring from quince-blossom to morning-
    glory—
With these I would be.
And with water: the waves coming forward, without cessation,
The waves, altered by sand-bars, beds of kelp, miscellaneous
    driftwood,

Topped by cross-winds, tugged at by sinuous undercurrents
The tide rustling in, sliding between the ridges of stone,
The tongues of water, creeping in, quietly.

3.

In this hour,
In this first heaven of knowing,
The flesh takes on the pure poise of the spirit,
Acquires, for a time, the sandpiper's insouciance,
The hummingbird's surety, the kingfisher's cunning—
I shift on my rock, and I think:
Of the first trembling of a Michigan brook in April,
Over a lip of stone, the tiny rivulet;
And that wrist-thick cascade tumbling from a cleft rock,
Its spray holding a double rain-bow in early morning,
Small enough to be taken in, embraced, by two arms,—
Or the Tittebawasee, in the time between winter and spring,
When the ice melts along the edges in early afternoon.
And the midchannel begins cracking and heaving from the
          pressure beneath,
The ice piling high against the iron-bound spiles,
Gleaming, freezing hard again, creaking at midnight—
And I long for the blast of dynamite,
The sudden sucking roar as the culvert loosens its debris of
          branches and sticks,
Welter of tin cans, pails, old bird nests, a child's shoe riding a log,
As the piled ice breaks away from the battered spiles,
And the whole river begins to move forward, its bridges shaking.

4.

Now, in this waning of light,
I rock with the motion of morning;
In the cradle of all that is,
I'm lulled into half-sleep
By the lapping of water,

Cries of the sandpiper.
Water's my will, and my way,
And the spirit runs, intermittently,
In and out of the small waves,
Runs with the intrepid shorebirds—
How graceful the small before danger!

In the first of the moon,
All's a scattering,
A shining.

From *The Collected Poems of Theodore Roethke* (Garden City, N.Y.: Double-day and Company, 1966).

XCI

Nard Jones

So far-flung is the state of Washington and so diverse are its parts that any attempt to identify its essence is a fleeting pursuit. It can never hold precisely the same meaning to any two people. Nard Jones (1904–   ), trusted spokesman for the state through a dozen books and a lifetime of journalistic writing, one of its most literate and loyal supporters over a period of some forty years, raised the issue in a lyric discourse on the significance of *belonging* to Washington in his volume *Evergreen Land*. Even he concluded with paragraphs that were as much an inquiry as a statement.

No Place Like Home

I was born in the State of Washington and I have lived there for almost forty years, off and on. I have regarded it from the perspective of Manhattan and Canada, the Aleutians and Mexico, Los Angeles and New Orleans. I still am not sure just what it is, in addition to being a great piece of land of almost unlimited possibilities. I do not know whether it is a way of life or a state of mind, and I think it is a little of both.

It is inevitable that the State of Washington is something a little different to every Washingtonian. . . . When you mention home to a man from Washington there is no telling what he may be thinking of. He could be thinking of a canoe in the tule rushes of Lake Washington, with the moon shining down, and a pretty girl from the University. . . . Or he could be thinking of riding along on a high bluff of scab rock in the hot sun, listening to the dry wind scuttling through the sage and the tumbleweed.

He could be thinking of the Horse Heaven Hills, caught snug in the sharp bend of the Columbia, and could be hearing the creak of his saddle and the light music of the bit-rings. He could be remembering himself at the wheel of a fishing boat in waters off Point Roberts, that shred of Washington that can be reached by land only through Canada because it juts down over the International boundary. Or it could be down by Dungeness, watching the stern rise and fall in the swell that is rolling up old de Fuca from the greatest of the oceans.

Mention home to a Washingtonian and he might be thinking of Alaskan Way, that noisy, smelly, bustling street that hooks up Seattle's wharves. He could be seeing the yellow-white fir being loaded for Hawaii, and the Wenatchee apples slinging aboard a reefer bound for Norway. He might think of the bright sulfur, picked up at the Gulf of Mexico and set down at the foot of Yesler Way; and the vital steel unloading from eastern mills—that vital steel that Washington hopes one day not to ask for from the East.

He could be seeing Walla Walla wheat, too, for Vladivostok, and a little coastwise carrier down to her Plimsole mark beneath a cargo of creosoted timbers. Surely he would be thinking of the freighters bound north for Alaska with every kind of merchandise for that far and wonderful place so much a part of Washington. And on the land side of the wharves he would be dreaming of the lines of motor trucks, four abreast each way, thundering north and south, paralleling the freight trains that were there before them but which have lost the name of the waterfront artery once called "Railroad Avenue."

Yet "home" need not mean the waterfront at all. A Washingtonian may never have gazed at the sea, and he may die east of the Cascades without seeing Puget Sound or the San Juans or the

Queen City whose towers were built on more than seven hills. Mention home to him, and he may think only of the rolling fields of wheat or rye grass and the Blue Mountains behind them in the haze. He may be thinking of an old house built tall and grey with narrow windows that is the only house visible around the whole horizon, and therefore the only house in the world to his young eyes.

He could be thinking of a Chinese pheasant whirring out of the bracken in the pink dawn, or of a doe leaping a fallen cedar in the forest so thick that it has never once been lighted by the sun. He might be thinking of the mountains only, the blue snows and the yawning crevases and the trees all twisted by the kind of winds that never descend to the valleys.

He might be dreaming of great salmon leaping the waterfalls of the rivers or flashing the surface of Elliott Bay.He could be thinking of a little fishing shack on the bank of the Hoh, or of a big old-fashioned summer place in the lee of Port Blakely, where folks came by cruiser or brought their cars on the ferry, to play tennis, or dig for clams, or drink highballs and talk politics in the cool shadows of the long porch. . . .

It is seldom that you can find half a dozen of us together at one time to whom Washington means quite the same thing. It is a big state, and each of its parts is a bit different from the rest. Therefore, too, the sum of its parts means nothing, except that those parts are bound on the north by Canada, on the east by an imaginary line, on the south by the great Columbia, and on the west only by the vision of our people.

Even those of us who were born in Washington cannot say with preciseness what it is we like about the state. . . . No man is ever alone in his feeling that there is no place quite like home. We are bound together and set apart by geography and by our natural resources on which almost all our welfare rests. We are bound together, too, by an uncomplex way of life to which, sooner or later, every one of us becomes dedicated as to a faith.

From *Evergreen Land: A Portrait of the State of Washington,* Nard Jones (New York: Dodd, Mead and Company, 1947).

KEY DATES IN WASHINGTON STATE ANNALS

1579 Pacific Northwest coast skirted by Francis Drake, named Nova Albion (New England) and claimed for Great Britain.

1592 Legendary discovery of strait between Vancouver Island and Olympic Peninsula by Juan de Fuca.

1774 Mount Olympus sighted by Juan Pérez and named Sierra de Santa Rosalia.

1775 Coast claimed for Spain by Bruno Heceta and Juan Francisco de Bodega.

1778 Visit of Captain James Cook.

1787 Strait of Juan de Fuca entered and named by Captain Charles W. Barkley.

1788 Juan de Fuca Strait explored and Mount Olympus renamed by Captain John Meares.

1790 Juan de Fuca Strait region formally claimed for Spain by Manuel Quimper.

1792 Columbia River discovered by Captain Robert Gray. Puget Sound explored by Captain George Vancouver and claimed for Great Britain. Columbia River explored to Point Vancouver by Lieutenant William R. Broughton.

1803 New interest in Northwest stirred by Louisiana Purchase.

1805   Descent of Columbia River by Lewis and Clark Expedition.

1810   Spokane House established by North West Fur Company.

1811   Astoria founded by Pacific Fur Company. *Tonquin* disaster. Columbia descended by David Thompson, who claimed for England all territory north of Snake River.

1813   Pacific Fur Company property on Columbia River purchased by North West Fur Company.

1818   Fort Walla Walla built by North West Company. Policy of joint occupancy in Northwest agreed to by British and Americans.

1819   Spanish claims to Northwest ceded to United States under Florida Treaty.

1821   Merger of North West and Hudson's Bay companies.

1825   Fort Vancouver established by Hudson's Bay Company.

1831   American Society for Encouraging Settlement of Oregon chartered in Massachusetts by Hall Jackson Kelley.

1832   Arrival of Nathaniel Wyeth's overland party at Fort Vancouver.

1836   Waiilatpu Mission established by Dr. Marcus Whitman.

1837   Jesuit mission opened near Kettle Falls.

1841   Wilkes Expedition.

1843   First major American emigration to Northwest.

1846   United States-Canadian boundary fixed at 49° North.

1847   Whitman massacre.

1848   Oregon Territory created.

1849   Fort Steilecoom established by U.S. Army.

1853   Separate Washington Territory created with temporary capital at Olympia. Isaac I. Stevens, first governor. White population, 3,965. Survey of northern route for transcontinental railroad started.

1855   Widespread Indian uprisings follow attempt to remove tribes to reservations.

1859   Indian treaties ratified by Congress. Oregon granted statehood. Gold rush in eastern Washington.

1860   Population 11,594.

1861   Territorial University opened at Seattle.

1863   Present eastern boundary of Washington set, following creation of Idaho Territory.

1864   Arrival of first "Mercer girls."

1870   Population 23,355. Work begun on Northern Pacific Railroad from Kalama to Puget Sound.

1872   San Juan Islands boundary dispute with Great Britain settled.

1880   Population 75,116.

1883   Northern Pacific Railroad from Great Lakes to Puget Sound completed via Columbia River route. Peak year of salmon canneries.

1889   Washington admitted as 42nd state.

1890   Population 337,232.

1893   Great Northern Railroad completed to Seattle.

1897   Klondike gold rush introduces explosive expansion to Seattle.

1899   Mount Rainier National Park created.

1900   Population 518,103.

1902   Irrigation projects in Okanogan and Yakima counties started under Federal Reclamation Act. Yocolt forest fire.

1907   Industrial Workers of the World (Wobblies) organized.

1909   Alaska-Yukon-Pacific Exposition.

1910   Population 1,141,990. Three million acres destroyed and 85 lives lost in great Northwest forest fire.

1915   Celilo Canal opened.

1916   Transcontinental telephone service extended to Seattle.

1919   Armed clash between Wobblies and American Legion at Centralia.

1928   Capital building at Olympia completed.

1934   General maritime strike in Seattle.

1938   Bonneville Dam completed. Olympic National Park established.

1940   Population 1,736,191.

1941   Main structure of Grand Coulee Dam completed.

1943   Construction of atomic plant at Hanford started.

1950   White Pass highway across Cascades opened.

1954   McNarry Dam dedicated.

1960   Population 2,853,214.
1962   Seattle World's Fair.
1964   Research facilities of Hanford atomic energy operation
       opened to private industry to promote peaceful uses of the
       atom.